Benedicta Egbo
University of Windsor

Teaching for Diversity in Canadian Schools

PEARSON

Prentice Hall

Toronto

Library and Archives Canada Cataloguing in Publication

Egbo, Benedicta, 1954–
    Teaching for diversity in Canadian schools/ Benedicta Egbo.

Includes index.

ISBN 978-0-13-613153-3

    1. Multicultural education—Canada. I. Title.
LC1099.5.C3E39 2008   370.117'0971   C2007-905524-9

ISBN-13: 978-0-13-613153-3
ISBN-10:   0-13-613153-0

Vice President, Editorial Director: Gary Bennett
Executive Acquisitions Editor: Christine Cozens
Signing Representative: Colleen Fraumeni
Marketing Manager: Toivo Pajo
Supervising Developmental Editor: Suzanne Schaan
Production Editor: Pearl Saban
Copy Editor: Gary Burford
Proofreader: Deborah Cooper-Bullock
Production Coordinator: Avinash Chandra
Composition: Laserwords
Art Director: Julia Hall
Cover Design: Anthony Leung
Cover Image: Veer Inc.

7 8 9 CP 15 14 13
Printed and bound in Canada.

Contents

Chapter 5   Initiating Praxis: Knowing Self, Students, and Communities   123

Preface

In writing this book, I set out to provide a Canadian perspective on an issue that should be of significant interest to all educators. One central question guided my thoughts as I developed the volume: What should educators, especially preservice teachers, know about student diversity in order to effectively educate all students—particularly those from diverse backgrounds? The answers were rather straightforward. Educators have to be cognizant of the various theories of diversity and understand the different views of why some students succeed in school while others have tenuous relationships with school systems. They should understand the dual role of schools as simultaneously empowering and disempowering social institutions. They should also understand how the various elements of diversity intersect with teaching and learning, as well as how students from certain backgrounds are disadvantaged in school as a function of their identity. Most importantly, they should be able to challenge the status quo and empower *all* students through the contents they teach and through the pedagogical practices they adopt. In short, they must understand how teaching for diversity is an imperative in a pluralistic democratic society such as Canada.

There are several target audiences for this book. While the primary audience is preservice and in-service teachers, the book has much to offer graduate students in faculties of education, policy makers, principals, and other administrators. Students in allied disciplines, especially sociology and cultural studies, will also benefit from the discussions in the book.

In developing the book, I have taken care to maintain a balance between theory and practice, although the contents tilt somewhat toward practice. Consequently, the book gives teachers a substantial repertoire of practical examples, strategies, and vignettes in accessible language to facilitate the process of teaching for diversity and equity. The major themes of the book are organized into eight chapters:

Chapter 1 examines some theoretical understandings of diversity. The purpose of the chapter is to establish a foundational and theoretical base within which the discussions in subsequent chapters are grounded. To achieve this, some commonly held views about the relationship between diversity and academic achievement are discussed. The chapter also examines different views of the school as a social institution, and ends with a discussion of the constituents of social justice.

In an analysis of how immigration policies have contributed to Canada's demographic profile, and in turn to diversity among students, Chapter 2 begins with an examination of the historical foundations of Canadian diversity. This is followed by a discussion of the unique case of First Nations peoples, and their quest for self-determination and just social and educational policies. Arguing that teaching for diversity is also a matter of fundamental rights, the chapter also looks at the implications of the Canadian *Charter of Rights and Freedoms* for Canadian diversity. Finally, models of some prevalent educational responses to Canadian diversity, such as multicultural and anti-racist education are explored.

Continuing the theme of Canadian experiences with diversity, Chapter 3 shifts the focus to the challenges and dilemmas that face various educational stakeholders, especially students and teachers, vis-à-vis diversity in schools. Although a complex web of interacting variables impact on diversity within the educational arena, the interface between the following aspects of Canadian diversity and schooling are specifically addressed: linguistic, religious, and socio-economic diversity, and gender-based differences. The discussion of these variables highlights their impact on the schooling experiences of students from nondominant group backgrounds.

Chapter 4 asks the perennial question that dogs educators and policy-makers, and has yet to be adequately answered: *What shall we teach, especially in contexts of student diversity?* In response, readers are introduced to the concepts of negotiable and nonnegotiable knowledge as authentic inclusive knowledge. Emphasizing the interconnection between teaching practices and student academic success, the chapter also discusses several progressive pedagogical frameworks that teachers can adopt to empower their students, (particularly those from nondominant groups), e.g., diversity pedagogy, critical pedagogy, and peace education. Furthermore, since global issues cannot be disconnected from teaching and learning in contemporary classrooms, the chapter outlines the intricate connections between Canadian diversity and the emergent globalized world. The key stance adopted in the chapter is that teachers need to create alternative visions of their classrooms, beyond the traditional practices and pedagogies that are, more often than not, unsuitable for the socio-demographic realities of their teaching environments.

Premised on the belief that action for changing unjust educational practices must begin with understanding and changing the "self" as a situated being, Chapter 5 examines the ways teachers and administrators can better understand their own biographies in order to initiate praxis. Their biographies inform their beliefs and practices, and so affect the ways they relate to their diverse students, and the communities within which they teach. In addition to providing educators with strategies for conducting self-analysis, the chapter also gives leaders a tool for conducting school audits, for use in determining the programs, practices, and policies that require diversity-related attention.

Chapter 6 provides teachers with "tools for practice" by way of practical strategies for creating a community of learners in diverse classrooms. In creating a community of learners, teachers must value, nurture, and draw on the experiences and perspectives of all their students to critically engage them in the teaching and learning process. A unique feature of this chapter is a collection of vignettes that serve as hypothetical examples of "teachable moments" — unanticipated opportunities that enable teachers to reflexively and proactively engage diversity issues in their classrooms. The chapter concludes with a discussion of fair and anti-bias assessment and evaluation strategies and practices.

The goal of promoting diversity in Canadian schools cannot be achieved without substantive structural reforms and policy changes at all levels of the educational system. Thus, Chapter 7 argues that policy and training matter: Progressive policies are essential components of educational responses to diversity, as are the training of new teachers and of educational leaders. Finally, Chapter 8 points to future directions and provides a concluding synthesis of the discussions in the book.

As a strategy for encouraging the "engagement" of the book, readers will notice that each chapter begins with a vignette and ends with several pedagogical features—a list of key terms, a set of discussion questions, suggestions for further reading, a series of questions to test readers' knowledge, and some websites of interest. Ultimately, my goal for this volume is to provide educators with a guide that will enable them to teach for diversity, as well as initiate critical change in school and society.

Benedicta Egbo
University of Windsor

Instructor Supplement

An *Instructor's Manual* is available for downloading from a password-protected section of Pearson Education Canada's online catalogue (vig. pearsoned.ca). Navigate to your book's catalogue page to download this supplement. See your local sales representative for details and access.

Acknowledgments

The completion of this book would not have been possible without the support and co-operation of a number of people. I am indebted to the editorial team at Pearson Education, which provided the necessary support. In particular, I owe a dept of gratitude to Shelley Murchison, my developmental editor, who worked closely with me to ensure the timely and successful completion of the volume. My gratitude also goes to the following reviewers whose comments and suggestions strengthened the final version of the book: Janette Holmes, York University; Valda Leighteizer, Mount Saint Vincent University; Mary Mallik, Lakehead University; Michael Marker, University of British Columbia; Dolana Mogadime, Brock University; Elizabeth Mooney, University of Saskatchewan; Mike Parr, Nipissing University; Ruth Rees, Queen's University; Shaheen Shariff, McGill University; Michael Warsh, Simon Fraser University. My thanks also go to my colleagues in the Faculty of Education, University of Windsor who encouraged me in very important ways. I also want to acknowledge my graduate assistant Esi Visiani Santi for the valuable research support she provided.

Finally, I am deeply grateful to my husband and our children; your love, support, and patience are truly inspirational. Rina and Ezekiel, I am forever indebted to you. You, my family, make it all worthwhile.

About the Author

Dr. Benedicta Egbo received her PhD from the University of Toronto (OISE/UT) and is an associate professor in the Faculty of Education at the University of Windsor. She teaches educational foundations in the preservice program, as well as courses in the graduate program. Her research interests are interdisciplinary, and include minority education, social justice and equity issues, multiculturalism and multicultural education, language and education, teacher education, and education policy. She has published widely in these areas. Dr. Egbo is the founding editor of the international publication, *Journal of Teaching and Learning*.

CHAPTER 1

Education and Diversity: Framing the Issues

VIGNETTE

Gina had been teaching only a few months and, like all new teachers, she had already faced quite a few challenges, beginning with her initial conference with Mrs. Watkins the school principal. Gina had gone to the meeting with a list of "house-keeping" questions but had spent most of the hour asking about the challenges she was to expect in her culturally diverse urban classroom. Mrs. Watkins had done her best to allay her fears, and Gina had left the meeting feeling that her fears were probably unfounded. After all, she was now a professional and should, therefore, not allow her imagination to run wild (despite the stories she had heard from other teacher candidates who had interned in "multicultural" schools). Unfortunately, her fears came true. While Mrs. Watkins and her colleagues had been very supportive, Gina was experiencing difficulties managing her culturally diverse class.

She knew that she loved and cared for all her fifth graders (including Jimmy who some would consider for lack of a better word, a "nightmare"), but that was a different matter. Returning her thoughts to the noise and chatter of her students running around the playground, she wondered how her seemingly all-knowing foundations course professor would have handled an incident that occurred last week. It had culminated in racially offensive name-calling between a minority student and a White student during recess. She had done her best to resolve the conflict, but one of the parents had not been satisfied with the way she had handled the matter and had reported the incident, and her as well, to the principal. Why was she having so much trouble dealing with her students she wondered for the umpteenth time? Was it her own background? She prided herself in her ability to treat people fairly and equally, including those that are different from her. Besides, she mused, did she not pride herself for being "colour blind"? Was she trying too hard? Was it a case of self-fulfilling prophecy, or was it simply that she had not understood what she had learned during her training? Yes, she had learned a lot of theory. She wished now that she had had more opportunity to put some of that theory to practical use during her field experience. But that had been difficult since her cooperating teachers had remained in charge of maintaining discipline in almost every class she had been assigned to teach. What was it her professor had said about the connection between theory and practice? "Theory is to practice as practice is to theory". She wondered if there was any link at all between both concepts. Sometimes, the reality in the field seemed to suggest otherwise. Despite her misgivings, Gina knew that both are inextricably connected.

INTRODUCTION: SETTING THE STAGE

Gina's thoughts are not an unusual phenomenon among teachers, novice and veteran alike, who teach in culturally diverse contexts. Student diversity became a stable reality in Canadian schools as a result of demographic shifts that changed the country's ethnocultural landscape, which in turn, influenced social policy directions. Dealing with diversity in our schools remains as much a challenge today as it was decades ago. Then, as a matter of necessity, both the government and society at large began to address the issue of the changing "faces" of Canada, and its implication for education systems. Today, critical questions persist, such as what, why, and how to teach children in ways that reflect the rich tapestry of their diverse backgrounds.

Canada's challenges in dealing with diversity are part of a pattern of increasing student diversity in many Western countries because of massive global population shifts. To provide the conceptual base for analyzing the discussions that follow in the rest of the book, some of the theories and assumptions that dominate discussions of this phenomenon must first be clearly understood. In this chapter then, I explore some theoretical views of diversity and schooling: how they are interconnected; how taken-for-granted practices in schools are implicated in the marginalization and exclusion of some groups in society; and how the ways in which schools reproduce the existing social order further alienate and disenfranchise some groups. I also examine how, paradoxically, schools also hold the key to changing the status quo through policies and practices that are not only socially just but that also validate the identities of all students. Finally, I explore various perspectives on the linkages between diversity and academic achievement.

UNDERSTANDING DIVERSITY

In its simplest conception, diversity refers to difference. Thus, it is possible to speak of human diversity, bio-diversity, diversity of opinions, religious diversity, linguistic diversity, cultural diversity, etc. My concern in this book is more with this latter meaning — **cultural diversity** in its different theoretical conceptualizations. But cultural diversity cannot be properly understood without an understanding of the meaning of culture. As a social artifact, culture is a complex phenomenon that has different connotations depending on the context of use (Erickson, 2001). It is sometimes used in reference to aesthetic interests such as the arts or to describe the life-styles of groups and sub-groups within a society. It is also used in a sociological and anthropological sense to describe people's heritage, historical origin, and way of life. Bullivant (1989) distinguishes between two possible ways of looking at culture — as the heritage and traditions of a social group and as a group's strategy for adapting to, and surviving in its environment. Drawing on Bullivant's conception, Fleras and Elliott (1992) define culture as

> [a] shared system of meaning and symbols that account for patterned behaviour between individuals and among groups. This shared reality allows members of the community to make sense of the world they live in and to construct plans for adaptation and survival. Culture in the anthropological sense encompasses a complex range of beliefs and values that (a) define and generate behaviour, (b) contribute to the security, identity, and survival of community members, and (c) impart meaning and continuity during period of social change (p. 137).

As the above definition suggests, culture is acquired knowledge and as a result, does not exist outside a historical context. Rather, conceptions vary across time and space. However, while an understanding of what constitutes culture may vary temporally and across societies, it remains a primary component of individual and group identity formation. Because culture is embedded in language and language is an integral part of people's identities, it too features prominently in the conception of culture adopted in this book. Thus, culture is defined as the knowledge, values, customs, attitudes, language and strategies that enable individuals and groups to adapt and survive in their environment. Finally, culture is pervasive and "is in us and all around us, just as is the air we breathe. It is personal, familial, communal, institutional, societal, and global in its scope and distribution". (Erickson, 2001: 31).

In some societies cultural diversity—the different ways of knowing, perceiving, and interpreting reality, becomes a source of social conflicts as various groups struggle for survival and control of power. These conflicts can occur even within institutions such as schools. However, the extent to which cultural differences become problematic in schools (and society) depends on whether or not such differences are perceived as boundaries or borders. When cultural differences are treated as boundaries, there is a recognition that real differences exist between people but, these differences need not cause problems. However, when treated as borders, cultural differences become politicized and subsequently, become sources of dissention (Giroux, 1992). Differences aside, because each one of us identifies with at least two or more cultural affiliations, each person has his or her own cultural identity. This, in conjunction with some biological or inherited traits, becomes a marker of personal identity. The issue of how people's identities and differences are influenced by biology and social and cultural factors is one I develop in the sections that follow.

Biological and Social Factors Influencing Identity and Diversity

The construction of individual identity is a function of two variables, inherited genes and one's environment. Although our primary concern is with the social construction of identities, since inherited properties also contribute to our overall sense of who we are, it is necessary to briefly examine the biological influences on identity formation.

Biological factors are properties with which we are born. An obvious biological difference among people is sex since human beings are born either male or female (although emerging claims of the existence of more than two genders now challenge this belief). Other biological factors include race, skin colour, personality, and cognitive ability. These latter two also interact with the environment as people's identities evolve. For example, while we are born with certain cognitive abilities, our experience and interaction with the social context in which we are immersed may affect the extent to which these abilities develop. Interestingly, this perspective is the starting point both for theorists who subscribe to the belief that some groups in society are culturally deprived, as well as for scholars and practitioners who argue for empowering and inclusive educational policies and practices.

Unlike biological factors, social or cultural factors are those differences that emanate from our interactions with our environment. Social factors are often ascribed by society and are therefore temporal, depending on the prevailing social order. But, like biological factors, they too mediate the construction of individual and group identities. Examples of social and cultural factors which contribute to who we are include language, religion, social class, nationality, citizenship, and education.

The Individual and Cultural Identity

We are all cultural beings and our cultural backgrounds influence our perceptions of the world and, therefore, constitute an essential part of who we are. In theory, each individual belongs to at least one culture. Also, because a person simultaneously belongs to at least one macro-culture (the national culture), and one or more subcultures (functions of biology and the environment), we can say that in reality, as Figure 1.1 shows, human beings are fundamentally multicultural. For example, hypothetically, Gina in the opening vignette can be described as a White, middle-class, female, Christian, Canadian, teacher, of Scottish descent. She therefore belongs to one macro-culture (Canadian) and at least six different subcultures based on her race (White), social class (middle-class), gender (female), religion (Christian), profession (teacher), and ethnicity (Scottish). All these attributes, some of which were inherited and others socially assigned, contribute to Gina's identity. People's cultural identity (their perceptions of who they are on the basis of their race, ethnicity, gender, social class, religion, etc.), are inextricably linked to their historical experiences, their worldviews, and the extent to which they participate in the groups or subgroups with which they identify (James, 2003). In the words of Hall (1993: 394), " . . . identities are the names we give to the different ways we are positioned by, and position ourselves within the narratives of the past". However, this does not mean that people who belong to the same ethnic or cultural group should be considered as homogeneous. On the contrary, far from engaging in essentialist generalizations, we must be careful in our conceptualization of cultural

FIGURE 1.1 Individual and Cultural Identity Profile

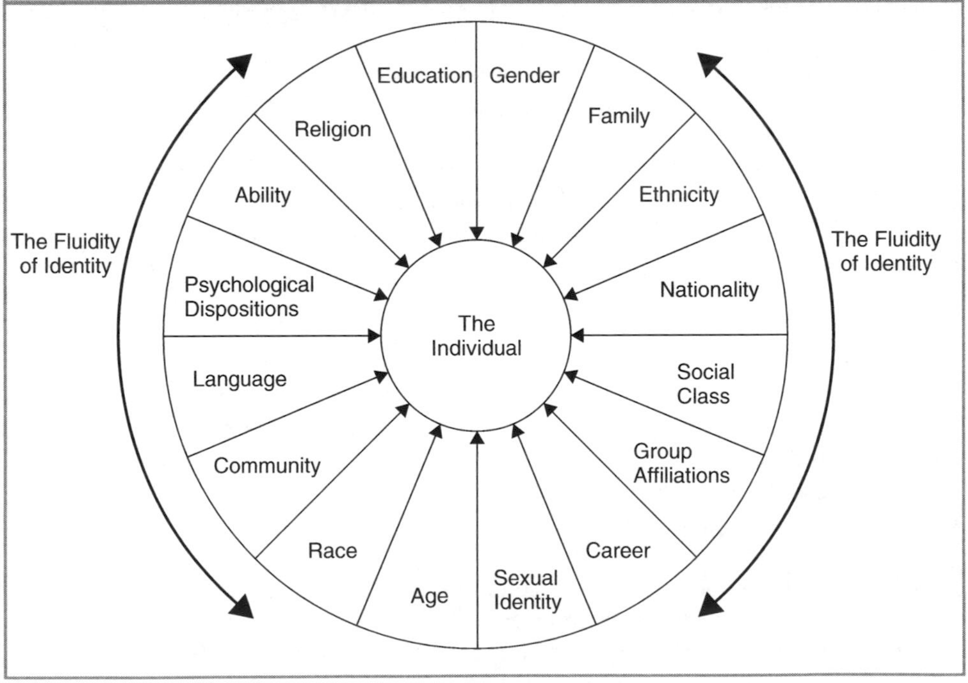

differences not to resort to **stereotyping** since membership in a culture or subculture is not an inevitable predictor of behaviour as Banks (2001) cautions:

> Although membership in a gender, racial, ethnic, social-class, or religious group can provide us with important clues about individuals' behaviour, it cannot enable us to predict behavior . . . Membership in a particular group does not determine behavior but makes certain types of behavior more probable (p. 13).

As will be established in the next section, schools, by their very nature as loci of social transmission, also contribute to the construction of individual and group identities through their **manifest** and **latent** functions, and their **explicit** and **implicit** curricula.

Our cultural background is our own personal possession and influences how we view ourselves. However, shared attributes link people to one another, and our perceptions of our selves and identities also change as our "spaces" change.

Certain social milieux influence our behaviour and perceptions of ourselves profoundly while others allow us to remain our authentic selves. Contexts where our identities are reaffirmed and legitimized will naturally contribute to higher self-esteem while the reverse is true in contexts where certain aspects of our identities are denigrated and stigmatized. For example, for many minority students, schools can be oppressive social arenas because of the devaluation of their worldviews, which are fundamental aspects of their identity. In making a case for the empowerment of minority students, Cummins (1996) argues that some minority students experience so much difficultly negotiating their identities that they begin to lose sight of who they are.

Race and Diversity

We have established above that several variables impact on diversity, and that identity can be fluid depending on one's environment or social positioning within a given space. One variable which contributes to our understandings of diversity and identity is the concept of *race*. Although there are biological bases for analyzing race, it is a deeply constructed phenomenon that is often shaped by social norms. This construct is then used by society to conveniently categorize groups of people who share similar physical features, including skin colour and other physiological differences (Chancer and Watkins, 2006). Race is therefore not a stable category; its conceptualization is dependent on the subjective interpretations of the dominant theory, often from the perspectives of the privileged group, during a particular historical period (Omi and Winant, 1993). Although the physiological distinction by skin colour may appear neutral, this is not so in reality because as Chancer and Watkins (2006: 50) posit, "[f]or many centuries, the Western world has accorded superiority to lighter skin types and relative inferiority to darker skin types, as biologically based shades of distinction came to reflect cultural and social prejudice".

How does this work in practice? Race becomes the basis of social discrimination when the dominant group, which considers itself the superior race, produces and distributes (but denies other groups or races) access to social rewards, thus placing the concept at the centre of discussions of power relations in society (Henry and Tator, 2006; Allahar, 1998; Omi and Winant, 1993). One question that is often asked within the Canadian context is "Does race matter?" The answer is a resounding yes. As Fleras and Elliott (2003) point out, even though Canadians are ambivalent about the concept, it will continue to count in everyday life and public policy:

> [N]ot because it is real, but because people respond as if it were real. Race matters not because people are inherently different or unequal, but because perceived differences may be manipulated as a basis for sorting out privilege and power. Race matters not because of biological differences, but because an exclusive preoccupation with genes detracts from scrutinizing those opportunity structures that are largely responsible for unequal relations. Race matters because reference to race has a controlling effect on those who are racially devalued (p. 52).

With regards to educational knowledge, there is indeed general agreement among critical writers that race is a variable which is commonly used to sustain inequality in schools, and subsequently in society (for example, Henry and Tator, 2006; Fleras and Elliott, 2003; James, 2003; Dei, 1996). But, in a reversal of this commonly held view of the link between race and inequality, educational and otherwise, Malik (1996: 39) argues that "it is not racial differentiation that has led to the denial of inequality but the social constraints placed on the scope of equality that has led to the racial categorization of humanity . . . it is not 'race' that gives rise to inequality but inequality gives rise to race".

This observation not withstanding, the fact remains as Ghosh (2002) points out, that the stratification of races is closely related to slavery and colonial processes, both of which were justified on the grounds of the superiority of the dominating race. Also today, sustained by the works of advocates of "scientifically-based" racial hierarchies, the belief in the superiority of certain races persists in Western societies such as Canada, the United States, the United Kingdom, and Australia, leading to **racism** and the continued oppression of minority groups. But, what is racism? James (2003: 136) describes racism as "the uncritical acceptance of a negative social definition of a colonized or subordinate group typically identified by physical features (i.e., race—black, brown, and yellow, red)". These groups are usually believed to be intellectually, physically, and culturally inferior, which gives oppressive groups "justifiable" reasons to dominate and oppress them by denying them power and privilege. Racism can be individual (operating at the level of one individual to another) or it can be institutional, structural, or systemic when "established policies, rules and regulations of an organization systematically reflect and produce differential treatment of various groups within that organization or institution and society more generally" (James, 2003: 137). This systemic, and most virulent, form of racism often denies subordinate and less powerful groups access to what society has to offer on the basis of their supposedly inferior skin colour. Institutional racism erects barriers that are sometimes insurmountable for nondominant groups.

Another variant of racism is cultural or ideological racism, which reinforces dominant group values by presenting them as normal and necessary for success in society and by practising them within social institutions such as the school. While all forms of racism are destructive, institutional racism is particularly inimical to the academic progress of children from non-mainstream communities. How does this happen? Henry and Tator (2006: 202) provide an outline of the ways through which racism is manifest within Canadian educational systems:

- racially biased attitudes of teachers and administrators
- Eurocentric curricula, and unfair and culturally biased assessment practices
- the construction of nondominant group children as "others"

- the harassment and excessive scrutiny of minority students
- the streaming of minority students into non-academic programs
- disciplinary policies that target minority students
- unrepresentative curricula, administration, and staffing
- the devaluation of nondominant group parents' and community involvement in schools

An example of how institutional racism operates in practice will illustrate the point. A school might, for instance, place a student with a limited knowledge of the English language in the same class as academically underperforming students even though he or she may, in fact, be an above average student. Similarly, schools sometimes (as a deliberate policy) place students whose first languages are variations of the English language, i.e., English as dialect students such as those from some parts of the Caribbean, in special needs classes. There is also the problem of the over-representation of minority students in vocational schools across the country.

Given the above argument, it is not surprising that progressive educators, in Canada and abroad who are committed to transformative change, have long argued that racism contributes in no small measure, to the tenuous relationship between minority students and educational systems. This is particularly true in contexts where there is cultural and racial incongruence between teachers and their students, and the latter are positioned as the "other" (Egbo, 2007; Delpit, 2006; Anyon, 2005; Razack, 1998; Ladson-Billings, 1994; Dei, 1996).

In her critically acclaimed book that analyzes the interplay between race and ethnicity in the classroom, Lisa Delpit (2006) argues that teachers can positively transform the lives of minority children if they dispense with prejudice, stereotypes, and cultural assumptions, which are in fact the consequence of miscommunications and miscues when primarily White educators teach *"Other People's Children"*. Critiquing what she refers to as a "culture of power" which is operational at the micro-level of the classroom, she argues that because the culture of power emanates from the perspectives of those who already control power in society (the dominant group), navigating the culture that schools transmit is easier for children from such backgrounds. To elaborate her point, Delpit (2006: 24) identifies five key aspects of this culture of power as follows:

1. Issues of power are enacted in the classroom
2. There are codes or rules for participating in power
3. The rules of a culture of power are a reflection of the rules of the culture of those who have power
4. If you are not already a participant in the culture of power, being told explicitly the rules of that culture makes acquiring power easier
5. Those with power are frequently least aware of — or least willing to acknowledge — its existence. Those with less power are often most aware of its existence.

She goes on to argue that in the first instance, the issues include the curriculum, the resources, the power of the teacher over students, and the explicit and implicit functions of the school. The codes in the second constituent of power include linguistic codes, communicative competencies, ways of self-presentation, ways of writing, etc. In this case, success in school and society depends on the acquisition of the cultural values or culture-bases (as I argue later) of dominant society, specifically those who control the resources. Delpit's fourth constituent of the culture of power argues that since schooling is a culturally and ideologically mediated experience, teachers are morally compelled to teach their non-mainstream students the codes that are necessary to succeed in society. The fifth point, which Delpit suggests is often neglected in related discourses, underscores the fact that many people who have power in society either by virtue of their numbers, social positioning, or race, are the last to acknowledge it. For them, power becomes a taken-for-granted phenomenon that is recognized and alluded to only by those without it. Delpit's argument brings to mind the well-known treatise on the impact of power, *White Privilege* by Peggy McIntosh (1990), which provides compelling insights into the taken-for-granted advantages that accrue to "Whiteness" institutionally, systemically, and in everyday life. Such privileges grant her certain rights and freedoms, as well as participation in a culture of power, that are not available to non-White members of society. Also, this privilege tends to be invisible and even denied by members of the dominant group. This is true of Canada as it is of many Western societies that ideologically subscribe to democratic-liberalism. Ironically, while its control of power can be invisible to the dominant group, it can also be invisible to the dominated through **hegemony**, which is akin to "invisible" power.

Returning to Delpit's (2006) account of teaching and cultural conflict in schools, the issues she raises transcend the curriculum and pedagogy. They involve, in a deeply profound way, the **life chances** of racialized and minoritized children. Life chances are opportunities that are provided by social conditions within a given society, and are a function of two elements — options and ligatures (Dahrendorf, 1979). Options provide choices and have implications for the future, while ligatures are bonds and linkages that individuals develop through immersion in a social context or by virtue of their social positions and roles in society. In many parts of the world, access to education (especially the valued kind) is often associated with two sets of life chances: increased life options, which means a greater range of future choices as a result of the acquired knowledge, and increased ligatures, which means individuals develop a greater range of connection with one another as a result of their shared experience in education (Corson, 1998). Both types of life chances are critical to the empowerment of any group, particularly those that have historically been at the margins of their societies.

Hegemony and Diversity

Hegemony relates to the "invisible" process of maintaining power and social control by dominant groups through state and social institutions. Through the process of normalization, oppressed groups internalize and accept their subordinate condition while they are oblivious to the colonizing process that is actually at work. As a concept, it offers insights into the study of power and the ways in which domination becomes reproduced as common sense thinking (Kincheloe, 2005). In simple terms, hegemony is unobtrusive power and its potency lies in its invisibility and subsequent acceptance by those who are oppressed. When hegemony is operational, dominant groups are able to eliminate resistance and opposition by (re)presenting imposed ideology as normal.

This concept relates to the analysis of diversity in Canadian schools because many of the oppressive structures and practices in schools are inadvertently reinforced by those who are at the receiving end. For example, members of certain social groups can internalize and reinforce the dominant group's negative perceptions of their academic abilities by resisting educational "success". This kind of behaviour, or "self-fulfilling prophecy," is a classic case of hegemony at work. While many anti-oppression advocates work hard to transform the system, some minorities will uncritically accept oppressive and exclusionary practices that are accepted as "normal". However, like most kinds of power, hegemonic power can exist only through the consent of those who yield that power. When people become consciousness of disempowering social structures, they develop resistance and challenge the status quo, including unfair practices, ideologies, and attitudes that are transmitted through the school's explicit and hidden curricula as noted above.

The Hidden Curriculum

The explicit goal of schools to socialize and educate the next generation is generally stipulated in the formal curriculum. However, a substantive amount of what students learn is not openly stated, even though such implicitly conveyed knowledge (the **hidden curriculum**) underpins student and teacher behaviour. Generally defined as the behaviours, attitudes, and knowledge the school unintentionally teaches through its content selection, routines, and social relationships, the hidden curriculum provides additional space for spreading dominant ideologies in schools and consequently promotes institutional racism (Henry and Tator, 2006; Bennett and LeCompte, 1995). Traditionally, schools are organized around hierarchical and monolithic models of instruction that de-emphasize the values, learning styles, ways of knowing, and worldviews of dominated groups. It is through the hidden curriculum that schools convey messages about who controls power in society, as well as whose voices matter (through what is included and omitted in the formal curriculum). Moreover, learning in school is not only done through textbooks and teaching, but also through participation and interaction in various school activities that promote dominant group norms and ethos. Since children differ in class, race, and other social indicators, so too will their understanding of the messages that are being conveyed to them through the hidden curriculum.

Within the Canadian context, the hidden curriculum is manifest in such school arrangements, like the school calendar, social and religious celebrations, concerts and festivals, hallway displays, the collections in school libraries, Eurocentric values, and the tacit acceptance of racism and discrimination (Henry and Tator, 2006). Some writers have argued that the oppositional subcultures or "creative maladjustment" (Kohl, 1994) that minority students tend to develop in schools, is collective resistance to the negative messages that are conveyed to them through the formal and hidden curricula. For this reason, any attempt at understanding how schools perpetuate inequalities, discrimination, and prejudice, must examine and deconstruct the hidden curriculum since it has as much impact on the construction of identities as what schools explicitly teach students.

Prejudice, Stereotypes, and Xenophobia

Very often, misconceptions about other races and people can lead to **prejudice**—"a set of rigid and unfavourable attitudes towards a particular group or groups that is formed in disregard of facts" (Banks, 1988: 223). While most people have some form of prejudice, it becomes particularly harmful when it is used as a basis for oppression, discrimination, and stereotyping. When people stereotype, they make misleading and inaccurate generalizations about others. One problem with stereotypes is that they can never be uniformly applied to a group (Fleras and Elliott, 2003) because among all social groups, there is as much intra-group as inter-group diversity. Take, for example, the common misconception that women do not have a strong aptitude for mathematics and the sciences. In reality, this stereotyped view is not supported by the evidence since many women, both nationally and globally, have excelled in the sciences and have gone on to build distinguished careers in their chosen fields. Similarly, stereotypes usually do not stand the test of time. For instance, for the first half of the 20th Century African Americans (and Blacks in general), were supposedly not endowed with athletic skills and were consequently excluded from competitive sports in the United States and other Western countries. However, their current dominance in many professional sports has led to revisionist perceptions of their athletic prowess. Despite the role that segregationist and racist policies played in excluding Blacks from sports preceding the civil rights movement, they are now widely believed to have genetically superior athletic abilities. Also, the stereotypical beliefs about the biological and cultural basis of minority students' academic underachievement have been discounted now that structural, institutional, and ideological variables are considered important contributors to the schooling outcomes of minority students.

At school, prejudice and stereotyping can have devastating consequences on teaching and learning as well as on the academic success of minority students. How does this happen? First, teachers and students do not come to school as tabula rasa and their pre-existing misconceptions of different groups in wider society may find the school to be fertile nurturing ground. Like anyone else, teachers are prone to the influences of stereotyping, but the nature of their job places them in a unique position to put their views to work (Corson, 1998). Second, stereotypical beliefs about some students' race or heritage may affect how teachers teach certain subjects and their expectations of, and the nature of their interactions with the students. Conversely, a student who believes that a teacher holds negative views of his or her race, group, or gender, may react in ways that do not support their academic progress. Over time, both the teacher and the student will develop **mutual resistance**, which makes teaching and learning very challenging. Unfortunately, as Cummins (2000: 7) points out "classroom interactions between educators and students [are] the most direct determinant of educational success or failure for culturally and linguistically diverse students". He further argues that while for some students' resistance can result in concerted effort to succeed in order to disprove their teacher's low expectations, the typical reaction is mental withdrawal or disengagement from an apparently coercive relationship which in turn, results in negative academic, social, and material consequences.

As experts suggest, prejudice is difficult to reduce in schools because, by the time children get to school, their perceptions of various ethnic and cultural groups are already formed as a result of cognitive immaturity and the need for parental approval (Aboud, 1992). Unfortunately, this attitude is legitimated in schools by curriculum content and through the behaviour of educational personnel. In fact, school responses to prejudice tend to treat it as the by-product of a few "bad apples", whose deviant behaviour is symptomatic of deficient home socialization.

Finally, another reason why prejudice is difficult to combat is the fact that people are reluctant to admit to it — in part because they are not often aware that they are prejudiced in the first place. However, a simple test of prejudice as provided in Table 1.1 is a starting point for identifying a person's propensity towards prejudice and discrimination.

A different kind of prejudice which is not often given the attention it deserves in Canadian society is **xenophobia**. Originating from two Greek words *xenos* (foreigner or

TABLE 1.1	Sample Test of Individual Prejudice

What is the first thing that comes to mind when you see or hear these words (arranged in alphabetical order)? Write down your first thought in the middle column and a relevant score in the right-hand column.

Word(s)	First Thought	Score
Asians		
Blacks		
Christians		
First Nations Peoples		
Gays and Lesbians		
Immigrants		
Jews		
Moslems		
People with Disabilities		
Refugees		
Whites		
Women		

Scoring

For each "positive" thought you earn 2 points, and for each "negative" thought, 0 points. A "neutral" thought (i.e. I don't care) earns you 1 point. Add up your points; the highest possible score is 24 points. A total score of 12 points or less signifies that you have a prejudiced attitude towards those that are different from you. A score of 13 to 20 indicates that you have some prejudices although for the most part, you are accepting of those who are different from you. A total score of 21 to 24 points means that you have a positive attitude towards those that are different from you; you are therefore not prejudiced.

stranger) and *phobos* (fear), xenophobia is a persistent fear of foreigners or people who are different. Xenophobia, particularly towards new immigrants, is becoming prevalent in Western societies because of massive global population shifts, and especially in a post September 11 context, which has witnessed increases in previously existing inter-group tensions (Giroux, 2002). These tensions can easily spill into schools, and without proper understanding of what is at work, educators are likely to miss early warning signs of conflicts that originate from xenophobic attitudes among their students.

The "Colour-Blindness" Syndrome

It is ironic that in a racialized and multicultural society like Canada, people tend to claim colour blindness (in a metaphorical sense), as the ultimate evidence of their aversion to racism, prejudice, and discrimination. For instance, it is not uncommon to hear teachers make comments like, "Black, White, blue, or green, I love all my students", "I do not see colour", "I treat everyone equally", or "As far as I am concerned, everyone is the same". Even if we concede that some people are less prone to racial biases than others, the absurdity of this kind of comment is self-evident. Even in culturally homogenous educational contexts it would be unnatural to make such claims of equal treatment. First, by the very nature of human beings, it is impossible to "love" everyone equally. Second, it is not realistic to claim that every student can be treated equally since there are significant individual differences (such as learning styles, abilities, disabilities, cultural differences, and personal circumstances) that mandate differential treatment if teachers are to effectively meet the learning needs of all their students. Third, without denying that such a statement is probably well-intentioned, it is impossible not to notice racial differences among students in the closed confines of a classroom. Claiming colour-blindness then, is analogous to denying peoples' existence or a negation of their identities. Gina in the opening vignette is clearly guilty of this faux pas albeit the result of ignorance. Differences do exist among people as noted above. The problem arises when differences are used as markers for unfair categorizations, prejudice, and distribution of social goods. Once we recognize this fact, we are then able to accept and talk about it, and thereby challenge oppressive structures that lead to the exploitation of differences in the first place.

SCHOOLS, SOCIAL POSITIONING, AND PRIVILEGE: THEORETICAL VIEWS

That schools are agents of socialization that play an important role in people's lives is a matter of consensus. That social positioning, privilege, and the knowledge that is produced in schools (at least in Western and pluralistic societies such as Canada), intersect in complex ways that affect school success or failure is also a widely accepted premise. What remains a source of raging debate is the nature and extent that role plays in creating social hierarchies. In the vast literature that has accumulated over decades of research and debate on all three issues, two broad perspectives emerge which subsume other views — the consensus and interrogative perspectives.

Consensus Perspectives

I use the term *consensus perspectives* inclusively to describe **conservative** and **liberal-democratic** views of schooling that dominated educational thought up to the 1970s. Informed by **structural functionalism** as proposed by sociologists Emile Durkheim (1956), Talcott Parsons (1951, 1959) and Robert Morton (1957), consensus theories see society as organized systems and structures in which equilibrium, stability, order, and social cohesion are its prominent features while agreement is the most prevalent social force. Similarly, consensus views of schooling see education as a liberating and requisite force for individual and social progress, which provides equal opportunities for all regardless of race, socio-economic status, gender, and cultural background. Education is also seen as a means of providing skills training and knowledge transfer, as well as basic societal values. In this linear conception of the role of schools, society is seen as a **meritocracy** and schools as level playing fields where all students have equal chance to succeed regardless of their background or gender.

Despite more informed analysis of the links between schooling and society, consensus views of schooling continue to be adopted by neo-conservative reformists who advocate "back to basics" educational policies such as those recommended in *A Nation at Risk (1983)* and the *No Child Left Behind Act of 2002* in the United States. In Canada, the current accountability and competency-based educational reforms (such as standardized curricula and standardized tests) are implicitly aimed at providing students with what policy makers believe to be basic knowledge (Corson, 2001). Entrenched reformists generally see education as a public good that serves the interest of both the individual and the commonwealth by preparing children for meaningful existence in society (Sowell, 2002; Coulson, 2002). There is in effect a refusal to acknowledge schools as sites where intergroup and class distinctions are reproduced or as arenas that do not serve the interests of less privileged members of society. By adopting a neutral view of schooling, consensus accounts of schooling absolve society from any culpability in the educational failure of children from disadvantaged communities. In contrast, the complicity of both state and social structures remains a point of convergence for other theorists. They believe that in addition to their explicit function of educating the next generation, schools are sites that perpetuate social injustices and politicize knowledge. These "interrogative" theorists see an inherent connection between education, social positioning, and power in society.

Interrogative Perspectives

In his book *Changing Education for Diversity*, David Corson (1998) asks a seemingly straightforward but profoundly complex and important question concerning ways of dealing with student diversity in plural societies:

> The key question . . . is whether the differences that exist between . . . diverse students and the majority of students in a given setting *are* [emphasis in original] educationally relevant. If they are relevant, then some different type of educational provision is warranted (p. 1).

Some writers have sought to establish this relevance by questioning the explicit and in particular implicit functions of education systems (e.g., Bowles and Gintis, 1976; Giroux, 1983, 1992; Bourdieu, 1977; Bernstein, 1977; Freire, 1970; Apple, 1982; McLaren, 2007). Used in this context (as an umbrella term for a wide range of theoretical views that question the ostensibly neutral role of schools), interrogative perspectives see education as politics-laden, and as such, the nexus of power struggles in society. The vast majority of theorists in this category believe that understanding the intersections of class, power, and privilege is critical to understanding how schools carry out their mandate. Two of these views, **conflict** and **critical** theories, provide the theoretical framework on which the views in this book are grounded.

Conflict Theories

Conflict theorists question the assumed neutral and value-free views of schools and expose how they serve the interests of the dominant group. They further argue that as institutions of socialization, schools reproduce the values, ideologies, and worldviews of the dominant group, and in so doing, reinforce existing economic, political, and social inequalities resulting in **social reproduction**. Two of the most influential perspectives for examining this paradigm are the economic reproduction and the cultural reproduction theories.

Schools and Economic Reproduction

Originating from the work of Samuel Bowles and Herbert Gintis, the economic reproduction theory asserts that one of the essential functions of the school is to sustain the labour force and capitalism along the lines of class and gender, and as a consequence, reinforce existing class-based inequities. According to Bowles and Gintis (1976), schools achieve this goal through differential socialization, which systematically teaches youths the skills, attitudes, and values that correspond to their expected future roles and positions within the labour force:

> The educational system helps integrate youth into the economic system, we believe, through a structural correspondence between its social relations and those of production. The structure of social relations in education not only inures the student to the discipline of the work place, but develops the types of personal demeanour, modes of self-presentation, self-image, and social class identification which are the crucial ingredients of job adequacy (p. 131).

Their central argument rests on the "**correspondence principle**", which asserts that there is a relationship between the unequal treatment less privileged students receive in schools and the hierarchical structure of the labour force. In their analysis, middle and upper class children are educated to occupy leadership positions within the capitalist economy while working class children and those from other disadvantaged segments such as minorities, women, and immigrants (the latter within the Canadian context) are trained to occupy subordinate positions. How does this work in practice? In Canada, minority students predominate in "compensatory" and special needs programs. Just as they constitute the majority in special needs programs, ethnic minority students are more likely to take courses that are less academically challenging than their White peers. In many Canadian secondary schools, students' courses are organized on a hierarchical basis of presumed level of difficulty. These range from the least difficult to the most difficult streams namely, basic/general, advanced, and vocational or university bound. Students then choose or are assigned courses based on educators' perceptions of their abilities or motivation to do the associated work (Young, Levin, and Wallin, 2007). More often than not, students who are considered less able (or less motivated) are "streamed" towards courses that are deemed less academically rigorous. The socio-psychological consequences of such groupings are obvious, especially for those in the lower streams. Unfortunately, immigrant and minority students overwhelmingly populate the general, basic, or vocational streams. This "sorting" function limits their future prospects and life chances.

However, while the correspondence principle is helpful in understanding how schools perpetuate social division and subordination through its "tailoring" function, it is flawed by its determinist position, its passive view of human beings, and the implicit message of futility in changing the existing social order. Moreover, the theory's failure to explain the resistance and conflicts that are inherent in social relationships in schools has been criticized. As Giroux (1983) argues, people do not always remain passive; they do put up resistance against the forces of domination once they have achieved the level of consciousness that will enable them to initiate transformative action.

Schools and Cultural Reproduction

Developing out of the works of Pierre Bourdieu (1977, 1991), Bourdieu and Passeron (1977), and Basil Bernstein (1977), cultural reproduction theory examines the mediating role of culture in reproducing social inequalities in society through institutions such as the school. Critical of consensus views of education (which suggest that educational systems offer equal opportunities to all on a meritocratic platform), its emphasis is on how class-based differences are legitimated in schools under the guise of neutrality. Bourdieu (1977) explains:

> among all solutions put forward throughout history to the problem of the transmission of power and privileges, there surely does not exist one that is better concealed . . . than that solution which the educational system provides by contributing to the reproduction of the structure of class relations and by concealing, by an apparently neutral attitude, the fact that it fills this function. (pp. 487 – 488)

Bourdieu goes on to argue that the educational system in fact favours majority group children who possess the **cultural capital** and **cultural habitus** that are compatible with those demanded by schools. Cultural capital is the knowledge-base that individuals have including their patterns of language skills and overall ways of viewing the world, while cultural habitus refers to class-based predispositions that a person possesses. The cultural capital that is valued in schools depends on who controls power and resources in wider society (which in Canada is that of middle-class society of European ancestry). Elaborating on the importance of cultural capital and habitus in school success, Bourdieu (1977) contends that the educational system

> offers information and training which can be received and acquired only by subjects endowed with the system of predispositions that is the condition for the success of the transmission and of the inculcation of the culture. By doing away with giving explicitly to everyone what it implicitly demands of everyone, the educational system demands of everyone alike that they have what it does not give. This consists mainly of linguistic and cultural competence and that relationship of familiarity with culture which can only be produced by family upbringing when it transmits the dominant culture (p. 494).

Bourdieu's views are important in understanding how culture is reproduced in school while diversity among students and human experience is eschewed. His views also underscore the inherent political and social processes at work in education, especially in pluralistic societies such as Canada. Furthermore, it exposes how certain forms of knowledge are privileged and others de-valued, based on who participates in what Delpit (2006) refers to as "a culture of power". What does this mean in reality? Bourdieu's views suggest that in the classroom, children from privileged backgrounds are more likely to be found intellectually endowed while less privileged children are likely to be found less capable of learning, in part because schools reinforce the cognitive and affective skills which the former already possess leaving the latter at a definite disadvantage.

Developing similar arguments, Bernstein (1977) uses the notion of linguistic codes to demonstrate how social inequalities are linked to language and communication patterns in the family. Relating this to schools curricula and pedagogical practices, Bernstein proposes that schools embody an educational code that dictates how power and authority are to be mediated. Working class families, he believes, develop "restricted" or "particularistic" linguistic codes (which are structurally deficient and incompatible with the language of the school), often leading to academic failure. Meanwhile, middle class families impart to their children complex and abstract codes that are more compatible with those of the school, and therefore help to ensure their academic success. Since, all else being equal, academic success mediates future success, existing class structures and inequalities are thereby reproduced.

The cultural reproduction theory offers compelling insights into the pattern of discrimination, domination, and institutional prejudice that reinforce the marginalized status of students from diverse and working class backgrounds. It also underscores how schools are by no means level playing fields, nor sites that promote diversity in socially significant ways. However, like the economic reproduction theory, it too falls short of proposing strategies for meaningful change or for dealing with diversity in schools.

Critical Theory

Arguing against the accounts of schooling provided by conflict theorists, critical theorists propose an alternative view of society that offers possibilities for changing its social institutions such as schools. With a focus on two issues (how schools help dominant groups maintain power and control, and how challenge and interrogation can interrupt the dominance), critical theory offers directions for change (McLaren, 2007; Kincheloe, 2005; Giroux, 1983; Peters et al., 2003; Apple, 2003).

Rejecting the view of schools as sites where all interacting variables are reducible to economics (or to uncontested wholesale transmission of dominant values and ideologies), critical theorists see schools as loci of power struggles between dominant and nondominant groups. However, while both conflict and critical theorists share the view that schools sustain class hierarchies and unequal power relations in society, they diverge on one important point — the potential of schools as sites for transformative **praxis**. Critical theorists believe that if schools subordinate some groups in society, they therefore hold the key for change through just and inclusive practices that affirm diversity. Thus, critical theory offers a framework that is germane to any discussion of diversity in schools. It sees the curriculum not only as a complex medium that perpetuates domination, but also as one that holds **emancipatory possibilities**.

Adherents of critical theory who are especially concerned about the role of schools in perpetuating social injustices (e.g., Giroux, 1983; Shor, 1992; Kincheloe, 2005a, 2005b; McLaren, 2007; Freire, 1970) advocate **critical pedagogy** that analyzes the relationship between knowledge and power in schools. Critical pedagogists emphasize how knowledge is constructed, situated, and contested within the context of power and marginality. They therefore critique, interrogate, and challenge educational practices that privilege certain kinds of knowledge while devaluing others. As discussed in more detail in Chapter 4, critical pedagogists see teaching as a politically charged, two-pronged activity that has the potential to either disempower students or raise their consciousness about unequal power relations in society. In the final analysis, critical theorists argue for transformative knowledge that would allow students to interrogate dominant assumptions about the social world, realign their worldviews, and gain a deeper understanding of the structures that impinge on their lives.

Post-modern Perspectives

Like critical theory, post-modern analysis of schooling tends to focus on the relationship between knowledge and power. Knowledge is seen as a site of struggle as the dominant group's control is challenged by less powerful groups in society. Postmodernists also critique dominant forms of analysis on which knowledge claims are based. They argue that such taken-for-granted **universal truths** should be challenged and deconstructed in order to reveal contradictions that are inherent in them. For postmodernists, knowledge is a fluid context-bound phenomenon wherein everyone's views matter. They also hold the view that because there are multiple realities and people construct knowledge differently, diversity should be celebrated rather than seen as a problem or inconvenience. Postmodernists therefore acknowledge differences (cultural, linguistic, racial, gender, sexual orientation, etc.), and emphasize the need to listen to previously silenced voices. Common criticisms advanced against postmodern theory are its relativistic stance (an implicit belief that "everything goes") and that it does not offer practical solutions for changing the unjust social and educational practices of which it is so critical.

DIVERSITY AND SOCIAL JUSTICE

One other perspective warrants examination in our analysis of the relationship between education and diversity. This is the commonly held view that valuing diversity in schools is a matter of fundamental human rights and **social justice** (Banks, 2006; Corson, 2001). Regardless of where on the political spectrum they are, theorists tend to agree on one point — social justice is a societal good worth aspiring to. Therefore, I briefly outline three dominant views of social justice that are relevant to the discussion here.

One common view of social justice is the account provided by John Rawls in his book *A Theory of Justice* (1971), which suggests that inequality in society is only justified if it benefits the disadvantaged. While belief in this perspective has traditionally produced liberal social policies that seek to ameliorate the condition of the less fortunate, Rawls' account of social justice has been criticized on two grounds: its predominant concern with economics and its view of the individual as the starting point for achieving a just society (Corson, 2001).

A second view (which is an improvement on Rawls' theory) sees social justice, or fairness, in terms of equal consideration of the claims of all stakeholders, even if the disadvantaged end up getting more than those who are better-off (Dworkin, 1978). In his analysis of individual and group rights in society, Dworkin makes a critical distinction between treating people equally and treating them as equals. In the former, everyone gets the same treatment regardless of their needs, while in the latter, everyone's needs are considered equally regardless of whether or not they get the same treatment. In other words, equality of treatment leads to injustice since equitable treatment means that the differences in peoples' needs are not taken into account during the distribution of social rewards (including fair access to educational opportunities). A hypothetical example will illustrate the point. Mark and Shane are two physically challenged grade 12 students in a high school that prides itself on its philosophy of "equal treatment for all". Both use motorized wheelchairs that double as their seats in class. While both students can write on regular desks, customized, adjustable desks would make their classroom experience less cumbersome and thus, increase their chances of having "equal" learning opportunities. While this would mean giving them differential treatment, the school would in reality, be living up to its pledge of equal treatment for all. Simply allowing the boys to write on the less-comfortable conventional desks amounts to social injustice. Another example will further explain the issue, and the concepts of equity and equality, which are implicit in the above example. To demonstrate how it is possible to have competing views of what constitutes equitable distribution of resources, Stone (1997) decides to share a mouth-watering chocolate cake in her policy class. She and the class decide to divide the cake into equal pieces before passing it around. It is instructive to note that, even though everyone had agreed to it, the students challenged the distribution strategy at the end of the exercise — on the grounds that what had been originally considered an equitable strategy for sharing the cake was, in fact, unfair. In all, there were eight different, but perfectly logical, reasons why the cake should not have been divided into equal slices. Taking stock of the cake-sharing experiment within the framework of "equality" meaning sameness, and "equity" denoting fairness, Stone concludes that sameness may in fact mean unfairness. Fair treatment may require unequal treatment, and the same distribution mechanism may be seen as equal or unequal, depending on one's point of view (p. 41).

Quite simply, in contexts of inequality, if one's goal is to achieve social justice, then fair treatment should result in differential treatment. Policies and programs (such as affirmative action in the United States and employment equity in Canada) that aim to improve the social and economic condition of traditionally disadvantaged groups (e.g., **visible minorities**, First Nations Peoples, women, and people with disabilities) were developed on the basis of such assumptions.

More recent perspectives have added other parameters to the constituents of social justice. In one such view, social justice is believed to transcend access to economic rewards and includes "relational and associational aspects — recognition and esteem of difference as cultural justice and equity of participation in social and political life" (Gamarnikow and Green, 2003: 210). An even more encompassing view of social justice is advanced by Young (1990; see also Gewirtz, 2001). Young's work provides a relevant analysis of social justice that is consonant with the discussion and ideas in this book. In Young's account of social justice, there are "five faces of oppression" as follows: **exploitation**, the transfer of the work of one group to another; **marginalization**, the exclusion of some segments of the society from access to social rewards; **powerlessness**, the lack of power, status, or authority of a group; **cultural imperialism**, the imposition of the culture of the dominant group on other less-powerful groups; and **violence**, unprovoked attacks on a perceived less-powerful individual (or group) for the purpose of humiliating the victim. Young's five dimensions of oppression are particularly important because they are congruent with the experiences of minoritized groups in many Western societies, including Canada.

The pluralistic accounts of social justice above recognize the fact that diversity is part of the human condition in which some groups are unfortunately marginalized. As such, they provide compelling reason why issues of cultural difference and schooling must remain at the core of public policy and educational discourse, certainly within the Canadian context. The need for such dialogue becomes even more urgent when we consider that racial and cultural differences are often used to explain differential levels of academic achievement among diverse groups.

DIVERSITY AND ACADEMIC ACHIEVEMENT

To fully appreciate the interplay between education and diversity, it is important to understand the key arguments that have been used to explain differential levels of school achievement between majority group children and children from minority backgrounds. Researchers, educators, and scientists have variously used biology, culture, and language-related factors to explain these differences.

GENETIC AND CULTURAL DEFICIT THEORIES

For much of the first half of the 20th Century, explanations of academic underachievement among students from certain ethnocultural backgrounds were bio-centric, i.e., the differences were believed to be the result of innate differences or a deficit in IQ (Jensen, 1969). In particular, scientifically racist explanations were drawn substantively from the field of psychology and from Darwin's theory of natural selection, which portrayed cognitive differences as a function of inherited traits (Winzer and Grigg, 1992). With regard to school achievement, the arguments were rather straightforward: students from certain races (e.g. Whites) were intellectually superior and therefore more likely to succeed academically, while the reverse was assumed to be true of racial and cultural minorities. The net result was that individual learners were considered solely responsible for their own success, and failure was attributed to a deficit in cognitive abilities. Such students (e.g., working class and non-White children) were accordingly labelled intellectually limited and subsequently treated in disempowering ways.

However, beginning in the 1960s, scathing criticisms of genetic deficit explanations, led to the emergence of a second framework for explaining the high rates of academic underachievement among students from non-mainstream backgrounds. According to the **cultural deficit** or **deprivation theory**, factors originating from students' home environment or cultural backgrounds (such as value systems, poor child-rearing practices, parental disinterest in their children's education, and lack of motivation on the part of the students), constrained their ability to achieve success in school. In many Western countries, the belief that academic failure among some racial and ethnic minority students was linked to culturally deprived environments led to the implementation of policies and programs that sought to remove (or at least minimize) the negative impact of the home environment on these students.

Unfortunately, deficit explanations of school failure persist in some quarters even though compelling empirical evidence has now challenged these assumptions. For example, Herrnstein and Murray (1994) and Rushton (1997) have re-insinuated the deficit argument into diversity and academic achievement discourse by making claims that by and large promote race-based explanations for differences in cognitive abilities. However, it cannot be emphasized enough that there is no evidence that biological or inheritable factors influence academic achievement in any significant way. Moreover, much evidence shows that factors such as racism, sexism, poverty, and homophobia have direct bearing on how well some groups perform in school. Although this will not necessarily end the controversy, some writers have suggested that it is more useful to speak in terms of ratios, i.e., how much of our cognitive abilities is the result of our genes, and how much is attributable to other factors. Finally, without discounting the fact that human beings differ from one another in their genetic make up, current knowledge clearly shows that factors that influence academic achievement are better explained by cultural differences and by structural inequalities that disadvantage students from poor and minoritized backgrounds.

Cultural Difference and Academic Achievement

One fact that seems to have gained acceptance among researchers in knowledge construction is the view of learning as an active and socially mediated experience. This means that in practice, as Levi Vygotsky (1962) asserts, the construction of knowledge is linked to how individuals interact with the world around them, both materially and socially. Therefore, in order to be meaningful, knowledge ought to be relevant to the experiences and meaning systems of learners, which should facilitate understanding and increase the chances of success. In a social constructivist view of learning, "learners create or construct their own knowledge through acting on and interacting with the world" (Woolfolk, 1995: 277).

A second noteworthy view of where cultural difference and school achievement intersect is the notion of schools as microcosms of society, in which (as I argued above), the majority group has a stranglehold on power. Consequently, practices within favour those who are already privileged in wider society, i.e., White students from middle-and upper-class backgrounds. Indeed, while much of the research over the last several decades emphasizes the importance of students' backgrounds in learning, students from subordinated groups are still expected to adapt to the monolithic culture that schools disseminate because of the devaluation of their cultural capital, including their first language (Cummins, 2000; Corson, 2001). The fact is that students from culturally different backgrounds often negotiate between two sometimes incommensurate worldviews or culture bases. I refer to these as a primary culture base (CB1) and a secondary culture base (CB2). CB1 is the worldview or cultural capital, including the first language (L1), that is acquired through home socialization. CB2 is the dominant culture, including mainstream language (L2), that minority students must acquire through immersion in the school culture in order to survive in wider society. The discontinuities between these two frames of reference not only create learning challenges for some minority students, they exacerbate inter-group tensions that may already exist outside the school (Bennett, 2007; Nieto, 2002; Erickson, 2001; Egbo, 2001).

Some researchers are convinced that much of the disadvantage and frustration that students from culturally different backgrounds experience in school invariably leads to feelings of disempowerment and alienation, which are precursors to dropping out. For example, in their study of dropouts among Black high school students in Toronto, Dei et al. (1997) link Black students' academic disengagement and readiness to drop out to school and structural variables that ignore their specific educational needs. To improve the chances of success among these students, Dei and associates propose (among other solutions), the establishment of **Afrocentric schools** that would impart African-centred knowledge to Canadian students of African descent. In a similar example, Bernhard and Freire (1999) discuss the case of a group of Latin American students in Toronto whose low academic performance was linked to teaching practices and educators' lack of knowledge (and attention to the perceptions, beliefs, and aspirations) of the students' community.

Besides micro-level educational practices, a host of writers has linked minority students' academic failure to discriminatory social policies in wider society. Cummins (1986: 32) sees the educational failure of minority students as "a function of the extent to which schools reflect or counteract the power relations that exist within broader society". In his discussion of the differences in rates of academic success among minorities Ogbu (1987, 1992) makes an interesting distinction between immigrant, or "voluntary", and native-born or "involuntary", minorities. He argues that what distinguishes (the more academically successful) voluntary minorities from (the less successful) involuntary minorities is neither genetic nor cultural environmental variables. Rather, the overriding factor is each group's perception of their status and place in society, which affects their perceptions of the value of education. A similar argument has been put forward to explain the low level of education and literacy among minority Francophones relative to Anglophones in Canada. For example, Wagner (1991, cited in Cummins, 2000) makes a distinction between two forms of illiteracy: illiteracy of oppression and illiteracy of resistance. In the latter, the minority groups (wishing to protect their language and culture), reject the kind of education that is provided by the dominant group. This resistance is a conduit to self-preservation. In contrast, illiteracy of oppression is the result of institutional processes that promote cultural assimilation with its resulting negative effects on identity.

Despite social obstacles, immigrants to countries such as the United States and Canada generally have a positive attitude towards their new country, and see the potential for better life chances in their adopted country as greater than that in their homelands. Thus, whatever problems they encounter are often perceived as temporary and surmountable through education and persistent hard work. On the flip side of the coin, involuntary minorities such as African Americans, Native Americans, and Canada's First Nations peoples, have no such recourse because their identities have been shaped within the context of a coercive and exploitative relationship with the dominant group. As Ogbu (1992: 8) puts it, "the more academically successful minorities [differ] from the less academically successful minorities in the type of cultural model that guides them. That is, in the type of understanding they have of the workings of the larger society and of their place as minorities in that working order".

There is some research evidence that immigrant minority students tend to aspire to lofty educational goals because education is highly valued in their families and communities. In a study of Punjabi Sikhs, Gibson (1987) found home support (parental attitude towards education) a significant factor in the considerable academic success of Punjabi immigrant high school students in Valleyside, California, because

> students are encouraged to excel academically and teased when grades and/or behaviour are poor. Parents remind their offspring that they have made great sacrifices for them and that the parents' lives would have been wasted if their children are not successful . . . Punjabis believe that they have the ability both to improve their lot economically, especially when they are well educated . . . (pp. 269, 271).

Hayes (1992), also reports positive attitudes towards education by a group of Mexican parents who believe in the power of education in improving one's life chances. In this case however, although there was an awareness of the value of education, a positive attitude did not appear to have produced academic success among the student sample. Ghuman (1980) and Ghuman and Wong (1989), in their studies of Punjabi parents and Chinese parents respectively, found that both groups value education very highly, both for education's sake and for the purposes of economic mobility. Similarly, Suarez-Orozco (1991) found that among Central American Hispanics in San Francisco, education is considered "the most significant avenue to status mobility in the new land" (p. 46). A Canadian study, *Youth in Transition Survey* (Statistics Canada, 2004), found that immigrant minority students have very high educational aspirations. According to this study, which examined the differences in the post-secondary aspirations of 15-year-old students, visible minority immigrant students had higher levels of education, reported higher grades, and were more engaged with school than their Canadian-born non-immigrant counterparts. The same study also reported that 79 percent of visible minority immigrant children aspire to acquire at least one university degree, compared with 57 percent of their Canadian-born nonimmigrant peers. In the same vein, 88 percent of visible minority immigrant parents and 59 percent of nonvisible minority immigrant parents respectively, shared the same educational aspirations with their children. Similarly, a study of Chinese parents' perceptions of their children's literacy, learning, and schooling in Canada (Zhang, Ollila and Harvey, 1998), found that parents from outside the mainstream (such as those in the study) have high expectations for their children's education, including a desire for their children to attend university.

If we accept Ogbu's claims and the findings of the studies cited above, then the link between diversity and academic achievement cannot be addressed outside the context of societal power relations. In effect, cultural difference per se may not necessarily lead to academic difficulties if students from culturally diverse backgrounds are treated inclusively, rather than as the "other", which is often the case.

Language Differences and Academic Achievement

Among educators, near-native proficiency in mainstream language (usually the formal language of the school), is often considered a correlate to academic success. As a consequence, there is a tendency towards discouraging students' use of their home languages in favour of the mainstream language. However, there is now sufficient anecdotal and empirical evidence that proves the importance of first language (L1) maintenance in the acquisition of a second language. In particular, researchers believe that substantive intellectual and cultural benefits accrue to minority students when active use of their first language is supported by educators (Corson, 1993, 2001; Cummins 2000, 2001; Ovando, 2001).

In Canada and other parts of the Western world, schools are no longer simply academic environments; they are also social sites where identities and power relations are negotiated and renegotiated with language issues featuring very prominently in the process (Cummins, 2000). Within this contested terrain, difficulties arising from limited proficiency in mainstream language often intersect with social positioning and access to social rewards. Those who have the requisite mainstream language tend to have more access to resources, whether one speaks of education or of other social capital. As Thompson (1991: 18) asserts, "The distribution of linguistic capital is related in specific ways to the distribution of other types of capital (economic capital, cultural capital, etc.) which define the location of the individual within the social space. Hence differences in terms of accent, grammar and vocabulary . . . are indices of the social positions of speakers . . . " Thompson's reference to accents delineates one language-related challenge that minority students face in school (which is not often given the attention it deserves in discussions of language and diversity) — accent-based discrimination.

Accent-based Discrimination

Accents are distinct manners of enunciation that are unique to an individual, group, or community of speakers. Quite often, as Lippi-Green (1997) asserts

> accent serves as the first point of gatekeeping because [people] are forbidden by law and social custom, and perhaps by a prevailing sense of what is morally and ethically right from using race, ethnicity, homeland or economics more directly. [People] have no such compulsions about language. Thus accent becomes a litmus test for exclusion, an excuse to turn away, to refuse to recognize the other . . . Accent discrimination can be found everywhere in our lives. In fact, such behaviour is so commonly accepted, so widely perceived as appropriate that it must be seen as the last back door to discrimination (pp. 64, 73).

A major rationale for accent-based discrimination is the perception that people who speak a dominant language (e.g., English or French), with non-native accents, have difficulties communicating meaning, and therefore are not easily understood. This attitude permeates interpersonal relations in schools (as it does in broader society), and as a result the greater burden of making sense in verbal exchanges is often placed on the party with the accent. Since schools have set notions of the "ideal speaker" of mainstream language, those who do not speak with conversational fluency are usually pathologized, and the chances of their success in school are questioned (as demonstrated in the discussion between the two teachers in the opening vignette in Chapter 3). Ironically, while it is not often consciously perceived as such, communication is a two-way process, with two or more participants subconsciously accepting the responsibility of mutually exchanging verbal or nonverbal cues as the case maybe (Burbules and Bruce, 2000). The "tune-out" that Lippi-Green describes above, accounts for some of the perceived language difficulties that immigrant students (who speak the mainstream language with accents) have in communicating meaning to their listeners. This is especially true for standard speakers who refuse to assume a fair burden of the exchange, even in school settings.

Admittedly, students, whose primary language differs from the formal language of the school sometimes experience difficulty when enunciating certain sounds as a result of mother tongue interference. For example, it is not uncommon to find speakers of academic (or standard) English, who are of Asian or African descent, mispronounce certain letters because their mother tongues have no corresponding sounds. However, even though these difficulties may not in any way hinder their academic progress, they are often treated as if their academic difficulties (where such exist) are directly linked to "imperfections" in speaking the mainstream language. This often results in accent-changing interventions that reinforce prejudicial attitudes and contribute to feelings of disempowerment among language minorities. It is not uncommon to find advertisements posted on notice boards on university campuses across Canada inviting "international students" to enrol in English conversational classes that would help them lose their accents (Dei, 1996). What those who write this kind of notice (who probably have the best of intentions) seem to miss is the fact that accents are integral attributes of a person's identity. Asking people to lose their accents through a deliberate or coercive effort in order to become successful in Canada (or any other country) is in essence asking them to lose a part of who they are. This has obvious socio-psychological implications. First, it is a way of saying to students who speak with accents that the way they (and their speech community) speak is not acceptable, thus taking the issue to the level of the negation of people's identities. Moreover, in time these students begin to internalize the messages of inadequacy, and therefore become unwitting partners in the perpetuation of linguistic hegemony (Egbo, 2001). Second, pathologizing the way such students speak, especially in elementary and secondary schools, may reduce their motivation to learn and precipitate a decision to drop-out of school.

Similar to accent-based discrimination is the issue of dialects — variations in mainstream language that sometimes provide a basis for language discrimination. For example, in Canada and the United States there is a belief that the English dialects spoken by some groups (e.g., First Nations peoples, Canadians of African and West Indian origin, Native Americans, Hawaiian Americans, African Americans, Hispanics, immigrants, and poor European-Americans) are all non-standard varieties that interfere with the acquisition of reading and writing skills and, perhaps, school success (Baron, 1997; Corson, 1995). Such perceptions among educators may lead to unfair assessments, and subsequent placement of dialect minority students in remedial education programs which may do more harm than good. In many ways, the extent to which minority students succeed in school depends on the extent to which their assessors consider them competent in written and oral language. Unfortunately, their inclusion or exclusion from certain programs and classroom activities also depends on such assessments. But, because the judgment of students' literacy skills, and thus their academic achievement, do not always depend on objective criteria (as we would like to think), assessment may provide widespread opportunity for language discrimination in schools (Corson, 1993). For example, as Edwards (1997) argues, teachers tend to react more unfavourably to reading miscues among dialect speakers than among standard speakers. Such attitudes may, in turn, lead to constant corrections that are detrimental because they send "a message to children that reading is concerned with word-for-word accuracy rather than meaning making" (p. 49). In the time-based environment of the classroom, constant interruptions may also reduce the amount of time students spend on reading and on learning in general.

Diversity and Preferred Learning Styles

There are countless studies that show that individuals vary in their approaches to learning. Some people learn visually, others aurally, still others learn experientially. Some prefer structured learning environments while others thrive in less organized environments. Another way of looking at learning styles is through the lens of the theory of multiple intelligences, which was developed by psychologist Howard Gardner. According to this theory, human beings possess several types of intelligence that enable them to solve problems in different contexts. Although Gardner originally proposed the existence of seven separate intelligences, he has since reformulated his theory to develop at least nine types of human intelligences (Gardner, 1999). These are linguistic intelligence, which is the ability to use language effectively (especially beyond everyday usage); musical intelligence, the ability to think in music; and logical/mathematical intelligence, the ability to understand causal links and manipulate numbers and quantities. Others include spatial intelligence, the ability to represent the spatial world in one's mind; naturalist intelligence, the ability to discriminate among living things and a sensitivity to other features of the natural world; and bodily-kinesthetic intelligence, the capacity to use the whole (or different parts) of the body to problem-solve or for certain kinds of production (as in athletics and the performing arts). Gardner's last three intelligences are intra-personal intelligence, or in-depth self knowledge; interpersonal intelligence, the ability to understand others; and finally, existential intelligence, the ability and tendency to ask critical questions about life, death, and what constitutes reality (see Table 1.2). Although not often interpreted as such at first glance, underpinning Gardner's influential theory is recognition of individual differences, which means that students should not be treated the same. In Gardner's own words

> I regard MI theory as a ringing endorsement of three key prepositions: We are not all the same; we do not all have the same kinds of minds (that is, we are not all distinct points on a single bell curve); and education works most effectively if these differences are taken into account rather

TABLE 1.2	Gardner's Multiple Intelligences
Type of Intelligence	**Ability to**
Linguistic	use language effectively, beyond everyday usage
Musical	think in music
Logical/Mathematical	understand causal links and manipulate numbers and quantities
Spatial	represent the spatial world in one's mind
Naturalist	discriminate among living things and a sensitivity to other features of the natural world
Bodily-kinetic	use the whole (or parts) of the body to problem-solve, or for production (as in athletics and the performing arts)
Intra-personal	acquire and consider in-depth self knowledge
Interpersonal	understand others
Existential	ask critical questions about life, death, and what constitutes reality

than denied or ignored. Taking human differences seriously lies at the heart of the MI perspective. At the theoretical level, this means that all individuals cannot be profitably arrayed on a single intellectual dimension. At the practical level, it suggests that *any* uniform educational approach is likely to serve only a small percentage of children optimally (1999, p. 91).

Just as learning styles differ from one individual to another, research has demonstrated that they also vary across cultures, although these differences may be subtle and variable (Parkay et al., 2005). For example, Au and Mason (1981) reported a substantial improvement in reading among a group of students at the Kamehameha Early Education Program (KEEP) in Hawaii when reading was taught in a manner that reflected the Hawaiian communicative style of cooperative story building. Based on their various researches, Ladson-Billings (1994), Dei (1996), and Ramirez (1982, cited in Scott, 2001), suggest that Black and African American students tend to prefer cooperative learning environments more than their White counterparts do. Similarly, Hampton and Roy (2002) in their study designed to identify ways in which university professors can facilitate the success of Canadian First Nations students, found that cooperative learning models are the most effective for engendering academic success among Aboriginal students.

Similarly, Grossman (1995) argues that there are significant ethnic differences in the extent to which students develop dependent or independent attitudes as a consequence of home socialization. He states that when compared to European American students, students from non-European American backgrounds (e.g. Hispanics, Filipino Americans, Native Americans, and South Asian Americans), are more likely to seek their teachers' direction and feedback.

In another study, May (1994) reports a positive learning environment, in a multiethnic and multilingual inner city school (Richmond Road) in New Zealand, through the revolutionary leadership of an educator who initiated a meaningful pluralistic classroom organizational structure. Through a complex system of vertical groupings, culturally inclusive curricula, and school/community partnerships, the school was able to accommodate the language and academic needs of all stakeholders.

La Escuela Inter-Americana in Chicago is another example of a school that has successfully incorporated cultural congruency into classroom activities (and education more generally), through the collaborative efforts of members of the community, educators, and students' families. According to a report by the National Coalition of Advocates for Students (NCAS, 1994), by adopting a philosophy of providing integrated education in a multicultural and bilingual setting (English and Spanish), this school has been successfully preparing students for harmonious existence in a culturally and linguistically diverse society.

Overall, the evidence seems to point to a preference for cooperative learning among nondominant group students. It should be noted, however, that learning-styles research has faced intense criticism. Woolfolk (1995) summarizes these arguments. First, the validity of some of the research has been called into question. Second, it may be arguably dangerous (e.g., racist and sexist) to identify learning styles and preferences on the basis of race and ethnicity. Indeed, it cannot be emphasized enough that learning styles are not racially or ethnically produced. Rather, they are culturally produced. The third point follows from the second. It should not be assumed that every member of a culture will learn best within one style since, as has already been established, individuals differ considerably even if they share a similar culture. One way of resolving this problem is to see learning style in terms of an individual attribute that is learned within a cultural context. The assumption that all members of a group have a preference for similar learning styles borders on stereotyping, which as argued earlier can produce very harmful consequences for those at the receiving end.

These criticisms not withstanding, adapting instructional strategies to the different learning styles of students has been found to be a useful means of optimizing academic success among diverse learners. In fact, in contexts of student diversity, this argument is one of the premises on which progressive theorists build their case for culturally relevant curricula and pedagogy. A similar argument is also often advanced by feminist scholars and activists in support of girl-friendly educational practices since, as the argument goes, schools reflect and reproduce male norms, values, and ways of viewing the world. Establishing learning contexts that are congruent with both boys' and girls' (and subsequently men's and women's) ways of knowing is also an important aspect of any attempt at effectively dealing with diversity in schools.

Gender-Based Differences

Gender, which is a socially constructed category based on sex or biological distinctions between men and women (Coates, 2004; Chancer and Watkins, 2006), is a significant marker of difference among individuals. Very early in life, children develop gender schemas — knowledge about what it means to be a male or female—that help them to mentally organize society's traditional expectations of them (Egbo, 2006). However, while men and women are physiologically different, research on the biological links between gender and achievement is inconclusive. In general, the evidence shows that while boys and girls achieve equally in mathematics and science during the early years of schooling, by the time they arrive in high school, boys have started to outperform girls in these areas. Girls on the other hand, appear to have a degree of superiority in language-related competencies.

It is, however, not clear whether innate qualities, socialization, or a combination of both, account for these differences (Egbo, 2006; Corson, 1993). It is no wonder then, that emerging knowledge on the link between gender and academic achievement cautions against the binary thinking that results in the over-simplification of a relationship that is far from being straightforward. To add to the confusion, the bulk of the research, including international assessments conducted by the Organization for Economic Cooperation and Development (OECD) through its Programme for International Student Assessment (PISA), suggests that many variables (such as modes of socialization, parental influence, sex-role stereotyping, individual motivation, and the school environment) contribute to any differential academic outcomes for boys and girls. Moreover, the argument that men and women have differentiated discursive norms, which in turn influence linguistic behaviour and practice both in and out of school, may have some significant implications for gender-based differences in schooling outcomes.

With particular reference to schools, the research findings tend to converge around several issues, the most salient being that pedagogical and classroom practices tend to silence girls. For example, for decades researchers have argued that prevalent classroom discourse, with teachers acting as enablers, tends to exclude girls, while boys tend to dominate classroom talk and initiate dialogue (Spender, 1982; Sadker and Sadker, 1986). However, during the last several decades, the language of education (and the classroom in particular) has taken an inclusive turn. This change has also shifted, to some degree, the language of texts and textbooks, which are now less stereotyped and paternalistic and more nuanced and neutral. Nevertheless, some writers have argued that the linguistic neutrality that now pervades educational texts simply masks the continued dominance of male norms under the pretext of egalitarian educational discourse (Bjerrum-Nielsen and Davies, 1997).

Besides biased language practices, a number of classroom observers have catalogued gender bias in the ways teachers interact with students. Boys appear to have more interactions with teachers, are called upon more often, and generally have more contact time with teachers. Teachers are also said to be more favourably disposed to boys' participation in class (Sadker, 2002; Shakeshaft, 1986; Sadker and Sadker, 1986). Taken together, these factors provide better outcome-oriented learning environments for boys.

But, not everyone agrees with the above assessment. There are views that suggest that the disproportionate attention that boys receive in class may be the result of teachers' frequently reprimanding their misbehaviour rather than deliberate discrimination against girls (Sunderland, 2000). Moreover, studies of classroom social interactions have shown that both genders sometimes behave in unpredictable ways. For example, based on the evidence from an **ethnographic study** of her own classroom, Gallas (1998) concludes that girls sometimes cross gender borders, put up resistance, and generally act in unpredictable ways. She also contends that while stereotypes may exist, heterogeneity may be more reflective of classroom interaction than is normally assumed. Also noteworthy are recent developments on the gender and achievement discourse. Emerging data suggest that girls are now catching up with, or doing better than boys in achievement levels as a result of long-standing advocacy for girl-friendly educational policies and practices (Murphy and Invinson, 2004). Indeed, the findings of a recent study conducted by the United States Department of Education (Freeman, 2004) concluded that

> [I]n elementary and secondary school and in college, females are now doing as well as or better than males on many indicators of academic achievement and educational attainment, and . . . large gaps that once existed between males and females have been eliminated in most cases and have significantly decreased in other cases. [However], women are still underrepresented in some fields of study . . . (p. 1).

These new developments provide additional support to the social influences theory of the link between gender and academic achievement. In fact, any suggestion to the contrary remains extremely controversial. For example, in January 2005, the former president of Harvard University, Lawrence H. Summers, unleashed a firestorm of controversy when he suggested (at a conference on women and minorities in the science and engineering workforce) that males' apparent superior performance in the sciences and mathematics is the result of natural aptitude (*Boston Globe*, January 17).

However, as with the case of the link between race-ethnicity and academic achievement, there is no conclusive evidence that shows that differences in cognitive abilities account for disparities between boys, and girls, academic achievement. Any gender-related differences that might affect how boys and girls learn, appear to be linked to patterns of socialization, which are context-dependent and therefore changeable. Indeed, seeing things this way (that school-based interventions can make a difference, as opposed to the natural aptitude paradigm) should enable educational systems to develop and adopt policies and practical strategies for not only responding to gender inequities but also to diversity in schools, more generally.

Summary

The purpose of this chapter was to establish a foundation and a theoretical base for analyzing and understanding the issues that are addressed in the book. Consequently, the chapter examined different views of the school as a social institution. Two broad paradigms, the consensus and interrogative perspectives, which subsume other views, were examined. In addition to exploring how schools contribute to sustaining the status quo in society, some commonly held views about the relationship between diversity and academic achievement were discussed. There seems to be no empirical evidence that shows that differences in academic achievement between culturally and racially diverse students and those from dominant backgrounds are attributable in any significant way to innate properties. Rather, a myriad of structural and contextual variables account for differential school achievement between various groups of students as well as that between boys and girls. Cognizant that there is as much intra-group diversity as there are intergroup differences, the chapter also examined the implications of learning styles for meeting the needs of all students, especially those from diverse backgrounds. Given that ethnocultural diversity is a stable Canadian reality, the chapter also examined the interactions between race, diversity, and education, as well as the concept of social justice (which should be the end result of transformative praxis). To contextualize the discussion in the rest of the book, Chapter 2 will examine the origins of Canadian diversity as well as its social, policy, and educational implications.

Key Terms

Afrocentric schools

Cultural capital

Cultural habitus

Ethnographic study

Liberal-democratic
ideology

Prejudice

Social reproduction

Universal truths

Critical pedagogy

Cultural deprivation
theory

Hegemony

Life chances

Mutual resistance

Racism

Stereotyping

Visible minorities

Critical theory

Cultural diversity

Emancipatory possibilities

Hidden curriculum

Meritocracy

Praxis

Social justice

Structural functionalism

Xenophobia

Questions to Guide Reflective Practice

1. Before reading this chapter, what was your understanding of diversity?
2. What is the link between culture and diversity?
3. How are theory and practice connected?
4. What are your views on the interconnections between (a) culture and academic achievement, (b) language and academic achievement, and (c) gender and academic achievement?
5. Map out your own cultural identity profile. How does your cultural identity affect how you relate to people who are different from you?
6. In your opinion, is racism a pervasive problem in Canada?
7. What is your understanding of the concept of social justice? Should the distribution of social rewards be based on the principles of "equality" or "equity"?

Case Study Analysis: Chapter Opening Vignette

1. Analyze Gina's perception of herself as "colour blind". How do you treat people that are different from you?
2. Why do you think Gina is experiencing difficulties in managing her culturally diverse class? What would you do differently?
3. Is Gina's problem a case of self-fulfilling prophesy?
4. Should Gina have reported the incident between the two students to the school administration?
5. Assume that you are Gina's mentor. Develop strategies to help her meet the challenges of managing diversity in her classroom.

Test Your Knowledge

1. Studies have shown that Canadians have a certain attitude towards "race" and related issues. Research and identify these attitudes. What is the general attitude of Canadians towards those who are different from themselves?

2. Develop a hypothetical policy for achieving social justice in Canadian society. Distinguish between the concept of "equity" and "equality".

3. In this chapter, Ogbu (1987, 1992) talks about "voluntary" and "involuntary" minorities. Does Canada have involuntary minorities? Who are they and what is their status?

4. According to the United Nations, there are more than two races in the world, research and identify these races.

5. Racial minorities are often referred to as "ethnics". Is this an accurate description? Is there anyone who does not have a race, culture, or ethnicity? Research and outline the perspectives of various writers and theorists on this issue.

6. Do the school boards in your province include the principles of social justice in their guiding philosophy?

For Further Reading

Chancer, L., and Watkins, B. (2006). *Gender, Race and Class*. Malden: Blackwell Publishers.

Cook, V. (Ed.) (2003). *The Effects of the Second Language on the First*. Clevedon: Multilingual Matters.

Delpit, L. (2006). *Other People's Children: Cultural Conflict in the Classroom*. New York: The New Press.

Essed, P. (1991). *Understanding Everyday Racism: An Interdisciplinary Theory*. Newbury Park: Sage Publications.

Freire, P. (1970). *Pedagogy of the Oppressed*. New York: Herder & Herder.

Gardner, H. (1999). *Intelligence Reframed*. New York: Basic Books.

Giroux, H. (1983). *Theory and Resistance in Education. A Pedagogy for the Opposition*. South Hadley: Bergin & Garvey.

Henry, F. and Tator, C. (2006). *The Color of Democracy: Racism in Canadian Society*. Toronto: Thomson/Nelson.

Isajiw, W. (1999). *Understanding Diversity: Ethnicity and Race in the Canadian Context*. Toronto: Thompson Educational Publishing.

Kohli, W. (2005). What is Social Justice Education. In W. Hare and J. P. Portelli (Eds.), *Key Questions for Educators* (pp. 98–100). Halifax: Edphil Books.

Lippi-Green, R. (1997). *English with an Accent: Language, Ideology and Discrimination in the United States*. London: Routledge.

McIntosh, P. (1990). White Privilege: Unpacking the Invisible Knapsack. *Independent School,* Winter: 31–36.

McLaren, P. (2007). *Life in Schools: An Introduction to Critical Pedagogy in the Foundations of Education*, 5th Edition. Boston: Pearson Education.

Peters, M., Lankshear, C., and Olssen, M. (Eds.). (2003). *Critical Theory and the Human Condition*. New York: Peter Lang.

The Jossey-Bass *Reader on Gender in Education* (2002). San Francisco A: Jossey-Bass Vincent, C. (2003) (Ed.) *Social justice, Education and Identity*. London: RoutledgeFalmer.

Websites of Interest

www.socialjustice.org/ Centre for Social Justices

www.cfc-fcc.ca/socialjustice/index.cfm Community Foundations of Canada

www.oise.utoronto.ca/research/cld/diversity.htm Centre for Leadership and Diversity

www.cea-ace.ca/foo.cfm?subsection=edu&page=map Canadian Education Association – Multiculturalism and Diversity

www.crr.ca/ Canadian Race Relations Foundations

CHAPTER 2

Social, Policy, and Global Trends Affecting Canadian Diversity and Education

VIGNETTE

Jeanne Elbbar had spent a good part of her day in court. As a lawyer who specializes in education law, she often represents those who are either challenging the constitutionality of some educational policy or defending the constitutionality of some decision made concerning the education of children. Today's case had been particularly nerve-wracking and had required even more preparation than usual. She had represented a group of parents who were defending their right to home school their children based exclusively on their cultural values, on the grounds that such rights were protected under the constitution. Of course, the matter was not quite as straightforward as her clients had presented it. The Crown attorney had adopted a prima facie interpretation of the province's philosophy of "equal education for all". Except in rare circumstances, every child must receive the same kind of education. He had implored Judge Kohle, who had the reputation of being very knowledgeable about the law, not to set a precedent that would open a Pandora's box because minority and advocacy groups in the province, particularly new arrivals to the country, would demand to educate their children according to the cultural values of the "old country". The resulting litigation would tax the resources of the courts, he added, never mind that some First Nations communities had been granted limited rights towards the control of their children's education: their case was unique, as First Nations peoples did not see themselves as "minorities", based on their status as premier Canadians. In arguing her case, Jeanne had invoked some sections of the *Canadian Charter of Rights and Freedoms* as well as several international covenants. She wondered how well she had presented her arguments. Uncharacteristically, she had not been able to gauge the judge's position on the case. She wondered: Why shouldn't every group that wants to educate its children as it sees fit have the right to do so? Why should the provinces and school boards demand that every child must learn a prescribed curriculum? Whose knowledge really counts or should matter in a country that considers itself a *cultural mosaic*? What would be the social consequences of a ruling in favour of her clients? Even as she reflected on these questions, she knew that the answers were extremely complex. Moreover, whatever the decision, it was going to be a long wait since Judge Kohle would not render her verdict for another eight weeks.

INTRODUCTION: AN IMMIGRANT NATION

Individuals and groups going to court to defend what they believe to be their constitutional right to educate their children according to their cultural beliefs is not an unusual phenomenon, especially within the context of a country that is generally considered an immigrant nation. Beginning with early European settlement, all accounts of Canada's non-First Nations history are linked in one way or the other to immigration. Contemporary Canadian ethnocultural diversity is the result of the convergence of the decline in natural population growth (it is estimated that by 2020, population increases by birth will drop to "zero" percent), and liberalized immigration laws that resulted in an upsurge in immigrants from non-European countries. Historically however, Canada has always been a culturally and linguistically diverse society. To begin with, First Nations Canadians had inhabited the land for centuries before the arrival of the first European settlers – the French and the British – who were followed by other immigrants from Western and Eastern Europe. For well over a century, the source of immigration to Canada was predominantly Europe, due to racist policies that were designed to exclude people from non-White regions of the world. However, these policies were determined by a host of variables that were in one way or another linked to the diffuse understandings of what constitutes Canadian diversity, a phenomenon that still dogs the nation as it consolidates its well crated identity of a "mosaic".

THE POLITICS OF CANADIAN DIVERSITY

Canadian diversity has always been dependent on the political environment of a given epoch, since the nation's immigration policies have always rested on the prevailing ideology of the day. Despite its national and international image as an immigrant nation, immigrants have not always been welcomed, as they are sometimes seen as liabilities by members of the majority group. While visible minorities have always been at the receiving end of racially induced discrimination, at one point in Canada's history, some White ethnic groups were considered subordinate to other Whites, and even White immigrants from certain social classes were considered inadmissible (Porter, 1965; Isajiw, 1999). White Europeans who were excluded from entering the country included those who were considered " . . . illiterates, . . . sick, . . . physically defective, revolutionaries and anarchists, enemy aliens and anyone who might become a public charge". Instructions were issued to overseas immigration officers to discourage the immigration of Ukrainians, Russians, and Finns, on the grounds that they were not "readily assimilable" (Isajiw, 1999, p. 82). Thus, whether we speak in terms of the relationship between White and non-White citizens, the Anglo-French rivalry, or between the two charter European groups and the First Nations peoples, Canada's dominant-subordinate relations have never been static. As a result of this fluidity, these once "inadmissible" White immigrants now constitute part of the dominant group that wields significant power and determines the modus of the distribution of social rewards, including the nature and type of access certain groups have to education.

Sustained through various orders-in-council and immigration acts, Canada subscribed to a deliberate policy of maintaining a racially homogeneous society until the end of World War II. Then, domestic needs and global events necessitated a major ideological shift in immigration policy. Due to its enormous implications for diversity, and also for conceptual clarity, the evolution of Canada's immigration policies and laws is discussed here from a broad temporal framework.

PRE-WORLD WAR II IMMIGRATION POLICIES

The period before the conquest of New France by the English marked an era of immigration that was exclusively focussed on the colonization of Canada by the French. Between 1760 and 1812 large numbers of British immigrants came to Canada and became the second group of colonizers. This period, which also witnessed an influx of immigrants from the United States, was followed by the post-1812 arrival of other immigrants such as the Germans, Black enslaved peoples, and Sioux Indians (from the United States). Between 1880 and World War I, immigrants from Eastern Europe and Asia also began to settle in Canada. Since this was the era of industrial revolution, many of the new arrivals went straight to work in factories, thus providing cheap labour for the expanding Canadian economy. Besides the Asians who were brought in mainly for the purpose of working on the Canadian Pacific Railway, Jewish refugees, and immigrants from Hungary, Russia, East India, and Japan also entered the country at this time. This trend continued until reductions and restrictions were imposed between World War I and II by the *Immigration Act of 1919* and the *Chinese Immigration Act of 1923*. Like earlier immigration acts (see Table 2.1), both acts served to limit the number of non-British immigrants entering Canada. They also denied admission to groups such as Blacks, Asians, Germans, and others who were considered illiterate, sick, and unsuitable. This exclusionary practice continued until the end of World War II when global events, and an emerging social order within the North American context, compelled the government of Canada to enact more inclusive immigration policies.

TABLE 2.1	Important Canadian Legislation Affecting Immigration and Diversity
Legislation	**Purpose**
• *Immigration Act of 1910* (Order-in council)	• To stop immigration from India
• *Immigration Act of 1919*	• To reduce the number of non-British European immigrants (produced a list of prohibited immigrants)
• *Chinese Immigration Act of 1923*	• To limit the number of Chinese immigrants
• *Immigration Act of 1952*	• To give sweeping powers to the Minister responsible for immigration
• *Immigration Act of 1976*	• To liberalize immigration laws (removed race as a criterion for immigration)
• *The Official Languages Act 1969* (Revised in 1988)	• To officially designate Canada as a bilingual nation
• *The Charter of Rights and Freedoms* (Constitution Act, 1982, Part 1)	• To guarantee various rights and freedoms to citizens (reaffirmed Canadian multiculturalism)
• *Multiculturalism Act of 1988*	• To officially make Canada a multicultural nation
• *The Employment Equity Act of 1995*	• To ensure equal access to job opportunities to all Canadians
• *Immigration and Refugee Protection Act of 2001* (Bill C-11. Came into effect in June 2002)	• To add flexibility to immigration laws and aid refugee claimants

POST-WORLD WAR II IMMIGRATION POLICIES

The end of World War II marked another turning point in the development of Canada's immigration policies. Based on the government's recognition that immigration was a necessity for economic growth and development, Canada for the first time began to accept large numbers of immigrants from diverse and non-Caucasian countries. Between 1946 and 1967 there was a significant change in the demographic profile of the country as a result of the liberalization of immigration laws. Most significantly, with the establishment of the 1967 *Immigration Act,* which removed racial identity as an integral part of the existing policy, national origin, and by implication race, was removed as a condition for immigration. In passing this Act, the government officially replaced blatantly racist policies with more inclusive ones. The 1976 *Immigration Act* designated refugees as a distinct category of immigrants and introduced a point system based on several predetermined criteria (education, proficiency in official languages, employment experience, age, and adaptability). This further knocked down immigration barriers and boosted the intake of immigrants from non-traditional sources, making Canada the multicultural, multilingual, and multiethnic society that it is today.

It is estimated that between 1967 and the 1970s, immigration from developing countries rose by about 40 percent with the vast majority of people coming from Asia, Africa, the Caribbean, and Latin America (Ghosh and Abdi, 2004; Statistics Canada, 2003), a trend that continues to date. For example, of the 1.8 million who were admitted into Canada between 1991 and 2001, 58 % came from Asia (including the Middle East), 20 % came from Europe, 11 % from the Caribbean, Central and South America, 8 % from Africa, and 3 % from the United States (Statistics Canada, 2003). These increases are even more staggering when one considers the insignificant number of non-European immigrants before 1961, as shown in Figure 2.1. In 2001, 5.4 million people or 18.4 % of the total population were born outside Canada (Statistics Canada, 2003).

In addition to overall increases in immigration levels, Canada's visible minority population is growing at a much faster rate as a proportion of the total population. According to Statistics Canada (2003), in 2001, there were 4 million visible minorities in Canada, comprising 13.4 % of the total population, compared to 3.2 million (11.1 %) in 1996, and 1.1 million in 1981, accounting for 4.7 % of the population (see Figure 2. 2). At the dawn of the 21st Century then, there is compelling evidence that Canada's diversity will continue to increase. At the very least, the 2002 *Immigration and Refugee Act,* which affirms Canada' dependency on immigration for its population growth, guarantees such increases. In its 2007 Annual Report to Parliament given by Diane Finley, Minister of Citizenship and Immigration, the government reiterated this dependency on immigration as follows:

> Immigration will play an increasingly important role in supporting Canada's economic prosperity and competitiveness. In a few short years, given our aging population, Canadians who leave school for the workplace will only offset the number of retirements. Immigration will therefore be a key source of labour force growth in the future. Moreover, the country is currently facing significant labour market shortages in some sectors and regions. Immigration can contribute to addressing both short- and long-term labour market needs by attracting people with the right mix of skills and talents to support economic growth today and in the future (Citizenship and Immigration Canada (CIC), 2007 Annual Report to Parliament on Immigration).

Since 1981, Canada has had a proportionally higher intake of immigrants compared to other immigrant-receiving countries such as Australia and the United States. Demographic estimates suggest that immigrants will constitute a significant portion of the Canadian population by the

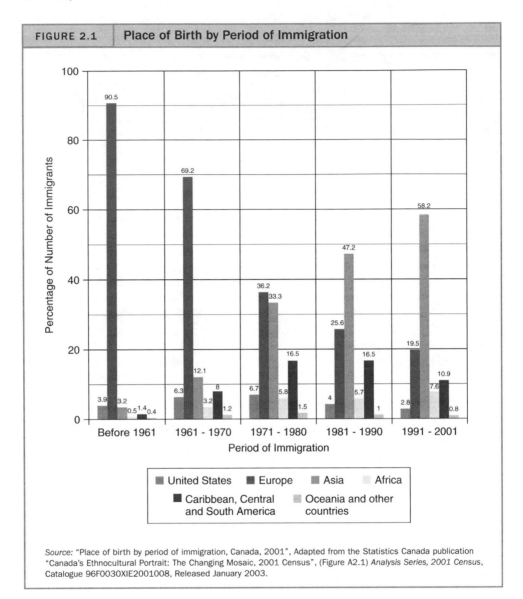

FIGURE 2.1   Place of Birth by Period of Immigration

Source: "Place of birth by period of immigration, Canada, 2001", Adapted from the Statistics Canada publication "Canada's Ethnocultural Portrait: The Changing Mosaic, 2001 Census", (Figure A2.1) *Analysis Series, 2001 Census*, Catalogue 96F0030XIE2001008, Released January 2003.

year 2017 as Figure 2.2 shows. Currently, immigrants constitute one-fifth of Canada's total population. With an official annual immigration target of 300 000 (approximately 1 % of the population), more than 200 000 new immigrants, mostly from Asia, the Middle East, Africa, and the Caribbean, settle in Canada each year. Of these, 60 % do not speak either of the two official languages at home. Not surprisingly, there are currently over 200 ethnic groups in Canada.

OVERVIEW OF CANADIAN EDUCATION

Based on the constitutional mandates of the *British North America Act 1867*, provinces have jurisdiction over education in Canada through publicly funded schools. By laws that are detailed in the various provincial education acts and regulations, the provincial ministry or

FIGURE 2.2	Visible Minority Population Projections 2001–2017

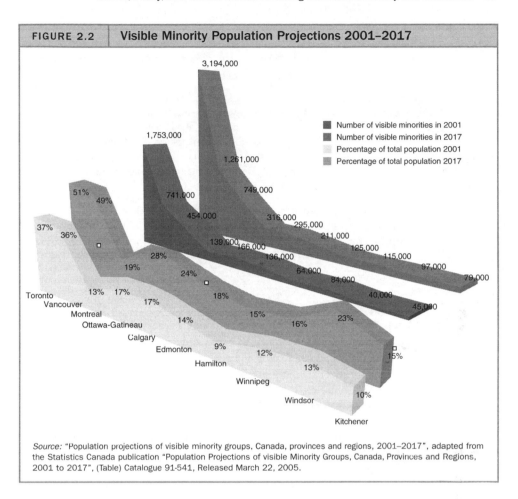

3,194,000

1,753,000

1,261,000

741,000

749,000

454,000

316,000
295,000

211,000

139,000
166,000

125,000

115,000

97,000

136,000

79,000

64,000

84,000

40,000

45,000

■ Number of visible minorities in 2001
■ Number of visible minorities in 2017
  Percentage of total population 2001
  Percentage of total population 2017

51%   49%

37%   36%

28%

19%

24%

13%   17%

17%

18%

15%

16%

23%

15%

9%

12%

13%

10%

14%

Toronto
Vancouver
Montreal
Ottawa-Gatineau
Calgary
Edmonton
Hamilton
Winnipeg
Windsor
Kitchener

Source: "Population projections of visible minority groups, Canada, provinces and regions, 2001–2017", adapted from the Statistics Canada publication "Population Projections of visible Minority Groups, Canada, Provinces and Regions, 2001 to 2017", (Table) Catalogue 91-541, Released March 22, 2005.

department of education creates curricula, sets standards for diplomas and certificates, and provides funding for school boards. However, while policies and funding are generally controlled at the provincial level, implementation is generally done at the local level. Unlike most industrialized countries, Canada does not have a national education system or national Minister of Education. While education is a provincial affair, the federal government can however, exert its influence on education through several mechanisms. The federal government's participation in formal education in Canada is through its involvement in areas of national interest. At present, this is tied to the allocation of funds and grants to nongovernmental organizations that are involved in the development and implementation of multicultural and citizenship education policies (Joshee, 2004). For example, Canadian teachers' associations and unions have policies and programs that are directly geared towards diversity and citizenship education, as do many community and advocacy organizations. Many of these programs are integral parts of the school curriculum at various levels of the educational system.

While each province varies in the policies and services that it provides to educational communities, there are however, commonalities that bind these policies together. For example, even though education is a provincial affair, the Council of Ministers of Education Canada (CMEC) generally organizes annual pan-Canadian meetings in which they discuss educational issues that are common to all provinces and territories. Besides the nationally decentralized structure, the Canadian educational system as a collectivity faces the challenging task of determining the most appropriate direction for education in the country. This perennial tension, which has been exacerbated by global forces, is summarized by Young, Levin, and Wallin (2007):

> Today, forces such as increased interprovincial and international mobility and the development of a global economy, coupled with efforts to equalize educational opportunities and to see schools play a role in promoting and sustaining a sense of Canadian identity, have produced pressures for increased standardization of schools and curricula across the country . . . Yet, at the same time, countervailing pressures require schools to acknowledge the linguistic, regional, and cultural diversity of the country, and to give individuals and communities more control over the school experiences of their children (p. 32).

The issue of providing a national education that also meets the diverse cultural and linguistic needs of Canada's children has become a cause celebre among scholars — both those who have a penchant for standardization and uniformity, and those who advocate educational justice for historically marginalized groups.

IMMIGRATION AND SCHOOLS

Canadian school populations mirror the ethno-cultural and linguistic diversity that exists in wider society, especially in large urban centres or Census Metropolitan Areas (CMAs) such as Toronto, Vancouver, and Montreal, where the majority of new immigrants settle. For example, in 2005, 30 % of the elementary and secondary school students in Toronto were born outside Canada in 175 countries; approximately 49 % had a language other than English as their first language; and about 10 % had arrived in Canada within the preceding three years (Toronto District School Board, 2006). A similar situation prevails in Vancouver and Montreal where a significant number of the students were also born outside the country. One issue that is not often mentioned but deserves special attention is the impact of refugees as a special category of immigrant on Canadian school systems. Traditionally, Canada has not always opened its doors to refugees, however, the rising number of displaced people resulting from global strife, has increased the annual intake of refugees. As shown in Figure 2.4, refugees constituted a sizable number of immigrants admitted into Canada between 1981 and 2004. During this period, 14 000 - 35 000 people were admitted into the country each year as refugees (Citizenship and Immigration Canada, 2004). Canada defines a refugee according to Article 1(A)(2) of the 1951 United Nations Geneva Convention, as any person who "has a well-founded fear of being persecuted for reasons of race, religion, nationality, membership in a particular social group or political opinion and is either: outside the country of their nationality; and is unable or, by reason of that fear is unwilling, to avail himself/herself of the protection of that country; or not having a country of nationality, and is outside the country of his/her former habitual residence, and is unable or by reason of that fear, is unwilling to return to that country" (Citizenship and Immigration Canada, 2006).

Based on the above definition, Citizenship and Immigration Canada (CIC) recognizes three classes of refugees. The first class is the *Convention Refugee Abroad Class*, which applies to persons outside their country of origin but unable or unwilling to return there for a well-founded fear of persecution, for reasons related to race, religion, political views, or affiliation in a particular social group. The second class is the *Country of Asylum Class*, which applies when the applicant is outside his or her country of origin, but has been and continues to be personally affected by civil war or armed conflict, or has experienced violations of his or her human rights and is unable to resove the problem within a reasonable period of time. Usually, this category of refugee would have adequate resources to support themselves and any dependants. The third class is the *Source Country Class*, which applies to those who reside in a country that has been designated as a source country, or still reside in their country of origin but experience, or continue to be adversely affected, by civil war, armed conflict, or human rights abuses (for reasons that are associated with race, religion, nationality, and social group affiliation).

Until 1976, when the government enacted the *Immigration Act*, Canada had no clear regulations for dealing with refugees. During that time, the government accepted its refugees on an ad hoc basis. The government's admission policy was simply based on the perceived ability of the refugee to adapt to life and survive in Canada (Howard, 1980; Dirks, 1984; Kaprielian-Churchil, 1996). Today, once a person is admitted as a refugee, the sponsor (either governmental or private) is responsible for his or her needs. The government may provide financial assistance or loans through the Resettlement Assistance Program and Immigration Loans Program. The duration of this assistance is usually one year, and includes the provision of food, lodging, health care, clothing, travel assistance, language training, legal aid, etc. (Kaprielian-Churchil, 1996). Current Canadian refugee policies are covered under the mandate of the 2001 *Immigration and Refugee Protection Act*. One of the most important

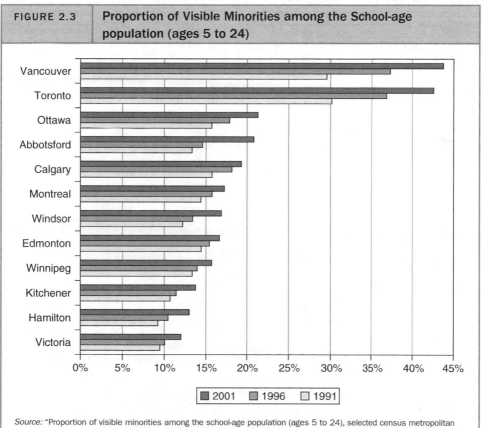

| FIGURE 2.3 | Proportion of Visible Minorities among the School-age population (ages 5 to 24) |

Source: "Proportion of visible minorities among the school-age population (ages 5 to 24), selected census metropolitan areas, 1991, 1996, 2001", Adapted from the Statistics Canada publication "Education Indicators in Canada: Report of the Pan-Canadian Education Indicators Program", (Figure A2.2) Catalogue 81-582-2005, no. 04, Released April 12, 2006.

instruments for accelerating the resettlement of refugees in Canada is education, as Flukiger-Stockton, 1996 writes "for people who have lost all their other assets, education represents a primary survival strategy. Education is the key to adaptation in the new environment of exile. Education is the basis upon which to build a livelihood. For some, education will be the decisive factor for resettlement in a third, normally richer country" (quoted in Hannah, 1999).

There are several ways that Canadian refugee policies have impacted the educational systems. First, many refugee children come from post-conflict and stress-prone situations that have health-related implications to which schools must respond. Second, like other immigrants, refugee students bring different cultures, languages, traditions, backgrounds, and values into schools to which systems must also respond (Kaprielian-Churchill, 1996). Third, confusions emanating from fluid government policies sometimes leave refugee children hanging in the balance, even though there is a provision in the current refugee policy that states that a foreign minor child in Canada does not require special authorization to study at the elementary and secondary school levels, unless he or she is the child of a temporary resident who is not authorized to work. A 1996 study by Kaprielian-Churchill found a host of issues related to the education of refugee students. One such issue involves bridging a problematic gap between educational institutions and the immigration system; this occurs primarily because education falls within the purview of the provinces, while immigration is federally regulated. Conflicts arise because interpretations of revisions to immigration regulations can vary from one school district to another across the country. For example, to be admitted, one school may require a student refugee to have completed the required papers for immigration, while another may choose to admit any child that has just arrived in Canada. A second finding of the study delineates the importance of early intervention in meeting the special needs of student refugees, which can be quite substantial, challenging, and complex given the history and (often traumatic), experiences of the students. As Grossman (1995) argues, students who have experienced the trauma of war,

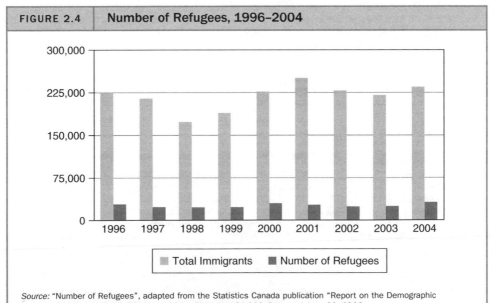

FIGURE 2.4   **Number of Refugees, 1996–2004**

Legend: Total Immigrants   Number of Refugees

Source: "Number of Refugees", adapted from the Statistics Canada publication "Report on the Demographic Situation in Canada", Table 2003 and 2004, Catalogue 91-209, Released June 30, 2006.

famine, persecution, and other suffering in their home lands, or have stayed for extensive periods of time in internment camps before arriving in a new country, bring additional problems which may impact on their performance and functioning within the school. Many student refugees who come to Canada often have, like their parents, experienced violence including murder, rape, unrelenting threat to life, genocide, and a host of other unspeakable acts that leave lasting emotional damage. As a consequence, schools must always be prepared to provide the necessary services, including psychological counselling, for these students.

THE POLICY OF MULTICULTURALISM

Another policy that has had a far reaching impact on Canadian diversity is the official designation of the country as a multicultural society. As discussed above, Canada has always been a de facto diverse society, even though the French and the English have dominated its historical and political landscape to the neglect of the First Nations peoples and other non-dominant groups. However, fermenting nationalist sentiments among French Canadians who had been marginalized relative to English Canadians led to the establishment of the *Royal Commission on Bilingualism and Biculturalism* by the government of Lester B. Pearson in 1963. Although the commission's primary mandate was to explore ways of developing a federal state that would be based on a doctrine of equal partnership between the two charter groups, it was also charged with "taking into account the contribution made by other ethnic groups to the cultural enrichment of Canada and the measures that should be taken to safeguard that contribution". This accounting was in response to the demands for a voice in Canada's affairs by other established ethnic groups such as the Ukrainians, Italians, Polish, Portuguese, etc. In publishing its report and recommendations, the commission devoted a volume to the important contribution of Canada's other ethnic groups, which resulted in 1971 with the adoption of the policy of *Multiculturalism within a Bilingual Framework* by the government of Pierre Elliot Trudeau (see Table 2.2). The social implications of this policy were enormous, the most obvious being that while Canada had two official languages, it had no official culture — as far as the government was concerned, every culture mattered.

According to some scholars and analysts, the policy was an attempt by the government to appease the French, English, and other Canadian ethnic groups. Much more noteworthy is the government's shift from an assimilationist and integrationist social ideology to a pluralist ideal, which recognized that beyond Canada's often-assumed dual character, ethnocultural diversity had become an inescapable social reality. To promote and support the new policy, the federal government made a commitment to assist all cultural groups that demonstrated a desire and effort to continue to grow and develop in Canada. The government would assist all such groups to overcome the barriers that impeded their full participation within the Canadian society. In addition, immigrants would be provided the assistance required for the acquisition of at least one of the two official languages (English and French) and finally, it would promote positive intercultural interaction in the interest of national unity.

Federally, successive Canadian governments (regardless of ideological affiliation), have strived to support the policy both in principle and in practice. It is not surprising therefore, that years after the official adoption of the policy, Prime Minister Jean Chrétien enthusiastically declared the following regarding Canada's ethnocultural diversity:

Canada has become a post-national, multi-cultural society. It contains the globe within its border, and Canadians have learned that their two international languages and their diversity are a comparative advantage and a source of continuing creativity and innovation. Canadians are, by virtue of history and necessity, open to the world (2000).

However, its endorsement and adoption by successive federal and provincial governments not withstanding, the policy has been extensively critiqued within the Canadian public policy discourse. Friesen (1992) identifies several recurring criticisms of the policy. One criticism is that multiculturalism is antithetic to the spirit of nationhood, and may emphasize differences rather than promote the ideology of a "Canadian" culture (Burnet, 1984; Bissoondath, 2002). This could inadvertently prevent minorities and ethnic groups from equally enjoying opportunities within the larger society.

A second criticism concerns equitable funding, the argument being that multicultural funding has been selective and unfair, and may result in further splintering of groups due to resource related in-fighting. Related to this is the problem of regional imbalance. For example, a significant proportion of the populations of Ontario, British Columbia, Alberta, Manitoba, and Quebec are made up of non-European ethnic groups, including new immigrants, visible minorities, and First Nations peoples. Provinces such as Newfoundland and Labrador, Prince Edward Island, Nova Scotia, and New Brunswick are primarily populated by members of the two charter groups. Due to the differences in provincial demographic profiles, issues related to the policy do not resonate in provinces with predominately European or Caucasian Canadian populations, while it is central to social and educational discourse in provinces such as Ontario, British Columbia, and Quebec.

There is also an urban-rural dichotomy (Dreidger, 2003). Many ethnic minorities, especially new immigrants, tend to settle in large inner cities and CMAs, which means that issues related to multiculturalism are often considered to be more relevant to these communities. Yet as discussed in Chapter 7, promoting fairness and social justice in Canadian schools requires collaboration with members of the dominant group in ways that will awaken their consciousness and appreciation of their privileged position relative to minority "others". Any model of empowerment that excludes White Canadians is exclusionary and can at best have marginal results, since change should not emanate from those who require justice *as they already see the need for change.*

Also, the direction and nature of the debate surrounding multicultural policies tend to be shaped by the vociferousness of the most visible minority groups within a locale. For instance, the high proportion of African Canadians in Toronto may be one of the reasons why discourse on diversity tends to focus on the intersections of race, ethnicity, and education within the city, while the interplay between race and education is more nuanced in Vancouver (Carrington and Bonnett, 1997). Thus, even within nonmainstream communities, those whose voices are less audible are further marginalized.

A third criticism of multiculturalism is that it has become a matter of political expediency for politicians trying to garner votes from minority groups — it is simply an ideology that is disguised as a political reality. In other words, once it has been established, multiculturalism masks the inequities that exist in society under the guise of a policy that values inclusion (Ng, 1995). Indeed, as John Porter, the eminent Canadian economist argued in his landmark work the *Vertical Mosaic: An analysis of social class and power in Canada* (1965), Canada's mosaic, is in reality asymmetrical. Access to social rewards (including occupations) is still a function of one's location on a vertical continuum of ethnicity, class, and power within the so-called mosaic. People of British ancestry are at the apex of the hierarchy. What is particularly relevant to our discussion is that for all practical purposes, the perception of Canada as an egalitarian mosaic may be an illusion that sustains the status quo.

Quebec's opposition to the policy constitutes a powerful and collective critique of multiculturalism. Fearful that the policy would subordinate the province's issues, Quebec's leaders have persistently criticized the policy and instead advocated inter-culturalism, (which although not explicitly stated) may accelerate integration and by implication, Francofication of new immigrants to the province. Like Quebecers, First Nations peoples (who have traditionally resisted being acculturated into Euro-Canadian culture), have also been dismissive of the policy because it infringes on their special and premier status within the Canadian confederation. Finally, there seems to be an emerging consensus among both its supporters and detractors alike, that almost four decades later, multiculturalism (and its spin-off programs), has not delivered what it promised. Fleras and Elliott (2003) provide a compelling précis of the various charges against multiculturalism:

> The paradoxes and ambiguities implicit within multiculturalism make it an easy target: Critics on the left have pounced on multiculturalism as ineffective except as a mantra for politicians and industry leaders to trot out for dignitaries or public relations. Multiculturalism is portrayed as a colossal hoax perpetuated by vested interests to ensure minority co-optation through ideological indoctrination . . . . Those on the right repudiate multiculturalism as a costly drain on resources that runs the risk of eroding national unity. Those in the middle concede multiculturalism as a form of ideological indoctrination or symbolic redress, but whose social control functions are inseparable from society-building . . . Radicals flay multiculturalism as a capitalist plot to divide and distract the working classes. Minorities are ghettoized into certain occupational structures and residential arrangements, thereby preserving the prevailing distribution of power and wealth while hiding behind the mistaken belief that cultural solutions can solve structural problems (p. 300).

The above are all powerful arguments and it is natural for individuals and groups, no matter what side of the issue they are on, to see things through the prism of their own strategic interests. But the fact remains that whatever its weaknesses, multiculturalism is an undeniable attribute of Canada's identity, and consequently diversity is a reality that all social institutions, including schools, must address. In general, Canadians are supportive of multiculturalism and accepting of diversity. However, research has shown that Canadians also favour assimilationist ideologies — those who support diversity and multiculturalism in principle also believe that immigrants should seek to be "more Canadian". Furthermore, the findings of a 2000 Ipsos-Reid survey of 1500 Canadians indicate that a majority of Canadians value the contribution of immigrants to Canadian society. Overall, research suggests that Canadians are neither strongly racist, nor strongly assimilationist (Moodley, 1999). While the Canadian government is quite proud of its immigration policies, it should be emphasized, as James (2003) argues, that "in controlling entry into Canada these policies articulate a notion of who best qualifies to be a "Canadian" and who will remain a 'foreigner' - i.e., immigrant" (p. 241).

As many writers have pointed out, it is instructive that despite the rhetoric of multiculturalism (even from those who are well-intentioned), the nexus of education in Canada continues to be Eurocentric, even though the worldviews of other groups (including those of Aboriginal peoples), are sometimes accommodated through the implied benevolence of the two charter groups. In effect, more work needs to be done towards removing the cultural barriers and injustices that non-majority group children experience in school. At the very least, the policy of multiculturalism provides compelling moral and ethical reasons to do so.

Educational Implications of the Policy

As it had for various sectors of the Canadian society, the policy had both explicit and implicit implications for education. These include issues related to funding, the design of school curricula, pedagogy, and even the training of educational personnel: schools now require teachers (who were not culturally literate) to impart relevant cultural knowledge to their diverse students. However, as pundits contend, the implementation of corresponding educational policies has been patchy and inconsistent. For instance, because educational governance in Canada is decentralized, the development and implementation of relevant educational policies and programs has not been uniform across jurisdictions.

Provincial responses to Pierre Trudeau's vision of a multicultural Canada were mixed and varied, ranging from enthusiastic embrace to cautious acceptance, and to inaction (Friesen, 1992). For example, Manitoba was the first to develop a **multicultural education** policy in 1972. Saskatchewan followed with its own policy in 1974, while Ontario officially developed a multicultural education policy in 1979. New Brunswick and Nova Scotia responded cautiously in 1986 and 1989. Alberta adopted its multicultural policy in the *Alberta Cultural Heritage Act* in 1990. With the act, a multicultural fund was established to fund programs and services, including educational programs, that were related to its mandates. British Columbia responded rather slowly and did not develop a corresponding policy until 1993. Prince Edward Island was ambivalent at first but eventually responded formally. To date, Newfoundland and Labrador, Yukon, the Northwest Territories, and Nunavut have no formal multiculturalism policy. Quebec refused to acknowledge the term **multiculturalism** but, in 1981, enacted its own **intercultural** policy, which was aimed at preserving the province's French character while protecting the rights of minorities. Quebec's educational policies are grounded in the principles of its intercultural policy, which was revised in 1985, and then renewed in 1990. Despite these disparate responses, as I have already argued, students in Canada now come from a variety of backgrounds and encounters with diversity are commonplace in schools. As such, schools are morally and ethically compelled, beyond a superficial level that extols diversity in principle but de-emphasizes it in practice (Solomon and Levine-Rasky, 1996), to address ways of helping every student succeed. The situation becomes even more complex when juxtaposed with the education of children of Canada's premier citizens, the First Nations peoples.

TABLE 2.2	The Root of Canada's de Jure Multiculturalism – Prime Minister Pierre Trudeau's Seminal Proclamation

Right Hon. P. E. Trudeau (Prime Minister): Mr. Speaker, I am happy this morning to be able to reveal to the House that the government has accepted all those recommendations of the *Royal Commission on Bilingualism and Biculturalism* which are contained in Volume IV of its reports directed to federal departments and agencies. Honourable members will recall that the subject of this volume is "the contribution by other ethnic groups to the cultural enrichment of Canada and the measures that should be taken to safeguard that contribution".

Volume IV examined the whole question of cultural and ethnic pluralism in this country and the status of our various cultures and languages, an area of study given all too little attention in the past by scholars.

It was the view of the royal commission, shared by the government and, I am sure, by all Canadians, that there cannot be one cultural policy for Canadians of British and French origin, another for the original peoples and yet a third for all others. For although there are two official languages, there is no official culture, nor does any ethnic group take precedence over any other. No citizen or group of citizens is other than Canadian, and all should be treated fairly.

The royal commission was guided by the belief that adherence to one's ethnic group is influenced not so much by one's origin or mother tongue as by one's sense of belonging to the group, and by what the commission calls the group's "collective will to exist". The government shares this belief.

The individual's freedom would be hampered if he were locked for life within a particular cultural compartment by the accident of birth or language. It is vital, therefore, that every Canadian, whatever his ethnic origin, be given a chance to learn at least one of the two languages in which his country conducts its official business and its politics.

A policy of multiculturalism within a bilingual framework commends itself to the government as the most suitable means of assuring the cultural freedom of Canadians. Such a policy should help to break down discriminatory attitudes and cultural jealousies. National unity if it is to mean anything in the deeply personal sense, must be founded on confidence in one's own individual identity; out of this can grow respect for that of others and a willingness to share ideas, attitudes and assumptions. A vigorous policy of multiculturalism will help create this initial confidence. It can form the base of a society which is based on fair play for all.

The government will support and encourage the various cultures and ethnic groups that give structure and vitality to our society. They will be encouraged to share their cultural expression and values with other Canadians and so contribute to a richer life for us all.

In the past, substantial public support has been given largely to the arts and cultural institutions of English speaking Canada. More recently and largely with the help of the royal commission's earlier recommendations in Volumes I to III, there has been a conscious effort on the government's part to correct any bias against the French language and culture. In the last few months the government has taken steps to provide funds to support cultural educational centres for native people. The policy I am announcing today accepts the contention of the other cultural communities that they, too, are essential elements in Canada and deserve government assistance in order to contribute to regional and national life in ways that derive from their heritage yet are distinctively Canadian.

In implementing a policy of multiculturalism within a bilingual framework, the government will provide support in four ways.

First, resources permitting, the government will seek to assist all Canadian cultural groups that have demonstrated a desire and effort to continue to develop a capacity to grow and contribute to Canada, and a clear need for assistance, the small and weak groups no less than the strong and highly organized.

Second, the government will assist members of all cultural groups to overcome cultural barriers to full participation in Canadian society.

Third, the government will promote creative encounters and interchange among all Canadian cultural groups in the interest of national unity.

Fourth, the government will continue to assist immigrants to acquire at least one of Canada's official languages in order to become full participants in Canadian society.

Mr. Speaker, I stated at the outset that the government has accepted in principle all recommendations addressed to federal departments and agencies. We are also ready and willing to work cooperatively with the provincial governments towards implementing those recommendations that concern matters under provincial or shared responsibility.

Some of the programmes endorsed or recommended by the Commission have been administered for some time by various federal agencies. I might mention the Citizenship Branch, the CRTC and

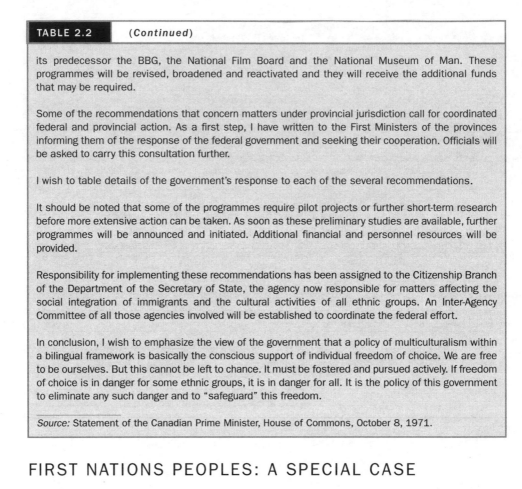

TABLE 2.2	(Continued)

its predecessor the BBG, the National Film Board and the National Museum of Man. These programmes will be revised, broadened and reactivated and they will receive the additional funds that may be required.

Some of the recommendations that concern matters under provincial jurisdiction call for coordinated federal and provincial action. As a first step, I have written to the First Ministers of the provinces informing them of the response of the federal government and seeking their cooperation. Officials will be asked to carry this consultation further.

I wish to table details of the government's response to each of the several recommendations.

It should be noted that some of the programmes require pilot projects or further short-term research before more extensive action can be taken. As soon as these preliminary studies are available, further programmes will be announced and initiated. Additional financial and personnel resources will be provided.

Responsibility for implementing these recommendations has been assigned to the Citizenship Branch of the Department of the Secretary of State, the agency now responsible for matters affecting the social integration of immigrants and the cultural activities of all ethnic groups. An Inter-Agency Committee of all those agencies involved will be established to coordinate the federal effort.

In conclusion, I wish to emphasize the view of the government that a policy of multiculturalism within a bilingual framework is basically the conscious support of individual freedom of choice. We are free to be ourselves. But this cannot be left to chance. It must be fostered and pursued actively. If freedom of choice is in danger for some ethnic groups, it is in danger for all. It is the policy of this government to eliminate any such danger and to "safeguard" this freedom.

Source: Statement of the Canadian Prime Minister, House of Commons, October 8, 1971.

FIRST NATIONS PEOPLES: A SPECIAL CASE

Despite revisionist accounts, Canada has always been a diverse society. It is a historical fact that by the time early European settlers arrived in what is now Canada, Aboriginals of various nations, including the Inuit and North American Indians, had already inhabited the land for centuries. This unique position warrants special attention to the nature of their experiences in any account of the trajectories of education and diversity in Canada. Although the European settlers considered them culturally homogenous, Aboriginal Canadians lived in culturally diverse societies that were constituted of different "nations", which not only spoke mutually unintelligible languages, but also had systems of self-governance and education (through oral modes of transmission) that enabled them to socialize the next generation. However, the assimilationist policies of the British colonizers, who saw Anglo-centric education as the vehicle for "redeeming and civilizing the savages", changed all that. In the words of Sir George Peckham, a 16th Century British colonialist, the education of North American indigenous peoples would redeem them:

> From falsehood to truth . . . from the highway of death to the path of life . . . from superstitious idolatory to sincere Christianity . . . from hell to heaven . . . . Besides the knowledge of how to till and dress the ground, they should be reduced from unseemly customs to honest manners, from disordered riotous routs and companies to a well-governed commonwealth, and with all that should be taught mechanical operations, arts and sciences (cited in Corson, 1998: 26)

To achieve their mandate, the Europeans developed an aggressive policy of re-culturalization, which required institutionalizing Canada's First Nations children in the now infamous residential schools, where compelling evidence shows they were subjected to the most brutal forms of oppression, degradation, social and legal injustices (Battiste, 2002; Royal Commission on Aboriginal Peoples, 1996).

Unfortunately, the assimilative policies of the colonialists devalued the culture and identity of, and eventually manifested in the dysfunctionality that exists in, many contemporary First Nations' communities and families (Isajiw, 1999; Ponting, 1998). Far from redeeming Aboriginal Canadians, the deprivileging of their cultural identities and the oppression and discrimination they experienced at the hands of the European colonizers, is an excellent example of the collective political, social, and psychological disempowerment of a people, which has impacted their overall life chances (as discussed in Chapter 1). Today, First Nations peoples have significantly less education relative to the general population. According to Statistics Canada, about 28 % of those living on reserves have only grade nine education compared to 5 % of the total population. While 15 % of Canadians have a university degree, only 4 % of First Nations peoples have attained this level of education (Barakett and Cleghorn, 2000; Statistics Canada, 1993). They are also significantly less represented in the work force as a percentage of the total population.

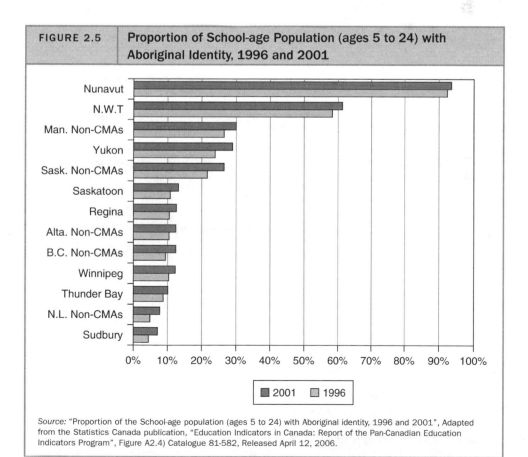

| FIGURE 2.5 | Proportion of School-age Population (ages 5 to 24) with Aboriginal Identity, 1996 and 2001 |

Source: "Proportion of the School-age population (ages 5 to 24) with Aboriginal identity, 1996 and 2001", Adapted from the Statistics Canada publication, "Education Indicators in Canada: Report of the Pan-Canadian Education Indicators Program", Figure A2.4) Catalogue 81-582, Released April 12, 2006.

It should be pointed out that Canada's policy of re-educating the "culturally deprived" as in the case of First Nations peoples, was not a unique phenomenon as Europeans have historically sought to "re-culturize" those who did not share in their culture and civilization (Henderson, 2000). Indeed, a similar trend existed in many parts of the Western world until well into the 1970s. In his 1970 book *How the West Indian Child is Made Educationally Subnormal,* Bernard Coard, a British educator of West Indian origin, provides a compelling account of the appalling conditions under which Black students who were considered intellectually inferior and thus sent to the so-called schools for the subnormal (ESN), were being educated in Great Britain. During the first half of the 20th Century, African Americans in the United States received similar treatment, until several court challenges (the most famous being *Brown v. Board of Education* in 1954), during the civil rights movement, began to change the status quo. Although some now argue that some of the progress gained as a result of the ruling is now eroding (Orfield, Frankenberg, and Lee, 2003), this landmark case accelerated desegregation of schools and ended the "separate but equal" doctrine as a deliberate policy, which had until then, provided the cover for unequal education between Whites and Blacks.

The First Nations Peoples and the Advocacy for Culturally Relevant Pedagogy

Unlike immigrants and other *diaspora* ethnic groups, Aboriginal Canadians have never accepted a "minority" status, given their unique position as the premier inhabitants of the land. Thus, despite a long history of subjugation, they have consistently resisted the governments' policy of forced assimilation, and instead have advocated the rights to self-determination and to educate their children according to indigenous epistemology — a worldview that is premised on the interconnectedness of all things (Battiste, 2002; Battiste and Henderson, 2000; Brant, 1990). For example, in stark opposition to the Eurocentric values that foster the exploitation and disruption of the ecosystem, indigenous Canadians have always lived in close harmony with nature and the land. This basic fact is the coalescing theme for curriculum development and pedagogy whenever they have had the opportunity to influence what their children learn in school, and in the last several decades they have continuously advocated for the right to do so. In response to these demands (and in an effort to correct past injustices), the federal Department of Northern and Indian Affairs Canada has developed policies to enable First Nations peoples to contribute to the education of their children in ways that are congruent with Aboriginal ways of knowing. Consequently, in many communities across Canada, including the Northwest Territories and Nunavut, Aboriginal peoples are actively involved in educational decisions, especially on the reserves. Also, the recommendations of the Royal Commission on Aboriginal Peoples (RCAP, 1996) have provided a policy compass for redressing the longstanding injustices that Canada's First Nations have experienced at the hands of mainstream society. The Royal Commission had this to say about Aboriginal people's control of education:

> We believe that Aboriginal parents and Aboriginal communities must have the opportunity to implement their vision of education. Aboriginal children are entitled to learn and achieve in an environment that supports their development as whole individuals. They need to value their heritage and identity in planning for the future. Education programs, carefully designed and

implemented with parental involvement, can prepare Aboriginal children to participate in two worlds with a choice of futures. Aboriginal people should expect equity of results from education in Canada (Volume 3, p. 442).

The Commission accordingly recommended some sweeping changes, including a call for the "Federal, provincial and territorial governments [to] collaborate with Aboriginal government, organizations or education authorities, as appropriate, to support the development of Aboriginal controlled educational systems" (vol. 3, p. 684). It is worth mentioning that in addition to the recommendations of the Royal Commission, international conventions also provide additional impetus to First Nations peoples' advocacy for the control of their own education. For example, Article 14 of United Nations *Draft Declaration on the Rights of Indigenous People* states

- Indigenous peoples have the right to establish and control their educational systems and institutions providing education in their own languages, in a manner appropriate to their cultural methods of teaching and learning.
- Indigenous individuals, particularly children, have the right to all levels and forms of education of the State without discrimination.
- States shall, in conjunction with indigenous peoples, take effective measures, in order for indigenous individuals, particularly children, including those living outside their communities, to have access, when possible, to an education in their own culture and provided in their own language.

Unfortunately, while there has been commendable progress towards improving their life chances, including the landmark September 2007 class action settlement in favour of the survivors of residential schools, negative and stereotyped perceptions of Canada's First Nations peoples persist as evidenced in their everyday encounters with some members of the non-native population (Battiste, 2002; Ponting, 1998). For example, the video *For Angela* (National Film Board of Canada, 1995), chronicles a true story of racial assault and verbal harassment: Rhonda Gordon and her daughter Angela were abused on a public bus by a group of White youths, as a result of their Native heritage. Motivated by the fear of a lasting negative impact of the experience on her daughter, Ms. Gordon refused to continue to be victimized and acted to stop the abuse. Enlisting the support of the administrators of the youths' school, Ms. Gordon initiated a dialogue that helps the students to understand the destructive consequences of their behaviour, which in addition to being prejudicial and racist, was also an infringement on their fundamental rights and freedoms as Canadians. A recent survey conducted for the Department of Indian and Northern Affairs Canada showed an increase of 10 % (compared to the last survey in 2003) in various forms of racism experienced by Canada's urban Aboriginal peoples. The survey also showed that 74 % of this racism was experienced at the hands of non-Aboriginal people. Given the injustices they have experienced and the concomitant tensions that have existed between the First Nations peoples and successive Canadian governments, Canadians often want to know what the nation's premier inhabitants actually want. As Fleras and Elliott (2003) argue in their poignant account in "Taking Aboriginal Rights Seriously" (see Table 2.3), First Nations people want what most Canadians want: equal rights and to live in a just and fair society where they are able to exercise those rights as protected under the Canadian *Charter of Rights and Freedoms*, and indeed under various United Nations conventions. They particularly want to be recognized for their inalienable right as the original owners of the land.

TABLE 2.3	Taking Aboriginal Rights Seriously

Aboriginal peoples define themselves as different and distinct. They categorically reject the view of themselves as Canadian citizens who happen to live in reserves. No less dismissive is the labeling of aboriginal peoples as yet another ethnic or immigrant minority. Aboriginal peoples claim to be a de facto sovereign political community ("peoples") whose collective rights to self-government ("nationhood") are guaranteed by virtue of aboriginality (ancestral occupation) rather than because of need, disadvantage or compensation. There is little enthusiasm for integration as an ethnic component into a Canadian multicultural mosaic, with a corresponding diminishment of their claims. Proposed instead is recognition of their sovereign status as the original occupants of Canada as well as a founding nation, not unlike that of the French in Quebec. Claims to sovereignty are defended either by reference to natural law or on spiritual grounds (Ahenakew 1985). As the original occupants whose inalienable rights have never been extinguished by treaty or conquest, aboriginal peoples do not seek sovereignty per se. Rather, they see themselves as having sovereignty, at least for purposes of entitlement, with only appropriate mechanisms required to put this autonomy into practice.

Aboriginal rights are different. Their differences are regarded as sui generis, that is, they differ from ordinary citizenship because only aboriginal peoples can possess such rights. Sui generis rights are based in sources of law that reflect the unique status of original occupancy (Borrows and Rotman 1997). These sui generis rights are collective and inherent: inherent, in that they are not delegates by government decree, but intrinsic to aboriginal peoples because of first principles, and collective, in that aboriginal communities can exercise jurisdiction over the individual rights of members of these communities (Denis 1997). Aboriginal rights encompass those entitlements that ensure their survival as peoples, including the right to ownership of land and resources, the right to protect and promote language, culture, and identity, the right to political voice and self-governance, and the right to aboriginal models self-determination (Mckee 1996).

What, then do aboriginal peoples want? The most direct response is, the same things as all Canadian citizens. Aboriginal peoples want to love in a just and equal society where they have the same rights as all citizens. But aboriginal peoples have also demanded their differences complement citizenship rights as the basis for reward or relationships. Recognition of difference is the constant that underpins all aboriginal aspirations. Without status differences, aboriginal people are in no position to press home their claims. Their claims have no more moral authority than those of other Canadians unless grounded in the motion that (1) they are different, (2) their differences must be protected, (3) these differences must be recognition and (4) differences must be taken into account as the basis for rewards and recognition. Equal opportunity or equality before the law is necessary but insufficient, since treating everyone he same merely freezes the prevailing distribution of power and resources, In the belief that equal standards cannot be applied to unequal situations without perpetuating the inequality, the principle of combining citizenship rights with aboriginal rights is proving provocative.

Source: Fleras, A., and Elliott, J. (2003). *Unequal Relations: An Introduction to Race and Ethnic Dynamics in Canada.* (4th Edition). Toronto: Prentice Hall. Reprinted with permission.

THE *CHARTER OF RIGHTS AND FREEDOMS*

The Canadian *Charter of Rights and Freedoms,* which superseded the Canadian *Bill of Rights (1960)*, is an integral part of the 1982 Constitution. It guarantees Canadians various fundamental rights and freedoms, including the freedom of conscience and religion, the freedom of expression, of beliefs, of democratic rights, of liberty and security as well as a plethora of legal rights. It also reaffirms Canadian official bilingualism, and the concomitant right of children to be educated in either language. Additionally, the rights of First Nations peoples are guaranteed as is the equality between men and women. Perhaps most relevant in the context of this book is that the *Charter* also reinforces Canadian multiculturalism and endorses programs and practices that are aimed at sustaining the nation's multicultural character. To complement the *Charter of Rights and Freedoms*, provinces have also developed their own Human Rights Codes, which outline the rights of citizens within each province and territory.

The *Charter*, Education, and Diversity

Explicitly and implicitly, some sections of the Canadian *Charter of Rights and Freedoms* have noteworthy implications for education, ranging from issues related to the rights of students, discipline, and compulsory school attendance to diversity, equity, and social justice. Consequently, the *Charter* has also had some impact on the extent to which provinces, territories, and school districts have responded to diversity in schools. Early debates on its impact on diversity and schooling tended to revolve around minority language rights, which are discussed in more detail in Chapter 3.

Today, the focus of the debate has shifted to discussions of the link between the empowerment of ethnic and minority groups within school systems, and the implication for educational policy and planning (Levin and Riffel, 1994). Many advocates for culturally relevant and inclusive education cite the provisions of the *Charter of Rights and Freedoms*, set out in the section on equality of rights, as an important starting point for analyzing the implications of the *Charter* for diversity (Levin and Riffel, 1994; Ghosh, 2004). To begin with, the *Charter* affirms Canadian diversity by endorsing programs that foster affirmative action. In so doing, it provides schools and society with compelling moral and ethical reasons for not only protecting the rights of students, but also for providing them with the kind of education that would increase their life opportunities and chances of succeeding academically. Specifically, sections 15, 23, and 27, which deal with equality of rights, minority language rights, and Canadian multiculturalism respectively, are particularly relevant here. Explicitly, section 15 not only outlaws discrimination by governments, it also makes allowances for programs, such as multicultural education, which seek to redress existing inequities (Young, Levin, and Wallin, 2007). For instance, subsection 1 of section 15 clearly makes "discrimination based on race, national or ethnic origin, colour, religion, sex, age, or mental or physical disability" illegal, and subsection 2 encourages programs and activities that are geared towards "the amelioration of the conditions of disadvantaged individuals or groups including those who are disadvantaged because of race, national or ethnic origin, colour, religion, sex, age or mental and physical disability". Interpreted in the light of the *Charter of Rights of Freedoms*, the dominance of Eurocentric knowledge in schools in many parts of Canada, an officially culturally diverse society, amounts to institutional discrimination and racism, and contravenes the principles of social justice. Ironically, the provinces and territories are not bound by the provisions of the policy of multiculturalism, as well as the *Charter of Rights and Freedoms* since both are federal legislation while education is a provincial affair (Ghosh, 2004). Nonetheless, many provinces and school districts have responded to student diversity by implementing various policies and programs.

EDUCATIONAL RESPONSE TO DIVERSITY

Early response to diversity by successive Canadian governments, particularly colonial administrations, was a policy of total assimilation, Anglo-conformity, and suppression of non-dominant cultures and languages. This policy of assimilation prevailed until well into the second half of the 20th Century, when Canada began to accept large numbers of immigrants from non-European countries. Beginning in the late 1970s and well into the 1980s, growing anecdotal and empirical evidence began to emerge that highlighted the fact that educational systems were failing to meet the academic and social needs of minority students in many parts of the Western world (Ryan, 2006; Wilkins, 2005). In Canada, the *Bilingualism Act* further accelerated schools' response to diversity, culminating in contemporary policies that are now in place for empowering students from diverse backgrounds, and providing equal educational opportunities for all. That said, specific programs and strategies are context-dependent, and are based on the perceptions of those whose voices hold sway in any particular context. In a discussion of alternative models for dealing with diversity in education, Ouellet (1992) identifies four ideological options that, in principle, serve as the basis for educational responses to diversity. The first option is the monocultural paradigm, in which the state imposes a "national culture", to which every citizen must adhere regardless of ethnicity. The educational aspect of this model would be **monocultural education**. In the second option the state's focus is on social cohesion, which fosters **intercultural education**. Consequently, enhancing the opportunities for harmonious relations between various ethnic groups, is a priority. In the third, transcultural option, citizens are encouraged to "go beyond the borders" of their ethnic group to creatively face the challenges that are inherent in a globalized world. This option by implication, emphasizes **transcultural education**. In the fourth, multicultural option, the state assumes the responsibility of helping all ethnic groups preserve their cultural and linguistic identities. This option provides the rationale for **multicultural education**, which is discussed in more detail below.

MULTICULTURAL EDUCATION

By far the most common policy and educational response to diversity, multicultural education grew out of the turmoil of the civil rights movement during the 1960s. While specific strategies are contingent on the milieu, its popularity increased significantly in the 1970s and 1980s when minority groups in countries such as Canada, the United Kingdom, the United States, and Australia began to challenge the privileging of Eurocentric worldviews in schools and demanded that their voices must be heard. Buoyed by the anti-oppression works of critical theorists and progressive educators (see Freire, 1970; Apple, 1982; McLaren, 2007; Giroux, 1983), they argued that it was fundamentally unfair that their children's ways of interpreting the world were not integral components of the curriculum.

Its emergence within the Canadian social and policy discourse was expedited by the nation's shifting demographic profile, as well as by the government's policy of "multiculturalism within a bilingual framework". The educational implications of this policy were quite significant. When the federal government adopted the policy, it expected the provinces, territories, and social institutions (including schools) to develop policies that would sustain Canada's emerging identity as a multicultural nation. Indeed, it can be argued that the emergence of multicultural education in Canada was a "neo-multiculturalism" movement, which symbolized the efforts of minority groups to challenge the prevailing cultural capital in schools (which was exclusively monocultural—either Anglo-centric in English-speaking Canada, or Franco-centric in Quebec). Setting aside the government's expectations, the demand that schools reform to reflect Canada's cultural diversity seems logical from a social justice perspective — especially if we concede (as argued in Chapter 1) that schools are complicit through their **explicit** and **hidden** curricula in the disadvantaged status of certain groups in society. However, globally, the concept has faced intractable difficulties since its emergence, beginning with problems associated with its definition.

There is no universal agreement as to what multicultural education really involves (May, 1994; Diaz, 2001; Banks, 1999; Banks and Banks, 2001; Bennett, 1999). Researchers ascribe different meanings to it according to their ideological position. What seems obvious is that in its various forms, multicultural education is intended as **applied multiculturalism** at least within the Canadian context. Fleras and Elliott (1992) sum up multicultural education from a Canadian perspective, as an organized attempt to manage and accommodate cultural diversity in schools, and it ideally "encompasses a comprehensive plan for transforming educational policies, programs and practice at all levels and across most domains" (p. 187). Such a transformation would also include changes in evaluation and testing procedures, curricula, teaching methods, teacher attitudes, institutional norms, and school-community relations, all of which should be formally reaffirmed in a school's philosophy and goals. The following definition from Banks and Banks, one of its best-known proponents, is representative of the common conception of multicultural education:

> Multicultural education is an idea, an educational reform movement, and a process whose major goal is to change the structure of educational institutions so that male and female students, exceptional students, and students who are members of diverse racial, ethnic language and cultural groups will have an equal chance to achieve academically in school . . . Each major variable in the school, such as its culture, its power relationships, the curriculum and materials, and the attitudes and beliefs of the staff, must be changed in ways that will allow the school to promote educational equality for students from diverse groups. . . . (2001, p. 1).

Making an argument similar to some of the critical theorists that are discussed in Chapter 1, Banks and Banks also contend that as currently structured, schools favour students from certain backgrounds and contribute to the academic underachievement of those whose cultural values are not reflected in their everyday encounters with academic knowledge. In effect, making what students learn culturally relevant would, in all probability, increase their chances of achieving success in school. Because of the difficulties that are inherent in the concept, there are as many models of multicultural education as there are theorists.

Models of Multicultural Education

Given the wide range of views, the greatest challenge that has faced multicultural education is determining which model to adopt. An analysis of various models, e.g., those proposed by Gibson (1977), Banks and Banks (2001), Rezai-Rashti (1995), and Magsino (1985, 1989), suggests that there are at least seven theoretical conceptualizations of multicultural education.

Multicultural Education as Education for Common Values

Targeting all students, this model is essentially monocultural if we follow Ouellet's (1992) proposition above. It is concerned with creating a sense of national identity. To achieve this goal, classroom practices would emphasize universal values and methodologies. Clearly, there is an incontestable wisdom in recognizing the links between unity and diversity, since in any nation-state there are macro values that must be nurtured for the common good, as well as to provide a sense of oneness and national identity as individuals communicate across cultures. As argued in Chapter 1, people typically identify with more than one culture or subculture, and the boundaries between these are often blurred. However, promoting universal values should not obviate the fact that peoples' views of the world are shaped by one predominant culture. Thus, valuing some cultures less than others in school, amounts to making those who subscribe to those cultures invisible. For all practical purposes therefore, this perspective of teaching and learning is not a transformative strategy for managing diversity in contemporary schools.

Multicultural Education as Education of the Culturally Different

This approach aims to equalize educational opportunities for culturally different students. There is an assumption that cultural differences create learning problems for students who do not have the cultural capital that is commensurate with that of the school. To remedy the problem, the school curriculum would relate course materials to minority students' cultural background as the starting point for their school success. The major flaw in this approach is the implicit notion of the superiority of one culture over others, which would ultimately lead to monocultural education. Also, since the model targets solely students from minority communities it negates the importance of engaging mainstream society, if critical praxis is the goal of progressive educational policies. Indeed, like their culturally different peers, White students have as much to gain from multicultural literacy as the students it is ostensibly designed to support.

Multicultural Education as Education for Cultural Understanding

According to Magsino (1985), this approach recognizes cultural diversity as a social reality in Canada, and it aims to promote cultural understanding and the appreciation of cultural similarities and differences in a plural and discrimination-free society. This means that schools would promote understanding and the acceptance of cultural differences, which would in turn foster social cohesion. In addition to removing cultural biases from textbooks, the model emphasizes the integration of cultural materials into the school curriculum to "ensure ethnic visibility". While this approach is an improvement on the first two, it would not empower students from non-dominant backgrounds in any meaningful way.

Multicultural Education as Education for Cultural Accommodation

This "accomodationist" perspective rejects segregationist ideologies. Rather, it sees cultural pluralism as a desirable social goal. Thus, each cultural group can become a politically viable interest group that is able to negotiate equitable distribution of social resources. The assumption is that the awareness of the power and dignity of one's ethnic group would enhance academic success, and subsequently lead to equality. The main beneficiaries of this approach (although intended for all students) would be children from diverse backgrounds since schools already promote the Western European culture of the dominant group. There is, however, a paternalistic overtone to this approach since minority communities are implicitly the beneficiaries of the benevolence of the dominant group.

Bicultural Education

According to Gibson (1977), bicultural education rejects cultural assimilation and " . . . seeks to produce a student who is able to operate across group boundaries". One underlying assumption of this approach is that while the retention of one's culture is essential, the acquisition of a second culture is also a worthwhile goal in culturally diverse societies. Thus, students from mainstream culture would also benefit from competencies in a second culture. It is also assumed that bicultural education would equalize economic opportunities for mainstream and minority students alike.

Multicultural Education as Education for Cultural Preservation

While this approach recognizes cultural difference as a social reality, its "segregationist" conception of multicultural education advocates the maintenance of ethnic boundaries — the "mosaic of segregated peoples" (Magsino, 1985: 6). Under this model, group interests would supersede the interests of wider society, and ethno-cultural groups would take control of their own destinies, including the education of their children in separate schools or schools-within schools. Magsino (1989: 61) suggests an outright rejection of this model since "it violates the principle of individual freedom, particularly for young people who are kept in ignorance and attain maturity unable to make decisions for themselves". To a certain extent, the advocacy for self-determination and for schools that are grounded in indigenous knowledge and pedagogy by Aboriginal Canadians and other ethnic groups stems from such a perspective.

Multicultural Education as Education for Multicultural Adaptation

This model aims to teach people competencies that would enable them to operate in two or more cultures within a society. All students would benefit from this approach and would be free to give up their original cultural affiliation, if they so desired. The model assumes that association with some ethnic or cultural group is essential for developing positive self-image. However, in order to determine the appropriate one, a person needs a "deep understanding of other cultures". Some of the pedagogical emphases of this approach include immersion classes, programs with courses taught in different languages, ethnic studies, multicultural extracurricular activities, and a good cultural mix of teachers.

Critique of Multicultural Education

While the various approaches to multicultural education have been tried and tested in different countries and educational contexts, its merits and limitations have been fiercely debated (May, 1994, 1999).Central to the debates are two diametrically opposing positions: the nature and extent of its transformative potential, and the thorny issue of individual versus collective rights. Moreover, even when there is some agreement as to its desirability, the challenge often remains in determining which version to implement. At the beginning of the 21st Century, educators and other stakeholders have yet to answer this fundamental question.

One of the underlying assumptions of multicultural education is that making education culturally relevant and inclusive would reduce the high incidence of school failure among culturally different students, and subsequently improve their life chances. Proponents also assume that learning about other cultures would reduce prejudicial and discriminatory attitudes among majority group children towards those who are different from them.

However, if multicultural education has received support from some educators and policy makers, wherever it has been introduced, conservatives have denounced it arguing that the structural reforms proposed under its umbrella are far reaching and would Balkanize society, weaken social cohesion, and obscure national identity (Bissoondath, 2002; Hirsh, 1987). For completely opposing reasons, advocates of more radical and progressive educational policies dismiss its efficacy as a framework for social transformation. In their view, multi-cultural education (as commonly advocated), is superficially symbolic and it inadvertently masks existing structural inequalities and divisions in society, by pandering to the cultural sensitivities of groups that advocate social justice for minorities. In so doing, they assert, it diverts attention from the real issues, which are power relations and social exploitation of race, class, and gender (Dei, 1996; Dei et al. 2000; Apple, 2006; McLaren 2007; Ladson-Billings, 1994; Giroux, 1983). As established in Chapter 1, an educational system does not exist in a vacuum and therefore cannot be separated from its historical context, nor can it be viewed apart from the larger political-power and economic structures within which it is located. As agents of socialization, schools impart the tenets, values, and belief systems characteristic of the worldview of the dominant group. In this way, the dominant culture is imposed on minority students, regardless of its effects upon them. This imposition that implicitly trivializes, de-emphasizes, and disrespects their culture, ultimately leads to disenfranchisement and ambivalence about their own culture and identity. The ultimate result is disempowerment.

The failure of the multicultural paradigm as commonly conceived and implemented in schools to address the unequal distribution of power and the question of social justice within larger society, constitutes one of its major flaws as Henry and Tator (2006: 214) posit: "Perhaps the most serious weakness of multicultural education was its failure to acknowledge that racism was endemic in Canadian society. While schools attempted to 'respond' to 'special needs' by affirming ethnic-minority children's background, culture, and language; by celebrating festivals; and by teaching 'mother' (heritage) languages; . . . the real problem of racial inequality was ignored". Put differently, diversity issues in Canadian schools cannot be addressed independent of a critical understanding of the power relations that exist within society, and how schools reinforce the status-quo. The argument continues that instead of multicultural education, what is needed is a critical analysis of institutionalized discriminatory policies and practices that are based on the colour of the skin, which keep minority groups powerless and voiceless. If multicultural education is to become social reconstructionist, it must translate rhetoric into action as well as focus less on histories, customs, and lifestyles. As Dei et al. (2000) argue

> the challenge of centring diverse epistemologies within the purview of standard educational practice, requires transcending the notion of multicultural knowledge and "experience" as rituals of song, dance and food. Instead, we must undertake a more substantive approach to knowledge production that situates education within a broad global epistemological frame of reference . . . extending our educational strategies beyond a "tourist curricula" (p. 171).

To challenge the status quo, critics of multicultural education propose an alternative approach, which they assert can better challenge the highly contested terrain of knowledge construction — anti-racist education.

ANTI-RACIST EDUCATION

Anti-racist education emerged as an alternative to multicultural education. Radical scholars and educators consider it a safe and apolitical response to the subordination of racial and cultural minorities in schools. As the term implies, its major emphasis is on combating discrimination against visible minorities, women, and other socially marginalized groups in society. It therefore addresses the problem of institutionalized racism and challenges traditional multicultural education, which is based on what Troyna (1993) refers to as saris, samosas, and steel bands. Proponents believe that the root cause of racism and prejudice is deeply embedded in social structures and institutional practices, and therefore cannot be adequately addressed by simply integrating superficial cultural and lifestyle knowledge into the school curriculum. Dei (1996) describes anti-racist education as

> [A]n action-oriented strategy for institutional, systemic change to address racism and the inter-locking systems of social oppression. Anti-racism is a critical discourse of race and racism in society and of the continuing racializing of social groups for differential and unequal treatment. Anti-racism explicitly names the issues of race and social difference as issues of power and equity rather than as matters of cultural and ethnic variety (p. 25).

Advocates of this paradigm are convinced that in the final analysis, education allocates power to individuals. If social equality is to be achieved, the fundamental barriers that prevent students from marginalized communities from the everyday sharing of power and social rewards must be broken down at the institutional level. The coalescing theme among the various arguments put forward by anti-racists is that neither the recognition of diversity per se, nor the preservation of one's cultural heritage, is enough to address the issue of unequal distribution of power in society. Besides their emphasis on racial patterns of oppression, anti-racists also point out the interconnectedness of all forms of oppression: including those that are based on race, class, gender, disability, and sexual orientation.

Although multiculturalists see anti-racism as analogous to multicultural education, anti-racists point to inherent differences between the concepts, arguing that the issue of race is treated differently in the two paradigms. They contend that multiculturalists tend to see racism as a product of ignorance and individual bias, but they believe that "the issues of 'race' and racism cannot be abstracted from the broader political, historical and social processes of society which have institutionalised unequal power" (Troyna,1987: 312). Despite the polemic between anti-racists and multiculturalists, there are similarities between the two concepts as both groups of theorists address the same fundamental issues — the subordinate status of racially and culturally different groups in pluralistic societies, and the ways in which educational institutions sustain it. Schools are therefore simultaneously the problem and the solution.

ALTERNATIVE SCHOOLS FOR MINORITIES

Currently, one of the most advocated responses to diversity in Canada is the establishment of alternative schools for minorities, in particular, Black-focused schools. Advocates of these schools argue that Canadian mainstream school systems have failed to empower minority students and that developing schools which are focused on their worldviews, cultural capital, and ways of knowing would reverse the trend of underachievement among these students (Dei, 1996; Dei et al., 2000). To its proponents, African-centred schools are critical to the empowerment of minority students in Canada and elsewhere. However, debates on the issue have been quite heated. In Ontario, where the issue has been particularly polarizing, there has been no consensus one way or the other. The opposition to the establishment of alternative schools for minorities tends to argue that ultimately these schools will become ethnic enclaves that have limited resources and attract only the poor. Current official government position in Ontario is to continue to educate all students in regular schools. Dei (1996), one of the key proponents of Black-focused or Afro-centred schools, provides a solution to how school systems can resolve the issues surrounding the creation of alternative schools for minority students. He argues that "the challenge is to move beyond the polemics of both advocacy and critique to concrete action, this means ensuring that African centered schools are not stereotyped and isolated but instead are given all necessary emotional material and other logistical backing to achieve what these schools are intended to accomplish for Black and other youth". One thing is certain, the issue will not be put to rest anytime soon. In Canada, the issues that surround the proposition for Black-focused or alternative schools for minority students are similar to those that have emerged from the resurgence of alternative schools for minorities, or "resegregation" as some refer to the trend in the United States (Orfield, Frankenberg, and Lee, 2002).

THE GLOBAL DIMENSION

In their edited book *Globalizing Education,* Michael Apple, Jane Kenway and Michael Singh (2005) argue that *globalization* has affected the way societies and education are organized. This is as true for Canada as it is for many Western societies. Within the Canadian context, it can be argued that ethno-cultural diversity is as much the function of global forces that have increased international population movements, as it is the result of progressive immigration policies. For instance, the increase in the phenomenon of displaced peoples has contributed significantly to the arrival of refugees from non-European sources on Canadian shores, which, as discussed earlier, has impacted on the ethno-cultural make-up of Canadian society and schools.

Educational policies are no longer made within the confines of national boundaries. For example, there is evidence that multicultural and anti-racist policies were to some extent influenced by complementary policies in Britain and the United States (Carrignton and Bonnett, 1997). Also, as McLeod (1992) argues, concerns about race relations in the United States led to the demand, in the 1980s, that multiculturalism must address the issue of race relations within the Canadian context. This demand had a spill-over effect in the educational arena, as school systems sought to introduce proactive race-related policies within their jurisdictions. Indeed, many multicultural and anti-racist policies in Canada were adopted during this time.

In addition to the mandates of the Canadian *Charter of Rights and Freedoms*, Canada is a signatory to various **international covenants**, which mandate that the rights of Canadians, especially marginalized and minoritized groups and, are safeguarded by the law. These covenants include The *Universal Declaration of Human Rights*, which was adopted by the United Nations in 1948, the *International Convention on All Forms of Racial Discrimination* (1965/1969), the *International Covenant on Economic, Social and Cultural Rights* (1966/1976), the *International Covenant on Civil and Political Rights* (1976), and the *Convention on the Removal of All Forms of Discrimination Against Women* (1979/1981). All these, in one way or another, inform the *Charter of Rights and Freedoms*, which in turn has had significant implications for Canadian education and diversity. As Power (2000) argues

> the broad international consensus that has emerged over the past 20 years on the rights of indigenous peoples has certainly played a key part in changing policy and legislation in at least 30 countries. While it would be fanciful to assume that these changes have eliminated centuries of injustice, prejudice and disadvantage there is a . . . veritable renaissance among indigenous peoples in their cultures, languages, histories and traditional ways of learning (p. 161).

Canada is not an exception in this regard. Although much work still needs to be done, First Nations peoples have benefitted from the global trend towards ameliorating their condition through education that is grounded in Aboriginal epistemology.

Summary

Historically, Canada is an immigrant nation. However, liberalized immigration policies since World War II have increased the admission of racial, ethnic, and linguistic minorities, resulting in significant demographic shifts in schools and society. With an official annual target of 300 000 (approximately 1 % of the population), more than 200 000 new immigrants, many of whom do not speak either of the official languages at home, settle in Canada each year. Currently, immigrants constitute one-fifth of Canada's population.

Collaterally, linguistic diversity in Canadian schools mirrors this ethno-cultural diversity, especially in large inner cities. Consequently, and also on the basis of the constitutional provisions of the Canadian *Charter of Rights and Freedoms*, as well as the policy of multiculturalism, social and educational policies have been developed to accommodate Canadian diversity. By far the most common educational response to immigration and diversity in Canada has been the adoption of empowering approaches to schooling. One of these approaches is multicultural education, which is premised on the rationale that school systems are morally bound to reflect the multicultural character of Canada, in order to equalize educational and social opportunities for all. In addition, it is also grounded in the principles of fundamental human rights and social justice, which reject monocultural and assimilationist educational ideologies in pluralistic societies such as Canada. However, the concept has been the subject of raging debate. Conservative opponents are united, and reject the concept on the grounds that it is antithetic to the concept of nationhood. Progressive educators diverge on one contentious issue — the efficacy of the concept as an empowering framework. While one group is quite supportive of the concept, the other argues that, although well-intentioned, multicultural education as commonly practised has been at best neutral, because it has failed to address the root cause of the marginalized status of minorities, which is the unequal distribution of power and thus the unfair control of educational knowledge by the dominant group. In effect, the argument continues, schools' policies towards education remain substantively assimilationist and monolithic. As an alternative to multicultural education, they advocate anti-racist education, which stresses the salience of race and social positioning in discourses on improving the life chances of minority peoples. The next chapter focuses attention on some specific attributes of Canadian diversity, e.g., language, religion, social and economic status (poverty in particular), and how these intersect with education.

Key Terms

Diaspora	Explicit curriculum	Globalization
Hidden curriculum	Intercultural education	International covenants

Monocultural education   Multicultural education   Multiculturalism
Transcultural education

Questions to Guide Reflective Practice

1. What are your personal views on Canada's contemporary immigration policies?

2. Based on your reading of this chapter, how does immigration intersect with Canadian diversity and education? How can school systems ensure that the worldviews of diverse learners are valued and respected?

3. What are the educational implications of Canada's multiculturalism policy?

4. The federal government once pursued a policy of assimilation regarding First Nations education against the backdrop of their resistance and research that suggested otherwise. In what ways was this an infringement of their fundamental rights and freedoms?

5. Based on the discussion in this chapter, with an emphasis on similarities and differences, do a comparative analysis of multicultural and anti-racist education. What is the most obvious difference between these paradigms?

6. In your opinion, what is the impact of globalization on education? What are the implications for Canadian diversity?

Case Study Analysis: Chapter Opening Vignette

1. Should all parents have a right to educate their children according to their cultural beliefs as Jeanne Elbbar suggests?

2. What is your interpretation of "equal education for all" given the discussion of social justice in Chapter 1?

3. How would you respond to Jeanne Elbbar's question "Whose knowledge really counts or should matter in a country that considers itself a *cultural mosaic*?"

4. In what ways are standardized curricula fair or unfair to students from culturally diverse backgrounds?

5. Assume that you are Judge Kohle; how would you render your verdict on this case?

Test Your Knowledge

1. Canada's First Nations peoples constitute part of the world's indigenous peoples. Name three indigenous groups from other parts of the world.

2. Identify ten countries in Sub-Saharan Africa.

3. Besides Mandarin, what other languages are spoken in China?

4. What is the law in your province regarding the enrolment of immigrant children in school immediately after their arrival?

5. What is your provinces' policy regarding the education of Aboriginal children?

6. How many new immigrants arrived in your province in the last two years?

7. What is Aboriginal epistemology?

8. Many provinces have formally established anti-racist networks that are designed to combat racism. Does your province or city have one?

9. List and discuss the achievements of five non-White Canadians. In what ways did the achievement of these individuals contribute to building Canada?

10. List at least three books that were written by non-White Canadians that you have read. What were these books about?

For Further Reading

Banks J. A., and Banks, C. A. M. (Eds.), (2001). *Multicultural Education: Issues and Perspectives*. (4th Edition). New York: John Wiley and Sons.

Bannerji, H. (2000). *The Dark Side of the Nation: Essays on Multiculturalism, Nationalism and Gender*. Toronto, Canadian Scholars' Press Inc.

Barakett, J., and Cleghorn, A. (2000). *Sociology of Education: An Introductory View from Canada*. Scarborough: Prentice Hall.

Bennett, C. I. (2007). *Comprehensive Multicultural Education: Theory and Practice,* 6th Edition. Boston: Pearson Education.

Derman-Sparks, L., and Phillips, C. (1997). *Teaching/Learning Anti-Racism*. New York: Teachers College Press.

Kauffman, J., Mostert, M., Trent, C., & Hallahan, D. *Managing Classroom Behaviour: A Reflective Case-Based Approach*, 3rd Edition. Toronto: Pearson Education.

Landsman, J., and Lewis, C. W. (2006). *White Teachers/Diverse Classrooms*. Virginia: Stylus Publishing.

May, S. (1999). *Critical Multiculturalism: Rethinking Multicultural and Antiracist Education*. London: Falmer Press.

Olssen, M. (Ed.). (2004). *Culture and Learning: Access and Opportunity in the Classroom*. Greenwich: Information Age Publishing.

Salili, F., & Hoosain, R. (Ed.). (2003*). Teaching, Learning, and Motivating in a Multicultural Context*. Greenwich: Information Age Publishing.

Wotherspoon, T. (1998). *The Sociology of Education in Canada: Critical Perspectives*. Toronto: Oxford University Press.

Young, J., Levin, B., and Wallin, W. (2007). *Understanding Canadian Schools: An Introduction to Educational Administration*, 4th Edition. Toronto: Thomson Publishing.

Websites of Interest

www.stemnet.nf.ca/CITE/canada2.htm Gander Academy: Resources on Aboriginal People of Canada

www.bced.gov.bc.ca/irp/be810/apcmul.htm British Columbia Ministry of Education: Multiculturalism and Anti-Racial Education

www.cea-ace.ca/foo.cfm?subsection = edu&page = map Canadian Education Association

www.albertaassociationformulticulturaleducation.ca/ Alberta Association for Multicultural Education

www.caslt.org/research/rep5e.htm Canadian Association of Second Language Teachers

www.cmef.ca The Canadian Multicultural Education Foundation

www.sasked.gov.sk.ca/docs/policy/multi/index.html Saskatchewan Learning: Documents on Multicultural Education and Heritage Language Education Policies

CHAPTER 3

Linguistic, Religious, and Socio-Economic Diversity and Schools

- ❏ Linguistic Diversity and Language Policies
- ❏ Immigrant and Minority Students' Experiences of Schooling
- ❏ Cross-cultural (Mis)Communication
- ❏ Religious Diversity in Schools
- ❏ Socio-Economic Diversity and Schooling
- ❏ Gender in Canadian Classrooms

VIGNETTE

Mrs. Mollard, who teaches seventh grade, and Ms. Glis who teaches fifth grade, are discussing the academic progress of Renaa (a relatively new immigrant student, whose family immigrated to Canada from a South Asian country two years earlier). As required by law, her parents had enrolled her in school immediately after their arrival. Following the school board's policy, Renaa had been placed in an ESL program that enabled her to receive additional English language instruction outside of her regular class. However, even with extra help in her ESL class, Renaa's current teacher was not satisfied with her progress in Language Arts, especially her conversational proficiency. She still had some difficulty communicating in English, and compared to the other students in her class, her reading level was below expectation. While Ms. Glis had been Renaa's first teacher in Canada, she was now in the seventh grade in Mrs. Mollard's class.

Mrs. Mollard: I am concerned that Renaa's proficiency in English language is not improving. I wonder what the problem is. You had her in your class two years ago just after she arrived, what do you think?

Ms. Glis: I don't know since I haven't taught her for a while, but I think you should give her more time.

Mrs. Mollard: How much time? I am worried that at this rate she may have problems making the transition to high school, which is less than one year away! A few weeks ago, I invited her parents for a conference, and we agreed that Renaa should be encouraged to communicate in English more often at home. However, this is difficult because both parents are also learning the language and speak their native language most of the time. In fact, that is a big part of the problem. How can she improve her language skills if she has limited opportunities to practise what she learns in her ESL class?

Ms. Glis: You may have a point there, but I still think that she needs more time. Think about it for a moment: Suppose the situation were reversed, and you found yourself studying in Renaa's home country, having to use her native language for educational purposes. How quickly do you think you would master the language? For precisely this reason, I try to be patient with my ESL students, and as you well know, I have quite a few! Every country and every language in the world seems to be represented in my class. Sometimes I wonder how I am able to deal with so much diversity. Besides cultural differences, my students also come from different socio-economic backgrounds. Sometimes, some of them (through no fault of their own) come to school without lunch. My class seems to be a reflection of some of the things I read in the papers and see on TV about socio-cultural differences among Canadian students. I must admit that I am sometimes overwhelmed, but I try to take it in stride and provide all the support I can for the students. That is probably what Renaa needs, your support and patience, otherwise your good intentions might actually do more harm.

Mrs. Mollard: You're probably right. I guess I'll have to try a different approach with Renaa. She really is a very bright girl, you know. Also, she is very conscientious with her homework and participates actively in all class activities. It's just that sometimes I feel that she is not trying hard enough to improve her language skills.

INTRODUCTION: THE "MOSAIC" IN SCHOOLS

Although the above vignette is a hypothetical scenario, it is a scene that is commonly played out in Canadian schools. Educators struggle to deal with cultural diversity issues and other types of differences among students, whether they concern new immigrants or other minorities whose families have been in the country for several generations. As noted in Chapter 2, Canadian classrooms, especially those in large urban centres, are not only culturally diverse — they are also a mosaic of linguistic diversity, as the home languages of many students differ from the two official languages (see Figure 3.1). As a result, many students experience language-related challenges. Unfortunately, teachers often interpret the students' difficulties in mastering mainstream (and instructional) language as a lack of motivation or requisite aptitude. But, as Ms. Glis in the above vignette suggests, let us reverse the situation for a moment. How easily would an English- or French-speaking Canadian teacher master Mandarin if he or she were to suddenly find him or herself as a student in

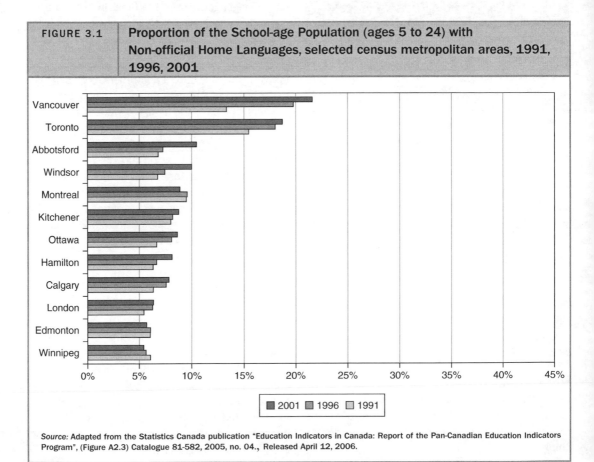

| FIGURE 3.1 | Proportion of the School-age Population (ages 5 to 24) with Non-official Home Languages, selected census metropolitan areas, 1991, 1996, 2001 |

Source: Adapted from the Statistics Canada publication "Education Indicators in Canada: Report of the Pan-Canadian Education Indicators Program", (Figure A2.3) Catalogue 81-582, 2005, no. 04., Released April 12, 2006.

China, or Swahili if the context was in East Africa? The excerpt from Howe (2003) in Table 3.1 explicates the point.

Howe's narrative of his experience illustrates the incredible challenges that many ESL or FSL students go through as they endeavour to acquire mainstream language. Fortunately, Howe's experience had a positive outcome because it enabled him to experience first hand, the incredible challenges these students face. But more importantly, this experience shapes his practice as an educator, enabling him to empathize with second language learners. Arguably, as an adult, these experiences were less traumatic for Howe than they would be for a young student in a new environment.

Language difference is, of course, only one dimension of Canadian diversity. The opening vignette serves as a springboard for introducing the various aspects of Canadian diversity discussed in this chapter. Chapter 1 centred on the general principles and issues that frame the debates on diversity in Canada and elsewhere, while this chapter discusses diversity issues that are specific to the Canadian context. An understanding of the unique characteristics of Canadian diversity, and how these intersect with schooling, are necessary precursors to dealing with diversity in our schools. Similarly, it is difficult to understand the effects of educational policies and practices in Canada without placing diversity at the core of our analysis. A complex web of interacting variables determines Canadian diversity within the educational arena, and the interface between the following aspects of our diversity

TABLE 3.1	Portrait of a Second Language Learner

It is a crisp spring day. The cherry blossoms are about to bloom and the noonday sun is streaming through the crowded spaces, reflecting off the glass and concrete office towers of Shinjuku. As the train comes to a halt I check the station sign — Sendagaya, yes that's right. I grab my knapsack and get off. As I head down the stairs, across the street to the large ominous building with the intimidating "Sendagaya Foreign Language Institute" sign, I am struck by the fact that I'm nervous and anxious. Why? Well, I deliberately overestimated my Japanese language ability in order to get into this pilot study language class . . . but how fluent is an "Intermediate" student anyway? Now I am about to find out. I enter the building, take the elevator up to the sixth floor where I am directed to a small, sparsely decorated classroom, dominated by a chalkboard and desk at the front. It is typical except for one feature — there are about 12 chairs arranged in a semi-circle facing the front. Many of the students are already present. "Konnichi-wa. Dôzo haitte kudasai," says a middle-aged woman I presume to be our sensei. I respond with a cautious, "Hai" and with a bow of my head I enter the room. It is quite a multicultural group as we discover in the introductions . . . entirely in Japanese. I am overwhelmed! Now I know what is meant by "immersion". The entire class is in Japanese. No English is used. Suddenly, I am no longer the "super-keener". The tables have been turned. I shrink into my seat when a question is asked. I am afraid of making a mistake. I feel way out of my league. Everyone seems so confident! I now fully relate to ESL students in Canada.

For the first time in my life, I felt the fear of making a mistake or raising my hand to volunteer information. At times I was totally confused—I had difficulty doing what the teacher asked of me. However, as an adult with a wider range of cross-cultural experiences, I believe I was better able to cope than most ESL students in Canadian classrooms. I have a great deal more empathy for ESL students, now that I have experienced what I perceive as their helplessness in a foreign classroom, as I was the Japanese foreign language equivalent of an ESL student in Canada.

Source: Howe, E. R. (2003). Curriculum, Teaching and Learning Within the Context of Comparative, International and Development Education. *Canadian and International Education.* Vol. 32 (2), p. 5. Reprinted with permission.

and schooling are addressed in this chapter: linguistic, religious, socio-economic, and gender. As one of the most vulnerable and at-risk populations in schools, this chapter also explores the status of minority and immigrant children in Canadian schools. To address this issue, the following questions will be explored: What are the experiences of minority and immigrant students in Canadian schools? To what extent are schools meeting the needs of the students? What is the nature of the relationship between minority students and those who teach them? The overarching aim of this chapter is to examine both the nature of the mosaification of Canadian schools, and the extent to which certain groups of students are either empowered or disempowered by the educational system.

LINGUISTIC DIVERSITY AND LANGUAGE POLICIES

Language matters have taken centre stage in Canadian social and policy discourses since Quebec's "quiet revolution" in the 1960s. This prompted the establishment of the Bilingualism and Biculturalism (B and B) Commission in 1963, and the subsequent institution of official *bilingualism* in 1971. Since the adoption of the *Official Languages Act of 1969* (revised in 1988), the federal government has been constitutionally and politically committed to the promotion of the duality of the Canadian confederation, and to the equal status of English and French as the official languages.

A second factor that has influenced language policies in Canada is the presence of (what is referred to interchangeably as) world, community, or heritage languages (Fleras and Elliott, 2003). These are languages that are spoken by ethnic groups who have maintained ancestral links with these languages. Also contributing to language policies is the massive post-World War II admission of immigrants from non-European countries. In reporting its findings, the B and B Commission (1970) was cognizant of Canada's de facto *multilingualism*, as it notes in Book IV of its report:

> The presence in Canada of many people whose language and culture are distinctive by reason of their birth or ancestry represents an inestimable enrichment that Canadians can not afford to lose. The dominant culture can only profit from the influence of these other cultures. Linguistic variety is unquestionably an advantage and its beneficial effects on the country are priceless (p.14).

To preserve this linguistic diversity, the Commission urged educators and school systems to explore ways of promoting heritage languages, provided that this was not done at the expense of the official languages. To fulfill this mandate, policy makers and school systems would have to adopt a progressive view that would value these languages as resources. Ruiz (1984) identifies three potential orientations in language planning: language as problem, language as right, and language as resource. According to Ruiz, the "language as problem" paradigm is grounded in hegemonic and assimilative language ideologies in which a dominant group marginalizes minority languages. This orientation fits Canada's colonial and pre-official bilingualism language ideology, when English was the dominant language of work, education, and everyday life. The "language as a right" perspective best describes Canada's rationale for the adoption of official bilingualism as a result of Quebec's increasing disenfranchisement. While it is the predominant French-speaking province in the country, and has a relatively smaller population than English Canada, Quebecers stake their claim that French be equal with English in Canada on the grounds of their charter status. Within the Canadian context, Ruiz's third orientation, "language as resource", embraces an ideology of **linguistic pluralism**, in which nonofficial minority languages are seen not only as resources (as noted by the B and B commission), but also alongside the official languages, as authentic media of instruction in schools.

Sustaining Official Bilingualism

As part of its commitment, the federal government provides funding for French language education (such as **French immersion** programs) across the country. A variant of bilingual education, French immersion programs began in St. Lambert, Quebec, as an outcome of political and educational factors and the aspirations of Anglophone parents who wanted to provide their children with quality education in English and French. It was expected that the students would acquire a significant level of proficiency in French while maintaining their proficiency in their first language, English. Although French immersion programs began tentatively as an experiment in second language acquisition, their success has been quite remarkable. In 1977–8 there were 37 838 students enrolled in the program nationally, and by 1998–9 there were 317 351 students in about 2000 schools (De Mejia, 2002). Despite the federal government's support for the policy, there is no uniform French immersion program in Canada as delivery structures vary from one province to another. There are also intra-provincial differences, because programs can differ from one school district to another within a province. However, in general there are two types of French immersion programs — Early French Immersion, in which students are enrolled in the program from kindergarten, and another variant, in which French instruction begins at a much later grade level. Pedagogically, most French immersion programs include instruction in French for half of the day and in English for the rest. One criticism often levelled at French immersion programs is that children learn the language in classroom contexts that provide very-limited-to-no contact with native speakers of the language (De Mejia, 2002).

Anglophone and Francophone minority language rights to education are protected under the Canadian *Charter of Rights and Freedoms*. Thus in many parts of Canada, schools try to meet the needs of official language minorities. For example, there are French-speaking Acadian communities in New Brunswick and other Atlantic provinces, and about half a million French-speaking Franco-Ontarians in Ontario, who have the right to educate their children in exclusively French schools. Similarly, despite Quebec's official *unilingualism* (which was established via Bill 22 (1974), making French the official language of the province as well as the language of commerce, work, and education, and the controversial Bill 101 (1977), banning the use of English within the public sphere), minority children whose parents were educated in English have a constitutional right to receive their education in English.

Notwithstanding constitutional guarantees and language policies that aim to promote bilingualism, the debate over language continues on three fronts. First, in the context of Quebec's fight for the preservation of the French language as an integral part of its overall struggle for a distinct identity. Handler (1988: 174) suggests this struggle "is also a battle on the ideological terrain over visions of the nation — Canada defined in opposition to the United States by the cultural characteristic of bilingualism, and Quebec defined as unilingual French in opposition to English Canada". Second, in the context of the adoption of just language and education policies that reflect the rapidly changing demographic landscape. Third, in the context of the nature, merits, and limitations of second language acquisition programs such as bilingual education and *English as a Second Language (ESL)* programs.

These in turn, invoke discussions of collateral issues such as the status of nonmainstream languages in schools and society, and the links between the exclusion of minority languages in schools and social justice (Corson, 1993; Cummins, 2000).

Diversity and Minority and Non-official Language Integration in Schools

One of the major concerns of linguistic minorities in Canada has traditionally been the exclusion of their languages as media of instruction in schools. The policy of multiculturalism (see Chapter 2) — which ensures equal status for all cultures and implicitly for their respective languages — provides a basis for the demand for heritage (or ancestral) language instruction in schools. As many writers have pointed out, the B and B Commission's recognition of the interdependence between language and culture is, in fact, recognition that non-official languages are integral aspects of any program that aims to affirm diversity. Similarly, the privileging of English and French in schools suggests that the languages of other groups in the mosaic are less valued. Thus, the exclusion of minority languages in Canadian schools amounts to a delegitimization of these languages, which is problematic in a self-proclaimed multicultural society.

Bilingual Education

One response to linguistic diversity has been the introduction of bilingual education, which in theory is intended to enable minority language students to achieve conversational and academic proficiency in a second language (L2), while retaining their proficiency in their first language (L1). Although there is substantial debate surrounding second language acquisition and the role of students' first languages, there is a body of research suggesting that minority language children generally profit from bilingual programs in which their first languages play a major role (Cummins, 2000; Corson, 2001). Generally referred to as *additive bilingualism*, a concept that was popularized by the work of Lambert (1975), the concept promotes the idea that proficiency in two languages is better than proficiency in one, and that the maintenance of the first language while learning a second one does not subtract from the acquisition of the second language. Cummins (2000) explains:

> The linguistic and academic benefits of additive bilingualism for individual students provide an additional reason to support students in maintaining their L1 while they are acquiring English. Not only does maintenance of L1 help students to communicate with parents and grandparents in their families, and increase the collective linguistic competence of the entire society, it enhances the intellectual and academic resources of individual bilingual students (p. 38.)

In practice then, this means that a significant amount of teaching and learning should be done in second language learners' L1, or these students should receive instruction in a nonnominant language (students' primary languages) during a substantial part of the school day. However, despite emergent research that supports the immense benefit of L1 in second language learning, what generally prevails is *subtractive bilingualism*, in which "a dominant language is learned with the expectation that it will replace the mother tongue" (Corson, 2001: 105). In this case, language learners are expected to de-emphasize the use of their first language.

Bilingual education programs in Canada can be broadly categorized as immersion programs in which students learn the second language and other subjects in that language for most of the school day. One example is French immersion as described above. A second approach is the transition program, in which students receive literacy lessons in their first language as well as in the second language, until they become proficient enough in the new language to be integrated into the mainstream classroom. Pull-out or "sheltered" programs, in which students are removed from regular classrooms to receive instruction in the target language or in their first language, is a third method of bilingual education. A fourth case is the maintenance program, in which the main objective is for students to become proficient in both the second and their first languages. A fifth way of providing authentic bilingual experiences to second language learners is through the adoption of two-way bilingual programs, in which native language English speakers are placed with students for whom English is a new language. As Nieto (2001: 161) contends, "Two-way bilingual programs validate both languages of instruction, and their primary goals are to develop bilingual proficiency, academic achievement, and positive cross-cultural attitudes and behaviours among all students". Research has demonstrated that two-way bilingual programs are effective in helping minority language students maintain their native languages while learning English. One example is the program that operates at Oyster Bilingual School in Washington, D.C. The program is organized as an English acquisition program for limited English proficiency students and is simultaneously a Spanish acquisition program for limited Spanish students. This program successfully provides proficiency in both languages to the students (Freeman, 1996, 1998). In Canada, a recurrent problem with the integration of nonofficial or heritage languages in school is deciding which languages to adopt as media of formal instruction.

Heritage Languages

Subsequent to the legal recognition of Canada's bilingual and multicultural identity, many provinces sought to integrate heritage languages into the curriculum. For example, in 1971, Alberta became the first province to formally allow languages other than English or French as media of instruction in public schools. This was primarily a result of the advocacy of the province's ethnic minority communities. Currently, Section 11 of the *Alberta School Act* gives school boards the power to authorize the use of languages other than English or French, as languages of instruction. Under the language art program, students can study Chinese, German, Spanish, or Ukrainian, in addition to some Aboriginal languages. Also, depending on the program and grade levels, students have opportunities to study further languages, e.g., Italian or Japanese. Besides the heritage languages that are taught through the formal curriculum, there are also two not-for-profit associations that promote international and heritage language education in the province: the Northern Alberta Language Association (NAHLA), and the Southern Alberta Language Association (SAHLA).

The second province to formally adopt heritage language instruction was Saskatchewan in 1978, followed by Manitoba in 1979. Currently, Manitoba pursues a deliberate policy of heritage language instruction (Manitoba Education and Training, 1993). Reasons for this include the promotion of self-esteem and self-identity, the preparation of students for living and working in cross-cultural environments, and to provide "the opportunity for all Manitoba students to study other languages, in addition to English and French, regardless of their ethno-cultural background". In addition to selected Aboriginal languages, Filipino, German, Japanese, Hebrew, Mandarin, Portuguese, Spanish, and Ukrainian are examples of heritage languages that are taught in Manitoba schools.

In response to the policy of multiculturalism, the government of Ontario, in partnership with some school boards, introduced several consultative initiatives that were aimed at examining ways of introducing heritage languages as a third language option in its schools. There was stiff opposition to its plan and after a series of compromises, Ontario adopted its official heritage language policy in 1989. The British Columbia Ministry of Education promotes heritage and international language instruction to enable students to learn second languages that are relevant to their communities. Non-official languages include German, Japanese, Mandarin, Punjabi, and Spanish, among others. School boards are generally encouraged to develop additional second language curricula that meet the needs of their communities. In addition to government initiatives, the British Columbia Heritage Language Association also offers heritage language classes in Cantonese, Japanese, Mandarin, Korean, Farsi, Portuguese, and German in various parts of the province.

While laudable attempts have been made by some provincial governments to integrate heritage languages into the formal school curriculum, English continues to be the predominant medium of instruction in English-speaking Canada, and through legislation, French remains the language of schooling in Quebec. Yet as advocates of heritage language teaching point out, for multicultural education to be meaningful, heritage languages can neither be ignored nor relegated to supplementary status in Canadian schools (Lupul, 1987). Moreover, if we agree that language is part of people's cultural capital, then privileging some languages over others in a multicultural society goes against the principles of social justice, which most Canadian public institutions aspire to achieve. Moreover, while language mediates our experiences as an integral part of our identity, it is at the same time the tool through which power relations are negotiated (and renegotiated) among social actors (Corson, 1993). Taken a little further, language is *who we are*. The power of language becomes even more significant when access to certain languages becomes associated with life chances. In Canada and other Western societies, the possession of high status (usually mainstream), language is often essential for access to social power, and the devaluation of minority language amounts to a negation of the speaker's identity.

As noted in Chapter 1, Bernstein's (1977) arguments about the linkages between language and power in schools, is in the end, about how language contributes to access to opportunities in society. Logically, those whose languages are marginalized are basically excluded from access to power. It is no wonder that language has historically been used as a tool for the socio-cultural assimilation of nondominant groups. Nation states attempting to create socially cohesive societies often resort to linguistic genocide to achieve such ambitions (Skutnabb-Kangas, 2000). For example, the loss of their mother tongue facilitated the domination of Africans who were "imported" to the West as slaves. In the Caribbean Islands, plantation owners deliberately tried to ensure that Africans who spoke the same language were separated from one another, as a means of political and social control (Beckles, 1997). A similar attempt was made to dominate Canada's First Nations peoples by the European colonialists, through forced assimilation and the devaluation of their languages. As Corson (1993) argues, a starting point for increasing the life chances of people from nondominant groups is the adoption of just language policies that protect their linguistic and cultural interests. Unfortunately, through the workings of **hegemony**, as discussed in Chapter 1, minorities inadvertently contribute to the marginalization of their languages.

For example, minority students are sometimes reluctant to speak their native languages in schools. This is either because they are embarrassed or because schools encourage limited use of first languages among second language learners, as evident in the opening vignette. Another example of minorities reinforcing linguistic hegemony (Michie, 1999, cited in Apple, 2006) documents the case of some Chicago students in a Chicago school who avoided interacting with other students who spoke only Spanish. In part, this was because they were experiencing culture clashes and also because of the school's policy. To help the students counteract their negative attitude towards their language and culture some of the students, in conjunction with Michie, developed a culturally relevant audio production of a popular book that provided the students with spaces to learn about their own culture in ways that had not been previously used in the curriculum.

The study by Dei et al. (see Dei et al 1997, 2000) on Black students' disengagement from schooling in Ontario, identified the exclusion and negation of the students' languages as one of the contributing factors to their alienation. This led the researchers to conclude that "if language, culture and other such identity factors could be integrated into main-stream education, the Eurocentric model of schooling practiced today would shift towards an inclusive environment where minoritized students could develop a sense of space, place and belonging within their schools" (2000, p. 107). Minorities tend to view their languages as the most powerful symbols of their ethnic identities, and often wish that schools would be more linguistically inclusive. In response to the lack of minority languages in schools, minority parents in Canada often enrol their children in community or privately run heritage schools, usually organized on Saturdays or after regular school hours, where they receive instructions in their heritage languages.

English as a Second Language (ESL) Programs

By far the most common educational response to linguistic diversity in Canada has been the adoption of language programs that are designed to accelerate language- and immigrant-minority children's acquisition of competencies in the official languages. Across Canada, ESL programs are intended to provide limited English proficient students (LEP) with extra support to accelerate their acquisition of English. Unfortunately, instead of teaching it in ways that encourage the maintenance of students' first languages (L1), schools respond in ways that de-emphasize primary languages. This deficit approach to the acquisition of L2 contrasts sharply with current research that shows the substantive cognitive and cultural benefits that accrue to children when their first language is maintained during the learning of a second one (Corson, 1993, 2001; Cummins, 2000; Ovando, 2001). There is an implicit assumption that exclusive focus on the teaching of ESL will facilitate minority students' successful integration into the education system and mainstream culture. However, as many writers have argued, schools have to make an ideological shift that will give greater recognition to the advantages of maintaining students' home languages while learning a second language.

Such a shift would see students' cultural capital as a resource rather than as a handicap. Students are not likely to succeed academically if they have a low sense of their own identity, of which language is an integral part. This is not to say that language- and immigrant-minority students do not experience language-related difficulties in school. On the contrary, problems do occur. For example, mother tongue interferences sometimes happen, although when such interferences are successful they are hardly noticed by educators, but when they are unsuccessful they are considered obstructive (Ariza, 2006). Also, it is not uncommon to find English speakers of Asian and African origin who mispronounce certain words because their mother tongues have no corresponding sounds (Egbo, 2001). That being said, these problems do not necessarily present academic difficulties for minority students, and limited English proficiency is quite often not the only cause of problems that may exist. The overall point is that de-emphasizing students' use of their first language, as Mrs. Mollard in the opening vignette suggests, is not a pedagogically useful strategy. This is particularly so, given that research shows it takes five to seven years for most ESL students to acquire a level of competency that enables them to begin to deal with ordinary classroom activities (Corson, 2001).

Beyond the ethical questions involved in deciding whether dialect students need remedial help, researchers have made several recommendations that may be useful to educators who are at a crossroads as to how to deal with the issue. A Canadian study researching students who spoke English as a dialect noted that students who were experiencing difficulties with classroom language found that unobtrusive but focussed attempts (using a preventive approach) produced promising results, although the study recommended more deliberate and direct intervention for older children (Morrison et al., 1991).

In Canada, the most common format for ESL instruction is the pull-out approach: students are removed from their regular classes for a specified time to work on their language skills. This approach enables these students to bond and share in their common learning experience, but it is exclusionary, and the tremendous pressure to learn and speak only English with minimal use of their first language can be disempowering. Although it has its associated problems, the increased integration of ESL students into mainstream classrooms, due in part to limited resources, may provide ESL students with opportunities to speak English alongside native speakers.

The Special Case of Aboriginal Languages

One issue that has been neglected in discourse on diversity and education in Canada is the question of the integration of Aboriginal languages into the mainstream curriculum. Yet researchers consistently argue that Aboriginal languages are the fundamental media for the survival of Aboriginal epistemology, culture, and values (Battiste, 2000, 2002; Leavitt, 1993). Not only that, Aboriginal languages provide a distinctive lens through which Canadian indigenous cultures can be understood. However, the evidence shows that while many First Nations students do speak their heritage languages, the most prevalent method of learning these languages is as second language instruction (see Table 3.2). Unfortunately, the acquisition of these ancient languages as a second language may not be enough to ensure their survival, given their marginal status in Canadian society and schools. Concerns about the declining status of Aboriginal languages as well as its commitment to preserving, protecting, and revitalizing these languages, prompted the federal government to initiate the Aboriginal Languages Initiative (ALI), which was designed to address issues of Aboriginal languages acquisition and retention at home. A 2003 Canadian Heritage report stemming from the evaluation of this project had this to say about the status of Aboriginal languages:

> Many Aboriginal languages are in a critical state of decline; with only three given a strong chance of survival. For many languages, the only fluent speakers are elders, with knowledge and usage weakest among the young. Preserving Aboriginal languages is an extremely high priority, because of the link between cultural preservation and language — without language, the main vehicle for transmitting cultural values and traditions no longer exists (Canadian Heritage, *Aboriginal Languages Initiative Evaluation*, Final Report, p. 26).

TABLE 3.2	The Status of Aboriginal Languages: A Portrait

Currently, only a minority of the Aboriginal population in Canada is able to speak or understand an Aboriginal language. According to 2001 Census data, of the 976 300 people who identified themselves as Aboriginal, 235 000 (or 24 %) reported that they were able to conduct a conversation in an Aboriginal language.

This represents a sharp drop from 29 % in 1996, and appears to confirm most research which suggests that there has been substantial erosion in the use of Aboriginal languages in recent decades. Another definite indicator of the erosion is the declining percentage of the Aboriginal population whose mother tongue is Aboriginal. In 2001, just 21 % of Aboriginals in Canada had an Aboriginal mother tongue, down from 26 % in 1996.

However, the decline in mother tongue population has been offset to some degree by the fact that many Aboriginal people have learned an Aboriginal language as a second language. In 2001, more people spoke an Aboriginal language than had an Aboriginal mother tongue (239 600 versus 203 300). This suggests that some speakers must have learned their Aboriginal language as a second language. It appears that this is especially the case for young people.

Over the 20-year period from 1981 to 2001, most Aboriginal languages, whether considered viable or endangered, experienced long-term declines in their continuity (see "What you should know about this study" for definitions). And not surprisingly, the endangered ones suffered the most. Among endangered British Columbia languages like Haida and Tlingit, for example, continuity levels declined to practically nil by 2001; indeed, each of these languages currently has fewer than 200 first language speakers. At the same time, while the more viable languages like Inuktitut have retained their linguistic vitality, several larger viable languages like Cree and Ojibway saw steady long-term declines in continuity over the two decades.

[The] issue is even more salient in Aboriginal communities (that is, reserves, Inuit communities and settlements). In 1996, about two-thirds of comparable communities reported that most Aboriginal speakers had learned the language as their mother tongue; by 2001, the proportion had dropped to less than half. In contrast, the number of communities where many speakers had acquired it as their second language doubled from 8.5 % to 17 %. All told, about 33 % of communities enumerated in 2001 could be classified as being in transition from a mother tongue to a second language population.

Learning an Aboriginal language as a second language cannot be considered a substitute for learning it as a first language. Nevertheless, increasing the number of second language speakers is part of the process of language revitalization, and may go some way towards preventing, or at least slowing, the rapid erosion and possible extinction of endangered languages. Indeed, the acquisition of an Aboriginal language as a second language may be the only option available to many Aboriginal communities if transmission from parent to child is no longer viable.

As well, in gaining the ability to speak the language of their parents or grandparents, young Aboriginal people will be able to communicate with their older family members in their traditional language. It is also thought that the process itself of learning an Aboriginal language may contribute to increased self-esteem and community well-being, as well as cultural continuity.

Source: http: Statistics Canada, Norris, M. J. *Aboriginal Languages in Canada: Emerging Trends and Perspectives on Second Language Acquisition.* Retrieved on June 2, 2007, from//www.statcan.ca/english/freepub/11-008-XIE/2007001/11-008-XIE20070019628.htm#1

Aboriginal languages are suffering from the consequences of cultural hegemony, and past colonial and present government policies that have focused on monolingual English education for First Nations students. As the excerpt in Table 3.2 shows, many Aboriginal languages are already at the brink of extinction. It is ironic that many First Nations' children now acquire their ancestral language as a second language, rather than as their first.

As has been the case with other markers of Aboriginal identity in Canada, the de-privileging of Aboriginal languages is directly linked to attempts at assimilating First Nation's peoples into mainstream culture through education. A feature that distinguishes Aboriginal languages from Canada's official languages is that until recently indigenous knowledge was transmitted through oral tradition. Despite the importance of the written word as a technology of communication, it should be emphasized that the ancient ways of storing this knowledge are also at risk without the renaissance of Aboriginal languages. Thus, not only are these languages at risk of extinction, the modes of communicating Aboriginal knowledge more generally are also at risk. Battiste (2002) summarizes the link between education and Aboriginal languages:

> Indigenous languages and their symbolic, verbal and unconscious orders structure indigenous knowledge therefore, educators cannot stand outside of indigenous languages to understand indigenous knowledge . . . Where aboriginal languages, heritages and communities are respected, supported, and connected to elders and education, educational successes among Aboriginal students can be found. Aboriginal languages are irreplaceable resources in any educational reforms (p. 17).

While some provinces have made strides towards addressing the problem, very few school systems produce materials in Aboriginal languages (Battiste, 2002). Consequently, where such exist, Aboriginal language programs typically produce their own resources. Most notably, First Nations–operated schools are leading the effort to preserve Aboriginal languages. Like Battiste (2002), I believe that educational reforms need to redefine literacy in ways that affirm Aboriginal languages and consciousness as integral aspects of Aboriginal learning and identity.

Besides the historical, epistemological, and anthropological importance of Aboriginal languages, the loss of these languages has implications for First Nations students' learning and academic success. As argued throughout this book, language is an integral part of our identity and as such, intimate knowledge of our heritage language has important direct and indirect implications for our life chances. While projects such as the Aboriginal Languages Initiative (Heritage Canadian, 2003) constitute an important starting point, much more needs to be done towards the renaissance of Aboriginal languages in Canada.

IMMIGRANT AND MINORITY STUDENTS' EXPERIENCES OF SCHOOLING

Chapter 1 discussed how educational processes and practices contribute to the peripheral status of minority children in society. Drawing on the views of some of the theorists discussed in the chapter, I argued that far from consistently providing opportunities for upward mobility and increased life chances for all, schools routinely exclude minority groups. This occurs through structural, pedagogical, and curricular processes that negate their experiences — particularly those that do not conform to middle-class, male, heterosexual, and Christian values. These exclusionary practices create psychological boundaries between minority students and their predominantly White teachers in Canada (Ryan, 2006; Goddard, 1997).

The issues of racism, discrimination, and stereotyping are major sources of concern among minority students as many blame the educational system for reinforcing prejudicial attitudes that majority group children may already have. There are several factors that lead to the subordination of minority students, all of which collectively sustain and reproduce "otherist" perceptions of their status. These factors include the exclusion of minority students' history from the Eurocentric body of knowledge that is disseminated in schools. Yet other civilizations have flourished in Africa, China, and Latin America such as the Egyptians, Aztecs, the Mayans, etc. Similarly, few Canadian schools teach emerging (albeit controversial) issues, such as the origins of the alphabetic writing of the Greeks, which is the cornerstone of Western civilization, but has been traced to ancient Egyptian writing (Bernal, 1987). Another factor that diminishes the status of immigrant and minority students is the museum-like treatment they are often subjected to as representatives of "their people": to be put on display whenever the occasion demands it. Unfortunately, as Zine (2002) argues, being asked to "perform your culture for others, who seek knowledge of the "Other" through you, puts you [the minority] in the position of being the "native informant" in a tourist spectacle, when you know that your Anglo-Canadian classmates are never asked to do the same (Cindy, could you wear a traditional costume of your British ancestors to school for Canada Day?)". This museum-like treatment is an experience to which many minority students can relate. In a narrative that exposes how Canadian schools reinforce systemic racism, Isoki (2001) recounts his experiences of schooling as a Japanese-Canadian in an Ontario community. In one incident in grade five, his teacher put him and the only other "different-looking" child on either side of the front row for a class picture. Although pleased that he had been chosen for this special position, he was all the same perplexed since, in his previous class photos, he had always been placed somewhere in the middle as the smallest child in the group. The author narrates:

> Later, when the anxiously awaited picture arrived, the reasons for her actions [the teacher] became graphically apparent. Neatly framed between two different-looking children was the "real" class, those children for whom the school system existed. I think I realized even then that my humanity was, at the very least, inferior. I felt that I had been left on the periphery, looking in. I have that picture still. It serves to remind me not only of the subtlety with which a teacher . . . can harm a child, but also of the vigilance that must be maintained to avoid the damage that can so easily be perpetrated (p. 61).

Unfortunately, while educators may not be aware of the disabling consequences of their actions, the damage to minority students' self-esteem and perception of their individual identities (and ultimately, to the collective psyches of their communities) from this kind of experience is resilient and can last a lifetime.

Despite the rhetoric, the educational system does not promote equality of opportunity for all. For instance, the high drop-out rates among Black students in Ontario is a major problem. According to Radwanski (1987), Dei et al. (2000), and Ryan (2006) this is the result of the differential treatment these students receive, especially those who do not fit the preconceived mould of what a student should be or look like, as Isoki's narrative above indicates. There is of course nothing wrong with being different. Indeed, the central argument in this book hinges on the idea that difference ought to be valued. However, the problem is that difference can be used pejoratively as a code word for not being White. It should not come as a surprise then, that some nonmainstream students feel disconnected from the school system.

A study conducted by Blades et al. (2001) to identify issues of ethno-cultural difference related to specific secondary-school curriculum areas found that while teachers were generally aware of issues of cultural diversity and their implications for curricular practice, their "attentiveness to the cultural, ethnic and religious differences brought to the classroom by their students varied across subject areas" (p. v). The researchers also found that even in a subject area such as social studies education, which would normally allow the integration of diverse perspectives on immigration and Aboriginal issues, globalization, ethnic diversity, etc., there was no consistent pattern of integrating culturally relevant pedagogy as espoused by critical theorists (e.g., Ladson-Billings, 1994; Kincheloe, 2005a, 2005b; McLaren, 2007). While some teachers adopted inclusive pedagogies, others did not. This was mostly due to the limitations imposed by the provincial curriculum. As one of the participating teachers put it

> For the most part I think that our [province stated] curriculum is fairly Eurocentric. We spend a lot of time on European history and when we do touch on Asia, Africa, Latin America, different parts of the globe, I find it tends to be more of a negative context . . . I don't think students from non-European backgrounds have a real sense of the importance of their culture and the significant contributions that have been made. Within the Social 20 curriculum also, we look at interdependence — again, both in terms of the resources that are available and the way the curriculum is designed, it sort of sets up this north/south, first world/third world kind of division, which again is something that isn't really an accurate reflection of the experience of most of the students that we have (Blades et al. 2001, p. 35).

Yet, many Canadian analysts persistently argue that not only should epistemologies of other groups from Canada's cultural mosaic be included in schools' curricula, but past misrepresentations of various groups must also be corrected. They contend that unless such historical injustices are redressed, immigrant and minority children will continue to be marginalized in schools. Besides the exclusion of diverse perspectives from the curriculum, there's compelling evidence that shows that White teachers often treat minority students differently because of stereotypical beliefs about social groups who differ from themselves.

The disproportionate representation of minority students in special education classes is, in part, the result of institutional racism and discrimination. For instance, drawing on the findings of their research in the United States, O'Connor and Fernandez (2006) argue that schools contribute to the likelihood that minority students, especially those from poor socio-economic backgrounds, will be referred for evaluation and designated as special needs or disabled. Similarly, in their book *Why Are So Many Minority Students in Special Education?* (which documents the processes of labelling and social reproduction through which minority and low-income students are tracked into special education), Harry and Klingner (2006) provide compelling evidence of systemic racism and discrimination, when race and disability intersect in the United States. Their research also shows that special education placement is sometimes neither reflective of school quality nor real disability. "Rather, it reflected a wide range of influences, including structural inequities, contextual biases, limited opportunity to learn, variability in referral and assessment processes, detrimental views of and interactions with families, and poor instruction and classroom management" (p. 24). These practices were influenced respectively by each participating school's propensity towards a "culture of referral".

In Canada, minority students predominate in remedial and special needs programs. Just as they constitute the majority in special needs programs, the students are more likely to take courses that are less academically challenging than their White peers. In many Canadian secondary schools, courses are organized on a hierarchical basis of presumed level of difficulty ranging from the least to the most difficult streams, namely basic/general, vocational/advanced and university bound. Students then choose or are assigned courses based on educators' perceptions of their ability or motivation to do the associated work (Young, Levin, and Wallin, 2007). More often than not, students who are considered less able or motivated are "streamed" into courses that are less academically rigorous. The negative socio-psychological consequences of such groupings are obvious, especially for those in the lower streams. Unfortunately, immigrant and minority students overwhelmingly populate the general, basic, or vocational streams. This "sorting" function limits the future prospects and life chances of many minority students.

Besides the issue of tracking and referrals, a study by Duffy (2003) paints a discouraging picture of how Canadian schools are failing new immigrant minority students, especially refugees and those from poor families. On the basis of his findings, he concludes that

- while immigration levels from non-English speaking countries are increasing, funding for ESL and similar programs is being cut by school boards
- the integration of ESL students into regular classrooms is not serving their complex language needs
- there is a high dropout rate among immigrant high school students
- Black youths continue to be poorly served by the school system

Duffy goes on to argue that Canada risks creating an underclass if newcomers are not better served by the educational system. Of course, this is not to say that immigrant children come to school without problems, or that schools are the sole source of the difficulties immigrant students face. Indeed, like many members of their families and communities, they too have to deal with pre- and post-immigration stressors (Cole, 1998). These are not easily contained within the home environment, and therefore contribute to some of the challenges they might experience in school. As Corson (2001: 176) emphasizes, many "immigrant students are acutely aware of their family's lack of high status cultural capital and the power that attends it. They come from family circumstances where unemployment is common. Many others have parents who fill low-status and intermittent jobs, often spent with others from similar immigrant backgrounds". Immigrant children, particularly those from racial minority communities, come to school already aware that they and their families belong to the exclusive club of the systemically marginalized. In a society where power is the currency of access to all forms of opportunity, these children wield practically none. But Canadian schools can better serve the interests of these students through empowering programs and policies that are adequately funded and supported. It is important to remember as Igoa (1995) reminds us that, "[i]mmigrant children are more than "language minority" children. They are children who have been uprooted from their own cultural environment and who need to be guided not to fling themselves over-board in their encounter with new culture — for some, a "powerful" culture — and with a new language".

The negative experiences of minority students permeate all levels of Canadian education, including the institutions of higher learning. Overall, the literature suggests that like the first two tiers of education (elementary and secondary), Canadian post-secondary institutions are less welcoming to minority students than to those from mainstream backgrounds. For instance, in their study of the interactions between South Asian students and mainstream faculty in a predominantly White Canadian University, Samuel and Burney (2003) found that 100 % of the participating students believed that they had experienced both overt and covert racism as a result of cultural discontinuities between them and their professors. As one participant put it

> *Every single professor who has taught me is white* and I don't think we think the same. They don't understand the struggles and the burdens we bear. *When a third world issue is discussed I have to contribute and explain to the whole class.* The professors act like they want to make you comfortable in the class *but all they are doing is parade us in front of the whole class.* I have to constantly represent my culture and educate the masses. *That really makes me feel uncomfortable* (p. 96) [emphasis in original].

The same study found that some minority students do not feel that they are a cultural fit with their institutions of higher learning because they are culturally different from the majority of those who teach them. Perhaps even more worrisome, research shows that even in institutions of higher learning, perceptions of discrimination tend to affect minority students' self-esteem and academic performance, although many are resilient and choose not to drop out (as opposed to the case in high schools). According to Hurtado et al. (1999), such resilience may be due to the fact that the more academically confident minority students are, the more they are able to effectively deal with discrimination, even though they continue to feel marginalized.

Developing Resistance and **Oppositional Subcultures**

Psychologists have long acknowledged that people develop defence mechanisms as a way of coping with undesirable situations. One way that minority students cope with their subordinate social positioning and disempowering educational experiences is to develop counter-cultures opposing what they feel only marginalizes and alienates them. Drawing on the experiences of Blacks in the United States, Ogbu (1986) takes a provocative look into how Black students develop subcultures that are not only different, but are in opposition to the valued cultural capital of White mainstream society. In Ogbu's words

> Specifically, blacks and similar minorities . . . believe that in order for a minority person to succeed in school academically, he or she must learn to think and act white. Furthermore, in order to think and act white enough to be rewarded by whites or white institutions like the schools, a minority person must give up his or her own minority group attitudes, ways of thinking, and behaving, and, of course, must give up or lose his or her own minority identity. That is, striving for academic success is a subtractive process: the individual black student following

school standard practices that lead to academic success is perceived as adopting a white cultural frame of reference . . . as "acting white" with the inevitable outcome of losing his or her black identity, abandoning black people and black causes, and joining the enemy, namely, white people (cited in McLaren, 2007, p. 227).

Unfortunately, this kind of resistance to the monolithic culture they consider oppressive contributes to their academic underachievement (McLaren, 2007) and inadvertently helps to crystallize stereotypical views of their academic abilities held by their White teachers.

Although to a lesser degree than in the United States, the development of oppositional cultures by minority students is quite prevalent in Canadian schools. For instance, negative reactions to the exclusion of their worldviews and experiences from mainstream curricula contribute to academic failure among Aboriginal children. Research shows that high school dropout rates are proportionately higher among Aboriginal students, when compared to the general population. The situation becomes compounded when one factors in the strong tendency towards culture-related miscommunications between mainstream teachers and their minority students.

CROSS-CULTURAL (MIS)COMMUNICATION

One of the most obvious difficulties in culturally diverse schools, is the strong tendency for student-peer and student-teacher conflicts as a result of culture-related differential communication patterns. Banks (2001) provides a definition of **cross-cultural communication:**

> Cross-cultural communication involves the process of exchanging information between individuals from different social groups who interpret symbols and behaviour in similar ways. Cross-cultural communication doesn't just involve verbal communication. Most personal communication is non-verbal. It is estimated that about 65 % of all face-to-face communication does not involve speech. Touching, physical space, voice tone and volume, gestures, and use of the eyes are some of the ways people communicate non-verbally (p. 176).

Banks (1991) argues that when educational personnel work with people who differ substantively from themselves in culture, race, or ethnicity, mutually satisfying educational experiences do not always occur. Many of the difficulties emanate from the disconnect between the values and behavioural expectations of teachers and the students' values and culture. As Ariza (2006) points out, "Trying to decipher what another individual is truly conveying can be almost impossible without knowing the 'rules' of the other's cultural 'game' ". Moreover, making assumptions about what people from other cultures are trying to say can lead to erroneous conclusions. Since people's interactions with the world often begin with their culture, understanding cultural differences among students is essential for successful teaching and learning in contexts of diversity. Ethnicity is a shared awareness of a common culture, ancestry and sense of peoplehood. Summarizing the work of Longstreet (1978) who identified five aspects of ethnicity, Bennett (2007) argues that these five orientations (see Table 3.3), constitute valuable knowledge that teachers should have in order to meet the individual needs of their students. Three of these orientations, *verbal communication*, *nonverbal communication,* and *orientation modes,* are relevant to this chapter.

TABLE 3.3	Guidelines for Understanding Cultural Differences

Verbal Communication

- Grammar
- Semantics — meanings of words
- Phonology — sound, pitch, rhythm, and tempo of words
- Discussion modes — patterns of participating and listening

Nonverbal Communication

- Kinesics — body language
- Proxemics — personal space
- Haptics — frequency, quality, and location of touch
- Signs and symbols — meanings associated with artifacts, such as clothing, jewellery, emblems, flags, or traffic lights

Orientation Modes

- Body positions — unconscious movements and relaxation
- Spatial — architectural patterns and interpersonal distance
- Attention modes
- Time modes

Social Values

- Ideal behaviours — beliefs about how one ought or ought not to behave, such as seeking truth and beauty, being sincere, fair, compassionate, rational, loyal, or orderly
- Ideal goals — beliefs about some end-state that is worth or not worth attaining, such as security, happiness, freedom, equality, ecstasy, fame, power, or states of grace and salvation

Intellectual Modes

- Preferred ways of learning
- Knowledge most valued
- Skills emphasized

Source: Bennett, Christine I. (2007). Comprehensive Multicultural Education: Theory and Practice, p. 60. (6th Edition), Boston: Allyn and Bacon. Reprinted with permission.

Verbal Communication

Chapter 1 noted that differences in the way people communicate verbally can be a function of cultural differences that are identity makers for a group of speakers of a language or dialect. Thus, when students from diverse backgrounds speak English with different enunciation than speakers of standard English, it should not be construed by educators as language problems or limited proficiency. From the Canadian perspective, and in particular Saskatchewan, Heit and Blair (1993) have identified four levels of difference (pronunciation, grammar, vocabulary, and discourse norms), between standard English and the versions that are spoken by First Nations peoples. Collectively, these differences, or mother tongue interference, manifest in spoken language when speakers of indigenous languages unconsciously transfer the rules of their language to English:

> There is evidence that people who speak an Indigenous language tend to organize and tie together their English speech or writing in the same way they way they do the Indigenous

language . . . some research indicates that speakers of Athapaskan languages such as Dene organize their narratives in two's and four's rather than in three's (beginning, middle, and end), which is typical of English discourse (p. 120).

Like differences in utterances, differences in discussion modes, the way members of an ethnic group engage in discussion among themselves, at home, at parties, etc., are quite often sources of cross-cultural miscommunication (Bennett, 2007). Unfortunately, unaware of the cultural bases of the differences, educators often interpret them as deficiencies, a misconception that has significant implications for the academic success of all diverse learners.

Nonverbal Communication and Orientation Modes

It is not only utterances that create cross-cultural miscommunication; various patterns of nonverbal communication can exacerbate intercultural tensions between educators and their culturally diverse students. As Table 3.3 shows, categories of nonverbal communication patterns include **kinesics**, which is the study of body language, **proxemics**, or personal distance, and **haptics**, which is communication through touch. **Paralinguistics** or the study of vocal effects that affect speech production, is another nonverbal communication category. Each of these can potentially lead to cross-cultural miscommunication. How does this happen in practice? Take for instance the popular Canadian hand symbol for "OK". To North Americans, it is simply a positive gesture that signifies approval. To a Japanese person, the symbol refers to money, but to a Brazilian the gesture is obscene and has sexual connotations. Similarly, in some cultures, people look away when being spoken to as a sign of deference and respect, while within the Canadian context avoiding eye contact is interpreted as shiftiness or an indication of dishonesty or having something to hide. In another example, in some cultures, spatial distance is highly valued while in others proximity is encouraged. Also, paralinguistic features vary from one culture to another, and as such, limited understanding of vocal effects and their impact on the way people speak can result in misunderstanding. Finally, in some Asian cultures, people are encouraged to respond to questions indirectly. This means that within the classroom setting, some Asian students may respond to a teacher's questions in ways that do not provide direct answers, thus providing opportunity for cross-cultural conflict.

In his analysis of the link between Aboriginal Canadians' cultural values and their learning styles, Brant (1990) identified, among other factors, an ethic of non-interference, whereby cultural protocols prevent coercion in making people do what they do not want to do. Brant also argues that Aboriginal Canadians and other indigenous North Americans have a culture of non-competitiveness, emotional restraint, and a behavioural norm that values sharing while disdaining individual accumulation of material goods. Furthermore, Aboriginal people have a flexible concept of time, and they rarely show or verbalize gratitude or approval. Quite clearly, these values are in opposition to those espoused in Canadian schools' **Eurocentric ideologies**. Brant's assertions have been corroborated by cross-cultural research on cultural congruence and identity issues in the education of Aboriginal children (Nickels and Piquemal, 2005; Katz and McCluskey, 2003). Unfortunately, the cultural underpinnings of Aboriginal students' behaviour norms are often misinterpreted by teachers as disinterest or lack of motivation. Such conflicts become even more problematic when placed in the wider context of intergroup relations outside the school.

George and Louise Spindler (1994, cited in Gay, 2000) explain how cultural conflict can affect the relationship between teachers and students:

> Teachers carry into the classroom their personal cultural background that perceives students all of whom are cultural agents, with individual preferences and preconceptions. Students likewise come to school with personal cultural backgrounds that inflame the perceptions of teachers, other students, and the school itself. Together, students and teachers construct mostly without being conscious of doing it, an environment of meanings enacted in individual and groups behaviours, of conflict and accommodation, rejection and acceptance, and alienation and withdrawal (p. 9).

Related to difficulties arising from cultural miscommunications, is the matter of differential value orientations. Educators in culturally and linguistically diverse settings have to deal with issues that create ethical dilemmas. Some solutions may require major paradigm shifts, or unlearning values that were shaped by a teacher's personal experience and identity. A Canadian study (Solomon and Levine-Rasky, 1996) shows that despite theoretical support for inclusive pedagogies such as anti-acist education, teachers in five urban schools were reluctant to implement related principles in actual classroom practice. Teachers continued to perform their teaching duties

> in a generally traditional fashion . . . *in spite of their reports that they believe in doing otherwise* . . . . a disturbing number of teachers . . . demonstrated reluctance in acknowledging race, racial difference and racism as subjects for classroom or professional development (p. 30). [emphasis in original]

Another study on the same issue (Carr and Klassen, 1997) found that racial minority teachers were generally more supportive of anti-racist education than their White counterparts. The practical implications of this are obvious since White teachers make up the bulk of the teaching force in Canada. If they are reluctant or unable to make the ideological shifts that are the prerequisites for implementing culturally responsive education, then the schooling of minority students is likely to remain disempowering.

Even when educators strive to be inclusive and equitable in the classroom, and they integrate relevant aspects of race, ethnicity, gender, etc., they can still manage to "obliterate the realities of many of the children they teach" (Khayatt, 2000). Yet others, who are well-intentioned and cognizant of the salient issues, including the challenges minority students face, are sometimes blindsided by looking at these difficulties solely as the student's problems. Cummins (2000) provides an insightful vignette of how teachers sometimes fail to formulate the issues. A White Canadian science teacher had written a letter to a newspaper expressing how frustrated he was with the limited English skills of the (albeit bright) English language learning (ELL) students in his class. While the teacher's letter indicated that he was a caring and committed educator, who respected and made efforts to help his students, he failed to accurately diagnose the problem, which he believed, resided exclusively with the students. Cummins relates that nowhere in the teacher's letter did the teacher indicate how his incompetence, micro- and macro-level structural factors, or power relations among dominant and non-dominant groups in society, might be implicated in the issue. Crossing such a threshold would have required viewing the problem "as a socio-political issue related to power relations in the broader society" (Cummins, 2000; p. 250).

RELIGIOUS DIVERSITY IN SCHOOLS

Publicly funded education in Canada developed from the Christian ideologies of the two charter groups and consequently, early Canadian education systems were closely linked to Christian churches. Predominantly Anglican, United, and Presbyterian in English Canada, and Roman Catholic in Quebec, these churches organized residential schools that aimed to mould character on a foundation of Christian doctrine (Sweet, 2005). At the same time, First Nations children were forcibly removed from their homes into the now infamous residential schools. The rights of these groups to organize education were entrenched in the constitution. Importantly, early Christian beginnings in Canada were marked by characteristic intolerance that dominated interactions among and between the Christian colonizers and other non-charter groups (see Sweet, 2005, for a detailed review). However, as is the case with other aspects of Canadian life, the exponential growth of non-European populations has increased religious diversity. According to the 2001 census, religion still matters in our lives, as over 80 % of Canadians claimed some type of religious affiliation. As the data in Figure 3.2 show, the number of Canadians who reported affiliations with such religions as Islam, Hinduism, Sikhism, and Buddhism increased significantly in 2001 when compared with data from the 1991 census (Statistics Canada, 2003). Although the data from the 2006 census has not yet been published, past trends suggest likely increases in the number of Canadians who report affiliations with these religions. This means that as with other dimensions of diversity, religious diversity continues to increase as people from different religious backgrounds settle in the country. It also means that the number of students from diverse religious backgrounds has increased and will continue to increase in schools.

Constitutionally, all Canadians have the freedom to practise their religion. Religion in schools has become part of the larger debate on diversity, since religious minorities now challenge the privileging of Christianity in publicly funded education. One question that features prominently in debates on religious diversity in Canada is, "If Roman Catholics have a constitutional right to their own publicly funded schools, why not other religious groups?" Osborne (1999: 138). As Morgan (2001) puts it, while it may be a step in the right direction to include a survey of world religions in social studies curriculum

> it does little for those families with a bona fide commitment to a life of study and adherence to the teachings of classical Hebrew, Arabic, or Sanskrit texts. . . . Culinary multiculturalism is fine as a metaphor, but it cannot literally be the singular manifestation of pluralism in our society. Taking multiculturalism seriously means fostering an environment that also accounts for the needs of those whose cultural, intellectual and religious life requires a form of education impossible to achieve in public schools (p. 73).

Couched in the language of "choice in education", and following lengthy legal challenges in some instances, British Columbia, Alberta, Saskatchewan, Manitoba, Ontario, and Quebec now provide some form of public funds for independent denominational schools. In nondenominational schools, the respect for cultural diversity has precipitated the accommodation of the religions observances of nondominant groups. For example, in many jurisdictions there have been policy changes to prayers in schools, as well as to religious holidays. Several school boards have banned explicitly Christian prayers and have instituted more multicultural spiritual recitations. For instance, the Toronto Board of Education, in collaboration with people of different faiths, compiled

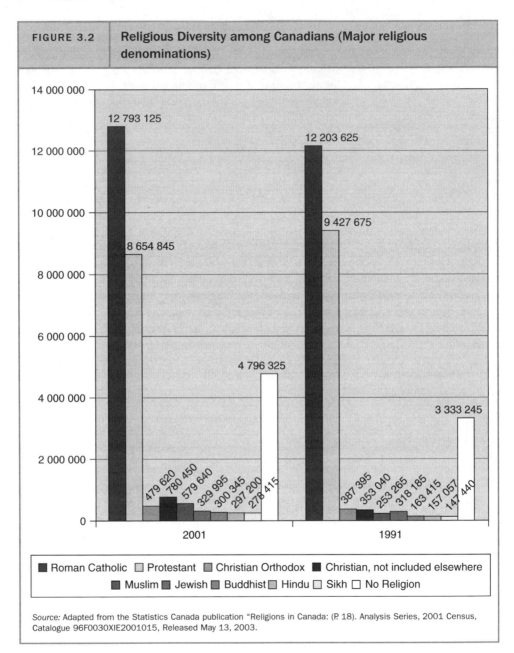

| FIGURE 3.2 | Religious Diversity among Canadians (Major religious denominations) |

Source: Adapted from the Statistics Canada publication "Religions in Canada: (P. 18). Analysis Series, 2001 Census, Catalogue 96F0030XIE2001015, Released May 13, 2003.

a multifaith book of readings and prayers that is used in school as an alternative to the formerly compulsory Christian Lord's Prayer (James, 2004).

Besides school-based initiatives, some community-based organizations are also engaging in efforts to broaden students' awareness of interfaith issues. One example is the "Meeting the Intercultural Challenge in Schools: Respect for Faith and Diversity Initiative" in Edmonton. Funded by Heritage Canada in partnership with Edmonton's

Society for Safe and Caring Schools and Communities (SACSC), the United Nations Association of Canada (Edmonton Branch), and Edmonton's Interfaith Centre, the project is designed to teach youth the consequences of religious intolerance.

Despite these accommodations, issues of religious freedom and the rights of religious minority students remain unresolved. Religion in schools continues to engender public debate, and legal challenges that have sought to remove religious exercises, to ban religious instruction completely, to include religious instruction in curricula, or to stake a claim for the public funding of denominational schools (see Dickinson and Dolmage, 1996; Clarke 2005). More often than not, the plaintiffs in these legal battles invoke the *Charter of Rights and Freedoms* in support of their positions (Sweet, 2005). The problem with this reasoning however, is that while the *Charter* guarantees freedom of religion, it "blocks tax-funded, school-based, religious teaching in non-denominational schools . . . " (Martin, 1996: 42).

Besides religious instruction, another contentious issue deals with the rights of students to carry religious symbols such as kirpans or to wear hijabs in schools. In some instances, this has required the intervention of the courts, resulting in different interpretations of the *Charter of Rights and Freedoms*. For example, the Ontario Divisional Court upheld the decision of the Ontario Human Rights Commission to allow the wearing of kirpans in one school district because "[The] Board of education's policy of prohibiting such religious symbols had an adverse effect on Sikhs." The Commission subsequently argued in favour of wearing kirpans to school within the board's jurisdictions as long as they "were reasonable in size and could be worn under clothing". But, in a similar case, *Multani c. Commission scolaire Marguerite-Bourgeoys*, citing safety concerns, the Quebec Court of Appeal (2004) struck down the decision of a lower court that had allowed a student to wear his kirpan to school.

Another thorny issue that continues in schools is the extent to which the observances of faiths other than Christianity should be recognized. Part of this problem stems from the provincial and localized nature of educational governance in Canada: there are no uniform policies to guide educational institutions. Moreover, regional differences in the demographic profile of communities make it impractical to apply uniform strategies when dealing with religious diversity in schools.

SOCIO-ECONOMIC DIVERSITY AND SCHOOLING

One marker of diversity in most societies is socio-economic difference. Research has found that social class differences, such as family income, account for up to 50 % of the difference in academic achievement among children. This is the single most reliable predictor of school achievement (Levin, 2004; Lee, 2000). Specifically, poverty is associated with higher incidences of poor health, riskier environments, and riskier behaviour among children (Lee, 2000) — all of which negatively impact school performance. Children from low-income backgrounds are also more likely to drop out and less likely to pursue higher education. Some children from poor families arrive at school hungry and exhausted, due to a lack of basic necessities such as food or home heating (Morse, 2000). This can in turn lead to problems such as low self-esteem, reduced motivation, lower educational aspirations, less extra-curricular participation, fewer student-teacher interactions, interrupted attendance, delayed development, illiteracy, being streamed into less challenging programs, academic

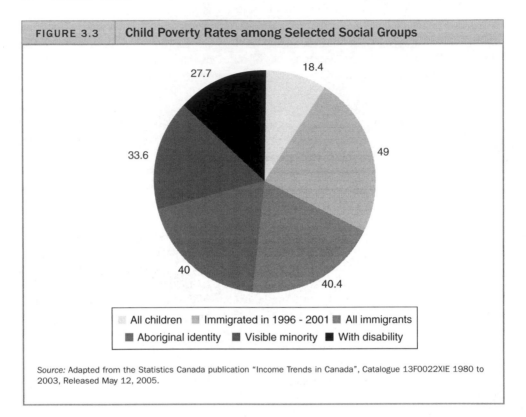

FIGURE 3.3   Child Poverty Rates among Selected Social Groups

Source: Adapted from the Statistics Canada publication "Income Trends in Canada", Catalogue 13F0022XIE 1980 to 2003, Released May 12, 2005.

underachievement, and ultimately to increased risk of dropping out (Levin, 1995). A study conducted in 1998 by the Canadian Council on Social Development, found that 35 % of children from poor families have delayed vocabulary development compared with only 10 % of children in higher income families (Morse, 2000).

Poverty rates among Canadian children have been a major concern of successive Canadian governments. Yet despite significant economic growth since 1989, when Parliament adopted a resolution to eliminate child poverty, the situation has grown progressively worse (Morse, 2000) and socio-economic disparity remains entrenched in Canadian society (Levin, 1995, 2004; Young, Levin, and Wallin, 2007). According to the 2005 *Campaign 2000 Report Card* on child poverty in Canada, 1.2 million children still live in poverty, and child poverty rates have remained around 18 %. Notably, poverty rates among Aboriginal, immigrant, and visible minority children more than doubled the average for all children (see Figure 3.3).

The Role of Schools in Perpetuating Poverty

Schools are not primarily responsible for creating poverty. However, they perpetuate and sustain it through structural and pedagogical practices that subjugate minoritized and impoverished students. As discussed in Chapter, schools serve a sorting function (through which students are provided the kind of education that is thought to be requisite to their future role in society), primarily along the lines of class, gender, and socio-economic status. This is particularly prevalent in schools in urban and ghetto areas, where the poor, minorities, and immigrants live. Research has documented that these schools do not enjoy the same infrastructure, facilities, and services that are available to students in more affluent neighbourhoods (McLaren, 2007; Ryan, 2006, Anyon, 2005).

Drawing on her extensive research work on schooling and inequality in New Jersey, Jean Anyon (1980, 1981, and 1997) has provided significant insight into how schools short-change students from minority and low-income backgrounds, sustain patriarchy and racism, and generally reinforce social stratification. In her book *Radical Possibilities: Public Policy, Urban Education and A New Social Movement* (2005), Anyon makes a compelling yet hopeful case that sees schools simultaneously as part of the problem of, and the solution to, reducing social inequalities in society. As she sees it, because "[education] is an institution whose basic problems are caused by, and whose basic problems reveal the other crises in cities: poverty, joblessness, and low-wages, and racial and class segregation" (p. 177) schools lend themselves to a social praxis that has transformative possibilities.

While Anyon's critique draws on her work in the United States, some Canadian studies have uncovered similar trends. For example, a study by Lee (2000) demonstrates that the vast majority of Canada's urban poor are recent immigrants. While an average of 30 % of immigrants in Canadian cities lived below the poverty line in 1995, only 21.6 % of urban poor were Canadian born. Figure 3.3 also shows that child poverty rates are highest among recent immigrants, followed by Aboriginal children with the rates of 49 % and 40 % respectively. A longitudinal study conducted between 1980 and 2000 found low-income rates had risen among immigrant populations, while they had fallen among the Canadian-born population (Picot and Hou, 2003). One of the best-known accounts of the state of schools in less economically privileged Canadian communities is documented in Peter McLaren's *Cries from the Corridor: The New Suburban Ghettos* (1980). This book, which chronicles his experiences teaching in a school in Toronto, ignited a national debate on the state of urban schools in Canada that precipitated some positive changes. However, some argue that schools in less affluent Canadian communities continue to face difficulties related to under-resourcing.

Schools also sustain class and economic inequality through pedagogical practices that are not relevant to the needs and interests of children from lower socio-economic backgrounds (Olson, 1995). There is also the danger that schools might erroneously use poverty as a rationale for categorizing some students as likely to face learning-related challenges (Young, Levin, and Wallin, 2007) thereby predicting their failure before they even have a chance to demonstrate their abilities. This means that educators are unlikely to pay as much attention to them as they would normally pay to students whose academic success is considered as a given. Similarly, programs for privileged students such as classes for "gifted" children and private schools also contribute to widening the chasm between students from privileged and marginalized backgrounds (Curtis, Livingstone, and Smaller, 1992).

Nevertheless, the situation is not immutable. Schools can help improve the lives of students from low-income backgrounds through sustained proactive and practical initiatives. For example, Maynes (2001) analyzed the successes of two schools participating in the Toronto District School Board's *Project School* initiative. He identified seven institutional and structural variables that can facilitate the academic success of children living in poverty. The first variable is a sense of wholeness. In both schools there was a shared sense among all participants that everything that happened appeared to be interconnected — all while the schools managed to continuously adapt their programs as necessary — an indicator of successful improvement. The second variable is leadership. There was evidence of democratic, collaborative, and distributive leadership in both project schools: the principals not only practised democratic leadership, they ensured that everyone contributed to the success of the initiative. (See the discussion of diversity-oriented leadership in Chapter 7.) A third factor is a collaborative school culture. The teachers worked collaboratively and as teams, and the schools' culture facilitated and fostered in-school professional development. A fourth variable is an orientation towards student achievement. In both project schools, there was a deliberate and sustained effort to ensure that students performed well on provincial standardized tests. Even so, this focus on successful test performance did not preclude efforts to support them in other areas.

A fifth variable is resources. Each school received additional resources that facilitated their ability to provide extra support to the students, such as giving teachers more time to deal with the psychological and emotional issues typically prevalent in inner city schools. The sixth factor that enhances a school's ability to proactively support poor students is curricular orientation: the teachers were able to adapt the traditional curriculum to the needs of the students. While they focused on the academic needs of the students, such as improving their literacy skills, they also addressed diversity and social justice issues. The teachers recognized that their students were marginalized by the regular curriculum, which essentially excluded their voices. In addition to attending to diversity issues, the schools also worked collaboratively with parents, thus creating a community of interested stakeholders. Other research confirms that successful collaboration with families and communities is an integral part of any program geared towards improving the lives of minority and low-income students (Delpit, 2006; Ladson-Billings, 1994; Ryan, 2006; Dei et al., 2000). A final variable is the action of the board, which provided the required resource support. As noted in Chapter 7, without district office support, it is difficult to successfully implement policies and initiatives at the micro-level of the school.

GENDER IN CANADIAN CLASSROOMS

Gender is a critical dimension of diversity — a point previously established in Chapter 1. The question addressed in this section is the extent to which gender intersects student empowerment in our classrooms. Although Canadian girls and boys have achieved near educational parity numerically, the nature of the schooling experience of both genders remains a contentious issue.

While it must be emphasized that there are various forms of feminism and that gender experiences (male or female) inextricably intersect with race, class, and social space, women as a group do not have equal status with men in Canadian society. They earn less, face the proverbial glass ceiling in the labour market, and are less likely to be elected to political office. In short, Canadian women still suffer from various forms of discrimination and prejudice (Osborne, 1999). While there are many reasons for this inequality, one cause can be traced to the differential socialization that boys and girls receive in schools, based on societal expectations of male and female roles in society. Thus, for decades women's voices were excluded from the curriculum, textbooks, and discourse norms as men were portrayed by and large in dominant and assertive roles. Schools also reified the status quo by tacitly encouraging boys and girls towards certain academic disciplines. This accounts for the very limited number of women in the areas of science and technology, even though the first degree granted to a woman in Canada was in science (Bellamy and Guppy, 1991). It is also not a coincidence that women predominate in certain professions. For instance, women make up the bulk of the teaching personnel in the first two tiers of education, but this is not reflected at the leadership level of school administration and supervisory personnel. Besides curricular exclusions, women also suffered physical and sexual harassment in schools (Larkin, 1994).

Largely due to feminist advocacy and to women's general struggle for equal rights (which paved the way for changes in the curriculum and increased awareness of sexism), Canadian schools are now more empowering to female students. To begin with, significant progress has been achieved in changing the images of girls and women in textbooks since the publication of the report of the Royal Commission on the status of women in 1970. Also, in many subject areas girls now perform as well as, or better than, boys. For example, the Pan-Canadian Council of Ministers of Education's 2002 School Achievement Indication Program (SAIP) test showed that among 13 - 16 year olds, girls performed at significantly higher levels than boys in writing. The Program for International Student Assessment (PISA) 2006 literacy tests confirm that Canadian girls have better reading skills than boys at a certain age. Similarly, a four-year study to determine the relationship between gender and test scores of grades 3, 6, and 9 students in Alberta (Pope et al 2006) found some correlation between gender and test scores in most subject areas. While boys scored higher than girls in mathematics and science, girls out-performed boys in language-based areas. Indeed, within the Canadian public policy and educational discourse, a school of thought is now emerging that asserts that the lack lustre performance of boys in reading, writing, and literacy indicates that the tide has turned and schools are now disadvantaging boys rather than girls (See Gaskell and Eyre, 2004; Froese-Germain, 2004).

In Canada and the Western world, media accounts of gender and achievement are sounding alarm bells about an emergent gender gap in which boys, in a reversal of fortune, are falling behind girls. So great is the concern about this new gender gap that as Froese-Germain (2004) puts it

> "What about the boys?" has become the familiar rallying cry of critics who believe schools are failing young males. Some feel that boys have been neglected as a result of earlier efforts to bridge the gender gap for girls, that gains for girls have been made on boys' backs. "Feminization" of the curriculum, school culture and teaching profession, so the argument goes, has worked against the interests and strengths of boys.

The belief that the gains made by girls have come at some cost to boys is so strong among some educators that efforts are being made in several educational arenas, especially in school districts, to improve boys' lack lustre performance in the areas of reading and writing (Bodkin, 2004).

It is noteworthy that different from earlier arguments advanced about girls' limited aptitude in mathematics, technology, and the sciences, researchers for the most part attribute boys' literacy challenges to patterns of socialization at home and through the media that suggest that it is not masculine to read. Anecdotal evidence aside, research seems to support the "boys and failing grades" hypothesis. For example, a Quebec study by Bouchard and associates (2003) confirmed a link between the degree of students' adherence to socially constructed gender stereotypes and school achievement. Others have attributed the problem to structural variables, such as the dominance of women in the teaching profession — the argument being that increasing gender parity within the profession would be a step in the right direction. However, as Froese-Germain (2004) cautions, while gender equity in the profession is a laudable ambition, "it's an open question whether simply having more men teachers in classrooms will of itself influence boys to read more and improve their writing skills" (p. 4).

While on the surface it may appear that women now have equal footing with men, despite the progress that has been made, there are still gender-based power differentials in Canadian society. There are inequities at all levels of the educational system including institutions of higher learning (Bellamy and Guppy, 1991; Litner et al., 1992: Williams, 1990). This has significant implication for the life chances of girls and women. As in other advanced societies, gendered educational practices, such as language construction, pedagogical practices, and discourse norms in schools, continue to be implicated in the extent and nature of women's access to social rewards and positions of power in Canada. Moreover, schools continue to emphasize behavioural norms that are commonly associated with men, such as competition. Overall, school curricula explicitly and implicitly continue to under- or misrepresent women's experiences and ways of knowing. This is because the epistemological assumptions of school curricula in Canada remain for the most part, male-biased. Subject choice is still gendered, as more boys than girls choose the sciences. Any attempt at managing diversity in schools should, as Barakett and Cleghorn point out, "include . . . not only the writing and life experiences of [Canadian] women, but also women's accounts and interpretations of history, as well as their analyses of the body of knowledge (produced mainly by men) that has come to be considered the appropriate content for all" (2000: 86).

Eliminating gender imbalances within the educational arena also requires that policy-makers desist from thinking in terms of "gender neutrality", as for all practical purposes Canadian society is still patriarchal. Thus, while both female and male needs should receive equal consideration in our school systems, the outcomes of such scrutiny should lead to differential treatment for women, as they comprise a marginalized group. This argument may appear to contradict the *Charter of Rights and Freedoms* (which guarantees equal rights to both sexes), however, the *Charter* also provides redress for unjust practices, and amelioration for those who have been discriminated against. It is important to take into account the dynamics of the complex situations which certain (e.g., Aboriginal, immigrant, and minority) women face. I refer to this as "triple jeopardy" in society (and the classroom). First, the subjugated status of their communities. Second, their sex. Third, their interactions with authority (and teachers) are often confined within others' perceptions of their social positioning within their cultural communities. For example, pressure from educators to assimilate often forces immigrant high-school girls to cede some of their cultural capital in favour of Western values. In McLaren's (1980) narrative of his teaching experiences in a Toronto school, he posits that the West Indian female students in his class had a particularly difficult time. Not only did they have to deal with family-related challenges, they also had to face everyday racism in school. The "tough girl" stance of some of the girls was only a defensive façade — a symbolic response to societal constraints, structural inequalities, and experiences of difference (which contrasted sharply with those of their middle-class teachers and peers). Unfortunately, educators often interpret such behaviour as rebellion against their "repressive foreign culture", without recognizing the systemic racism that is at the root of their "resistance" in the first place (Rezai-Rashti, 1995). There is evidence that minority women from certain socio-demographic strata (such as immigrants and refugees) are the least visible group in schools. This is a result of the stereotyping that portrays women as passive victims of male dominance within their own communities — an image with which they would rather not be associated (Corson, 2001). The problem is that this stereotyped perception often affects how such girls are received in school, which in turn may affect their self-esteem, school performance, and life chances.

Summary

Chapter 1 discussed some fundamental issues surrounding diversity and difference. Chapter 2 examined some specific issues that are related to Canadian diversity. This chapter continued this theme and explored other elements of diversity from a Canadian perspective. Taking linguistic diversity as a starting point, the chapter examined the interface between Canada's official bilingual and de facto multilingual identity and schooling. Issues such as the viability of an inclusive language policy in schools, as well as the status of minority language students were addressed. Along the same line, second language learning programs such as French immersion and ESL programs were examined. One critical issue that is persistently neglected in debate on education and diversity is the nature and possibility of integrating Aboriginal languages as formal media of instruction for First Nations students. The chapter examined the issue arguing, as do Aboriginal scholars, that a prerequisite for the revival and preservation of indigenous knowledge systems in Canada is to affirm Aboriginal languages in Canadian education. The undermining of Aboriginal languages remains one of the most problematic social issues. Indeed, unless immediate action is taken to remedy the situation, there is a strong likelihood that the use of Aboriginal languages will continue its downward trend.

As marginalized groups with distinct needs, the experiences of immigrant and minority students in school were also discussed. There is compelling evidence that minority students have a tenuous relationship with schools due to systemic racism, exclusionary educational practices, and Eurocentric ideologies which not only negate their identities, but also devalue their cultural capital. The chapter also examined the cross-cultural miscommunication between educators and their non-majority-group students. Finally, a critical aspect of diversity, the intersection of gender and schooling, within the framework of women's less powerful social positioning in society, was also discussed. Regardless of the emergent view that boys, not girls, now need equity attention in Canadian education, the consensus remains that boys and girls experience schooling differently.

Key Terms

Assimilation

English as a Second
Language (ESL)

Hegemony

Multilingualism

Paralinguistics

Bilingualism

Eurocentric ideologies

French immersion

Kinesics

Mutual resistance

Proxemics

Cross-cultural
communication

Haptics

Linguistic pluralism

Oppositional subcultures

Unilingualism

Questions to Guide Reflective Practice

1. Should all new immigrant children be required to minimize communicating in their primary languages in order to accelerate the acquisition of mainstream language?

2. With some of your peers, research and discuss the advantages and disadvantages of supporting second language learners' primary languages while learning a second language.

3. Besides biases in the educational system, identify other ways in which women are disempowered in Canadian society.

4. Develop a hypothetical plan to help schools provide more empowering schooling experiences for minority students.

5. "Another study . . . found that racial minority teachers were generally more supportive of anti-racist education than their White counterparts". Why do you think that some White teachers are more resistant to authentic change in some educational contexts?

6. To what extent do you believe schools should accommodate the worldviews and voices of the diverse groups that make up the Canadian mosaic?

Case Study Analysis: Chapter Opening Vignette

1. Identify two critical issues that are raised in this vignette.

2. How would you describe Mrs. Mollard's attitude towards Renaa: racist, impatient, or supportive?

3. How would you advise Mrs. Mollard to deal with the situation?

4. Besides Ms. Glis' advice, in which other ways can Mrs. Mollard help Renaa?

5. According to Ms. Glis, her class is a reflection of some of the things she reads in newspapers and sees on TV "about socio-cultural differences among Canadian students". What is the nature of the information you receive from the media regarding Canadian diversity?

Test Your Knowledge

1. How are schools meeting the needs of minority and immigrant students in your community? What are the barriers to change?

2. Research and identify three non-Christian religions in your community and province. What are the pillars of these religions?

3. Canada's Aboriginal peoples have a wealth of indigenous languages that are used as media of communication in First Nations communities. Identify several Aboriginal languages; in what provinces and communities are they spoken?

4. Are there gender equity programs in the schools in your community?

5. Besides those cited in the chapter, research and identify two legal cases in your province that in some way involved an aspect of Canadian diversity.

For Further Reading

Anyon, J. (2005). *Radical Possibilities: Public Policy, Urban Education, and a New Social Movement*. New York: Routledge.

Apple, M. W., and Buras, K. L. (Eds.). (2006). *The Subaltern Speak: Curriculum, Power, and Educational Struggles*. New York: Taylor & Francis.

Bourdieu, P. (1991). *Language and Symbolic Power*. Cambridge: Polity Press.

Clarke, P. (2005). Religion, Public Education and the Charter: Where Do We Go Now? *McGill Journal of Education*, 40(3): 351–381.

Cummins, J., and Danesi, M. (1990). *Heritage Languages*. Montreal: Our Schools/Our Selves Education Foundation.

Dickinson, G. M., and Dolmage, W. R. (1996). Education, Religion and the Courts in Ontario. *Canadian Journal of Education*, 21 (4): 363–383.

Freeman, C. E. (2004). Trends in Educational Equity of Girls and Women: 2004 (NCES 2005-016). U.S. Department of Education, National Center for Education Statistics. Washington, DC: U. S. Government Printing Office.

Igoa, C. (1995). *The Inner World of the Immigrant Child*. New York: St. Martin's Press.

Landsman, J., and Lewis, C. W. (2006). *White Teachers/Diverse Classrooms. A Guide to Building Inclusive Schools, Promoting High Expectations, and Eliminating Racism*. Sterling: Stylus Publishing.

Larkin, J. (1994). *Sexual Harassment. High School Girls Speak Out*. Toronto: Second Story Press.

Lippi-Green, R. (1997). *English with an Accent: Language, Ideology and Discrimination in the United States*. London: Routledge.

Morris, S., McLeod, K., and Danesi, M. (1993). *Aboriginal Languages and Education: The Canadian Experience*. Oakville: Mosaic Press.

Sears, C. (1998). *Second Language Students in Mainstream Classrooms: A Handbook for Teachers in International Schools*. Clevedon: Multilingual Matters.

Sweet, L. (2005). Accommodating Religious Differences: The Canadian Experience. In C. James (Ed.), *Possibilities & Limitations: Multicultural Policies and Programs in Canada*. Halifax: Fernwood Publishing.

Websites of Interest

www.sasked.gov.sk.ca/docs/policy/multi/hert.html Multicultural education and heritage language education policies

www.languagestore.com/canada/ Language Planning, Language Policy, and Language Research in Canada

ww.wsd1.org/programs/language.htm Aboriginal Heritage Language Vocabulary

www.ocol-clo.gc.ca/ Official Language Website of Commissioner of Official Languages

CHAPTER 4

Transformative Frameworks for Promoting Diversity

VIGNETTE

It was going to be one of those days in Gregory Dymes' third-year sociology class: *Race and Ethnicity*. A heated debate about the twin concepts of prejudice and discrimination was unfolding, and as usual, opinions were divided along racial lines. While there was some consensus that discrimination is a problem in Canada, at issue was its nature. Is it an individual or a systemic phenomenon? Who or what groups are most likely to be victims of discrimination and prejudice? Most of the White students (who constituted the majority) insisted that prejudice and discrimination are individual problems that are neither sanctioned nor reified by social institutions. "It's people's attitudes that are prejudiced, not institutions'" declared Jason, "the system does not tell immigrants to get off welfare and get jobs. Fair or unfair, it's people who say such things". In contrast, virtually all the minority students (who made up about 18% of the class) agreed that systemic discrimination is as rampant, if not worse, than that of the individual. "What do you mean it is not the system? Don't

you pay attention to the media, which, as far as I am concerned, is the mouthpiece of the system?" retorted Wang, a Chinese student. Listening with rapt attention, Professor Dymes, who encouraged students' engagement with the topics addressed in his class, wondered why opinions about such issues are often divided according to community affiliation. He was also intrigued with the extent to which debates about "difference" have changed since he first began teaching, some 29 years ago. Then, such discussions often centred on other aspects of difference other than racial discrimination and immigration. Not that these issues were not discussed, they simply did not take centre stage in social discourse, nor incite as much fervour, as they do now. He did an unobtrusive scan of the room and was rather surprised at the number of non-White students in the class. As a student at the various levels of the educational system, his classes had been very homogenous. Things had indeed changed dramatically. He was quite aware of the demographic projections that, over the next few decades and perhaps even beyond, an increasing proportion of school-aged children will come from non-White populations. Returning his thoughts to the issue at hand, he knew from experience that the debates would become even more contentious as the course progressed and the class delved into even more controversial issues concerning Canadian diversity. What seems to baffle him each time he has taught this course is the degree of difficulty students experienced when challenged to suggest or develop frameworks for dealing with socially unjust policies and practices in school and society. Yet, every member of the class would typically agree that these problems existed and needed to be addressed proactively.

INTRODUCTION: FRAMEWORKS FOR ACTION

Professor Gregory Dymes makes a valid point — it is often easier to debate the issues than to provide solutions for them. This is even more challenging when the issues involve the contested terrain of education, which is often mired in group interests. Thus, even after years of debate on education and diversity, one of the challenges that still faces educators is the adoption of critical practices that disrupt cultural imperialism through education and initiate social praxis. Indeed, while some progressive policies instituted in Canada over the last several decades have aimed to make schools more inclusive, many of them (and their associated practices) have had only limited success. Otherwise, the search for empowering ways of dealing with student diversity would have been laid to rest by now, assuming that this is even possible.

There are several reasons why teaching for diversity in Canadian schools remains an elusive goal. First, teachers and other educators at the front line of implementing progressive policies are not often knowledgeable about the various theoretical and practical frameworks that can help them provide inclusive learning environments for their students. Second, more often than not, those who are familiar with these frameworks acquire only a cursory knowledge of a benign framework such as mainstream multicultural education, which as Chapter 1 shows provides only superficial solutions. Moreover, because such knowledge is limited in scope, the effects are typically minimal. What teachers need is access to an array of potent tools to enable them to meet the needs of their diverse students.

This chapter is the first of several that provide specific frameworks for responding to diversity in Canadian schools. It attempts to do three things. First, it provides a potential solution to the perennial question that dogs educators and policy makers, "What shall we teach students especially in contexts of diversity?" (Young, 1984; Aoki et al., 1984; Osborne, 1999; Pike, 2000). To explore this question, the chapter introduces the reader to the concepts of **negotiable** and **non-negotiable knowledge** as authentic inclusive knowledge. Second, it proposes several progressive pedagogical frameworks that teachers can adopt to help them empower their students, particularly those from non-mainstream backgrounds. These frameworks include **diversity pedagogy, critical pedagogy,** and **peace education,** all of which might ideally culminate in **transformative learning.** The rationale for exploring various frameworks is based on the recognition that realistically, teaching for diversity in authentic and life-changing ways depends on the adoption of an eclectic program that integrates elements from various models across the curriculum. Standing alone, each of these frameworks can facilitate emancipatory practice, but intimate knowledge of several frameworks can enable teachers to adapt those that are best suited to their particular context. The ultimate goal of the frameworks and practices that are discussed is **transformative praxis,** which is also briefly discussed. Finally, this chapter explores the reasons why teachers (and other educators) are sometimes resistant to the idea of adopting praxis-oriented pluralistic perspectives in the first place.

THE CONCEPTS OF NEGOTIABLE AND NON-NEGOTIABLE KNOWLEDGE

A quick analysis of the problem facing York County's curriculum committee (see Table 4.1) will show that it is not an uncommon one in multicultural, multiracial, and multilingual societies. While the debate over what to include in Canadian publicly funded school curricula is as old as the country itself, in the last several decades it has assumed some urgency as a result of increasing student diversity. What kind of knowledge should students acquire (especially those in which diverse populations and other socially constructed minorities are

TABLE 4.1	York County Curriculum Committee Meeting

The school district's curriculum committee was having its biennial meeting, which usually involved an in-depth analysis of the problems that had been identified in the current curricula. Again, judging from the enormous pile of complaints from parents and advocacy groups within the minority communities, the social studies curricula were the most problematic. Some changes had been proposed during the last meeting, but they had been put on hold because the committee could not arrive at consensus, even though most of the changes had sounded quite straightforward. The major criticism of the curricula was that they relegated the historical contribution of some members of society, including First Nations' peoples, immigrants, Black Canadians, and women, to a mere footnote. The committee was well aware that the contribution of these groups clearly needed to be integrated into the curriculum, but the question was, where to begin? While some members of the committee were quiescent about the proposed changes, others contended that enough change had already been made to the existing curricula. From the looks of things, the committee was once again facing an impasse.

represented)? What knowledge base do students need in contemporary Canadian society? The answers to these ostensibly simple, but operationally complex questions are often missing in much of the discourse on diversity in our schools. Also lacking is the acknowledgement of a changing world order, of which Canadian students are an integral part. Thus, it is essential to teach knowledge that is congruent with the needs of Canada's pluralistic society, in order to increase the life chances of all children, especially those from nonmainstream communities. But we must not lose sight of emergent global realities that mandate the acquisition of knowledge, which simultaneously allows the individual to maintain her or his identity while transcending cultural boundaries. As some writers have argued (e.g., Banks, 2006; Noddings, 2005a; Bennett, 1992) we must move towards conceptions of diversity and multiculturalism that affirm individual and group identity while recognizing a shared set of values. Banks (2006) sums up the rationale for education that is cognizant of the global world we live in:

> Because we live in a global society that is highly interconnected an effective education for the 21st century prepares students for thoughtful citizenship in their communities, their nation, and the world. Worldwide immigration and globalization raises new questions about how to prepare students for thoughtful and active citizenship. Multicultural societies are faced with the problem of constructing nation-states that reflect and incorporate the diversity of their citizens and yet have an overarching set of shared values, ideas, and goals to which all of its citizens are committed (p. 151).

This melding of the local, national, and to a limited extent, the transnational provides the philosophical foundation for the development of the interrelated concepts of negotiable and non-negotiable knowledge.

What is non-negotiable knowledge? Non-negotiable knowledge is essential knowledge that all students must acquire in a diverse society. It takes as a starting point the view that curricular knowledge (including the hidden curriculum), must be analyzed, critiqued, reoriented, and deconstructed to create spaces for empowering minority students and all others. However, different from frameworks that advocate inclusive knowledge in pluralistic societies, non-negotiable knowledge is cognizant that in any nation state, there are macro-values that provide a sense of social cohesion, as people must communicate between and across cultures. Affirming diversity and people's identity must always remain the material and fundamental objective of the adoption of non-negotiable knowledge.

In contrast to non-negotiable knowledge, negotiable knowledge is context driven and is geared towards promoting specific local epistemologies and values. That is, it is designed to teach students what they must know about their immediate communities. As Figures 4.1

and 4.2 show, each concept has specific dimensions all of which constitute inclusive knowledge in diverse societies.

DIMENSIONS OF NON-NEGOTIABLE KNOWLEDGE

The question that guided the development of non-negotiable knowledge was "What should Canadian children learn, given the degree of diversity among school-aged children?" In response to this question, a cluster of critical knowledge areas were developed. These include culturally relevant academic knowledge, **critical multicultural** or **intercultural education, global awareness, critical language awareness, critical thinking,** knowledge about indigenous people, knowledge about the environment and **biodiversity,** and knowledge about information and communications technology.

Culturally Relevant Academic Knowledge

The first and critical component of non-negotiable knowledge is culturally relevant academic knowledge. This is the core, or explicit, curriculum that schools formally teach across most jurisdictions in Canada. It is a given that students must be taught formal knowledge in order to acquire the necessary skills for survival in society. However, what is advocated here is that these subjects be explicitly designed as culturally relevant knowledge, using content that reflects the cultural capital of all students — making the information more closely aligned with their frame of reference. Ladson-Billings (2006: 3) illustrates how academic knowledge can be adapted to become culturally relevant:

> [I]n a culturally relevant high school English class the teacher may understand that he or she has to teach *Romeo and Juliet* but would couch that book in the context of students' own struggles with parents over dating. . . . [T]he teacher may include some films, popular music, or other stories that take up the theme of young, forbidden love (p. 34).

While Ladson-Billing's comments refer to adolescent sub-culture, which is relevant to most high school students, *Romeo and Juliet* can be adapted to the heritage cultures of minority students. For example, virtually all cultures have beliefs and norms about dating, i.e., what is taboo and what is permissible. Teachers in heterogeneous classrooms can explore this angle by asking students to relate the central themes in the book to what pertains to their own culture.

The overarching outcomes of culturally relevant academic knowledge should be students knowing and valuing their own culture, as well as understanding the dominant culture they must navigate, in order to become accomplished citizens. Ladson-Billings (2006) describes this as cultural competence, although in a different sense than the idea of teachers, or other service professionals becoming familiar with the cultural nuances of their clients. Rather, Ladson-Billings is referring to the kind of cultural competence that enables "students to recognize and honor their own cultural beliefs and practices while acquiring access to the wider culture, where they are likely to have a chance in improving their socioeconomic status and making informed decisions about the lives they want to live" (p. 36). She argues that teachers have an obligation to expose their students to the dominant culture that marginalizes them. The rationale is that "without the skills and knowledge of the dominant culture, students are unlikely to be able to engage that culture to effect meaningful change" (p. 36). Indeed, the entire argument in this volume hinges on the idea that while academic knowledge is essential knowledge, making it culturally relevant is a prerequisite for empowering all students — especially those from nonmainstream backgrounds. What students learn should not only refer to their culture bases, it must also be supported with culturally responsive teaching practices.

Critical Multicultural and Intercultural Education

The adoption of critical multicultural education and intercultural education, in this context, is based on the recognition that while both concepts are interconnected, they are often treated discretely. Critical multicultural education is implementing structural and institutional changes beyond the usual rhetoric, which culminates in exoticizing minority groups. Intercultural education focuses on fostering cross-cultural understanding. Critical multicultural education is about social justice (see Chapter 1), and it is also about diversity and critical pedagogy (see below). Thus, embracing both concepts involves redefining the way knowledge is taught and learned within the context of a rapidly changing world, including dramatic demographic shifts, globalization, and the proliferation of information and communications technology (ICTs). When we factor xenophobia (see Chapter 1) into the equation, learning to live together becomes one of the most challenging tasks that students face in the 21st Century. Why is intercultural education a particularly important dimension of non-negotiable knowledge within the Canadian context? First, it suggests the equality of Canada's various cultures without necessarily subscribing to the problem of cultural relativism. Second, it addresses the problem of mainstream multicultural education, which is that it ostensibly creates a dominant Canadian culture (English or French) against which other cultures are measured. Bannerji (2000: 78) captures the essence of this argument, "[d]ue to its selective modes of ethnicization, multiculturalism is itself a vehicle for racialization. It establishes Anglo-Canadian culture as the ethnic core culture while 'tolerating' and hierarchically arranging others around it as 'multiculture'."

Even in stable democracies such as Canada, there is broad consensus that intercultural understanding is not a given, as racism, religious intolerance, prejudice, and other forms of discrimination still permeate institutional, interpersonal, and inter-group relations (Henry and Tator, 2006; James, 2003; Fleras and Elliott, 2003; Razai-Rashti, 1995; Moodley, 1999). Most people fail to realize that most of the world's contemporary conflicts are linked to a rejection of pluralism and diversity of voices within national boundaries. Oppression and discrimination are not just something that happens "out there". Just as nations must strive to maintain harmonious coexistence with one another, they also must strive towards intercultural understanding within their own boundaries.

Indeed, inclusive school knowledge has, now more than ever, become a mediating variable in social relations (both nationally and internationally), and intercultural education is not only a conduit for fostering such understanding, it is also a tool for promoting social justice. But intercultural education involves more than simply understanding why people act or speak the way they do: It necessarily means changing the way one sees the world. It also involves acquiring intercultural competencies such as intercultural communication (communicating effectively across cultures), as discussed in Chapter 3. Furthermore, understanding other peoples' cultural frames of reference is not particularly productive if one maintains a dogmatic stance towards one's own. Daniel (2001) identifies several key components of intercultural education:

- It must foster respect and equality between individuals and challenge existing power relations.
- It should promote participatory and democratic environments in which everyone can express his or her opinions.
- It is based on the experiences of students, and constructed with the teacher as facilitator, rather than the depositor of information.

- It is inclusive, such that it provides access to all in ways that everyone has the same opportunities.
- It respects differences while it recognizes similarities among individuals.

In addition to Daniel's suggestions, intercultural education is a praxis-oriented framework that aims to achieve the following:

- facilitating cross-cultural understanding
- providing educators and students with the tools for exploring national and global inter-connections
- enabling educators to adopt inclusive practices that simultaneously focus on empowering individuals and identifying commonalities
- positioning equity and social justice as the nucleus of intergroup understanding

Global Awareness

As a component of non-negotiable knowledge, global awareness means more than a cursory knowledge of the world beyond students' local community and country. Such knowledge is grounded in the understanding that all parts of the world are interconnected, and that every-one has a stake in its survival. Global awareness transcends the traditional social studies cur-riculum that provides surface descriptions of select parts of the world and focuses on such questions as "Where is China on the world map?" or "What is the capital of Kenya?" Rather, it entails a deep engagement with evolving world issues, including conflicts, geno-cide, famine, and global politics, for appropriate grades and in appropriate ways. As recent events demonstrate, it is an illusion to assume that we are immune from what happens out-side our immediate environment. This is true whether we speak of catastrophic diseases (e.g., HIV/AIDS, tuberculosis, and malaria), global warming and pollution, or natural dis-asters (e.g., hurricanes, tsunamis, earthquakes, and volcanic eruptions). We are all witness to how problems that occur in other parts of the world can change the world as we know it in an instant. The events of September 11, 2001, in New York City and Washington, D.C. come to mind. Global pandemics, such as Avian Flu or the fatal outbreak of Severe Acute Respiratory Syndrome (SARS) in Canada in 2003, also demonstrate the unpredictability and interconnectedness of world issues. Although these events were rooted in other parts of the world, their impact continues to reverberate in Canada and elsewhere by way of policy changes of international magnitude. For better or worse, as Pike (2000: 231) claims, "the nation is no longer the primary arbiter of our private fate". Global awareness in the context of a rapidly changing world enables learners to gain in-depth understanding of the interface between their immediate community and the proverbial "global village".

In Canada, global awareness is usually taught through global education programs. Many school districts have implemented some variant of the program, sometimes in col-laboration with international partners and networks. Given the discussion above, what is global education? Drawing on the definition from the Association for Supervision and Curriculum Development, Tye (2003) describes global education as a program that

> involves learning about those problems and issues which cut across national boundaries and about the interconnectedness of systems — cultural, ecological, economic, political and techno-logical. [It] also involves learning to understand and appreciate our neighbors who have different cultural backgrounds than ours; to see the world through the eyes and minds of others; and to realize that other peoples of the world need and want much the same things (p. 165).

To further explicate Tye's latter point, which is particularly relevant here, I draw on two diametrically opposing views of culture — the emic and the etic perspectives. The etic perspective has to do with abstract and universal notions of culture. To teach culture in an etic sense means teaching the phenomenon from the perspectives of an outsider looking in. On the other hand, the emic perspective has to do with context-based notions of culture. Following the same logic, to teach global awareness in an emic sense means adopting approaches that enable students to immerse themselves in that particular culture or issue (or at the very least, approximate what it feels like to be part of it). Canadian educational institutions generally teach global and cross-cultural issues from an etic stance, thus allowing students limited opportunity to empathize (see Chapter 8) with those who are different from them. The general point is that when teaching global awareness, Canadians schools ought to be doing much more than they are at the moment. That being said, there is cause for hope: Canadian students are becoming more globally aware through virtual classroom programs that connect them with their peers in other parts of the world (see Table 4.3). Additionally, many school boards now integrate global education into the curriculum in more meaningful ways than the traditional one. There is also the prospect of institutionalizing global education, because as Pike (2000) points out

> Canadians' passion for internationalism, coupled with a federal immigration policy that is diversifying and expanding the physical and cultural make-up of the country's population, indicate both a need for, and a receptivity to, the wide-spread implementation of global education (p. 231).

In summary, authentic global awareness programs should facilitate students' developing knowledge and skills in the areas described in Table 4.2.

A common misconception about teaching global awareness is that it excludes knowledge about local communities and local issues. On the contrary, both are interconnected. As Willinsky (2004) argues, the onus is on Canadian teachers "to help students see how learning about their own communities and learning to present their new knowledge skilfully can help them inform public thinking about both local and global issues" (p. 25).

Critical Language Awareness

Critical language awareness is also an important dimension of non-negotiable knowledge. Students, and adults for that matter, are not often aware of the implications of the language they use or how harmful words can be when inappropriately used. Indeed, as a powerful

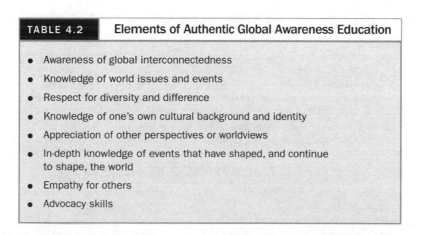

TABLE 4.2	Elements of Authentic Global Awareness Education

- Awareness of global interconnectedness
- Knowledge of world issues and events
- Respect for diversity and difference
- Knowledge of one's own cultural background and identity
- Appreciation of other perspectives or worldviews
- In-depth knowledge of events that have shaped, and continue to shape, the world
- Empathy for others
- Advocacy skills

TABLE 4.3	Promoting Diversity and Global Awareness through Virtual Classrooms

Several Canadian and international web-based global awareness programs deserve mention here. Collectively, these programs showcase the diversity of Canadian and human experience.

The first is the Associated Schools' Project of UNESCO (ASP). By far the largest international program on global education, the program aims to encourage educational institutions to organize programs that are designed to increase students' knowledge and understanding of world issues and problems.

The second is the iEARN program (International Education and Resource Network). Launched in 1988, it promotes collaboration between students and educators transnationally. It is a non-profit organization that invites teachers and students from around the world to connect with one another through various curriculum-based online projects. Subject areas include language, science, social studies, and the arts. Headquartered at the University of Calgary, iEarn Canada is affiliated with iEarn and has been in existence since 1992. Students between the ages of 5 and 19 are eligible to participate in the projects offered by iEarn. Examples of global projects in which the program has enabled Canadian students to participate include the Child Soldiers project, the Bullying project, and the Environment Online (ENO) project (which is coordinated from Finland). Overall, there are 300 schools from 90 countries that participate in the program. The purpose of this program is to raise students' consciousness of the problems and issues that face the world, and how they can contribute to alleviating these problems, both at home and abroad.

Funded by the Canadian International Development Agency (CIDA), Butterfly208 is another program to promote global awareness among students. Named to represent the approximately 208 countries in the world, and using the butterfly effect to denote the interconnectedness of every country, Butterfly208 allows Canadian students to get involved in international development. The project holds annual contests in various categories, for schools, teachers, and students. Through CIDA, Butterfly208 also provides numerous resources to be used in classrooms throughout Canada.

The Global Classroom Initiative (GCI) is a research-based program also sponsored and funded by the Canadian International Development Agency (CIDA). Since 2002, organizations such as teachers' federations and school boards may apply for funding for projects that concern international development. These project ideas can take a variety of forms and use different media, including the internet and print media.

The Global Virtual Classroom (GVC) is another program to foster global awareness. Created in 1996 and managed by the Give Something Back International Foundation (GSBI), it is an educational website that provides free online connection for students from various countries to interact with one another. GVC emphasizes integrating technology into the classroom, and it holds an annual web design contest. Each design team consists of three schools from three different continents. Embarking on a project together, the three schools must interact and learn from one another.

Although somewhat in a different category from those mentioned above, Canada's Community Access Program (CAP) connects students, teachers, and other individuals to the internet, and implicitly to the rest of the world. Established in 1995 by the government of Canada through Industry Canada, CAP provides resources to access centres for computers, internet access, and other forms of electronics. Schools, libraries, and community centres act as the main access points. CAP also has a youth initiative that allows students aged 15-30 to find employment and learn valuable technological skills to further their employability. The CAP has well established websites in British Columbia, Manitoba, New Brunswick, and Prince Edward Island. Also, CAP has over 1400 French access sites in Quebec. The Toronto District School Board and the Edmonton Catholic District School Board are among the many school boards that offer access sites. Lastly, Northwest Territories, Nova Scotia, Nunavut, Yukon, and Newfoundland and Labrador are CAP participants.

technology of communication, language can be an arbiter of empowerment or oppression. It follows logically that any knowledge that students acquire, particularly in contexts of diversity, should include critical language awareness (Fairclough, 1992). Critical language awareness helps students to understand the ways in which language, ideology, and power are connected. For example, it is through language that prejudice and negative stereotypes such as racial slurs, epithets, and name-calling are conveyed. We also use language to repress, label people, or distort reality. Similarly, the language we use shapes our perceptions and realities, as well as those of others with whom we interact (Corson, 2001). Consider for instance the following episode between a teacher and a female student in a male-dominated grade 9 physical education class. Ten minutes into the class, Kendra who is normally a phys-ed enthusiast, was still standing in a corner of the gym seemingly oblivious to the activities around her. When the teacher notices Kendra he beckons to her to come closer.

> **Teacher:** Kendra, why are you not participating?
>
> **Kendra:** Sir, I'm not feeling well.
>
> **Teacher:** What's the problem?
>
> **Kendra:** Sir, I'm not sure. I'm just not feeling well. Can I be excused from doing the exercises today?
>
> **Teacher:** (*looks at the boys conspiratorially*) Well, there must be something. You look decidedly unhappy. Having boy troubles?
>
> **Kendra:** (*looking indignant and embarrassed, replies emphatically*) No, sir! I told you; I'm just not feeling well!
>
> **Teacher:** (*turning to the boys, the teacher winks and says*) Guys! What else do you think it could be?

Revelling in what they saw as a funny (and welcome) interlude, the boys begin to laugh simultaneously. By this time, Kendra had had enough. She stormed out of the gym and walked straight to the principal's office.

How might we interpret this incident? Besides his obvious insensitivity and unprofessional behaviour, this teacher is engaging in gender-based stereotyping, or sexism, expressed through insensitive language. He trivializes Kendra's problems, and humiliates and alienates her by assuming that her problems must in one way or the other, be associated with boys. There is of course a myriad of problems that Kendra could have been experiencing. Yet, he makes a stereotypical assumption about teenage girls — that most of their personal problems are linked to relationships with boys. While the teacher was probably just trying to be funny and did not intend any harm, this type of sexist action and attitude (expressed through language), belittles, disempowers, and psychologically damages as much as direct verbal harassment. (See Chapter 2 for the case of Rhonda Gordon, as documented in the video *For Angela*). Although the above vignette is a hypothetical scenario, the teacher's attitude epitomizes the kind of typecasting that Ng (1995) refers to as "common sense sexism", which occurs more frequently in schools than we would like to think. Children are particularly oblivious to the consequences of improper language usage, thus as in other areas of the teaching/learning dichotomy, teachers must model critical language awareness by paying attention to their language practices in and out of the classroom. Practical strategies for promoting critical language awareness among students include

- modelling positive language use, e.g., avoiding prejudicial and put-down language
- examining text and other resource materials to remove sexism, bias, and stereotypes

- integrating critical language awareness across the curriculum
- helping students to understand the linkages between language and identity
- providing students authentic opportunities to deconstruct texts
- teaching how other forms of communication (e.g., body language) convey prejudice
- teaching the connection between thought and language
- teaching critical thinking skills.

Critical Thinking

Critical thinking is a deliberate process of reasoning that enables people to move from a restricted to a more abstract level of thinking. According to Paul and Elder (2004: 1), "[c]ritical thinking is a process by which a thinker improves the quality of his or her thinking by skilfully taking charge of the structures inherent in thinking and imposing intellectual standards upon them". Used here in a Freirian sense that has emancipatory possibilities, critical thinking allows learners to see the "big picture" through a deliberate process of dialectical thinking (Freire, 1970) that involves reflection, probing, questioning, and finally reconfiguring the information they receive in a way that relates to their own experiences and meaning systems.

There are a number of reasons why critical thinking should be foundational and therefore non-negotiable knowledge for all students. First, there are immense individual and societal benefits that result from logical thinking. Second, we live in complex and turbulent times in which as Paul (1995: 13) asserts, "critical thinking will become a survival need, an external imperative for every nation and every individual who must survive on his or her own talents, abilities and traits". Some would argue that critical thinking is already part of our survival needs in contemporary society. The problem is that we fail to either recognize or accept this reality, and when we do, we fail to adopt it as part of a robust curriculum. Third, it allows students to become active participants in their own learning in ways that appeal to their own meaning systems. Fourth, it enables students to deconstruct and then reconstruct the information they receive in order to ask important, thought-provoking questions. Research has shown that the ability to think critically is associated with prejudice reduction and a reduction in dogmatic thinking. However, despite its salience among the various dimensions of non-negotiable knowledge, critical thinking is the most difficult to teach because it involves requiring people, in this case students, to change the way they think. As Paul (1995) puts it

> We cannot escape the brute fact that there are no algorithms for doing one's own thinking. Critical thinking, by its very nature, is principled not procedural thinking. Critical thinking requires thinkers to continually monitor what they are thinking by means of questions that test for clarity, accuracy, specificity, relevance, consistency, logic, depth, and significance. Since critical thinking often involves thinking with multiple points of view in terms of reference, it often *yields multiple, possible solutions* (p. 283). [my emphasis]

We all interpret the world through our cultural lenses, and human beings are creatures of habit. If we think about it for a moment, how often do we as adults change the way we think? Imagine how much more challenging this can be for students — especially at the first two levels of the education system. To be effective, teachers must also model critical thinking: students cannot become critical thinkers if teachers themselves are not willing to critique and modify their own thinking behaviour. Moreover, students are unaware of what highly skilled thinking looks like, as they rarely see it modelled in traditional school systems (Paul and Elder, 2004).

Thus left on their own, students cannot understand ways of critiquing their own thinking and assumptions about ideas, events, and issues and people (especially those that are different from them). In sum, critical thinking skills should enable students to

- improve their thinking skills
- avoid uncritical acceptance of information they receive by analyzing the various options
- become informed consumers of knowledge
- become open to new ideas, perspectives, and worldviews
- adopt the practices of critical reflection and deliberate reasoning
- change perspectives when such is warranted
- empathize with others
- become agents of change by acting to transform undesirable social policies and practices

Knowledge about Indigenous Peoples

Why should knowledge about indigenous people be considered foundational knowledge in contemporary Canadian classrooms? Why should it be non-negotiable knowledge? As previously argued, Canada's First Nations peoples have historically been subjected to injustices at the hands of the Europeans, since their arrival in North America. As a consequence, both groups share a tenuous relationship as the Royal Commission on Aboriginal Peoples (1996) aptly observes in the introduction of Volume 2 of its report:

> the relationship that has developed over the last 400 years between Aboriginal and non-Aboriginal people in Canada . . . was built on a foundation of false premises — that Canada was for all intent and purposes an unoccupied land when the newcomers arrived from Europe; that the inhabitants were a wild, untutored and ignorant people given to strange customs and ungodly practices; that they would in time, through precept and example, come to appreciate the superior wisdom of the strangers and adopt their ways; or, alternatively, that they would be left behind in the march of progress and survive only as an anthropological footnote.

Consequently, for far too long the history of First Nations peoples was all but nonexistent in school curricula, as a result of European ethnocentrism even though as the Royal Commission (1996) also points out "this country was not *terra nullius* . . . the newcomers did not 'discover' it in any meaningful sense". While recent attention to diversity and social justice issues has increased the presence of Canada's first people in curricula, this is often taught in ways that do not allow students to engage the issues substantively. Moreover, their immense contribution to Canadian confederation, and their unique epistemology still do not receive the attention they deserve (Battiste and Henderson, 2000). But, political and social justice issues aside, non-First Nations Canadians have much to learn from **indigenous knowledge** systems, which are gaining attention as consequential thought systems (Dei, 1996; Semali and Kincheloe, 1999). What is indigenous knowledge? While a detailed rendering is beyond the scope of this work, a brief sketch follows.

However, before proceeding we must address a long-standing misconception about indigenous knowledge: that it refers exclusively to the worldviews of "native" or "traditional" peoples. This is an erroneous assumption. In reality, every knowledge-base is indigenous to a group or cultural entity. Thus, the monocultural knowledge that is disseminated in Canadian schools is based on Eurocentric ideology, which is indigenous or native to Western European peoples. The assumption that indigenous knowledge is synonymous with only non-Western worldviews is akin to the belief, held by some members of the dominant group, that non-White people do not have a culture. We know of course, and this is the essence of the argument of all critical educators and theorists, that everyone belongs to a cultural community. We also know, as argued throughout this book, that the culture that prevails in Canadian schools is that of European Canadians. Thus, the problem is that the knowledge-base which is indigenous to some groups, such as First Nations peoples or those of African descent, is not highly valued in schools. Viewed from this perspective, in this volume the use of this terminology to refer to the ways of knowing of minoritized groups, particular First Nations peoples, is a matter of conceptual convenience.

Different from Western canons, indigenous knowledge encompasses the entire realm of knowledge that the Royal Commission on Aboriginal Peoples (1996, 4: 454) describes "as a cumulative body of knowledge and beliefs handed down through generations by cultural transmission, about the relationship of living things . . . with one another and their environment". Additionally, it comprises specific areas of knowledge, including humanistic, traditional ecological, scientific, human health, and spiritual knowledge (Brascoupé and Mann, 2001; Grenier, 1998). Central to indigenous epistemology is the practice of oral tradition (Loppie, 2007). Most of the world's indigenous peoples, including Canada's First Nations peoples, have a profound sense of community and experience nature as an integral part of their day-to-day existence. These values are increasingly acknowledged as essential for survival in an era of global strife and environmental degradation. Indigenous systems of thought are of significant benefit to non-Aboriginal people because of the vast repertoire of knowledge that has been accumulated over many centuries. For example, the Inuit know much more about Arctic wildlife populations and the environment than other Canadians do (Grenier, 1998). Similarly, indigenous traditional holistic medicine is now used outside Aboriginal communities both nationally and globally. Furthermore, teaching them indigenous knowledge will provide students with another view of how knowledge is produced in diverse contexts. There is indeed much that Canadian students can learn from indigenous knowledge. Battiste and Henderson (2000) offer the following as the common structure of indigenous ways of knowing:

> (1) knowledge of and belief in unseen powers in the ecosystem; (2) knowledge that all things in the ecosystem are dependent on each other; (3) knowledge that reality is structured according to most of the linguistic concepts by which Indigenous describe it; (4) knowledge that personal relationships reinforce the bond between persons, communities, and ecosystems; (5) knowledge that sacred traditions and persons who know these traditions are responsible for teaching "morals" and "ethics" to practitioners who are then given responsibility for this specialized knowledge and its dissemination; and (6) knowledge that an extended kinship passes on teachings and social practices from generation to generation (p. 42).

Besides the ecological benefits, teaching Canadian students about indigenous knowledge will expand their knowledge about Canada's First Nations peoples. An underlying cause of the stigma and stereotyping that is sometimes associated with First Peoples (such as the incident in the video described in Chapter 2) stems from a distorted view of who they are — a view mostly gleaned from media misrepresentation. It would not be far-fetched to suggest that teaching indigenous knowledge should be part of the curriculum in all teacher preparation programs. As Howard (2006) suggests in his book *We Can't Teach What We Don't Know*, it would be illusory to expect that teachers would be able to infuse and teach indigenous knowledge if they themselves do not understand what it entails. Another rationale for the advocacy to make indigenous knowledge an integral part of the curriculum in Canada and globally, is to repair some of the damage that has been done to the ecosystem by Western thought (Dei, 1996; Semali and Kincheloe, 1999).

The Environment and Bio-diversity

In the annals of world history, February 2, 2007, will be remembered as the day the world received a wake-up call to the impact of global warming and other environmental abuses on the survival of the planet. On that day in Paris, France, the world's leading climatologists presented a report on the climatic condition of the planet based on scientific evidence from their work. The report painted a gloomy picture of the consequences of environmental degradation if the world does not reverse its human-initiated destructive course. The social and educational implications of this report are obvious, but one may ask "What does this have to do with Canadian diversity?" While perhaps not immediately obvious, both are linked in very important ways. First, most of Canada's environmental education programs give pre-eminence to diversity issues. The practices of Canadian environmental educators are informed "by critical pedagogy, popular education, feminism and eco-feminism, environmental thought, environmental justice, . . . holistic education or indigenous knowledges" (Russell, Bell, and Fawcett, 2000: 199). As will be apparent later, some of these paradigms also inform the work of critical and progressive educators. Second, while many parts of the world will experience climatic change, the bulk of the world's environmental degradation affects marginalized communities, including Aboriginal and urban communities. For example, award-winning Canadian environmental activist and Nobel Prize nominee Sheila Watt-Cloutier has been sounding an alarm about the gradual disappearance of the Artic, and the concomitant impact on the Inuit way of life — and perhaps that of the entire country (*The Globe and Mail*, May 24, 2006). A third reason why the environment and biodiversity constitute essential knowledge is that we live in a volatile world that is rife with environmental exploitation and degradation that can result in conflicts. Some of the world's most enduring conflicts can be traced directly to environmental exploitation, destruction of livelihood, and the subsequent population displacement. In fact, experts believe that there are more environmental than political refugees. Many of these refugees come from diverse backgrounds and immigrate to Canada in search of better life chances for themselves and their children. A fourth and perhaps most important reason why in-depth knowledge about the environment should be a requirement for all students is to teach students to become guardians of the environment. Noddings (2005) explains:

> Students should be involved in direct, hands-on environmental projects as part of their practical education. Just as they should participate in care of the young, aged, and disabled, so they should contribute to cleaning up streams, planting trees, and maintaining gardens in parks and school yards. Such work may not only induce a lifelong commitment to environmental causes but might even inspire some students to consider related occupations: horticulture, architectural landscaping, city planning, civil engineering, forestry, artistic endeavours such as painting plants and animals, or journalism involving plants, animals, and the environment (p. 136).

Information and Communications Technology (ICT)

In an information age, knowledge of ICTs should be non-negotiable because it is now a prerequisite for successful living. In most Western societies, ICTs are integrated across the curriculum because they are considered an indispensable part of schooled knowledge. Unfortunately, despite their immense benefits (increased student productivity, increased engagement with language and literacy development, expanded opportunities for cooperative learning among students, virtual access to the world, etc.), many ethical issues have now arisen regarding ICTs and education. Their proliferation ushered in new possibilities and opportunities for social, economic, and educational progress, however, they have also created new forms of exclusion and diversity-related problems. One of which is the digital divide. Digital divide occurs when individuals either have or lack access to ICTs based on such variables as socio-economic status, race, ethnicity, geography (rural-urban differences), and gender (AAUW, 1998; Statistics Canada, 1999;). Additionally, there is the problem of language as many computer and software programs are written in English, which presents immense challenges for students with limited English proficiency (ELP). At the same time, the ability to use computers and related technologies has become a foundational skill for academic success. For equity-minded educators, these are problems that schools can help to ameliorate by making computer literacy non-negotiable rather than optional knowledge. Questions to guide policy and school-based action in this regard include the following:

- Who is excluded from access to ICTs?
- What are the potential consequences of this exclusion?
- In what ways can schools help to close the digital divide?
- How can teachers ensure that all students receive appropriate and meaningful instruction in ICTs?

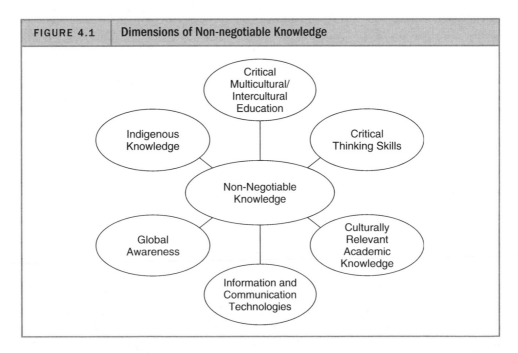

FIGURE 4.1   **Dimensions of Non-negotiable Knowledge**

- How does limited access affect the academic success of students from poor and marginalized communities?
- How can schools increase limited English- and French-proficient students' access to ICTs in school?

DIMENSIONS OF NEGOTIABLE KNOWLEDGE

In contrast to non-negotiable knowledge, negotiable knowledge is context sensitive. It is the kind of knowledge that is relevant to the needs of local communities. For instance, in high immigrant population areas, the heritage languages of the community would be negotiable, since each community would have to determine the languages that best reflect its ethnocultural dynamics. What do the contents of negotiable knowledge look like? As we explore some examples of negotiable knowledge, keep in mind that as contingent knowledge, negotiable knowledge will vary from one locale to another.

Community-Centred Values

Before discussing the idea of community-centred values it is important to emphasize, as Banks (2006) points out above, that there are common values that everyone should adhere to which must be cognizant of an emergent global world. So, what kind of values should schools teach in a pluralistic society? Wilkinson and Hébert (2003: 40) have identified 12 basic citizenship values that should be taught in Canada. These values are loyalty, sincerity, openness, civic-mindedness, freedom, equality, respect for self and others, solidarity, self-reliance, respecting the earth, a sense of belonging, and human dignity. They argue that there is an interrelationship between these macro-values, which can further be collapsed into four citizenship domains: the civil, the political, the socio-economic, and the cultural domain (which is of particular relevance here). It "refers to the manner in which societies take into account the increasing cultural diversity in societies, diversity due to greater openness to other cultures, to global migration and to increased mobility (p. 40).

Wilkinson and Hébert's framework provides a model for incorporating values into the curriculum. But, it must be emphasized that in teaching shared values, educators must not resort to reductionist universalism, whether purposeful or inadvertent, that positions hegemonic, assimilationist Eurocentric knowledge as worthy of perpetuation.

In addition to common values, every community has its own values, norms, and ethos that guide member behaviour. In this book, these values constitute negotiable knowledge. Thus, the onus is on every community to develop and teach specific values that foster tolerance, pluralism, and inter-group understanding within its own jurisdiction. For example, most communities have contextualized practices and beliefs that are associated with their dominant way of life. These values may be linked to specific religious beliefs, or they might even be related to local industries as sources of income generation. Teaching community-centred values should be guided by such questions as What kinds of values are needed for peaceful co-existence within our community? How should these values be developed? Whose cultural values are to be appropriated? How can these values be integrated across the curriculum? How can we ensure that everyone's voice is included? Teaching community-centred values should begin with values that are most desirable within each individual classroom.

Community Awareness

If we were to ask a typical high-school student to identify the ethnic groups that live in her or his community, chances are that he or she would fail that "test" dismally. Some neo-conservatives (who adhere to "one size fits all" social and educational ideologies) may see this knowledge gap as evidence of the existence of a macro-Canadian culture that should obviate all talks about diversity. This would not be in the best interest of the community, however. As a bilingual, multicultural — and as we have seen — de facto multilingual society, it makes sense for people to get to know members of their community (used in the broad sense) to enable cross-cultural understanding and tolerance. Thus, another dimension of negotiable knowledge is teaching students about the diverse ethnic groups and cultures that exist in their own communities. It is equally important for students to learn about the various religions that are practised locally. Perhaps even more important, students have to know and appreciate the contribution of various groups (including new immigrants and refugees) to the development of their communities. Ensuring students' knowledge of their communities is a proactive way of affirming diversity in schools.

Heritage Languages

The federal government provides funding to support heritage language programs (see Chapter 2). Thus, in response to increasing diversity among students, school boards and community organizations now offer courses in community or heritage languages. Although teaching heritage languages is extremely important, it is however, negotiable knowledge because these languages vary from one community to another. Since each community has predominant languages, it is important that school systems determine which languages have enough representation to warrant formal instruction. For instance, while in some communities Urdu, Chinese, Vietnamese, Gujerati, and Polish may be the most widely spoken non-official languages, in another Arabic, Swahili, Korean, Hindi, and Tamil may be the most commonly spoken. Patterns of immigration and settlement vary from one Canadian community to another, so we can expect that the heritage languages that are taught in Grand Prairie, Alberta, will differ from those in Windsor, Ontario. Similarly, the non-official languages that are supported by Montreal schools will be markedly different from those in Vancouver. This is not to say that the same heritage languages are not spoken in different regions of the country. Clearly, people speak Mandarin in various cities across British Columbia as they do in Ontario, Manitoba, Saskatchewan, or Quebec. The main argument is that each community would have to negotiate the inclusion of its languages as part of the core curriculum — rather than the common practice, as after school or Saturday programs.

Local Ecosystem

As experts argue, students in the 21st Century mandatorily must become generally environmentally literate. This includes intimate knowledge of the local ecosystem. It also means teaching students the various forms of life that exist in their communities in ways that emphasize their interconnection.

Having discussed what students should generally be taught in schools in pluralistic societies, we now turn our attention to a discussion of some specific frameworks through which educators can teach these knowledge areas, beginning with diversity pedagogy.

FIGURE 4.2	Dimensions of Negotiable Knowledge

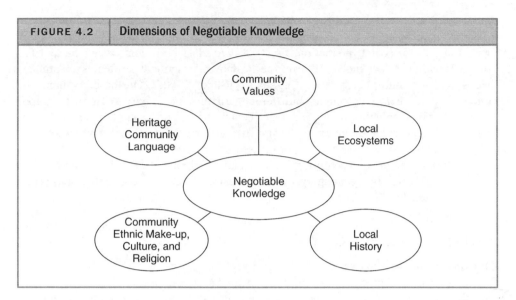

DIVERSITY PEDAGOGY

Diversity pedagogy is an emergent theory that proposes a set of principles that emphasize the interconnectedness of culture, cognition, and schooling. According to one of its major proponents Rosa Hernández Sheets, diversity pedagogy "represents a union between classroom practice and theoretical scholarship explicating the role of culture in the social and cognitive development of children. . . . [It] views the natural connectedness of culture and cognition as keys to linking the teaching-learning process to elements of diversity" (2005: 19).

The theory states that culturally inclusive teachers should be able to observe and identify individual and group cultural behaviour patterns, and then apply such knowledge in identifying student skills and competencies. These observations would, in turn, help teachers make informed instructional decisions and create optimal conditions for the academic success of their culturally diverse students. While the theory stresses the enormous importance of teachers in the teaching and learning process, it also emphasizes the important role that students play in their own learning. This is akin to constructivist approaches to learning, which see individuals as active participants in the process of knowledge construction.

There are eight dimensions of diversity pedagogy, each of which is divided into two parts: teacher pedagogical behaviours and student cultural displays (Sheets, 2005). Teacher pedagogical behaviours include teachers creating classroom conditions that enable students to become their authentic selves. For example, when teachers create culturally validating learning environments through their instructional activities and interpersonal behaviours, students are encouraged to act in ways that validate their identities as individuals, and as members of other social formations. There is in effect, a correspondence between teacher pedagogical behaviours and student cultural displays.

How do these sets of variables interact? Sheets postulates that most students exhibit culture-related behavioural patterns (cultural displays) to which teachers can respond in two different ways: they can either respond positively or remain indifferent (which is to act in traditional ways). Teachers who recognize and respond to student cultural displays develop diversity consciousness, promote ethnic identity development, provide opportunities for social interaction, create a safe classroom context, encourage language learning, select inclusive resources, adapt instructional strategies to students needs, and use multiple assessment strategies (Sheets, 2005). On the other hand, she argues that teachers who remain indifferent will promote binary reasoning, support assimilationist ideologies, promote teacher-centric classrooms, maintain a stressful climate, de-emphasize heritage language use, use generic instructional content and universal methods, as well as use limiting assessment criteria. By acknowledging the intersection of culture and cognition in the social development of children (and implicitly learning), diversity pedagogy provides educators a valuable conceptual and practical tool for teaching for diversity.

CRITICAL PEDAGOGY

Drawing on the seminal works of McLaren (2007), Kincheloe (2005), Giroux (1983), Freire (1970), and Apple (2004) (works with which all educators should be, but typically are not, familiar), **critical pedagogy** as adopted in this book focuses on two dialectic views of education: how power mediates academic success, and how challenge and interrogation can interrupt the control of dominant society over education. As a substitute for the politically expedient knowledge that students receive in schools, advocates of critical pedagogy propose an alternative view that offers possibilities for social transformation. As a framework for changing educational practices that are premised on inflexible worldviews, which in turn reinforce the oppression of less powerful groups, critical pedagogy aims to improve schooling outcomes for all students. Proponents also argue that such improvement requires classroom practices that are not only cognizant of the diverse backgrounds of learners, but are also grounded in a sound understanding of the politicized nature of current education, in which some discourses are privileged and others devalued.

Although there are multiple strands of critical pedagogy — the "libertarian, the radical, and the liberationist, all with points of difference and fusion" (McLaren, 2007: 193) — there are some common threads that connect all strands. For example, advocates agree that changing undesirable educational practices at the school level requires educators who are reflective practitioners, adopt democratic practice, and are culturally literate. They advance the cause of social justice with the ultimate goal of exposing oppressive social structures, and empowering the marginalized in society. In the view of one of its most notable proponents Joe Kincheloe (2005)

> Critical pedagogy is dedicated to resisting the harmful effects of dominant power. Advocates of critical pedagogy work to expose and contest oppressive forms of power as expressed in socioeconomic class elitism, Eurocentric ways of viewing the world, patriarchal oppression, and imperialism . . . In this context, white people must learn to listen to non-whites' and indigenous people's criticism of them and of the cultural norms they have established and imposed on people of a lower socioeconomic class and non-European peoples . . . (p. 34).

Critical pedagogists believe that schooling and its various practices are inherently politically contested spaces where oppositional discourses are silenced. As such, they challenge educators to become critical of mainstream understandings of what education and being educated entail, to question the canons and assumptions that underlie the curriculum, and to understand that issues of social justice cannot be separated from teaching and learning.

Moreover, critical pedagogists challenge educators to expose the power dynamics that are at work in school settings through educational policies that were developed and adopted as "neutral" by the dominant group. Critical pedagogy enables students and educators to read the "word and the world" (Freire, 1970), while espousing teaching practices that value, nurture, and draw on the experience and perspective of diverse students.

However, for critical pedagogy to succeed, teachers must embrace democratic communication practices, in which the teacher's role becomes more than that of a transmitter of knowledge. As advocates point out, democratic or **dialogical communication** is a precursor to student empowerment. Student-centred and teacher-directed dialogical discourse aims to facilitate the development of critical thought and expression and to eliminate what Shor (1992) refers to as teacher talk. Shor posits that teacher talk is "the one-way discourse of traditional classrooms that . . . alienates students, depresses their achievement and supports inequality in school and society" (p. 85). He argues that because teacher-talk suppresses critical thought, students put up resistance that sabotages their desire to learn. In contrast, dialogical classroom discourse encourages students' critical thinking and is essential in critical pedagogy.

Student-centred and teacher directed, **dialogical classroom communication** aims to facilitate participatory communication, which engages rather than disengages students. In dialogue-centred classrooms, students are encouraged through teacher modelling, to ask provocative questions about issues that relate to power, knowledge, and social positioning. Although the complexity of the question and discussion will vary according to the level of education, in a dialogue-centred classroom the teacher creates a comfortable, non-threatening environment that affirms differences, and multiple perspectives and experiences. In short, what ultimately emerges from such a milieu is a community of learners where knowledge is created and shared by both teacher and student (Shor, 1992; Cummins, 2000; Villegas and Lucas, 2002). Such "engaged pedagogy", in which education is seen as the practice of freedom (hooks, 1994), should in turn engender meaningful student participation in classroom discourse and activities. In summary, the goals of critical pedagogy include but are not limited to the following:

- interrogating and disrupting the dominance and dissemination of monocultural Eurocentric knowledge in pluralistic societies such as Canada
- challenging the assumptions that inform the construction of the knowledge that students are taught in school
- providing culturally relevant teaching that engages, rather than disenfranchises, students
- centring the voices and experiences of all students in teaching practices
- increasing the life chances of minority students through just educational practices
- encouraging students to critically question and engage **dominant narratives,** in particular the contents of the curriculum
- having teachers recognize and engage the socio-political environment within which their profession is embedded

- having teachers and other educators become critical of their own biographies
- exposing how the language educators use produces particular practices that exclude some students
- emphasizing a curriculum that is responsive to the everyday knowledge that is relevant to students' diverse experiences
- integrating the experiences of women and other nondominant groups into the curriculum
- engendering transformative learning.

TRANSFORMATIVE LEARNING

Transformative learning, manifested in both educators and their students, should be the culminating effect of the implementation of the various frameworks for teaching for diversity discussed in this chapter. Although there are different conceptions of transformative learning, one coalescing theme links its various approaches — the idea of a profound change in consciousness or perspective in the learner (Mezirow et al., 2000; Cranton, 1994). While the nature and extent of perspective transformation varies in individuals, especially in young learners, such change involves a re-alignment of the learner's worldviews, as well as a deeper understanding of the structure of her or his world. By awakening the interrogator in learners, transformative learning allows them to challenge entrenched assumptions, and to embrace problem-posing educational approaches which according to Freire (1998) enable people to

> develop their power to perceive critically the way they exist in the world with which and in which they find themselves; they come to see the world not as a static reality, but as a reality in process, in transformation . . . Teacher-students and student-teachers are continually reflecting on themselves and the world, establishing an authentic form of thought and action.

While transformative learning is most often associated with learners, educators also benefit from it through a process that allows them to engage in self-analysis. Specific strategies for engaging in authentic self-analysis are discussed in Chapter 5.

PEACE EDUCATION

One of the causes of intolerance, discrimination, and prejudice (e.g., racism, sexism, or homophobia) in society is people harbouring distrust of those that are different from them (see Chapter 1). Conflict among students and teachers is sometimes the residue of intergroup distrust in society, which can be deep-seated in immigrant receiving countries such as Canada. Juxtaposed onto global conflicts that spill into classrooms when children from dissenting groups come face-to-face, peace education has become part of the discourse about diversity, multiculturalism, and intercultural understanding.

What is peace education and why should it be an integral part of diversity programs? Article 26 of the *Universal Declaration of Human Rights* describes peace education as "directed to the full development of the human personality and to the strengthening of respect for human rights and fundamental freedom . . . " that promotes *"understanding, tolerance and friendship among all nations, racial or religious groups"*. In their book *Educating for a Culture of Peace*, Yaacov Iram and associates (2006) outline why peace education is a correlate of diversity education. The authors argue that to achieve a culture of peace, societies must first teach positive values, which are critical to sustaining pluralism, tolerance, human rights, and multiculturalism. According to Yaacov Iram, peace education is a diversity-oriented framework that aims towards "promoting knowledge, values, attitudes, and skills conducive to peace and non-violence, and . . . an active commitment to the building of a cooperative and caring democratic society. It aims at promoting social justice, equality, civil responsibility and solidarity . . . and practices of peaceful conflict resolution and non-violence" (2006, pp. 7-8). Although rarely conceptualized as such, Iram's definition provides a compelling rationale for making peace education an empowering educational model for affirming diversity and cross-cultural understanding. Thus, as often presumed, peace education is not simply about resolving existing conflicts, it is also about preventing conflict, and promoting tolerance, prejudice reduction, and diversity.

There are various approaches to implementing peace education programs, but the adopted model should be dependent on contextual factors. For example, Salomon (2001) identifies three possible regions where peace education can occur: in regions where there is ongoing violent conflict between enemies, in regions of tension where there is a lot of racial, inter-ethnic, and tribal tensions between the majority and minority, and in regions of tranquility where there are no obvious conflicts (in which case peace education serves to maintain the relative tranquility locally and to export peace understanding to conflicted areas). Canada fits into this latter category.

A second approach to peace education purports that peace education is most effective if the peace educator adapts his or her own approach to the different conditions that affect societies. Bar-Tal (2002) suggests that peace education should not only highlight behavioural patterns, it should also be a type of socialization process, engaging people in the active process of change. In this model, the success of peace education depends on educators addressing relevant issues, such as diversity in society. For example, students need to examine issues related to social injustice as perpetuated in the real world by exploring various books with characters from different backgrounds and racial identities. Also, deconstructing and understanding racial identity issues can help promote peace and facilitate informed social action among students.

A third peace education paradigm focuses on violence prevention, whether physical, psychological, or structural (Harris, 1996). The latter is of particular relevance here because it involves institutionally sanctioned social injustices such as denying people their basic rights and freedoms, excluding them from access to empowering kinds of knowledge, excluding their experience from the curriculum, etc.

Another framework for teaching peace education is the model put forward by *The Earth Charter*, which is a declaration of the fundamental principles for building an equitable, just, and sustainable global world. Overseen by the Earth Charter Commission, the *Charter* outlines the skills, ideas, and attitudes that young people need for survival in the 21st Century. The four major themes identified as essential knowledge areas for young people by the *Charter* (as described by Carlsson-Page and Lantieri, 2005) are respect and care for the community of life, ecological integrity, social and economic justice, and democracy, nonviolence, and peace.

As recent hate-related incidents have shown, some groups in Canada live in fear of unprovoked harassment, attack, stereotyping, and prejudice simply because of who they are (Henry and Tator, 2006; Fleras and Elliott, 2003). Ultimately, peace education is about tolerance, respect for human rights, validation of personal identity, and cross-cultural understanding — principles that are at the heart of Canada's official policy of multiculturalism. Consequently, peace education should be an integral part of the teacher knowledge base—starting with what student teachers learn in teacher education programs. Swee-Hin and Cawagas (2002) identify several aspects of peace education that preservice programs should promote, in order to ensure that Canadian educators can teach a culture of peace:

- integrating comprehensive peace education into the curriculum
- stressing the importance of classroom management models that proactively include conflict resolution
- engendering educator commitment to teaching nonviolence
- engendering teacher commitment to working with all stakeholders in education, e.g., parents, community groups, social agencies, and political bodies, in order to design and establish peace education programs
- fostering in teacher candidates the ability to challenge social injustice, environmental destruction, human rights violation, and manifestation of violence
- emphasizing the importance of becoming involved in research that promotes peace and prevents violence
- working collaboratively with other institutions to ensure that teacher candidates understand ways of teaching peace across the curriculum
- providing teachers with the authority to challenge anti-peace measures — this aspect is particularly important since frequently educators are unable to embrace critical frameworks as a result of situational and institutional constraints.

BARRIERS TO EDUCATORS' ADOPTION OF CRITICAL AND PLURALISTIC PERSPECTIVES

There are several frameworks that teachers can adopt to affirm diversity in schools. Unfortunately, studies have shown that teachers are often resistant to embracing progressive educational policies and practices (Solomon and Levine-Rasky, 1996; Carr and Klassen, 1997). McKenzie and Scheurich (2004) have identified what they refer to as "equity traps", which teachers and other educators may fall into, thereby preventing them from adopting equitable practices. Their study, to determine White teachers' perceptions of students of colour, their own racial identity, and their perceptions of the relationship between the two, found that teachers tend to fall into four equity traps, which they and their school leaders must address. The first equity trap is a deficit view of students' achievement, which sees students as deficient because their families and communities are deficient. A second equity trap is "racial erasure", which means the kind of illusory thinking that racism will go way if only society would stop talking about it. A third equity trap is the "gaze", which is persistent monitoring of students' behaviour. The fourth equity trap is "paralogical behaviour" through which people rationalize their behaviour by holding others responsible for it, as one participating teacher in their study did:

> The anger of the kids caused me [to act this way]; I've gotten sucked into their anger. I mean I've never spoken to kids the way I have spoken to them this year. I mean it's just, I am just this far out

of control in my classroom on more days than I want anybody to repeat (McKenzie and Scheurich, 2004: 624).

The research recommended that principals play a significant role in overcoming barriers to equity in diverse school contexts. However, barriers to embracing praxis-oriented strategies also stem from structural or institutional factors. There are several variables that are inimical to progressive practices in contexts of diversity. Note that although these variables are discussed separately for conceptual clarity, in practice they can exist simultaneously.

1. *Personal beliefs and value systems* One of the most obvious reasons why teachers and other educators find it difficult to adopt critical perspectives is their own values and personal beliefs. We all see the world through the prism of our own backgrounds, which can make it challenging to embrace multiple perspectives or paradigm shifts. Furthermore, because most Canadian educators come from the dominant Anglo-European culture, they have different value orientations from many of their culturally diverse students. In her book *White Teacher,* Vivian Paley chronicles a poignant account of her personal journey and progress towards dealing with Black students at an integrated school in a predominantly White middle-class neighbourhood in the United States. What is particularly compelling about her account is her revelation of the enormous difficulties that are inherent in trying to change one's worldviews. Through insights gleamed from her experiences, Paley offers the following advice to teachers: "[T]he challenge in teaching is to find a way of communicating to each child the idea that his or her special quality is understood, is valued, and can be talked about. It is not easy, because we are influenced by the fears and prejudices, apprehensions and expectations, which have become a carefully hidden part of everyone of us" (preface, p. xx). Nevertheless educators, especially those who teach in diverse contexts, must make the paradigm shifts that diversity necessitates in their professional milieu.

2. *Adherence to orthodoxy* Although many educators embrace inclusive pedagogy in principle, the corpus of literature on the subject (Solomon and Levine-Rasky, 1996; Carr and Klassen, 1997; McLaren, 2007) indicates that they are often ambivalent in practice, as most continue to adhere to the traditional pedagogical orientations that informed their training. The popular assertion that teachers generally teach the way they were taught is not unfounded, as many are reluctant to think "outside the box". Moreover, educators tend to see their role less as an agent of change and more as a means of transmitting official knowledge that they have been mandated to teach. The problem of orthodox thinking is one that teachers should address if they plan to teach for diversity (see Chapter 8).

3. *Fear of being an outsider* Many teachers work in conservative environments, and as in most organizational settings, people need to fit in. Even teachers who genuinely want to make a difference in the lives of their diverse students are constrained by the fear of exclusion. No one ever wants to be at the periphery of a social space: indeed, being a minority in any context always engenders feelings of discomfort and alienation. Unfortunately, this important point is often lost on many educators, partly as a result of their training. Still, there are teachers who want to make a difference and make every effort to do so even if, like some of their students from minoritized communities, they have to put up resistance.

4. *Initial professional training* Researchers have long believed that the initial professional training teachers receive is partially responsible for society's failure to make education more responsive to the needs of culturally and socially different children (Ladson-Billings, 1994; Solomon, 2000; Cochran-Smith, 2000; Villegas and Lucas, 2002). In Canada, 95% of teachers are White and come from culturally homogenous communities, as do most preservice teacher candidates. For many teachers then, contemporary Canadian classrooms that must cater to diverse populations are different from what they remember about their own schooling experiences. They are in effect, unprepared to deal with student diversity. Yet, with few exceptions, teacher education programs are silent on this issue (see Chapter 7). Also, data from Statistics Canada show that about 30% of the school-age population (especially in urban centres such as Toronto, Vancouver, Montreal, Hamilton, and Windsor) is non-White. This is not to suggest that White teachers cannot address issues of diversity — the point is that preservice education programs need to provide more training in ways of responding to diversity in their classrooms.

5. *Institutional structures and policies* Very often, the educational system itself presents barriers that prevent teachers from embracing alternative worldviews. As Ladson-Billings (1994) points out, in many cases teachers who challenge oppressive educational structures and embrace progressive models (such as culturally relevant pedagogy), often work in opposition to the system that employs them. In some cases they resort to subterfuge. When school systems do not embrace diversity as official policy and so create structures to support it, it is unrealistic to expect teachers to do so in their everyday practice. That being said it is important to emphasize, as Cummins et al., (2005: 42) assert, that all educators, regardless of their backgrounds, always have choices. They can either continue to transmit sterile knowledge or "go beyond curricular guidelines and mandates".

6. *Limited knowledge of students' background* Knowledge of the recipient is a critical component of communication. This is particularly important in the context of diversity. As experts tell us, it is only when teachers know who their students are (especially those that come from marginalized communities) that they are able to address their specific needs. But, beyond the issue of empowering disadvantaged students, knowing and understanding students is a critical component of effective teaching.

7. *Inadequacy* Sometimes even teachers who want to adopt empowering strategies as routine practice are constrained by a lack of procedural knowledge about integrating learning strategies across the curriculum. What generally prevails is a haphazard infusion of strategies into subjects such as social studies and history. Perhaps even more telling, teachers who ostensibly are at the front line of advocating for all their students are not often conversant with empowering frameworks.

8. *Perceived irrelevance of diversity issues* As already stated, the bulk of Canadian teachers are White and from middle-class backgrounds. In contexts where students are culturally and ethnically homogeneous (in most cases White), there is a tendency to exclude diversity issues on the rationale that diversity issues "are for minorities". This is however an erroneous assumption (see Chapter 5).

9. *Curricular constraints* For many critical education theorists, the school curriculum is considered a form of cultural politics — as it is inextricably linked to the "sociocultural dimension of schooling" (McLaren, 2007). That Canadian school systems

promote a Eurocentric body of knowledge, which in turn sustains asymmetrical distribution of power and cultural imperialism while excluding the voices of some segments of society, is a view that many scholars share (e.g., Dei, 1996; Dei et al., 2000; Tator and Henry, 2006; Fleras and Elliott, 2003; James, 2003; Joshi, 2004; Moodley, 1999). As a consequence, most curricula do not foster the adoption of anti-oppressive paradigms. Thus, curricular constraints stemming from system-wide policies that negate other worldviews may prevent teachers from embracing pluralistic pedagogies even when they want to do so. See Chapter 3 for a case when a teacher asserts that curricular limitations prevent her from integrating more culturally responsive materials into her lessons.

10. *Professional isolation* At the micro-level, teachers generally work in autonomous contexts within the confines of their own classrooms. This limits opportunities for interacting and sharing ideas (including diversity issues) with their colleagues. Although some school systems provide opportunities for diversity training through workshops, the knowledge acquired is difficult to implement without sustained dialogue with peers.

The list above is a starting point for transformative praxis. They are not immutable barriers, since teachers who really want to become change agents can do so, once they are privy to the factors preventing them from providing the kinds of empowering educational experiences that students and their families have a right to expect. Nevertheless, transcending these barriers can be quite challenging, and it requires systematic, deliberate, and sustained effort.

Summary

This chapter examined three distinct but interrelated issues: what to teach students in pluralistic societies, critical frameworks for empowering all students (especially those from subordinate backgrounds), and the underlying causes of educator resistance to embracing progressive pedagogies. To address the first issue, i.e., what to teach in Canadian schools, the concept of negotiable and non-negotiable knowledge as requisite knowledge bases was introduced. Important dimensions of non-negotiable knowledge include critical multicultural/intercultural education, culturally relevant academic knowledge, global awareness, critical language awareness, critical thinking, knowledge about indigenous peoples, knowledge about the environment and biodiversity, and information and communication technologies. Examples of negotiable knowledge include community-centred values, knowledge about the community, heritage languages, and knowledge of local ecosystems.

Researchers have established that educators' knowledge about and adoption of critical frameworks for empowering diverse learners can be problematic. The chapter discussed several progressive frameworks: diversity pedagogy, critical pedagogy, and peace education, all of which should engender transformative praxis in students and their teachers. The discussion of these frameworks follows from the analysis of multicultural and antiracist education (see Chapter 1) as the two most common frameworks for addressing diversity in Canadian schools. Finally, it advanced several reasons why educators are resistant to embracing critical and inclusive pedagogies in schools as integral aspects of their everyday practice. The next chapter explores how teachers, and administrators alike, can overcome these barriers, particularly those that are within their spheres of influence.

Key Terms

Biodiversity	Critical language awareness	Critical pedagogy
Critical thinking	Dialogical classroom communication	Diversity pedagogy
Dominant narratives	Global awareness	Indigenous knowledge
Intercultural education	Negotiable knowledge	Non-negotiable knowledge
Peace education	Transformative learning	Transformative praxis

Questions to Guide Reflective Practice

1. Assume that you have been given the opportunity to develop an inclusive seventh grade curriculum. What knowledge areas would you include?

2. Besides the frameworks that are discussed in this chapter, conduct research to find other potential frameworks for responding to diversity in schools. In what ways do these differ from the frameworks (i.e., critical pedagogy, diversity pedagogy, and peace education) discussed in this chapter?

3. Examine your local school board's curriculum documents for several grades. To what extent do the knowledge areas align with the concept of negotiable and non-negotiable knowledge?

4. Organize a mock debate with a group of friends on the topic of the purposes of education.

5. In your opinion, is all learning "consciousness-raising" and "transformative"? Justify your response.

6. Compared to many parts of the world, Canadians enjoy peaceful coexistence with one another. Why then, should peace education be an integral part of the school curriculum?

7. How are environmental and diversity issues interconnected?

8. Define your understanding of a) critical multicultural education, b) inter-cultural education, c) critical pedagogy, d) diversity pedagogy, and e) peace education.

Case Study Analysis: Chapter Opening Vignette

1. Professor Dymes, who actively encouraged student "engagement" with the topics addressed in his class, wondered why opinions about such issues are often divided along racial or ethnic lines. Describe your understanding of "engagement" in this context.

2. Do you believe that issues related to diversity deserve more attention in Canadian schools than they currently receive?

3. Situate yourself in Professor Dymes' class. What is your position regarding the debate?

4. Why do you think it is difficult to devise strategies for dealing with diversity?

5. Based on Professor Dymes' declaration that there is usually potential for conflict as the course progresses due to its controversial nature, should he change his strategy of "active engagement"?

Test Your Knowledge

1. Before reading this chapter, to what extent were you familiar with the concepts of diversity, pedagogy, critical pedagogy, and peace education?

2. What is the policy of your local school board regarding the use of information and communication technologies?

3. What global awareness initiatives exist in the schools in a) your community, and b) your province? Are global awareness and environmental education part of the core curriculum?

4. Research and determine the differences between indigenous knowledge and Western knowledge.

5. Who determines what heritage languages are to be taught in your local community? How are the programs organized? Are they part of the core curriculum, or taught in "weekend" schools?

6. Interview two teachers who teach in culturally diverse contexts. What are their views on the issue? What are the challenges they face on a daily basis?

For Further Reading

Alred, G., Byram, M., and Fleming, M. (Eds.). (2003). *Intercultural Experience and Education*. Clevedon: Multilingual Matters.

Banks, J. (Ed.). (2004). *Diversity and Citizenship Education: Global Perspectives*. Princeton: Princeton University Press.

Battiste, M. (2002). Indigenous Knowledge and Pedagogy in First Nations Education: A Literature Review with Recommendations. Apamuwek Institute. Ottawa: National Working Group on Education and the Minister of Indian Affairs, Indian and Northern Affairs Canada (INAC).

Battiste, M. (2000). *Reclaiming Indigenous Voice and Vision*. Vancouver: UBC Press.

Freire, P. (1970). *Pedagogy of the Oppressed*. New York: Herder and Herder.

Goddard, T. (1997). Monocultural Teachers and Ethnoculturally Diverse Students. *Journal of Education Administration and Foundations*, 12(1): 30–45.

Goldstein, T., and Selby D. (Eds.). (2000). *Weaving Connections: Educating for Peace, Social and Environmental Justice*. Toronto: Sumach Press.

Kincheloe, J. (2005). *Critical Pedagogy Primer*. New York: Peter Lang.

Paley, V. (2000). *White Teacher*. Cambridge: Harvard University Press.

Reagan, T. (2005). *Non-Western Educational Traditions: Indigenous Approaches to Educational Thought and Practice,* 3rd Edition. Mahwah: Lawrence Erlbaum Associates Publishers.

Semali, L., and Kincheloe, J. (1999). *What is Indigenous Knowledge?* New York: Falmer Press.

Websites of Interest

www.criticalthinking.org Foundation for Critical Thinking

www.coun.uvic.ca/learn/crit.html Learning Skills Program — Thinking Critically

www.peace.ca/index.htm Canadian Centres for Teaching Peace

www.cultureofpeace.ca Canadian Culture of Peace Program

www.un.org/cyberschoolbus/peace/home.asp UN Peace Education

www.sasked.gov.sk.ca/docs/policy/multi/hert.html Multicultural Education and Heritage Language Education Policies

www.statcan.ca:8096/bsolc/english/bsolc?catno=11-008-X20000025165 Passing on the Language — Heritage Language Diversity in Canada — Statistics Canada

www.peace.ca/hero.htm Canadian Peace Educators and Their Work

CHAPTER 5

Initiating Praxis: Knowing Self, Students, and Communities

- ❑ Teachers and Self-knowledge
- ❑ Teacher Diversity Awareness Compass (TDAC)
- ❑ Teacher Diversity Research
- ❑ Critical Leadership Action
- ❑ Administrator Diversity Awareness Compass (ADAC)
- ❑ Knowing Students

VIGNETTE

Ms. Dante's eleventh grade class was engaged in a discussion about racism, prejudice, and stereotyping. Considered one of the "liberal" and "progressive" educators in the school, Ms. Dante believed that everyone deserves a fair chance in life, and she had little patience with intolerance. Compared with some of her colleagues, she seemed to have the uncanny ability of "connecting" effortlessly with students from diverse backgrounds, which enabled her to take liberties with issues that other teachers would rather avoid. By all accounts, Ms. Dante was the most popular teacher among the non-White students in the school. To introduce this particular topic, she asked her students to identify some stereotyped beliefs about certain racial groups in Canadian society — beginning with stereotypes of Blacks. She repeated the exercise for Asians, East Indians, First Nations' peoples and Arabs. At the end of the exercise, Ms. Dante moved on to a different aspect of the topic when suddenly a student of Arab decent raised his hand and said, "Ms., you skipped a group". "Which group is that?" she asked. "Well, what about White people? There are some stereotypes about them too," he responded. Ms. Dante casually replied that she did not discuss stereotypes associated with Whites for fear of "stepping on too many toes". After the class, and out of the teacher's earshot, the student expressed his anger and disappointment with Ms. Dante's attitude to the other minority students that had been in the class. The other students agreed, stating that they too were shocked and disgusted with Ms. Dante's insensitive remark. What's more, they all agreed that they felt inferior and subordinate to their White peers who Ms. Dante had not dared to offend. As far as they were concerned, if she had not wanted to "step on the toes" of the White students, she clearly did not have any problem stepping on theirs.

INTRODUCTION: INITIATING PRAXIS

The preceding chapter discussed frameworks that teachers can appropriate in order to teach for diversity in their classrooms. However, teaching in contexts of student diversity requires more than just embracing new ideas. It requires a new mindset, which can be achieved only through critical and ongoing self-analysis. It also requires the examination of the educational structures that may contribute to the oppression (and silencing) of some groups of students, along with members of their communities. Furthermore, critical self-analysis is crucial for praxis because our perception of ourselves, including our beliefs, attitudes, and interactions with others, can change dramatically upon close inspection. Indeed, teachers can only empower their students when they understand who they are and how their identities intersect with the pedagogical choices they make in their practice. As an example of how self-analysis can illuminate and improve practice, let us examine the case of Ms. Dante in the opening vignette. She considers herself a progressive educator who believes in the principles of social justice, and has little patience with people who show intolerance to others. Unfortunately, she exemplifies the well-meaning teacher who inadvertently nurtures racism in an institutional setting. In attempting to tackle a controversial and sensitive issue head on, she sabotages her own efforts at empowering her students by accentuating dominant group power within her classroom. In so doing, her actions result in the diminution and disempowerment of her minority students. Had she conducted a critical self-analysis to better understand herself as an educator, she would have discovered that beneath her veneer of tolerance, she actually harbours, or at least acknowledges, the same Eurocentric ideologies (as her remarks indicate) that she finds abhorrent. She would also have discovered that she enjoys certain privileges that accrue to her as a member of the dominant group in Canadian society.

Premised on the belief that critical action for changing unjust educational practices must begin with understanding and changing the "self" as a situated being, this chapter examines the ways teachers can better understand themselves, their diverse students, and the communities within which they operate. The chapter also explores the pivotal role of educational administrators, in particular principals, in culturally diverse settings. It begins with a brief analysis of how teachers (and other educators) may contribute to the silencing of some voices by virtue of their role as disseminators of socially sanctioned and value-laden knowledge.

TEACHERS AND SELF-KNOWLEDGE

The Teacher's Situated Self

There are many who hold the view that teaching is a neutral activity. However, contrary to popular belief, it is fundamentally a political project as Nieto and Bode (2008) tell us:

> Knowledge is neither neutral nor apolitical, yet it is generally treated by teachers and schools as if it were. Consequently, knowledge taught in . . . schools tends to reflect the lowest common denominator — that which is sure to offend the fewest (and the most powerful) and is least controversial . . . . Every educational decision made at any level, whether by a teacher or by an entire school system, reflects the political ideology and worldview of the decision maker . . . All the decisions . . . educators make, no matter how neutral they seem, may have an impact on the lives and expectations of . . . students (p. 55).

Like Nieto and Bode, Villegas and Lucas (2002) provide two contrasting views of teachers and teaching that have direct bearing on how teachers approach their practices. At one end of the continuum is the view that sees teaching as an apolitical activity. Thus, teachers are technicians whose primary function is to "use accepted and proven means to impart knowledge and skills prescribed by the curriculum, which is designed by experts and selected administrators and policy makers, none of whom work in the classroom" (p. 55). From this perspective, the distinction between teaching and indoctrination is blurred since schools can be conceptualized as instruments of socialization that aim to mould students according to the values that society considers desirable for social cohesion. By disseminating these ideologies, teachers inadvertently become part of the ideological apparatus through which, according to Althusser (1971), the dominant group exerts control and subjugates less powerful groups.

In Canada, this control is explicitly exercised through the contents of the curriculum, which by commission and omission excludes the voices of some segments of society (Henry and Tator, 2006; Fleras and Elliott, 2003; Dei et al., 2000; Rezai-Rashti, 1995; Joshee, 2004; Moodley, 1999). Moreover, the widespread phenomena of provincial control of the curriculum, standardized testing, and frequent measurement and assessment of teacher effectiveness, are all structural evidence of the moulding function of education. This moulding favours the dominant culture and values, which results in the reproduction of asymmetrical power relations in wider society (see Chapter 1).

In contrast with the view of teaching as a neutral activity Villegas and Lucas (2002) suggest that at the other end of the continuum are beliefs that see teachers as agents of change who are committed to challenging social inequalities through their everyday practice. One hallmark of the behaviour of such teachers is that, rather than de-politicizing their personal and professional philosophies, they re-politicize themselves to the realities of the social environment in which they work, as a strategy for instituting sustainable educational praxis. In embracing a social justice paradigm, they recognize that certain students are disempowered by school systems. Therefore they reject meritocratic educational ideologies that blame the students (and their families) for their failures as a result of presumed genetic inferiority and cultural deprivation (Nieto and Bode, 2008; see also Chapter 1). These teachers also acknowledge the relevance of power relations in wider society to understanding educational policies and practices. Even more salient, they understand that by virtue of their privileged position, teachers themselves are authority figures who have considerable power over their students. Teaching therefore, has much to do with the exercise of power and power relations even though, as bell hooks (1994) admonishes, for all those who teach

> the classroom remains the most radical space of possibility . . . for renewal and rejuvenation in our teaching practices. Urging all of us to open our minds and hearts so that we can know beyond the boundaries of what is acceptable, so that we can think and rethink, . . . create new visions . . . celebrate teaching that enables transgressions — a movement against and beyond boundaries (p. 12).

The movement beyond boundaries and towards socially just praxis must however begin with self-critique. Such scrutiny includes an analysis of teachers' value and belief systems, teaching practices, and their role in reproducing social hierarchies in Canadian society. As argued previously, we all grow up in cultural environments that promote the rationality and superiority of our own worldviews over those of others. It is therefore illogical that educators are able to empower others if they do not understand the values that inform their own practices. Palmer (1998) provides a very compelling argument for teacher self-knowledge:

> Teaching, like any truly human activity, emerges from one's inwardness, for better or worse. As I teach, I project the condition of my soul onto my students, my subject, and our way of being together. The entanglements I experience in the classroom are often no more or less than the convolutions of my inner life. Viewed from this angle, teaching holds a mirror to the soul. If I am willing to look in that mirror and not run from what I see, I have a chance to gain self knowledge — and knowing myself is as crucial to good teaching as knowing my students and my subject . . . In fact, knowing my students and my subject depends heavily on self-knowledge. When I do not know myself, I cannot know who my students are. I will see them through a glass darkly, in the shadows of my own unexamined life — and when I cannot see them clearly, I cannot teach them well . . . Good teaching requires self-knowledge: it is a secret hidden in plain sight (pp. 2, 3).

Unfortunately, while educators often ask questions regarding what to teach and how to teach it, they hardly ever inquire who the "teaching self" is (Palmer, 1998). This failure to inquire about the teaching self often results in teachers remaining unaware of their own values, norms, beliefs, and biases, which subsequently "limits a teacher's ability to connect and appropriately facilitate the learning process of students who operate from a cultural paradigm different from that of the teacher" (Irving, 2006: 196). Critical introspection is therefore, particularly important in demographically complex contexts such as Canadian classrooms, where the ethnocultural composition of teachers differs significantly from that of the students they teach (Goddard, 1997; Solomon et al., 2005). Not only would such introspection help teachers to develop an inclusive theory of practice, it would provide them practical insights that can engender change and successful educational outcomes for all their students. However, for self-knowledge to occur, certain self-directed processes that serve as catalysts or **triggers** must be initiated. Cranton (1994: 214) outlines the precursors of educator self-development and transformation:

> [T]he educator, in order to develop the meaning perspective of *being an educator* would: increase self-awareness through consciousness-raising activities, make his or her assumptions and beliefs about practice explicit, engage in critical reflection on those assumptions and beliefs, engage in dialogue with others and develop an informed theory of practice.

Teachers currently work under stressful, disempowering, and challenging conditions, and must navigate complex webs of internal and external demands, including the hierarchical culture of the school, policies that foster social inequities, orthodox professional training, etc. (Nieto and Bode, 2008). It is, however, ever more important in these fluid times that teachers become forces of empowerment through the practices they adopt in their own classrooms as facilitators and instructional leaders. Teachers may have limited opportunity to influence macro-level policies, however, they can create environments that foster positive educational outcomes for their students by beginning with an understanding of their own situated selves as "cultural workers". Figure 5.1 presents a multidimensional framework of the **Teacher Diversity Awareness Compass (TDAC),** which was designed to facilitate the process of self-analysis and awareness of diversity issues among teachers. Specifically, the five stages of TDAC include critical self-reflection, role reversal or role-playing of the "other", attitude and value appraisal, perspectives review and realignment, and self-directed **transformative action.**

TEACHER DIVERSITY AWARENESS COMPASS (TDAC)

Critical Self-Reflection

Perhaps the most important component of TDAC, critical self-reflection involves asking a series of id questions, e.g., Who am I, and how do my personal history, identity, and social positioning impact my practice? The ultimate objective of self-reflection is to enable educators to become practitioners who engage in regular self-monitoring, in order to identify and so modify undesirable practices (especially those that contribute to culture, language, gender, or other socio-demographic related chasms in the classroom).

A results-oriented reflection would also include an examination of the moral, social, and philosophical assumptions that frame a teacher's classroom practices. Uncovering the contradictions in their personal and professional beliefs is critical for teachers since these may contribute to the reinforcement of the status quo. Also, Price (2006) has identified another important rationale for understanding the teaching self. She argues that knowing who they are enables teachers to unleash their personal power — the "spiritual internal force that every person is born with that enables him or her to know that he or she can indeed create positive change for himself or herself and others" (p. 124). Price further argues that a teacher's interaction with students depends on how she or he decides to use this personal power, which can add to, subtract from, divide, or multiply her or his students' school success. Obviously, teachers who choose to use their personal power positively will empower their students — especially those who come from marginalized backgrounds.

An in-depth analysis of the relevant literature reveals that there are seven areas that require attention for conducting effective self-reflection: personal history and values, pedagogical beliefs and approaches, knowledge of diversity issues, knowledge of students, assumptions about learning, and assumptions about knowledge, and beliefs about society. These areas are discussed below, while Table 5.1 provides sample questions for conducting effective teacher self-reflection and analysis.

Personal History and Values The purpose of examining one's personal history is to develop an autobiographical framework that will serve as a foundation for addressing the other components of TDAC. This includes basic background information about the teacher and an examination of the core values and beliefs that underlie his or her practice. In a pluralistic society such as Canada, a critical analysis also exposes the privilege or oppression associated with the teacher's ethnic group. Peggy McIntosh's (1990) analysis of the privileges that accrue to her as a result of her "Whiteness" is a classic example of critical self-analysis with the concomitant conscientization that should lead to transformative action. Her uncovering of the now well-known list of privileges (which enable her to lead a life where she is free to exercise her civil liberties as she chooses) enabled her to see the unfair advantages that Whites enjoy in society. She asserts

> I have come to see white privilege as an invisible package of unearned assets that I can count on cashing in each day, but about which I was "meant" to remain oblivious. White privilege is like an invisible weightless knapsack of special provisions, maps, guides, passports, code books, visas, clothes, tools, and blank checks (p. 31).

Like McIntosh, Gibson in her article *Teaching as an Encounter with Self: Unravelling the Mix of Personal Beliefs, Education Ideologies and Pedagogical Practices* (1998) provides a compelling narrative of the unravelling intersections of her own beliefs and ideologies as a White educator and her teaching practices. This was accomplished through a reflective analysis of a class she had taught to graduate students. The class discussion had focused on the learning pace and social separation of ethno-culturally different students. Through post-instructional analysis, Gibson realizes how she had "retreated" from discussing with her students the political implications of some taken-for-granted school practices such as tracking, which reinforce social hierarchies in society. Gibson contends that her confrontation with "self" and the interrogation of her own practices exposed prejudices that had been submerged. This leads her to conclude that "encounters with self as a cultural entity, as a teacher, and as a learner are critical components in the construction of culturally relevant pedagogy" (p. 361).

Pedagogical Beliefs and Approaches Why is it important for educators to examine their own pedagogical beliefs and approaches?

It is important because educators set the tone and the direction of any school program regardless of the formal curriculum based on their own beliefs. Ladson-Billings (2006) summarizes how teachers' beliefs influence their practices:

> Teachers who believe that society is fair and just believe that their students are participating on a level playing field and simply have to learn to be better competitors than other students. They also believe in a kind of social Darwinism that supports the survival of the fittest. . . . Teachers who . . . [are] **culturally relevant** assume that an asymmetrical (even antagonistic) relationship exists between poor students of color and society. Thus, their vision of their work is one of preparing students to combat inequity by being highly competent and critically conscious (p. 30).

A Canadian study (Vibert et al., 2002) was conducted to determine approaches to critical practice in three elementary schools. Overall, the three schools valued students' welfare, yet the extent to which each one adopted critical and empowering practices depended on staff conceptions of the curriculum. One of the study sites, a socio-economically diverse multiethnic inner city school, was located in an impoverished community. In this school, staff conception of the curriculum as a "fixed entity" resulted in the adoption of a deficit model of education that "emphasized the needs or deficits of groups of students instead of focusing on their ability to achieve academic success, to take responsibility to improve their situation, or to have a voice in constructing their own future" (p. 98). In the second school, located in an upper-class community, the staff embraced a more democratic and collaborative approach to learning, and had higher expectations for student success. However, the staff approach to critical practice still fell short of having students become actively engaged with the curriculum in substantive and transformative ways. At the third site, with an economically diverse student population, staff conception of the curriculum as critical practice was demonstrated through "on-going school and classroom discussions about the workings of power . . . [and] a frank and forthright accounting for social conditions attended by pedagogy of hope" (p. 97). The school's emphasis on a pedagogy of hope is particularly noteworthy because it suggests that, rather

TABLE 5.1	Checklist for Conducting Critical Self-Reflection and Analysis
Area of Self-Reflection	**Sample Questions**
1 *Personal History*	• In what ways do my personal history and worldviews affect my teaching practices? • What are the privileges or oppressions that come with my identity? • In what ways does my background facilitate or hinder my success in Canadian society? • What are my personal beliefs about diversity and equity issues?
2 *Pedagogical Beliefs and Approaches*	• What is my basic approach to teaching? • Does this approach best serve the interests of my diverse students? • In what ways could I be reinforcing stereotypes through my teaching practices? • In what ways do I create space for promoting democratic values in my classroom?

TABLE 5.1		*(Continued)*
		• How often do I reflect on my classroom practices?
		• What kinds of resources do I use in my everyday practice?
3	*Knowledge of Diversity Issues*	• What are the key debates about diversity in Canadian society?
		• How current am I with research on diversity?
		• What does the research say?
		• How can I become culturally literate?
		• What cross-cultural competencies do I have?
		• What do I know about the following groups in Canadian society: a) First Nations peoples, b) Visible minorities, c) Women in Canadian history, d) People with disabilities?
4	*Knowledge of Students*	• How well do I know my students?
		• To what extent do I interact with members of diverse communities?
		• What are the various first languages (L1) of the minority students in my class?
		• In what ways do I support first language maintenance among my students?
5	*Assumptions about Learning*	• What are my basic assumptions about learning?
		• What are my beliefs about learning styles?
		• To what extent is learning style socially and culturally influenced?
		• Am I meeting the instructional needs of my students?
		• What are my expectations for my students?
		• To what extent am I contributing to the success of all?
		• How relevant are my expectations to the life experiences of all my students?
6	*Assumptions about Knowledge*	• What are my basic beliefs about schooled knowledge?
		• What should Canadian students learn in school?
		• Who controls this knowledge?
		• Whose knowledge do students currently learn?
		• To what extent is this knowledge inclusive?
		• To what extent do I question and engage curricular materials?
7	*Beliefs about Society*	• What are my beliefs about how society functions?
		• Who controls power in society and how do I feel about this?
		• To what extent do I share in that power dynamic?
		• Do I believe that equity and social justice are marginal or important issues in Canadian society?
		• Who determines educational policies, and how do I feel about this?
		• What are my beliefs about the link between education and society?

than seeing the students' social position as intractable, it underscores the teachers' belief in possibilities. This is the message that Freire (2002) sends in his book *A Pedagogy of Hope*, an optimistic treatise on education's potential for changing the conditions of those who are less privileged under the right circumstances. While the social context of each school played a part, the differing approaches were defined by staff belief about pedagogy and the purposes of schooling.

Knowledge of Diversity Issues As argued throughout this book, all educators who work in pluralistic contexts need to become culturally literate. For example, teachers who are well versed in multicultural issues in Canada are better positioned to respond positively to student diversity (see Chapters 1 and 2). Understanding diversity issues requires theoretical and practical knowledge of all the issues discussed in this volume.

Knowledge of Students Knowledge of students is an integral part of effective teaching in any context. But it is imperative in contexts of student diversity. This issue is discussed in more detail below.

Assumptions about Learning Much of what teachers do in the classroom is influenced by their basic assumptions about teaching and learning. Additionally, it is important for teachers to understand how students come to know so that they can convey the information through these learning systems (Gay, 2000). Although only indirectly related to issues of diversity, the study by Vibert et al. (2002) above is also an example of how educators' perceptions of learning can influence related practices, both at the individual and institutional levels.

Assumptions about Knowledge An analysis of teachers' assumptions about knowledge enables them to determine how best to adapt the contents of the curriculum to reflect the cultural capital of their students. Even though many provinces have now adopted standardized curricula, teachers still have opportunity to adapt the knowledge they teach, thus making it more relevant to students' prior knowledge and worldviews.

Beliefs about Society Teachers' beliefs about how society works also affect their practice. Such beliefs are uncovered by questions such as "Who controls power, and who should control power and resources in society? Who is disadvantaged in Canadian society and why are they at the bottom of the social hierarchy? What are my feelings about the social positioning of disadvantaged Canadians?" The essential idea is for teachers to uncover the lenses through which they view societal issues. Chapter 1 discusses two possible conceptions of society — the consensus versus interrogative social ideologies. A teacher who views the workings of society from a consensus perspective will most likely adopt pedagogical strategies that are different from those of teachers who subscribe to interrogative perspectives with the latter being better positioned to adopt transformative educational practices.

Role Reversal or Role-playing the "Other"

The world we carry in our "heads" often prevents us from entering other peoples' worlds. Therefore, this stage involves educators role-playing "others" who are different from themselves. The goal of this exercise is to develop empathy for the experiences of students whose cultural values or worldviews are different from those commonly espoused in Canadian schools. In the case of Renaa (see the opening vignette of Chapter 3), her concerned teacher may have gained better insight into ways of helping had she empathized more with Renaa's situation as a new immigrant and ESL student. Additionally, the teacher could have contextualized Renaa's language difficulties by asking herself questions such as

- How is she coping with the everyday requirements of schooling in an unfamiliar culture?
- How does she negotiate her identity within the context of the school?
- Does her schooled knowledge connect with or reflect her cultural capital?
- How would I feel if I were Renaa?
- Would I be able to adapt as quickly as she is expected to adapt?
- How would I expect my teachers to respond to any learning-related challenges I might face?

In other words, Renaa's teacher may have better positioned herself to help had she engaged in role reversal. One problem with role reversal however, is that educators have few authentic opportunities to do so in contexts where they can receive feedback. Ergo, interactive sessions during professional development workshops are excellent opportunities for role playing because they enable educators to interact and share their experiences with their peers.

Attitude and Value Appraisal

Why should educators examine their values, and how they feel about their own racial or ethnic groups, or any other socially constructed category? Quite simply, to determine how they feel towards people who possess similar or dissimilar characteristics. Conventional wisdom suggests that we react more positively to those with whom we have more in common than to those with whom we differ. Nonetheless, understanding our taken-for-granted perceptions of people who are similar to us can be just as illuminating as examining how we feel about those who are different from us. For example, a systematic analysis may uncover that an individual has a propensity towards ethnocentrism — a predisposition that ordinarily may not be apparent in their interactions with others. In addition to understanding how they feel about those with whom they share commonalities, it is extremely important that teachers understand their attitudes towards "others" since this will, in part, determine their response to diversity among their students. Research (and educators' accounts of their personal experiences) indicates that White teachers are sometimes apprehensive about teaching non-White children (Delpit, 2006; hooks, 1994, 2003; Paley, 2000; Ladson-Billings, 2006; Howard, 2006), yet teachers hardly ever ask themselves why this is the case. Many have argued that the success of diverse students depends on teachers' willingness and ability to empower them, which in turn depends on their perceptions of those students and their respective communities (Cummins, 2000; Dei et al., 2000; Delpit, 2006). Guiding questions to facilitate value and attitude appraisal include the following:

- What values shape my educational practices?
- Are these values similar or different to those of all my students?
- What are my beliefs about those with whom I share a common identity? How do I interact with them?

- What are my basic beliefs about people who are different from me? How do I relate to them, especially as my students?
- In what ways could I be contributing to the silencing of some segments of Canadian society?
- In what ways do I validate or negate the identities of my students?

Perspective Review and Realignment

This involves becoming aware, or developing critical consciousness, in an emic sense (see Chapter 4) — seeing things through the lenses of others and making a conscious effort to remain open-minded and shift paradigms as needed. The concept of critical consciousness (see Chapter 4) was popularized by Brazilian educator Paulo Freire, and has been appropriated by many scholars to describe the condition in which people become aware, beyond a surface level, of issues that matter in their lives. As Freire (1970) explained, the nature and kind of education people receive can contribute significantly to the extent to which they achieve critical consciousness. Ryan (2006) summarizes what critical consciousness entails:

> Being critical means becoming more sceptical about established truths. Being critical requires skills that allow one to discern the basis of claims, the assumption underlying assertions, and the interests that motivate people to promote certain positions. These skills enable people to scrutinize the evidence and logic that proponents of a course of action employ to support their arguments and conclusions. Critical skills allow people to recognize unstated, implicit and subtle points of view and the often invisible or taken-for-granted conditions that provide the basis for these stances. People who possess a critical consciousness have a desire not only to engage in critique but also to act in support of their views (p. 114).

Critical consciousness is therefore a forerunner to perspective realignment, which ideally is accompanied by pedagogical changes that aim to empower students and their communities.

Self-directed Transformative Action

While perspective realignment involves a cognitive shift, self-directed transformative action involves the development of a series of action plans for changing the "self" and for empowering, and thereby improving the life chances of, students from marginalized communities. It is an outcome of critical self-reflection and it is the mechanism for translating the findings into praxis. It is important to note that TDAC is not a linear process. Also, in theory each step informs the other in a cyclical and continuous way, as the double-ended arrows in Figure 5.1 indicate. In practice however (with the exception of self-directed transformative action), the stages are not immutably sequential since individuals can begin the process at any stage of the cycle. For example, through role reversal, a teacher may achieve the level of critical awareness for initiating transformative action without necessarily completing all the stages in the cycle. Other activities that can be adopted by educators to increase self-understanding and diversity awareness include participation in interactive prejudice-reduction workshops, embracing progressive pedagogies (see Chapter 4), and reading diversity related journals.

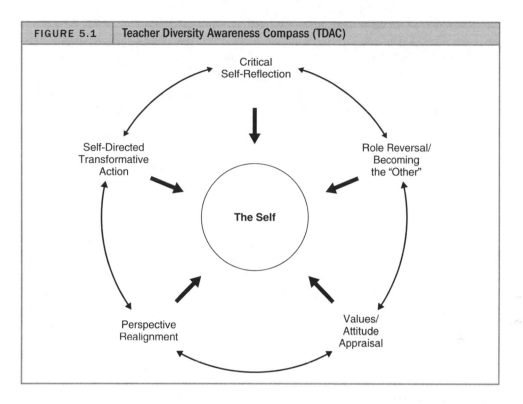

FIGURE 5.1 | Teacher Diversity Awareness Compass (TDAC)

TEACHER DIVERSITY RESEARCH

Teacher diversity research is part of the project of initiating praxis through self-study. It is also part of the broader concept of action research, where practitioners systematically study their own work with the intent of creating new knowledge, and so improve practice from their own stance as key participants (along with their students) in a community of learners (Arhar et al., 2001). Mills (2007) describes action research as

> any systematic inquiry conducted by teachers, researchers, principals, school counsellors or other stakeholders in the teaching/learning environment to gather information about how their particular schools operate, how they teach, and how well their students learn (p. 5).

Teacher diversity research is geared towards understanding the "teaching self" and activities, in relation to diversity issues. Thus, while action research deals with the general practitioner, teacher diversity research deals with the specific practices in which teachers engage that are purposely designed to empower their diverse students in inclusive learning environments. Usually, seasoned teachers engage in their craft without thinking about their actions and practices, as these have become part of their psyche and daily routine and activities. Almost intuitively, they know what activity follows the preceding one, which student needs to accomplish a certain task, what disciplinary action is warranted by a certain infraction as appropriate to each student, and when to group students for tasks. But, by engaging in diversity research, teachers can avoid pedagogical atrophy, replacing it instead with renewed enthusiasm as a result of the new knowledge gleaned from the research. Thus, teacher diversity research provides teachers with opportunity to see taken-for-granted everyday practice in new ways. Seeing things through different lenses is a powerful pre-cursor for developing new understanding and developing better ways of doing things in the classroom. Knoblauch and Brannon (1993) summarize the advantages of teacher research as an integral aspect of effective teaching practice:

> Teacher research . . . [aims] to construct new knowledge of educational life from the vantage points of its primary participants — teachers and students. It also aims to enfranchise teachers as authentic makers of that knowledge in order to enhance the quality of their participation in curricular planning, resource development, [and] instructional change . . . (p. 186).

Teacher diversity research enables practitioners to better understand the interpersonal dynamics between members of the classroom community, such as those between teachers and students and between students and their peers. It also interrogates the curriculum, the resources teachers use in their everyday diversity-related practice, and their pedagogical approaches. Above all, it allows teachers to better understand the intersectionality of a complex amalgam of individual, social, and institutional variables that affect educational outcomes for students, especially those from subordinate communities. As Kincheloe (2005) explains, teacher researchers understand

> [t]he complexity of the educational process and how schooling cannot be understood outside of the social, historical, philosophical, cultural, economic, political and psychological contexts that shape it. Scholar teachers understand that curriculum development responsive to student needs is not possible when it fails to account for these contexts (p. 18).

In effect, becoming a diversity researcher also enables teachers to examine the political nature of education. This is a dominant theme in critical pedagogy, in which (among other roles) teachers are to be scholar-researchers and knowledge brokers who continuously reflect on their practice. Viewed this way, teachers are not simply uncritical purveyors and implementers of programs that were developed in contexts far removed from the school. Rather, they become agents of change who reject traditional and deskilled models of teaching that reduce teachers to receivers and not producers of knowledge (Kincheloe, 2005). What does deskilled teaching look like? Kincheloe (2005: 19) provides an example:

Teacher says:	Class, take out your pencils.
	[teacher waits until all students have their pencils in hand]
Teacher then says:	Class, turn to page 15 of your textbook.
	[teacher waits until all students have turned to correct page]
Teacher says:	Read pages 15–17. When you are finished, close your books and put your hands on top of your desk. You have ten minutes.

This kind of teaching reduces knowledge to sterile and rehearsed rote learning that is particularly damaging in culturally diverse contexts.

Steps in Teacher Diversity Research

Teachers often ask how to initiate teacher research, particularly the kind that is designed to improve practice in contexts of student diversity. While there are various approaches, below is a basic model (illustrated in Figure 5.2), that can be adapted to specific contexts depending on student dynamics and the issues of concern.

1. *Problem definition* As with most research projects, the first step in teacher diversity research is defining the particular problem that the teacher intends to explore.

Usually, this is an issue about some aspect of difference among students with which the teacher feels some dissatisfaction and therefore would like to improve. For example, the issue might be a teacher's perceived inadequacy in the extent to which multiple perspectives are integrated into the curriculum. Another issue may be the nature of the interactions between the teacher and her or his minority students, or it might be exploring ways of deconstructing textual materials for bias and stereotypes. A common issue of concern among teachers in contexts of diversity is the search for innovative approaches and strategies for supporting ESL and new immigrant students.

2. *Development of a research tool* Once an issue to be investigated has been identified, the next stage is to develop a tool, which may be a series of relevant questions (as shown in Table 5.2), to serve as a guide during the data collection process. It may be possible to identify an extant research instrument that can be adapted to a teacher's particular teaching context. However, because diversity action research is issue specific, it would probably be more appropriate to develop a contextualized tool.

3. *Data gathering* Following the identification of the research tool, the next (and perhaps the most significant) stage is information or data gathering. Depending on the topic being explored, one of the most results-oriented methods for conducting teacher diversity research is **focused observation**, or the extended observation of a specific pre-identified problem. Even more productive is the use of multiple sources of data collection, including one-on-one student interviews, class discussions, analyses of the teacher's daily journal and of student work, student surveys, etc. Another advantage of using multiple data sources is that it provides teachers opportunities for triangulating, or confirming the validity of the data that has been uncovered (Arhar et al., 2001). Depending on the chosen technique, it is important to determine the optimal time during the school day that the data should be collected.

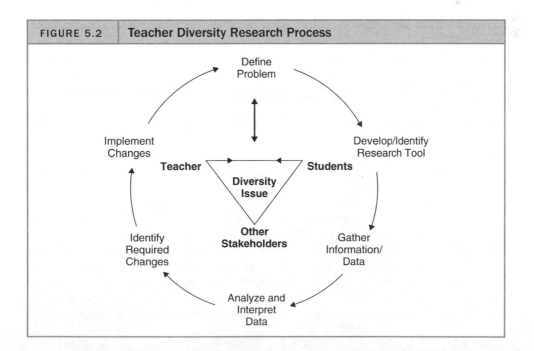

FIGURE 5.2	Teacher Diversity Research Process

However, it should be pointed out that, as a correlate of action research, teacher diversity research becomes part of a teacher's daily routine, once he or she has mastered the process.

4. *Analysis and interpretation* Following the data gathering stage, the teacher critically analyzes all the information that has been uncovered through the research. The goal is to determine the recurrent themes or issues that emerged from the data, and to interpret what they mean. Interpreting the data can be quite daunting and requires careful review.

5. *Identification of changes* This is the stage when the teacher determines the necessary action required as a result of the findings of the study. The changes might be substantive, minor, complex, or incremental and in some instances, may require consultation with the school administration and parents. For example, a teacher might conclude that a certain text contains a level of bias that makes it untenable as a text in her or his diverse classroom. This would clearly have school-wide policy implications, and would therefore require the input of various stakeholders, including the principal, other teachers, parents, and perhaps the school board.

6. *Implementation of changes* This is the stage when the teacher implements the required innovations as an extension of the research. It is critically important to monitor the implementation process on an ongoing basis, as is required of any educational change process (Fullan, 1993). One authentic way of determining the success of the changes implemented on the basis of the findings of the research, is to solicit feedback from students, parents, and other stakeholders, as appropriate. This can be done through class discussions and simple surveys. It is also important to keep meticulous notes or daily journals throughout the research process. Collectively, these notes will become the teacher's narrative of the research journey, as well as a foundation for future diversity research.

Teacher diversity inquiry is a useful strategy for helping teachers improve their practice in pluralistic classrooms; however, like most types of research, it is not without its limitations. For instance, teachers may be blindsided by their supposedly neutral working environments and therefore fail to recognize how their everyday practices are in reality grounded in other peoples' belief systems. Another problem arises from the possibility that a teacher's proximity to the situation (since he or she is playing the dual role of researcher and subject) may skew both the data and the overall results. These limitations notwithstanding, many researchers are now cognizant of the fact that traditional forms of educational research have not significantly altered the life chances of non-majority group students and their families (Corson, 1993; Egbo, 2005). Teacher diversity research is therefore only one way of initiating and contributing to change by enabling teachers to teach towards equity and social justice.

In addition to self-analysis and teacher diversity research, teachers can also engage in hypothetical simulations or troubleshooting. Based on their personal and expert knowledge of their own classrooms, they can determine the scenarios likely to occur in their day-to-day interactions with students. For example, what kinds of problems are likely to occur in the next reading class? Who is likely experience difficulty with the text, and how might I be able to help them? Additionally, being a reflective practitioner is not enough in most diverse contexts. Teachers also must become reflexive practitioners, who are able to react to situations almost instinctively. Also, it is not only teachers who must be adept at problem-solving in contexts of student diversity. Administrators, whose leadership is critical in making schools inclusive learning environments, must also be prepared to deal with issues as soon

TABLE 5.2	Sample Questions for Analyzing Texts for Bias and Stereotypes

1. To what extent does the text present any groups in Canadian society in a stereotypical and unflattering way?

2. Does the text present women in a demeaning way?

3. Who is accorded power in the text, and who is presented in a subordinate position?

4. Is the text insensitive to diversity related issues, e.g., slavery, the Underground Railroad, religion, ethnicity, race, residential schools?

5. Is the text biased in its presentation of the contribution of different groups in the building of Canada?

6. Does the text make generalized and sweeping claims about some groups in Canadian society?

7. Does the text present non-European Canadians in a negative light?

8. Are the images in the text predominantly those of White Canadians?

9. Does the text present the contribution of males and females in Canadian society in an equitable manner?

10. Will the text enable students to engage the curriculum?

11. Is the text likely to offend some groups of students in the classroom?

12. Does the text present the issues from an inclusive perspective?

13. Will the text meet the general approval of *all* parents?

14. Is the text written in fair and unbiased language?

as they occur. The next section discusses ways administrators can prepare themselves for empowering leadership in Canadian schools beginning with critical self-analysis.

CRITICAL LEADERSHIP ACTION

Education legitimizes dominance and power, and it also serves to interrogate and interrupt power, but only through the concerted effort of all stakeholders in the community of learners. Teaching for diversity and social justice in Canadian schools will be difficult goals to achieve without site-based administrators assuming dynamic leading roles. As educational leaders, they are uniquely positioned to counter practices that serve only elite interests and promote social injustice, at least within their own schools (Ryan, 2006; Corson, 2000).

Although there are competing models of effective leadership, current scholarship on socially just educational practices emphasizes the importance of school leaders in implementing and sustaining inclusive practices that empower students from non-majority backgrounds. For example, Corson (2000) proposes emancipatory leadership, which would shift administrators' focus away from protecting sectional interests and toward increasing the life chances of their students. Brown (2004) proposes a transformative agenda through "leadership for social justice and equity", while Shields (2003, 2004) advocates transformative and dialogic leadership.

By advocating a shift from traditional understandings of leadership to more political, activist, and contested interpretations, these writers along with critical pedagogists (see Chapter 4) are promoting leadership practices that identify, deconstruct, and challenge the attitudes, values, and ideologies that contribute to unsatisfactory schooling experiences for students from diverse backgrounds.

What then constitutes critical leadership action in contexts of student diversity? In discussing an emancipatory theory of leadership, Corson (2000) provides a compelling rationale for developing praxis-oriented strategies to guide practice:

> Educational leaders do try to cope with sociocultural complexity, but often, they lack the means for developing intercultural and interclass dialogue. As often, they are without the culturally precise insights needed to make well-informed decisions . . . [these] professionals are often defeated before they begin, because they are asked to plan in advance, from the interests of their own dominant group, what arrangements would be chosen by other people whose interests might not be understood readily by anyone who is not from the relevant class, sex, or *culture* (p. 114). [my emphasis]

Critical leadership action in contexts of student diversity should involve practices that not only empower students and subordinates, they should also transform the leaders themselves in a deep and far-reaching way, just as teachers must shift paradigms. As Starratt (2003) advises, school administrators need to reinstate the humanistic values of education: moving from practices that reinforce the status-quo to those that are context-based, interactive, and dialogic. This means that in current contexts, success in leading schools depends on the degree to which educational administrators, such as teachers (as discussed in the previous section), are committed to self-study, self-reflection, and critique, as well as furthering their understanding of the broader socio-political contexts within which their professional activities are embedded.

ADMINISTRATOR DIVERSITY AWARENESS COMPASS

To facilitate the process of self-analysis, Figure 5.3 introduces the **Administrator Diversity Awareness Compass (ADAC),** a two-pronged tool that enables school leaders to conduct diversity-related self- and institutional analysis. As an analytical and diagnostic tool, ADAC increases the chances of administrators' success as they negotiate the complex amalgam of variables that comprise the context of student diversity. Success is defined as leaders' achievement of making their schools inclusive learning environments, where nonmainstream students are not only made to feel welcome, but are also given opportunity to participate in relevant and age-appropriate decision-making processes. The process of self-analysis in ADAC is fundamentally the same as for TDAC (see Figure 5.1). The second part is however, more complex — performing **diversity audits** within the school to determine which programs, practices, and policies require diversity attention. Overall, the compass challenges administrators to ask uncomfortable questions of themselves and the educational systems within which they work. Leader self-analysis is particularly critical because studies show that many administrators are reluctant to admit that there are diversity-related problems in their schools. Like teachers and other members of the dominant group, they are also prone to denying the existence of prejudice in their schools. In a study that explored the challenges associated with ethno-cultural diversity in schools, Ryan (2003) reported that many of the administrators, who were drawn from among principals in two large Canadian school districts, were reluctant to acknowledge incidents of racism in their schools. Moreover, those who did acknowledge it tended to downplay its significance or pervasiveness. For example, one of the participating principals believed that students' use of racial slurs was usually out of frustration, and not out of an intentional desire to be racist. According to the principal, students

> attack the colour of the person and often times it is done in the fashion of 'it is the only mechanism that I have to get back at this person, so I will do that'. It is not done in an ongoing sort of way and I think there's a difference there . . . it is very easy to target someone's skin color because it's right there at your fingertips (p. 151).

This principal's comments are clearly illustrative of the tendency towards the denial of discrimination and prejudice that is pervasive in Canadian society, to which many writers have alluded (Henry and Tator, 2006; Dei et al., 2000; Solomon et al., 2005). In any case, this administrator appears to have missed an important point: there is no excuse for resorting to biased language as a tool for dealing with conflict situations, even among children.

Diversity Audits

As a self-initiated institutional assessment, a **diversity audit** determines the extent to which a school affirms and promotes diversity and develops a vision of an inclusive school that is cognizant of the intersections of leadership practice, institutional structure, and student empowerment. An important rationale for conducting diversity audits is that schools differ in their various characteristics. For instance, they have their individual strengths and weaknesses, and may differ in their approach to educating children based on the beliefs of their teaching staff as we saw in the study by Vibert et al. (2002), above. Similarly, programs that are particularly effective in one school may only be partially successful in another. Therefore, diversity audits should be done within the context of the variability among schools. Several broad questions to guide diversity audits include

- How do teachers acknowledge and value the cultural capital that students bring to school?
- What are the core perceptions of diversity in the school? Is it considered a resource or a problem?
- How does the school support students from diverse backgrounds?
- What is the nature of the relationship between the school staff, parents, and the community?
- What structures have been instituted in the school specially to support diversity?
- What kind of resources are used in the school?
- Is there any pervasive racism among students and teachers in the school?

Research shows that in most instances where schools see diversity as a resource, they foster a positive climate, which increases the chances of positive educational outcomes for all students. In their study across several levels of schooling in the United States, Henze et al. (2002) found that leaders in each school used different approaches to foster positive interethnic relations. These differences took into account the students' level of development, as well as the sizes and structures of the schools. The researchers also found that not only were the principals pivotal in setting a positive tone in the study sites, they also engaged in critical self-introspection:

> One of the characteristics of proactive leaders in the schools visited during the study was their courage. They were able to look within themselves and honestly confront their own biases and shortcomings, and they did the work they needed to do in the world. They seemed to share an assumption that internal work is necessary in order for external work in the school community to be authentic and effective. This courage to start with yourself and examine deeply held beliefs is also one of the essential qualities of leaders who foster resiliency in their schools (p. 17).

As Skrla et al. (2004) suggest, audits are important tools for facilitating change in contexts of diversity. In the model proposed here, all audits must, however, be preceded by a school population inventory or **environmental scan**.

Environmental Scan

The term *environmental scan* describes the process of appraising the composition of the student body in the school, beginning with a simple but often ignored question "Who are the students in my school?" Many writers argue that educators who know their students are better positioned to initiate praxis (e.g., Sheets, 2005; Villegas and Lucas, 2002; Gay, 2000). Also, educators who know their students understand that within the Canadian context many students constantly negotiate between two often antithetical culture-bases (see Chapter 1). The results of an environmental scan can go a long way in helping administrators make informed decisions about the appropriate pedagogical strategies, materials, language support needs, community partnerships, etc., which are necessary for achieving positive learning outcomes for all students.

While an environmental scan should be an integral part of a principal's tasks, detailed systematic scanning is necessary only during the first few weeks of each school year. This is because it is essentially diagnostic and therefore redundant once teachers and administrators know who their students are. So, as the school year generally begins in September in Canada, a principal needs to engage in intensive environmental scanning only during the months of September and October (depending on socio-demographic variables such as the size, location, and degree of parental involvement in the school). Nevertheless, it must be emphasized that while environmental scans need not be on-going, many students come and go during the course of a school year. Such students must not be allowed to fall through the cracks, and educators must also make a concerted effort to get to know them.

Structural Audits

Very often school authorities assume that the procedures, practices, and policies that have been instituted to improve learning outcomes are yielding intended results when majority group students and their families appear satisfied with the status quo. Unfortunately, this lack of objection often masks the fact that the interests and needs of other segments of the school community (such as girls, students with disabilities, from poor and working class families, or from minority communities) are not being met. The fundamental function of *structural audits* is to expose these contradictions and anomalies. While specific areas will vary from one institution to another, the following are areas that generally require structural audits: hiring policies, programs and practices, instructional resources, school culture and climate, and disciplinary policies.

1. *Hiring policies* Most Canadian teachers are middle class, White, and monolingual, and they are teaching a student population that is increasingly diverse in race, language, culture, ethnicity, ability, and social class. Auditing a school's hiring policies to determine the degree of diversity provided among the teaching staff is therefore a necessity in a pluralistic society. Students from diverse backgrounds need to see themselves reflected in the school community of which they are an integral part. Imagine the psychological impact of visible minority students seeing only White teachers at a school. Just as it is important to diversify the teaching staff, it is also necessary to ensure the diversity of the support and peripheral staff, as they too interact with students on a regular basis. More often than not when we talk about diversifying the school staff, the focus is on mainstream teachers who teach diverse students, and not on the other staff who provide valuable and visible ancillary support.

2. *Programs and practices* While the core programs in most Canadian schools are prescribed by provincial mandate and legislation, schools still have opportunity to develop additional support programs based on school-wide needs assessments. In diverse school contexts, these programs are conduits to student empowerment. For example, a targeted program audit can be used to evaluate whether a school has established a framework for increasing intercultural understanding among the whole school community, and if so, it can be used to assess the success of this program. Several questions serve as the basis of the assessment:

- What programs have been implemented to promote diversity and social justice?
- To what extent are the programs achieving intended the goals?
- Who is included or excluded from the programs?
- What changes are required and how can these be implemented?
- Who should be involved?

Besides conducting program audits, principals should also examine the school's practices, especially those at the micro level. For example, as religious diversity is now an emergent phenomenon in urban Canadian schools, a principal could conduct an audit to find out the school's specific practices for accommodating the needs of students from nonmainstream religious backgrounds. Other structural audits could include examination of patterns of student groupings for instruction, which cultural observances a school supports, and what channels of communication have been instituted to increase parental involvement.

3. *Instructional resources* The purpose of auditing instructional materials is to determine the relevance of the resources being used to the needs of all students. Sheets (2005) suggests three types of instructional resource analysis. The first is availability, which is a cursory analysis, early in the school year, to determine which materials are available and what kind of instructional support they may provide. A second type is determining the appropriateness of the materials in meeting the individual and group needs of the students, in areas such as ability levels, language, strengths, and interests. The third type of resource assessment (of particular relevance here) is "an in-depth critical analysis . . . to examine the culturally influenced substance, meanings, and perspectives present in the instructional resources" (p. 129). To facilitate this process Sheets identifies four general categories of analyses for establishing the degree to which instructional resources are culturally inclusive. These are message, the ideological, political, and cultural values embedded in the resource, and authenticity, the extent to which groups are accurately represented. The last two categories, language and illustration serve the function of reinforcing the message and authenticity (see Table 5.3).

In the Canadian context, researchers argue that the instructional resources used in many classrooms are unconnected to the worldviews of students from minority and First Nations communities (Battiste, 2000, 2002; Dei et al., 2000). Perhaps even worse, educators sometimes use materials that are insensitive to nondominant group students. For example, Allingham (1993) criticizes the insensitive practice of including such culturally biased books as *Huckleberry Finn* and *To Kill a Mockingbird* in the secondary school English curriculum. While it can be argued that these texts provide a platform for engaging in robust and informed debate, teaching such texts must be done in a way that does not disenfranchise the visible minorities in the classroom. Resource audits require the collaboration of teachers and school leaders since teachers and students are the consumers of these materials.

TABLE 5.3	Checklist for the Analysis of Culturally Inclusive Instructional Material					
Message		1	2	3	4	5	N/A
1. **The status, accomplishments, ideals, norms, and values of a cultural group are presented as one of many groups that comprise our nation's diversity.** (i.e., a particular group does not have a privileged or superior position; people of colour are not presented as helpers to European Canadians, nor as social problems with special needs, nor as objects of oppression to be pitied.)							
2. **The work promotes national unity.** (i.e., all citizens are given equitable racial, ethnic, cultural, gender, political, and social status. They all enjoy degrees of communality, such as same language, common market, and protected legal entitlements.)							
3. **There is diversity within the group being discussed.** (i.e., differences of people from the same ethnic group are shown in the variety of careers held, and in racial markers such as skin hue and facial features, and differences in skills, strengths, and needs. There are various economic levels, leadership positions, social backgrounds, and academic roles present, as well as variety in food, clothes, art, and musical preferences.)							
4. **The content is academically and historically accurate and presented from multiple perspectives.** This includes the viewpoints of all groups under discussion (i.e., there is balance between the struggles and accomplishments of all cultural groups.)							
Authenticity		1	2	3	4	5	N/A
1. **The author has authority based on insider cultural knowledge, or has expert experiential knowledge of the cultural group under discussion and is able to tell the story from that group's viewpoint.** (i.e., authors are from the culture they are writing about; the ethnicity of the author is identifiable and the work does not misrepresent or exploit the cultural group; the resource is accurate in history, heritage, values, attitudes, norms, and worldviews of the culture or event under consideration.)							
2. **The main purpose of the work is to extend students' knowledge of culture, provide new insights, and promote understanding.** (i.e., economic benefits resulting from the sale of multicultural materials do not appear to be the author's primary objective).							
3. **All cultural groups' accomplishments to the nation's past, present, and future economical, political, cultural, and social growth are presented realistically, authentically, and accurately.** (i.e., visible minorities and other nonmainstream groups are not presented as only making contribution to the established, dominant society.)							
Language		1	2	3	4	5	N/A
1. **The language is fair, realistic, accurate, and honest.** (i.e., it does not demonize, romanticize, idealize, stereotype, typecast, or classify some people with substantial or token status, with meaningful or insignificant knowledge, or any with invisible or silent roles.)							
2. **The language is inclusive.**							

TABLE 5.3	*(Continued)*						
3. **Students** (considering their age and maturity) **can handle the presence of overloaded, biased, inflammatory, insulting, offensive, or prejudicial language.** (i.e., does the author use expletives, racial slurs, or homophobic language? Examine the author's word choices such as slaves/enslaved people, etc. Are differences in colours, values, languages, and practices described as strange, colourless, exotic, ugly, or foreign?)							
Illustrations		**1**	**2**	**3**	**4**	**5**	**N/A**
1. **The illustrations reflect the realities of a culturally pluralistic society.** (i.e., there is a balanced representation of diverse racial and ethnic groups, gender, ability differences, socio-economic class, sexual orientation, and family lifestyles.)							
2. **Peoples, events, places, maps, and cultural artifacts are represented accurately.** (i.e., unique racial, ethnic, and cultural differences are evident in the illustrations, there is no prevalent generic model, a specific racial or ethnic group can identify people, and maps are realistically proportioned.)							
3. **The pictures are not stereotypical and do not exhibit overloading of cultural symbols.**							

Source: Adapted from Sheets, Rose Hernandez (2005). *Diversity Pedagogy: Examining the Role of Culture in the Teaching-Learning Process*, pp. 133–134. Published by Allyn & Bacon, Boston, MA. Copyright 2005 by Pearson Education. Adapted by permission of the publisher.

4. *School culture and climate* In contexts of student diversity, classroom interactions can either be a source of learning and empowerment, or a source of conflict and disagreement. Moreover, just as culture and climate can moderate the nature of the interactions between the various members of the school community, they can also impact on the schools' support of diversity. Most of the intergroup conflicts in wider society can be exacerbated by the proximity that the school environment fosters. Therefore the promotion of teacher leadership, which aims to empower teachers to empower their students and to provide a learning environment that supports positive inter-group interaction, is important. Ryan (2006: 72) suggests several empowering institutional arrangements that can formalize teacher leadership practices:

   - decision-making arrangements that give teachers real power
   - a locally controlled process that allows teachers to frame a definition of empowerment
   - roles that are clearly specified yet not overly constraining
   - a climate that supports risk taking
   - a mechanism for providing adequate resources
   - schedules that provide teachers with the time they need to participate in leadership activities

5. *Disciplinary policies* In a video titled *Quick to Judge*, developed by TVO and used as a resource for teaching about racial prejudice, a Black student's hopes for winning a poster competition are dashed when he gets into a fight with a White student. Out of frustration from feeling that he has been discriminated against, the student tears up the poster on

which he has expended considerable effort. His problems are compounded when the White student misplaces his own poster. In the investigation that follows, both the teacher and the school principal accuse the Black student of being connected with the disappearance of the White student's poster, despite his insistence of his own innocence. Although the Black student is eventually exonerated, in their rush to judgment, the school staff stereotypically finds him guilty of the offence.

Although only a vignette, incidents like this, which sometimes lead to suspensions, happen frequently in Canada and the United States, so much so that there is now widespread belief among researchers that violence prevention policies instituted over the last several years are increasingly targeting minority students unfairly. For instance, studies show that minority (especially Black) students are disproportionately suspended and expelled under the zero tolerance polices that many school boards have adopted to stem the tide of escalating school violence in Canada. One study (Ruck and Wortley, 2002) found that students from the four participating racial groups (Black, South Asian, Asian, and other) were significantly more adversely affected by zero tolerance policies than their White counterparts. The study also showed that compared to the three other minority groups, Blacks were more likely to view themselves as being discriminated against by zero tolerance policies. A study by Upshaw conducted for the Halifax Regional School Board, (2003, cited in Henry and Tator, 2006), found that 40 % of Black high-school students in Halifax have been suspended at least once (with 35 % in junior high and 8 % in elementary schools having also been suspended). The report also showed that the Black community in Halifax continues to feel disenfranchised and excluded by the school system. Similarly, the 2006 annual report of the Advisory Committee to the Halifax Regional School Board concluded that the board's disciplinary policy was generally discriminatory against minority students.

Many visible minority communities in Ontario have expressed similar concerns about that province's zero tolerance policies under its *Safe Schools Act, 2000,* which provides the legal basis for the province's disciplinary policies. So great was the concern that, in 2005, the Ontario Human Rights Commission launched a formal complaint against the Ministry of Education. It declared that the policy had a disproportionately negative impact on visible minority (especially Black) students, those with disabilities, and students from low income backgrounds. In a settlement that promised to provide alternative disciplinary measures, rather than suspensions and expulsions, the government agreed to make changes to the policy and pledged to provide those compelled to leave for serious behaviour infractions with alternative educational opportunities. In June 2007, new legislation introduced to revise the zero tolerance policy and to add other safe schools measures passed unanimously (Ontario Ministry of Education, 2007). The new amendment, Bill 212, *Progressive Discipline and School Safety*, replaces mandatory suspensions and expulsions (except in limited circumstances) and requires school boards and principals to respond to behavioural infractions in more appropriate ways. This gives them more discretionary power over student discipline, and also under the new bill, education authorities are to take mitigating circumstances into account before suspending or expelling a student. Given what has been outlined above, audits of disciplinary policies must be an integral part of any school's internal self-assessment.

Cross-Cultural Sensitivity Audits

The purpose of **cross-cultural sensitivity audits** is to examine the relationship and interactions between the various members of the school community (such as those between

TABLE 5.4	Sample Questions for Conducting School Disciplinary Policy and Practices Audit

- Are the school's rules for behaviour written in clear and bias-free language?
- Are there robust mechanisms for a thorough investigation of allegations of unfair discipline practices?
- Is there fair application of disciplinary policies?
- Is there documented evidence that a particular group of students is disproportionately suspended or expelled?
- Are students consulted, or encouraged to participate in, the development of school disciplinary policies and rules?
- What are the most common problems that have originated as a result of the schools discipline policies?
- Are students and their families aware of the disciplinary policies present at the school?
- How does the school respond to victims of violence?
- To what extent does the school proactively foster a violence-free culture?
- Are the province's, ministry's, or board's disciplinary policies being enforced appropriately?

students and their peers, teachers and non-majority students, and teachers and their colleagues), especially those from different ethnocultural backgrounds. The principal's leadership style is also a critical factor since he or she sets the tone of the school by modelling, developing, and sustaining policies that promote cross-cultural understanding. Overall, conducting effective cross-cultural sensitivity audits involves asking a series of diagnostic questions:

- What structures have been established to promote cross-cultural understanding in the school?
- Are there diversity-related conflicts between the students and teachers or between students and their peers?
- What is the frequency and nature of conflict between teachers and their diverse students? (The essence of these conflicts is a good barometer for gauging the extent of culture-related misunderstandings in a school).
- How might school practices foster prejudice, stereotypes, and xenophobia within the school and surrounding communities?
- Has the school instituted programs to support students from diverse backgrounds?
- To what extent are other religious observances (besides Judeo-Christian traditions) acknowledged or celebrated?
- How are language minority students supported in the school?
- What opportunities are available for fostering school-community collaborations?
- What community values are included and validated in the school's programs and practices?

At first glance adopting the **Administrator Diversity Awareness Compass (ADAC)** may imply additional work for school leaders, but administrators do not have to work longer hours to make their schools inclusive learning environments. They simply have

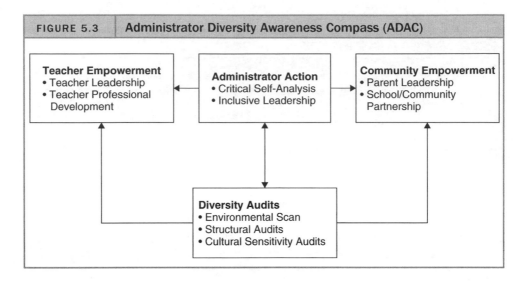

FIGURE 5.3 | **Administrator Diversity Awareness Compass (ADAC)**

to work differently — by critiquing the ways in which some practices affect students from marginalized communities. Finally, conducting effective diversity audits requires that, like teachers, school leaders have in-depth knowledge of who their students are, beyond the foundational information that environmental scans provide.

KNOWING STUDENTS

There are two ways that educators can strive to better get to know their students. The first is through working with students as co-participants in a community of learners, and the second way is working with parents and the communities where each school is located.

Understanding Students

Just as it is important for educators to understand themselves and how their identities and personal histories intersect with their classroom practices, it is essential for them to know who their students are. Villegas and Lucas (2002) suggest types of information that teachers need to know about students from diverse backgrounds. These include students' lives outside the school, their relationships to subjects, students' perceptions of school knowledge, their belief in schooling to improve their lives, and students' community life.

Specifically, knowing students' lives outside of the school means understanding their family and social life. Knowing students' perceptions of school knowledge includes an understanding of students' past educational experiences, and knowing students' relationships to subjects centres on the premise that prior knowledge must be recognized when seeking to gain new knowledge. Finally, teachers knowing students' community life involves, among other things, understanding community demographics, as well as what resources are available to members of the community. Besides having first-hand knowledge of students, the programs and strategies that teachers use to acquire such information are equally important. Thus, educators must seek information about their students from multiple sources, including discussions with community members and participation in community events.

An important strategy for getting to know the students they teach includes learning from the students themselves, as they have a repertoire of information about their own lives and communities. Due to the prevalence of cultural discontinuity between teachers and their diverse students, teachers have as much to learn from students as students have to learn from teachers. How can teachers learn from their students? Villegas and Lucas (2002) suggest conferencing directly with students, reading students' learning logs, and actively involving students in the construction of knowledge, as well as embracing a strategy of reciprocal teaching. As Palmer (1998) argues above, it is indeed difficult to teach if educators do not know who their students are, or cannot identify and draw on their students' prior knowledge and beliefs. Schools that do not take into account students' prior knowledge or use instructional strategies that are relevant to their lives run the risk of alienating them.

In her landmark 1994 work, *The Dreamkeepers*, Gloria Ladson-Billings explores the work of eight "excellent" teachers of African-American children, who empower their students through **culturally relevant pedagogy**. This approach focuses on teaching school knowledge by building on what students already know, thus making the students active participants in the learning process in very authentic ways. Ladson-Billings (1994) provides an example of how teachers can weave their in-depth knowledge of students into their teaching practices in ways that empower and speak to the students' funds of knowledge (Cummins, 2000) as well as meet their specific needs:

> Lewis, Devereaux, and Rossi know their students well. They know which ones respond to subtle prodding and which ones need a more forceful approach. For them, good teaching starts with building good relationships. Rossi knew that one of her students was considered a candidate for special education. However, she believed that it was important to include him as a part of the class and hold him responsible for meeting high standards. To ensure that these expectations did not frustrate him, she spent more time with him, guaranteeing incremental success. Devereaux knew that Michael had a troubled home life. . . . [H]is poor reading ability was tied to the problems he confronted at home. So she worked to fill his school day with literacy experiences. By calling on him to read — directions, daily messages, and recreational materials — she cemented her relationship with him while he built his knowledge base and skills (Ladson-Billings, 1994, p. 125).

In-depth knowledge of students also facilitates teachers' abilities to establish working relationships with families. Although it is possible for students to successfully complete school without teachers and parents forging a partnership, family connections with teachers provide additional motivation for students, especially those at risk of dropping out, to work harder in school.

Knowing and Working with Parents and Communities

Over the last several decades, the research on parent and community school involvement has pointed in one direction — school-parent partnerships contribute to positive educational experiences and promote academic success among students (Epstein, 2000; Cummins, 2000). For example, Jordan and Rodriquez (2004) conducted a review of relevant research on the impact of parent and community involvement in education. In instances when parents were actively involved in their children's schooling as an integral part of efforts to increase students' academic achievement, there were increases in grade point average and enrolment in more rigorous academic programs. Moreover, earned credits and classes passed improved, along with assiduous school attendance, as well as tangible improvement in behaviour and social skills both in school and at home. Another study (Boethel, 2003, as cited in Jordan and Rodriguez, 2004) reviewed the findings of recent research that focused on specific family and student variables such as race and/or ethnicity, culture and socio-economic status. It had limited results in terms of the extent to which the school involvement of parents from non-mainstream communities contributed to student's academic success. However, the study demonstrated that many parents, regardless of demographic variables, have high academic aspirations for their children. Results such as these further cement the seamless and dynamic relationship that should ideally exist between a school and its socio-cultural milieu. More importantly, virtually all writers agree that school-parent partnerships are particularly important where students come from different backgrounds than their teachers. Few would query the assertion by Cummins (2000: 47) that minority students are empowered depending on "[t]he extent to which culturally diverse communities are encouraged to participate as partners in their children's education and to contribute 'the funds of knowledge' that exist in their communities to this educational partnership". Parents do indeed have a vested interest in what goes on in schools, and they can, through their involvement, make a significant difference — especially in schools that are characterized by student difference.

In Canada, provincial legislation and policies have instituted formal channels for increasing parental involvement in schools. For example in Ontario (even though participation is largely symbolic as parents play an advisory role), provincial legislation allows for parental participation in school through membership in school councils. In Alberta, parents' involvement in their children's education may be actualized through the mandatory school councils that were established in 1995. Although council members play an advisory role within the education system, each one must include the principal, teachers, parents, and community representatives who do not have children in the school. Student participation in school councils is encouraged in high schools.

Saskatchewan encourages parental and community involvement in education through participation in school community councils that were established in 2006. Each council typically consists of the principal, teachers, parents and guardians, high-school students, and other community members. As in the case of the two provinces above, members of the council play an essentially advisory role to the Department of Learning.

Parental involvement in schools in New Brunswick may be facilitated through the Parent School Support Committee (PSSC). According to the District Education Councils (DEC) of New Brunswick, the PSSC consists of the principal, parents, teachers, student representatives, community members, and DEC members. The primary responsibilities of the PSSC include advising the principal on education and policy issues, working alongside the principal to develop and monitor school improvement initiatives, and participating in the hiring and performance evaluations of various school administrators. The New Brunswick parental involvement model provides parents and communities more opportunity to play a substantive role than the ones in most provinces.

In Quebec parents and community members may participate in their children's education in two ways. First, through a governing board that consists of an equal number of parents and school staff. The board is presided over by a parent, and its major responsibility is the evaluation, development, and implementation of regulation policies. Members may also contribute to other important matters. A second channel is through participation in the Parent Participation Organization in their child's school.

In British Columbia, parents and community members play an advisory role through the School Planning Council. Members of the council may also participate in school development planning, as well as work towards improving student achievement. Membership includes the school principal, a teacher representative, three representatives from the parent advisory council, and students in grades 10 through 12. Parent representatives are selected by the parent advisory council, which elects its members to the planning council by secret ballot. In addition, the parent advisory council seeks to maintain and promote collaborative communication between parents and the planning council.

In the majority of provinces, members of parents' or school councils, regardless of the model, come predominantly from majority group communities, and little attention is devoted to increasing the participation rates of minority communities. Thus, partnerships between teachers and diverse communities are still problematic even though researchers agree that such partnerships are a sine qua non for minority students' academic success (Dei et al., 2000; Ryan, 2006; Cummins, 2000). Parent/school partnerships are proactive and effective educational practice, and there are very practical reasons for advocating stronger ties between schools and diverse communities. Tension between minority students and their teachers can be significantly reduced if teachers understand the culture of the students. Cultural barriers can be overcome when teachers know the community's values. For example, it is easier for a teacher to understand why a particular student looks away when being spoken to if she or he understands that in the student's culture, it is a sign of respect for children to avoid direct eye contact when being spoken to by an adult (see Chapter 3). This is just as true of diverse communities as it is of other subordinate strata of society. Delpit (2006) describes this phenomenon as teachers' ignorance of community norms:

> Many school systems have attempted to institute 'parent training' programs for poor parents and parents of colour. While the intentions of these programs are good, they can only be truly useful when educators understand the realities with which such parents must contend and why they do what they do. Often, middle-class school professionals are appalled by what they see of poor parents, and most do not have the training or the ability to see past surface behaviors to the meanings behind parents' actions (p. 175).

Delpit provides her personal experience of how teachers' ignorance of community norms can create cultural barriers between themselves and members of non-dominant group communities. In one example, a group of parents in a predominately Latino school in Boston, repeatedly brought their first graders into the classroom in advance of the official start of the school day, despite teachers' request to the contrary. This eventually led to conflict when the teachers began to lock the school doors to prevent the parents from bringing the children in before the official time. Delpit argues that the conflict could have been avoided had the teachers understood that in that community's culture, parents view their 6 year olds as babies, and therefore could not fathom leaving them in the school yard without parents or teachers in attendance. A simple resolution, she asserts, could have been to have one of the teachers in attendance, or alternatively to have a parent volunteer remain, in the school yard with the children until they were permitted to enter the classroom.

Compelling evidence shows that many minority parents in Canada feel excluded from the decision making processes in their children's schools. (Dei et al., 2000; Bernhard and Freire, 1999). For example, while many immigrant parents want to participate in their children's schools unobtrusively (not wishing to interfere directly with the teacher's work), they would like to be consulted before important decisions about their children's education are made.

Thus, while parent-school involvement is considered an integral part of inclusive and democratic schooling, what often remains problematic is the nature of their participation. According to Ryan (2006), the levels of potential parental involvement, associated roles, and possible areas of participation, can run from inclusive to exclusive — roles may vary from informal to formal, and areas range from teaching issues to school-level administrative matters. However, while schools have a wide range of options vis-à-vis defining the nature of their relationship with communities, an inclusive and participatory model is far more results-oriented in contexts of student diversity.

Co-opting White Students and Their Communities

A common misconception among Canada's White communities is that diversity issues are not relevant to dominant group students. This fundamentally flawed assumption is also commonly held by dominant groups in other pluralistic Western societies. For example, according to Nieto and Bode (2008), even though multicultural education is an inclusive framework designed to benefit all students, the idea that it is solely for members of the minority community is a commonly held belief of the dominant group in the United States. According to these writers, even teachers have a tendency towards this kind of thinking:

> Teachers in primarily White schools might think that multicultural education is not meant for their students. They could not be more wrong. White students receive only a partial education, which helps to legitimate their cultural blindness. Seeing only themselves, they may believe that they are the norm and thus most important and everyone else is secondary and less important. . . . Feeling as they do, young people from dominant groups are prone to develop an unrealistic view of the world and their place in it (pp. 50–51).

The casual dismissal of the relevance of diversity issues to the White majority is one of the main reasons why the acceptance of diversity remains limited. The benefits of diversity education to minority students are frequently emphasized in schools, research, and scholarship. However, the reality is that most of the introspection and change must come from the White segment of society, to whom power and privilege overwhelmingly belong. Regardless of race, ethnicity, social class, or location (i.e., rural or urban), diversity issues have as much to do with Canada's White communities as they do with diverse communities. In fact, frameworks such as multicultural, intercultural, and anti-racist education are indeed particularly beneficial to dominant group students whose experiences markedly differ from those of their minority counterparts. Some members of the dominant group deny the existence of prejudice and discrimination in Canadian society, as the vignette in Chapter 4 shows (see also, Solomon et al., 2005; James, 2003). Such denials make it difficult to challenge oppressive structures and unwanted social biases. As Henry and Tator (2006: 1–2) observe, "White Canadians tend to dismiss evidence of their racial prejudice and their differential treatment . . . In a society which espouses equality, tolerance, social harmony, and respect for individual rights, the existence of racial prejudice, discrimination and disadvantage is difficult to acknowledge and therefore remedy". It is harder for those who have privilege in society to see the existence of social injustice perpetuated through institutional structures. It is therefore easier for members of the dominant group to see education as a meritocracy, in which everyone has an equal chance of success (see Chapter 1). Also, while most White Canadians support multiculturalism in principle, many resist the implementation of programs that support it (Carr and Klassen, 1997). Invariably, every community is interconnected, either by national or international events, or by government policies that have implications for the life of every citizen. Therefore, it cannot be emphasized enough that as members of a pluralistic nation, all Canadian students need to understand the importance of tolerance and peaceful co-existence. This is of course not yet the case, but with concerted commitment from every stakeholder — including members of the dominant group — to interrupt oppression, discrimination, and prejudice, it can be.

Summary

In general, the matter of education is complex and multifaceted because of the presence of competing ideologies and approaches. This issue assumes enormous proportions in contexts of student diversity. The practical task of reconciling the goals of social cohesion and of validating the cultural, linguistic, and ethnic identities of *all* students is challenging. This chapter argued that educators are able to make a difference through the practices they adopt, beginning with critical self-analysis. Educators are often concerned with the contents of the curriculum, but they hardly ever analyze the questions of who they are, and how their biographies affect the choices they make in the classroom. Such analysis is imperative in Canadian classrooms — where student diversity is the norm rather than the exception. The chapter also argued that in order for them to successfully support diversity, administrators, like teachers, must also engage in self-and institutional analysis. To facilitate teacher, administrator, and institutional analyses, two multidimensional tools — the Teacher Diversity Awareness Compass (TDAC) and Administrator Diversity Awareness Compass (ADAC), for teachers and administrators respectively — were discussed. Each tool has a component that specifically evaluates the "self", and ADAC has a second component for evaluating a school's commitment to affirming diversity and social justice.

Finally, it also argued that just as it is essential for educators to know themselves, they also must know and understand the students they teach. This can be addressed by using strategies that gain knowledge of student personal and cultural strengths, life outside of school, relationships to taught subjects, and student perceptions of school knowledge and beliefs about the role of schooling in their lives. Knowing students also entails understanding student cultures, home backgrounds, and communities. Educators who aim to work for change must develop dynamic working partnerships with the communities within which they operate.

Key Terms

Administrators Diversity
  Awareness Compass
  (ADAC)
Focused observation
Teacher diversity research
Triggers

Audits
Culturally relevant
  pedagogy
Structural audits
Transformative action

Cross-cultural sensitivity
Diversity audits
Environmental scan
Teacher Diversity
  Awareness Compass
  (TDAC)

Questions to Guide Reflective Practice

1. Think back to your elementary and high school days. What kind of relationships existed between your schools and your community?

2. This chapter argues that teaching is not a neutral activity; it is fundamentally a cultural phenomenon. Do you agree with this description of teaching?

3. Choose a friend from a different culture. Discuss each other's background and then reverse roles. How does it feel to be this person for a brief moment?

4. What kind of privileges or oppressions are associated with your ethnic background and community in Canadian society?

5. To what extent do you agree with the chapter's argument that self-knowledge is essential for effective teaching, especially in demographically complex educational settings? Justify your response.

6. Aside from the areas identified in the chapter, what other aspects of the school should receive diversity audits?

Case Study Analysis: Chapter Opening Vignette

1. What is your interpretation of Ms. Dante's comment that she did not want to "step on anyone's toes"?

2. In your opinion, are the minority students' reaction to Ms. Dante's remarks justified?

3. How could Ms. Dante have handled the situation?

4. Should teachers discuss stereotypes about different groups in Canada with their students? Justify your answer.

5. Do you think that Ms. Dante understood the implications of her comment?

6. What action would you advise the students to take?

Test Your Knowledge

1. Using the checklist in Table 5.1, conduct a critical self-analysis. The findings should reveal your attitude towards diversity.

2. There are parents' advocacy groups in virtually every community in Canada. Which advocacy groups exist in your community?

3. What is your province's policy on parental involvement in educational decision-making processes?

4. With a colleague, conduct a diversity audit of your school. If you are not currently teaching in a school, think back to your days as a student at any level. As much as your memory allows, conduct a diversity audit of your school using the model outlined in this chapter.

5. Research the kind of relationships that exist between teachers in two schools (one elementary and one secondary) and members of the community.

6. Interview two teachers: one from a diverse school setting and the other from a relatively homogenous school. Are there significant differences in their views about diversity? If there are, what conclusions can you draw from such differences in opinion?

For Further Reading

Begley, P. (1999). Guiding Values for Future School Leaders. *Orbit*, 30(10): 19–23.

Casella, R. (2005). What is Zero Tolerance? In W. Hare and J. Portelli (Eds.), *Key Questions for Educators* (pp. 128–130). Halifax: Edphil Books.

Epstein, J. (2001). *School, family, and community partnerships: Preparing educators and improving schools*. Boulder: Westview Press.

Ladson-Billings, G., and Tate, W. (Eds.). (2006). *Education Research in the Public Interest: Social Justice, Action, and Policy*. New York: Teachers College Press.

Mills, G. (2007). *Action Research: A Guide for the Teacher Researcher*, 3rd Edition. Upper Saddle River: Pearson Education.

Ryan, J. (2006). *Inclusive Leadership*. San Francisco: Jossey–Bass.

Van Manen, M. (2003). On the Epistemology of Reflective Practice. *Teachers and Teaching: Theory and Practice*, 1(1): 33–50.

Websites of Interest

www.canadianhomeandschool.com The Canadian Home and School Federation/ La Fédération Canadienne Foyer-école

www.ofhsa.on.ca Ontario Federation of Home and School Associations, Inc.

www.bccpac.bc.ca Confederation of Parent Advisory Councils (BCCPAC)

www.preventionviolence.ca Canadian Observatory on School Violence Prevention

www.safecanada.ca Government of Canada, School Safety

www.bullying.org Students Against Violence Everywhere Bullying

www.canadiansafeschools.com The Canadian Safe School Network

www.decnb.ca District Education Councils of New Brunswick

CHAPTER 6

Beyond Differences: Building Bridges and Creating a Community of Learners

❏ Instructing for Success
❏ Assessing Students in Diverse Contexts
❏ Classroom Management in Diverse Contexts
❏ Combating Prejudice and Discrimination
❏ Teachable Moments
❏ Modelling Behaviour
❏ Teaching Social Justice

VIGNETTE

Cascadia Secondary School is in Cascadia, a suburban community about 85 kilometres from the nearest urban centre. Despite increasing diversity in the surrounding communities, Cascadia had remained relatively homogenous. For the most part, teachers were used to teaching students who looked like them — Canadian-born children from White, Christian, middle-class backgrounds. Despite conservative community values, most of the teachers considered themselves progressive educators at least publicly. Privately however, many were thankful that they did not have to cope with the problems that big city schools face: drugs, violence, and increasing diversity (along with its attendant implications for schools). Recently, a group of refugees from a country in Southeast Asia (recently granted political asylum by the Canadian government) settled in the community. At first, everyone had welcomed the newcomers. The staff and students of Cascadia Secondary School were particularly supportive. But, as the year progressed, problems began to emerge. One of the first challenges that

faced everyone was the language barrier, since the refugee students were not proficient in English, the language of instruction. A second challenge was the nature of the relationship between the new students and their resident peers; after the first few months, the novelty had worn off. The newcomers were now quite isolated, and for the most part they interacted mainly with one another. They even sat together in class. They were also excluded from peer-initiated activities. Eventually, exclusion gave way to conflict, which degenerated into name calling and verbal harassment. To diffuse the growing tension, the principal invited several students from both sides for a discussion. During the conference, the, principal learned that some of the White parents were quite upset about the presence of the newcomers in their midst. The perception was that the "immigrants" would create all sorts of problems in their once pristine community. Shocked at what the students told him, the principal wondered what the best line of action would be. He wanted to enlist the help of some of his teachers, but was well aware of their various complaints about the immigrant students. The teachers had told him that some of the new students were "acting up", were "uncooperative", did not "follow instructions", and generally had a negative impact on life in their classrooms. He knew that if these complaints were true, the students' behaviour was probably one of two things; they were either going through post-immigration stress including culture shock, or their teachers did not know how to "engage" them. His knowledge of pedagogy and previous experience teaching in an urban school told him that the latter reason was most likely. He had to act, and fast.

INTRODUCTION: ENGAGING ALL LEARNERS

This chapter explores practical strategies for creating a community of learners in diverse classrooms. The key stance adopted is that teachers need to create alternative visions of their classrooms. These go beyond the orthodox practices and pedagogies that are, more often than not, incompatible with the socio-demographic realities of their teaching environments. In creating a community of learners, teachers must value, nurture, and draw on the diverse experience and perspectives of all students, critically engaging them in the teaching and learning process. Engagement is particularly important in contexts where students are either unfamiliar with, or have had tenuous encounters with, school systems (Cummins, 2000; McLaren, 2007). Yet, problems often stem from teachers not knowing how to engage such students in ways that enable them to become part of the learning community. This is precisely the problem in the opening vignette. The teachers have clearly not made a concerted effort to engage the students, nor have they gone out of their way to encourage a positive rapport between them and their peers. As some writers tell us, one of the most important strategies for creating a community of learners and teaching for success is establishing positive group dynamics in the classroom (Jones and Jones, 2004; Kronowitz, 2008). There are several reasons why this is crucial. First, there is greater potential for conflict in contexts of student diversity (as a result of culture-related miscommunication). This means that understanding who the students are, early in the school year, helps to minimize such tensions, which can result in significant classroom management challenges. Second, establishing positive group dynamics serves as an impetus for teachers to systematically study the backgrounds of their students. In trying to understand what makes each student "tick", teachers have no choice but to learn about the daily lives and communities of their students. Third, it provides a guide for prudent grouping of students for instruction and in-class activities. Some teachers may decide to group students who they believe share some commonalities, however, this may not be in the best interest of their students from minority backgrounds. Grouping students on the basis of mixed ability is probably the best strategy in contexts of diversity. The rationale is that this minimizes the isolation and labelling of students (which is usually the case when they are grouped according to race, gender, ethnicity, or any other socio-demographic variable). Fourth, it is in keeping with conducting diversity audits as discussed in Chapter 5. To a certain extent, the processes of establishing good group dynamics is akin to a micro-level environmental scan (see Chapter 5) as they both enable teachers to ask a fundamental question: "Who are my students and how can the dynamics of the group impact on teaching and learning in my classroom?" Fifth, and perhaps most important, establishing great group dynamics should be considered a prerequisite for an equity and success-oriented instructional environment.

How can teachers establish superb group dynamics? There is no foolproof way of doing this; however, Jones and Jones (2004) suggest several useful strategies: One strategy is to ask students to identify the students they would prefer to do their group activities with, or with whom they would like to eat lunch. A second strategy is to find out from each student which of their peers they know the least, and would like to know better. Another strategy is to have students respond to a questionnaire that asks them to identify their feelings about their position in the classroom, and their feelings about the group. Using an interview guide (see Table 6.1), teachers can also conduct one-on-one interviews with students to find out their interests and perceptions of schooling, and what their expectations are. To be effective, the questions

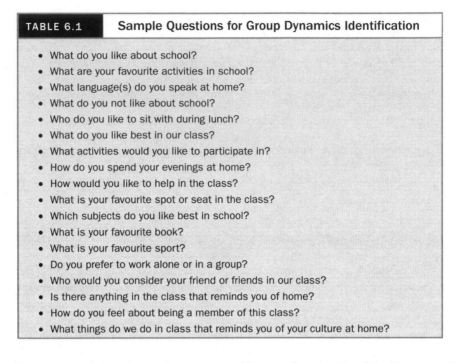

TABLE 6.1	Sample Questions for Group Dynamics Identification

- What do you like about school?
- What are your favourite activities in school?
- What language(s) do you speak at home?
- What do you not like about school?
- Who do you like to sit with during lunch?
- What do you like best in our class?
- What activities would you like to participate in?
- How do you spend your evenings at home?
- How would you like to help in the class?
- What is your favourite spot or seat in the class?
- Which subjects do you like best in school?
- What is your favourite book?
- What is your favourite sport?
- Do you prefer to work alone or in a group?
- Who would you consider your friend or friends in our class?
- Is there anything in the class that reminds you of home?
- How do you feel about being a member of this class?
- What things do we do in class that reminds you of your culture at home?

should be open-ended so that students can provide more than "yes" and "no" answers. The ultimate goal of establishing good group dynamics is to help teachers adapt lessons, pedagogy, and student tasks in ways that culminate in successful teaching and learning.

INSTRUCTING FOR SUCCESS

How then can teaching become more successful in contexts of student diversity? The strategies given here use a contingency approach — the specific strategies adopted by individual educators will vary according to context and to variables such as class size and the degree of diversity among the students. For conceptual convenience, the strategies are discussed from a temporal framework (from the perspectives of sequentially structured **instructional activities** as follows: **pre-instructional activities**, instructional activities, and **post-instructional analysis**). Although conceptually separate, all three phases are interconnected since the process is cyclical as Figure 6.1 illustrates. For example, while pre-instructional activities inform teachers' activities during actual instruction, the insights gleaned from post-instructional analysis guide preparations for subsequent lessons and so on.

Pre-Instructional Activities

The pre-instructional phase includes all preparatory activities that precede instruction. In addition to routine lesson planning, this stage is particularly crucial for teachers who wish to empower diverse students because their success or failure depends on what they do at this stage. Ultimately, this stage not only involves content planning, it is also the stage where teachers should conduct comprehensive content analysis to check for bias in language and resources.

Checking for Bias in Language (CBL)

One of the most important activities teachers should engage in during the pre-instructional stage is checking the proposed language of instruction for bias using templates that are similar to the one provided in Chapter 5 (Table 5. 2). This is critical in contexts of student diversity because some students may be sensitive to certain types of language and words that the teacher may have included in the lesson plan. It is during the pre-instructional stage that teachers have the opportunity to put theory into practice by ensuring that the language of instruction is culturally relevant and sensitive to the presence of some groups in the class. It is important for teachers to always remember that while it is easy to eliminate the most obviously biased language, sometimes the most offensive words are those that are ostensibly neutral. Take for instance the innocuous phrase "these people", which is commonly used in Canadian society. In certain contexts, it has the dubious function of creating an "us" and "them" dichotomy that implicitly suggests the superiority of the speaker. Some members of the dominant group often refer to First Nations peoples, new immigrants, and other minoritized groups as "these people", without realizing the derogatory connotation. In a similar vein, describing a group of people during lessons as "stingy", "pushy", or "underdeveloped" (in case of countries), while describing others as "smart" or "intelligent" should be avoided as much as possible (Allgood, 2001). Depending on the grade level, there are students who will take exception to the use of such words during instruction. Indeed, talking about any group of persons implying that they collectively have these shared characteristics is inappropriate.

Besides checking for bias, language screening also provides teachers the opportunity to ensure that they have adapted the language of instruction to meet the proficiency levels of their diverse students. For example, in instances where there are ESL students in the class, it is good practice to critically assess the provisions that have been made to accommodate their language needs and limitations. Overall, the purpose of pre-instructional language analysis is to ensure that no student feels excluded by the language of instruction.

Checking for Bias in Materials (CBM)

Just as it is essential to check for bias in language, it is also important to check for bias in the materials that a teacher intends to use. The purpose is to ensure that the resources are appropriate, inclusive, and relate to the lived experiences of the students in the class. To check for bias in materials assumes that teachers have assembled a repertoire of resources that are reflective of the diverse backgrounds of the students. For example in cases where there are First Nations children in the class, teachers must ensure that instructional aids have some relevance to the culture of Canada's First Nations peoples. Arguably, it may not be possible to include resources that are representative of the culture of every student in the class — the key is to be as inclusive as practically possible. A useful strategy for including materials that are culturally relevant is to select resources that cut across cultures. There are indeed as many cross-cultural teaching tools as there are monocultural resources.

Inclusive Pedagogy

Chapter 4 discusses the twin concepts of critical and inclusive pedagogy extensively. The major task for teachers during the preparatory stage then, is to flesh out the ways they plan to infuse the principles of critical and inclusive pedagogy into the instructional process. It is also during this stage that teachers must identify how they plan to engage students in ways that enable them to question the knowledge that is being taught. An earlier chapter discussed the importance of teaching and modelling critical thinking to students. During the pre-instructional stage, teachers have a unique opportunity to identify specific practical strategies for fostering critical and higher order thinking, guided by questions such as the following:

- Will students be actively engaged in the learning process or will they be treated as depositories of information?
- What kind of questions will be asked during instruction?
- Will students have ample opportunity to apply their critical thinking skills?
- Which group of students will benefit most from the lesson as designed?

Instructional Activities

As the nexus of teachers' pedagogical activities, the instructional stage should ideally begin with introductory or opening activities. Teachers, especially those who teach lower grades, do not often consider it necessary to engage in small talk with students, but in contexts of student diversity this can go a long way towards empowering students. This engagement, even nonverbal communication such as a nod or a smile, will put students at ease and serve as an acknowledgement that they are valued participants in that community of learners. Besides letting students know that they are valued, establishing a rapport with them is an affirmation of their identity. Everyday, many minority students walk into Canadian classrooms feeling apprehensive and tentative, as if they do not belong in that environment. Without particularly singling them out, imagine what even the most basic affirmation of their presence at the beginning of the day can do in terms of boosting their morale, self-esteem, and readiness to learn.

Differentiated Instruction

Differentiated instruction means targeted strategies that enable teachers to meet the individual needs of students according to their state of readiness, interests, abilities, strengths, and skills (Kronowitz, 2008). This is an invaluable strategy in cases of student diversity. A major strategy for successful differentiated, or adaptive, instruction is to give students multiple options that are matched with appropriate tasks. This facilitates their ability to learn individually and the teacher's ability to meet the individual needs of students. It is also important in contexts of student diversity that teachers use multimedia presentations, interactive discussions, and hands-on activities to try to motivate all students to learn. This has the added advantage of minimizing boredom and disinterest. Ultimately, the goal of differentiated instruction is to provide students with a nurturing, supportive, and non-competitive learning environment that reinforces diversity without compromising the quality of what students learn (Bennett, 2007).

Pacing and Transitions

Pacing — the speed at which a lesson progresses — is critical during instruction, but exceptionally so in contexts of student diversity because of wide-ranging differences among students. Indeed achieving instructional objectives, as well as students' comprehension, hinges on it. This means that in teaching content, teachers should pace lessons in ways that enable all students to follow what is being taught. There are times when it is necessary to slow down the pace just as there are times that require an accelerated pace. Jones and Jones

(2004) provide several strategies for pacing instruction that are as useful in contexts of diversity as they are in other contexts. One strategy is for teachers to develop an awareness and understanding of their own teaching tempo, which includes learning how to generate interest without being overly animated. Since becoming cognizant of one's teaching tempo can be quite challenging, Jones and Jones suggest that teachers videotape themselves during instruction. This gives them the opportunity to replay the tape as often as they like. By observing themselves teach, teachers will be able to determine whether they talk too fast or repeat themselves too often. Videotaping serves another important function in contexts of student diversity: it helps teachers assess the extent to which they have taken the diversity of their students into account. Additionally, it provides them invaluable opportunity to analyze the reactions of their students who for various reasons may not have actively participated in the lesson.

Related to pacing are transitions — when teachers switch from one activity to another, or from one subject to another, during a lesson. Often, this provides opportunities for behavioural problems to arise during instruction. It can be even more problematic in contexts of diversity because there may be students who did not fully understand the teacher's instructions for language-related reasons.

Monitoring for Comprehension

It is generally good pedagogical practice to monitor student comprehension during instruction. However, this assumes urgency in contexts of diversity, where a host of variables can impede students' understanding of the concepts being taught. One way to check for student comprehension is by monitoring their body language. Why is this a useful strategy? First, in diverse contexts, there are usually students who do not feel confident enough to alert teachers of any difficulties they might be experiencing. Second, and more important, there may be students in the class who come from cultures that do not permit children to express their feelings. For these students, asking questions for reinforcement or clarification is often not an option. For example, some language minority students may not understand a concept but may feel too embarrassed and self-conscious to ask questions.

Varying Instructional Style

Just as students have their preferred learning styles, teachers have preferred teaching styles that are "the teacher's pervasive personal behaviors and media used during interaction with learners" (Bennett, 2007). Teaching style research shows that teachers whose instructional styles approximate their preferred learning styles tend to experience more ease in teaching (Bennett, 2007). Implicitly, these teachers are better able to meet the learning needs of all their students. Beyond that, varying instructional style has long been established as a way of sustaining student interest in learning (Jones and Jones, 2004; Kronowitz, 2008). Varying teaching styles in contexts of student diversity is critical because it ensures that teachers are accommodating the learning styles of as many students as possible (Grossman, 1995; Sheets, 2005; Villegas and Lucas, 2002). It also serves as proactive classroom management because it helps to keep students interested in the lesson, since they become restless when they are faced with extended periods of monostylistic instruction. Moreover, teachers who use monostylistic instructional approaches do not promote equity in their classrooms because they are simply not meeting the needs of all their students.

As Ghosh (2002: 102) rightly argues, the teaching styles of many teachers in North America (including Canada) tend to be "based on the characteristics of male, white, middle-class norm . . . . [which] include task orientation; attention to parts rather than whole; emphasis on formal rules; linear thinking patterns; dispassionate but, attentive behaviour . . . ". This contrasts sharply with the learning styles of females and students from minority cultures and working-class backgrounds, which tend to emphasize personal interactions, attention to the whole, and contextualized information (Ghosh, 2002). In instances where teaching styles differ markedly from student preferred learning styles, students do not do as well as when there is correspondence with their favoured modes of learning and how they are taught.

Interacting with Students

This is particularly important in contexts of student diversity. As noted in Chapter 1, research shows that teachers tend to interact with, and generally call on, boys more often than girls (Sadker and Sadker, 1986; Sadker, 2004). They also tend to interact with, or call on, students from dominant group backgrounds more often than they do minority students. Unfortunately, this kind of selective interaction sends the wrong message to students from disadvantaged communities. Teachers' interactions with their students should be equitably distributed regardless of socio-demographic variables such as gender, racial or ethnic background, sexual orientation, or ability or disability. The bigger question then becomes how teachers overcome the problem of inequitable interactions with their students. First, they must engage in deliberate monitoring of who they call on to participate in classroom activities during and after instruction. For example, they should keep track of how opportunities to respond to questions during instruction are distributed. Second, they should deliberately vary the students they assign to leadership roles in the class. Third, they should, as much as possible, integrate group activities into the instructional process. This not only provides students with opportunities for cooperative work, it also enables teachers to interact with small groups, thus increasing the likelihood of interactions with all students during the course of the day.

FIGURE 6.1	Inclusive Instructional Process

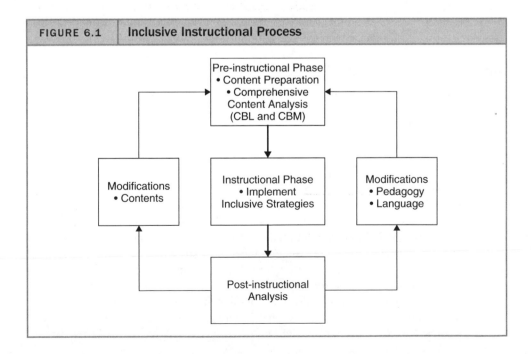

Cooperative Learning/Group work

A time-tested strategy for encouraging participation and collaboration among students is group work. There is general consensus among educators that small group activities encourage cooperative and collaborative behaviour, especially among students who would otherwise not participate. Small groups provide a valuable opportunity for students to build strong interpersonal bonds, thus creating an environment that enhances the quality of the classroom experience for all. Although cooperative learning has always been an important part of the teaching-learning process, it has evolved as an important pedagogical strategy in efforts to provide inclusive learning environments for all students. Additionally, a review of research on cooperative learning demonstrates that overall "cooperative learning does positively affect relationships between students of different races or ethnicities, while also increasing their achievement" (Slavin, 1983: 75). Drawing on the views of several researchers, Sapon-Shevin (2004) summarizes why cooperative learning is a particularly effective teaching strategy in heterogeneous classrooms:

> Cooperative learning is of value for all students including those who have been identified as "at risk," "bilingual," "gifted," and "normal". Cooperative learning encourages mutual respect and learning among students with varying talents and abilities, languages, racial, and ethnic backgrounds. . . . [C]ooperative learning is effective in reducing prejudice among students and in meeting the academic and social needs of students at risk for educational failure. . . . [It] can allow all students to work together, each student experiencing the role of teacher and of learner, and each student modeling recognition of and respect for many different skills and learning styles (p. 3).

In contexts of student diversity then, collaborative classroom work promotes cross-cultural communication among students because it provides them with opportunities to share their own views and perspectives on a given topic (Villegas and Lucas, 2002; Gay, 2000). Furthermore, cooperative learning has the additional advantage of enabling students from nondominant cultures to learn in less-competitive and less-threatening situations. While Canadian culture generally encourages and fosters competition among students, there are cultures that do not value or encourage competition. For instance, among First Nations peoples, competition is discouraged while collaborative work is encouraged (Brant, 1990).

There are several cooperative learning methods; four widely used approaches are briefly discussed below. Some of the most widely used cooperative methods were developed by Robert Slavin and his associates at Johns Hopkins University (Slavin, 1983). One of these models is Jigsaw II (a modification of the original Jigsaw developed by Aronson). In Jigsaw II, students are assigned to four-to-five member teams, and each student is given a topic on which to become an expert. Members from each team who have been assigned the same material are further grouped together and are expected to study the material, and then return to their original teams to teach what they have learned to their teammates. Students are quizzed and tested on all material assigned for cooperative learning. The knowledge that they will be tested gives every team member a powerful incentive to pay attention to their peer's instruction.

Another approach to cooperative learning is the Student Teams-Achievement Divisions (STAD). In this model, students are assigned to a racially, culturally, and mixed-gender heterogeneous groups of four to five members. Each week the teacher introduces new material, after which students study worksheets on the material. Following team practice, when all team members are confident of their mastery of the material, they independently take quizzes to earn points for their team. However, the value of each member's contribution to the team score depends on their past quiz average.

Another model developed by Slavin et al. is the Teams-Games-Tournament (TGT), which is a four-step process that enables students to work cooperatively, and a variant of STAD. First, as with STAD, the teacher teaches the material, then students are sent to study together in heterogeneous groups of four to five students to master the content. At the end of each week, students compete in tournaments. The unique part of TGT is that students compete in skills exercises against peers whose past academic performances are similar to theirs. This means that students are matched with those that have similar abilities, making the competition more equitable.

What is distinctive about the three approaches above is that they rely on equity-based scoring strategies in which success is based on effort and improvement rather than ability. Thus, every student, including a high-ability student, can potentially do well or poorly. Another variant of cooperative learning is the Team-Assisted Individualization (TAI) method. Developed originally for math, in TAI students are assigned to four-to-five member heterogeneous teams. Following initial diagnostic testing, students work through pre-identified math units individually. According to Slavin (1983), TAI is a unique approach because it uses

> individualized instead of class-based instruction . . . [and] was developed to be used when a class is too heterogeneous to be taught the same material especially when there are mainstreamed children who need the positive social interaction that takes place in the teams but also need to have material at their own level (p. 27).

Although it is a highly encouraging teaching method, especially in diversified contexts, cooperative learning comes with some challenges. First, as Jones and Jones warn, teachers should realize that when students work in groups (no matter how structured the activities are, nor how much they contribute to positive interdependence and individual accountability), there is never a guarantee that every individual in the group will be as productive as they could be. Another problem with cooperative learning arises from the variations in students' academic status. That is, a student's entry level skills, knowledge, proficiency in language, and status among peers can affect the outcome of the team effort. Another possible challenge with adopting cooperative learning is the potential for one high-achieving student to emerge as the leader of the group. However, teachers can counteract this by specifically appointing a low-ability student as the group expert and focusing on a task in which that student is already an expert. The student can then be asked to teach the knowledge to the group, the goal being to empower a student who ordinarily would not have the opportunity to "teach" others.

Post-instructional Analysis

Like the first phase, the post-instructional stage is also reflective, with the added benefit of hindsight since the focus of the analysis now shifts to determining the degree of instructional success. It is a stock-taking stage during which teachers decide which strategies to reinforce, refine, modify, or eliminate entirely — either because they worked or failed to contribute to the intended outcomes of the lesson. As quasi–teacher diversity research, (see Chapter 5), **post-instructional analysis** can also reveal the extent to which a teacher did adhere to diversity supporting strategies. How might teachers conduct successful post-instructional analysis? A useful strategy is to develop, and respond to, questions

TABLE 6.2	Guiding Questions for Post-instructional Analysis in Diverse Classrooms

- To what extent was the lesson inclusive?
- Why was it successful or unsuccessful?
- To what extent did I succeed in involving *all* my students?
- Which pedagogical strategies should be reinforced?
- Which strategies require modification?
- Did I dominate the class discussions?
- Did I provide all students with fair opportunities to participate in the lesson?
- Did I use language appropriately?
- Was the language gender and culturally inclusive?
- Was knowledge jointly created with my students?
- Who did I call on most often to respond to questions?
- What was the nature of my interactions with the students during instruction?
- What were the power dynamics in the class?
- Did I create an enabling environment for equitable student participation in the lesson?
- Were the resources as inclusive as expected?
- What were students' reactions to the resources?
- Did I vary my instructional style?
- Did I provide my students with opportunities for critical reflection during the lesson?

like those provided in Table 6.2. The answers to these questions provide valuable insight for planning subsequent lessons and activities.

To be very effective, post-instructional analysis must be conducted immediately after each lesson, or at the latest by the end of the day, while the proceedings are still fresh in the teacher's mind. Post-instructional analysis is by no means a time-consuming activity especially once the process becomes an integral part of a teacher's daily routine.

ASSESSING STUDENTS IN DIVERSE CONTEXTS

Assessment is an integral part of teaching (Grossman, 1995). It involves obtaining information that is used to make educational decisions about students, as well as giving feedback about their progress, strengths, and weaknesses. Information gathered through assessment is also used to judge instructional effectiveness and curricular adequacy (Gronlund and Cameron, 2004; Sheets, 2005; Ableser, 2007). Assessment can be diagnostic, formative, or summative. Although not often perceived as such, assessment and diversity are interconnected in very important ways. To begin with, there is significant diversity in the approaches and techniques that teachers can use to assess their students' performance. Second, constructivists have long acknowledged that students learn and construct meaning differently. It is logical that differential learning styles should also be reflected in the types of strategies and tools that teachers use when assessing students' performance. Moreover, as the Canadian Teachers' Federation maintains, "the assessment and evaluation of students whether carried out at the classroom level or beyond, must take account of gender differences as well as cultural, linguistic, socio-economic and other forms of diversity". Third, cultural and linguistic factors have significant impact on assessment, thus not all assessment tools are reliable across the board for all students. Furthermore, no assessment tool (especially test-based traditional variants), will achieve the same result across all ethnic or cultural groups although this fact is often ignored in schools. Corson (2001) argues:

> Often, culturally different children come to school knowing very different kinds of things from other children. Even when they use English words and other signs, the rules of use they have for them can be quite different. So, when they meet the assessment methods that teachers use, they sometimes are asked to display knowledge about "x, y", when what they really know about is "y, z". Often, in regular schools, they are never asked to display their knowledge about "y, z". Furthermore, they are usually asked to display their knowledge in unfamiliar ways (p. 119).

Besides the problem of incongruence, certain kinds of assessments have been indicted as being favourably skewed towards students from dominant group backgrounds. It is now a well established fact that standardized tests in countries such as Canada and the United States tend to be biased against women and minority students. A case in point — IQ tests (once the gold standard for assessing intelligence) have been found to be culturally biased because they measure indicators of intelligence only as defined within the dominant culture. Unfortunately standardized, and other school-based, tests continue to be used for sorting and segregating students, especially those from nondominant backgrounds or those whose primary languages (L1) are different from the language of instruction (Sheets, 2005; Nieto, 2002; Froese-Germain, 1999). Commenting on the current wave of high-stakes testing (and assessments more generally) that is sweeping across Canada, Froese-Germain (1999) has this to say:

> Not only is there little evidence to support standardized testing from a pedagogical standpoint, it is clear that standardized testing can have a detrimental impact on the most vulnerable students. Far from being a neutral practice, it perpetuates and intensifies educational inequities in two ways: through the misuse of test scores; and because test bias works against the interests of students from low-income groups, racial and ethnic minorities, girls and young women, and students with disabilities (p. 13).

Moreover, some of the standardized assessment tools in use are developed from the perspective of the "standard" student, which is a code word for students with a dominant group background. Teachers must always remember that while "tests maybe standardized . . . students are not" (Froese-Germain, 1999: 6). Similarly, Gillis (1993, cited in Froese-Germain, 1999) argues that "[a]nyone who expects students who are disadvantaged, impoverished, undernourished, neglected or severely disabled to score at the same level as students who are affluent, healthy, well cared for or able [bodied] is doomed to disappointment". While one must guard against simplistic over-generalization, Gillis makes a valid point that policy makers and educators in contexts of diversity should heed.

Recent approaches to measuring students' competencies tend to emphasize criterion-referenced, as opposed to norm-referenced, assessment. Criterion-referenced assessment measures student performance against set criteria, while norm-referenced assessment tools measure student achievement against that of their peers. Although it falls within the category of traditional assessment, criterion-referenced assessment is more suited to measuring student achievement in contexts of diversity because it is individual-oriented. Nevertheless, planning assessment strategies that take student diversity into account is a complex phenomenon: not only are teachers asked to teach culturally responsive pedagogy, they are also expected to develop culturally responsive measurement tools and strategies.

One strategy that is often considered equity-sensitive is authentic assessment, which emphasizes performance on tasks like those that exist in "real life" settings. Authentic assessment is versatile and covers a wide range of activities including oral presentations, collaborative group work, individual problem-solving projects, debates, videotapes of performance, dance, drama, exhibitions, experiments, observational data, peer- and self-assessments, and a multitude of other hands-on strategies (Gronlund and Cameron, 2004; Kronowitz, 2008). Why use authentic assessment? Ableser (2007) suggests some advantages of using authentic assessment that refer to its relevance in contexts of student diversity. First, because it is based on real-life problems, it draws on students' experiences. It enables them to use higher level thinking skills. Progressive pedagogy should provide students with opportunities for applying their critical awareness and critical thinking skills. Authentic assessment provides the springboard for students to engage in critical reflection and to participate actively in their own learning. It is useful in contexts of diversity because (unlike other assessment techniques), it focuses on process, thus allowing students wide latitude in demonstrating what they know. Also, it is more inclusive because it accommodates diverse learning styles. Finally, it focuses on students' unique strengths and competencies, and it motivates them to perform. Despite its advantages, Froese-Germain warns teachers to be cognizant of the fact that

> assessment, including authentic assessment, must be viewed first and foremost as part of a diverse strategy to improve the quality of education and address equity issues – other systemic reforms must be implemented in tandem that address broad social and educational conditions (p. 51).

In sum, several important issues from the above discussion deserve to be reiterated:

- When teaching students from diverse backgrounds, teachers must include assessment strategies that have written, verbal, and performance components to accommodate preferred learning styles. For example, students who do poorly on the verbal component due to language limitations, may do well on the performance component.
- In developing assessment strategies, educators must use approaches that are fair and bias free, particularly since assessment strategies tend to ignore cultural factors. Using a variety of assessment practices and strategies promotes learning.
- Assessing language minority students deserves particular attention. Several Canadian studies have documented bias in placement tests among language minority students, especially those given by psychologists who lack the knowledge-base or cultural competence to assess such students (Corson, 2001). Exemplary assessment strategies involve attention to cultural contexts, learning styles, and student language competencies.
- Assessment style is also pertinent in building culturally responsive teaching. It is important that assessment methods be geared towards promoting the development of student understanding, rather than promoting the memorizing of factual information. Also, as Villegas and Lucas (2002) assert, teachers (especially those who teach in culturally diverse settings) must interpret assessment results cautiously.
- Self-and peer-assessment are also important techniques for empowering students from nondominant groups, and indeed all students. Many school districts across Canada do not recognize these types of assessment as part of formal evaluations of student achievement. Nevertheless, teachers can use them as strategies for motivating their students to get involved and to take ownership of their own learning — especially those at risk for failure.

TABLE 6.3	Summary Guidelines and Strategies for Assessing Students' Work in Diverse Contexts

- Assessment must measure what has been taught.
- Teachers must use varied approaches to reflect differential learning styles.
- Whenever possible, assessment tools should be pre-tested for bias.
- Criterion-referenced and authentic assessments are more compatible with the principles of equity and fairness, but the data must be interpreted carefully.
- Assessment strategies should simultaneously build on students' strengths and help them grow in those areas that they demonstrate weakness.
- Multiple measures should be used to triangulate data on student performance.
- As much as possible, teachers must focus on authentic tasks that enable students to demonstrate their competencies, rather than testing them on competencies that they may not have.
- Tests and assessments must be constructed concurrently when planning lessons, rather than after the fact, so that there is congruence between differentiated tasks and assessment strategies.
- The language of assessment must be bias-free, as biased language can lead to student emotional reactions, which may adversely affect their performance on tests and activities.
- Teachers should adopt participatory assessment practices, and whenever possible, assessments should be designed collaboratively with students.
- There must be clarity and precision in the language used in assessment measures in order to facilitate student comprehension.
- Teachers must make accommodations in the tools used to assess the performance of second language learners, such as ESL or FSL students.
- In the interest of equity and fairness, teachers should provide additional time for students as needed when collecting assessment data.
- Perhaps most importantly, assessment tools must be culturally responsive.

But, a word of caution: In providing students with choices in assessment methods, teachers must be careful not to replace cognitively challenging assignments with watered-down options. As Sheets (2005: 177) asserts, while teachers should strive to "understand how cultural variations in students' home-rearing practices might affect assessment measures . . . [they should] not use cultural information to limit students' opportunities to learn or to shift responsibility for low achievement". For example, a teacher who believes that First Nations children perform very well in cooperative tasks should not limit their opportunities to also engage in independent tasks. The trick is to use fair, balanced, but equally challenging assessment measures.

CLASSROOM MANAGEMENT IN DIVERSE CONTEXTS

As a concept, classroom management involves much more than maintaining discipline in the classroom. It encompasses everything that teachers do (from organizing the physical space to managing student behaviour) to support an environment that is conducive to learning (Jones and Jones, 2004). The ultimate goal of effective classroom management is to reduce time spent on distractions so that more time can be devoted to teaching and learning

(Kronowitz, 2008). But with regards to managing their classrooms, much more is required of teachers in contexts of student diversity. To begin with, as noted in several instances in this book, culture- and language-related miscues often serve as conflict triggers in contexts of diversity. Moreover, students from nondominant backgrounds are more likely to be targeted by violence reduction policies. These have been instituted in many school districts across Canada, thus putting the students under constant watch, or the "gaze" (Henry and Tator, 2006) of teachers and school administrators (see Chapter 5). This creates resentment among minority students, further exacerbating whatever intergroup tensions may already exist.

On a different tack, it is important for educators to remember that behaviours considered "civilized" within any given context are usually socially constructed. This means that what Canadian schools consider appropriate behaviour reflects the choices made by members of the dominant group. Although not often perceived as such, this is one of the reasons why teachers set parameters for appropriate student behaviour at the beginning of each school year. Implicitly, this is recognition that behavioural norms vary from one context to another. Thus, while a student from a different cultural community may behave in ways that are deemed appropriate in that community, the same behaviour may be unacceptable in many classrooms. Some scholars consider the issue of differential interpretation of student behaviour as part of the invisible culture that creates problems in contexts of difference (Erickson, 2001). How a person experiences or displays emotional pain, how loud a person speaks, and how attentive a person appears to be in conversation may, in reality, be attributable to culture. However, the problem is not the difference per se but the interpretation. As Erickson asserts, the

> difficulty lies in our inability to recognize others' differences in ways of acting as cultural rather than personal. We tend to naturalize other people's behavior and blame them — attributing intentions, judging competence — without realizing that we are experiencing culture rather than nature (p. 39).

This is not to say that schools should not enforce disciplinary policies. The point, as argued in Chapter 3, is that many students in heterogeneous classrooms often negotiate between two culture bases. This tension extends to issues of what constitutes appropriate behaviour, as this can differ significantly in various cultures. Moreover, there has always been a tendency to look at urban schools in Canada as fostering juvenile delinquency, perhaps as a result of the overrepresentation of students from disadvantaged backgrounds. McLaren's (1980/2007) narrative of the experiences of students in an elementary school in a "ghetto" community date back the 1970s (see Chapter 3). Still, the unfavourable perceptions of minority students he describes often lead to unfair application of discipline in Canada (Dei et al., 1997; Ryan, 2003).Thus, in contexts of student diversity, teachers must adopt fair classroom and discipline strategies that are premised on the following principles.

A Sound Theoretical Base

All teachers require an in-depth understanding of the theoretical bases on which their classroom management practices are grounded. It is only through extensive knowledge of various classroom management theories that teachers can determine those that best suit their teaching contexts. Progressive theories that are student-centred, such as *collaborative management* are most results-oriented in contexts of student of diversity. This contrasts sharply with teacher-centred traditional approaches that exclude student voices from what goes on in the classroom. When teachers and students jointly share responsibility for managing behaviour, such collaboration encourages positive communication between all members of the classroom community.

Comprehensive Planning and Effective Instruction

The first part of this chapter examined inclusive instructional planning and teaching strategies in contexts of student diversity. But beyond issues of inclusion, comprehensive instructional planning and effective lesson delivery are proactive classroom and behaviour management strategies. Research supports the assertion that when lessons are well-prepared and taught effectively, major behavioural infractions are reduced.

Positive Interpersonal Relationship

Positive interpersonal relationship is foundational to establishing a positive climate in classrooms, and it is a conduit to the empowerment of students from marginalized communities. As noted in this volume and elsewhere, Canadian classrooms can be alienating to some groups of students, as a result of the devaluation of their cultural capital. Unfortunately, the hierarchical arrangement of classroom structures and modes of interaction generally emphasize the power differentials between teachers and students. It is therefore important that classroom activities revolve around teamwork, cooperative learning, and mutual understanding between teachers and their students, and between students and their peers. When students believe that they are valued by their teachers, their self-esteem goes up, making them more likely to behave in desirable ways.

Overall, the onus is on teachers to develop proactive classroom management strategies that encourage positive student behaviour. Creating environments that foster positive behaviour and interpersonal relationships in their classrooms means that teachers are going to spend less time on disciplinary issues.

The Physical Environment

The way teachers structure their classrooms contributes immensely to the extent that behavioural issues become problematic. Therefore, many Canadian teachers spend a substantial amount of time at the beginning of the year organizing their classrooms in ways that foster learning. For instance, a seemingly mundane activity such as a seating arrangement can reduce or increase behavioural problems. As a general rule seating arrangements should allow teachers to move around with relative ease, so that they can reach every student — especially those who need extra support. The way teachers organize student seating can also impact the overall climate of the classroom. Arranging students' seats in ways that create comfortable and informal learning environments has been known to increase students' interest and participation in class. It also tends to give them a sense of belonging, which in turn encourages increased interaction and cross-cultural communication among themselves. The end result is that students become much more relaxed and willing to participate in class activities, group projects, and other tasks. Also, organizing the physical environment of the classroom is essential for effective student learning and behaviour management. Teachers must remember that students spend a significant portion of their day in the classroom, and a physically chaotic or disorganized classroom will invariably translate into a space that is not conducive to learning. When the classroom is open, friendly, organized, and welcoming, students will respond more positively to instruction and collateral activities. Finally, in contexts of student diversity, it is important, and very empowering, for teachers to include artifacts from the representative cultures of their students as part of the classroom décor. In addition to displaying artifacts, teachers can use posters that include inspirational quotes from different cultures and parts of the world, and are written in different languages, especially those that reflect the heritage of the students in the class. Imagine how empowering it can be for students (especially language minority ones) to see these quotes posted around the classroom.

High but Realistic Expectations

These concepts are not necessarily as incompatible as people often think. If we believe the postulates of Levi Vygotsky (1962), students have a *zone of proximal development* — the point at which they need assistance in order for learning to continue. Thus, physical appearance and cultural issues aside, no classroom is ever homogeneous in the true sense of the word as students vary in abilities and learning styles. Juxtaposed with socio-demographic differences, Canadian classrooms are complex amalgams of students having diversified skills and ability levels, who due to structural and time constraints, teachers sometimes ignore. Similarly, teachers sometimes over- or under-estimate the abilities of their students. This is especially true for those who come from minoritized and impoverished backgrounds, for whom the bar is frequently set too low. Many observers of Canadian classrooms have long argued that teachers tend to have low expectations of minority students (Dei, 1996; Ryan, 2006; Corson, 2001; Cummins, 2000). Arguing from the perspective of schools in the United States, Landsman (2006) explains why this happens:

> There are teachers who rarely call home when young Black students are in trouble because they assume Black families are dysfunctional, illiterate, or unconcerned. I have talked with Black students in high schools who are aware that the teacher turns toward them when he or she has an easy question on a text and toward the White kids when he or she wants the answer to a more complex and difficult question. I have watched teachers allow Black students to saunter into class late with barely a recognizing nod of the head, whereas a White child who is late gets a frown and the mention of a phone call home (pp. 222, 223).

Landsman goes on to argue that teachers who send these kinds of subliminal disenfranchising messages are often not aware of their behaviour. These teachers also concede that until something triggers their awareness, or a switch just comes on, they automatically expect less from their minority students. Unfortunately, lowered expectations have lifelong consequences for the students at the receiving end. Thus, while it is important to set realistic expectations in order to prevent student frustration, alienation, and subsequent disengagement from learning, teachers must not compromise the quality and rigour of work that is expected from all students.

Moreover, it is important for teachers to understand how their expectations for their students can potentially affect the decisions they make about them. Nieto (2004) has the following to say about the impact of teacher expectations:

> Expectations are connected with the biases we have learned to internalize. If we expect children who come from economically poor communities to be poor readers, we may reflect this belief in the way we teach them. Similarly, if we expect girls to be passive and submissive, we may teach them as if they were. . . . Although our teaching approaches may be either unconscious or developed with the best intentions, the results can be destructive . . . . Having good intentions or even caring deeply about students is not enough. We need to consider our biases, which even the most [caring] teachers carry with them, everyday that we step foot into the classroom (p. 400).

TABLE 6.4	The Power of Expectations

A group of high school English teachers were participating in a diversity workshop. The facilitator was discussing how teacher expectations shape and influence how teachers may view their students and their work. He had also discussed how preconceived notions about certain groups can affect teachers' perceptions of students' abilities. While this does not happen all the time, it does happen often enough to warrant teachers paying particular attention that this does not happen to them, especially vis-à-vis their diverse students. To bolster his argument, he decided to conduct a test among a group of three volunteer participants. He gave each of them an identical copy of an impeccable analysis of an excerpt from Shakespeare's *The Taming of the Shrew*. He then instructed the teachers to read and then identify the author from a pool of three grade 10 English language students. To help the teachers make their decision, he gave them a brief bio of each as follows: The first student was from the UK and was attending school in Canada for one year through an international student exchange program. The second potential writer was a Black student described as a recent immigrant to Canada. The third student was described as a Canadian-born White student. At the end of the exercise the facilitator collected the work and not surprisingly, each educator had determined that the work was written by the visiting British student. The facilitator repeated the exercise among two other sets of teachers bringing the total number of participants to nine. Altogether, seven out of nine teachers believed that the literary analysis was written by the exchange student from the UK. The remaining two judged the writer to be the White Canadian student. None of the nine teachers thought that the work could have been written by the immigrant student. Needless to say, the teachers were shocked to find out that the analysis was written by the Black immigrant student. The facilitator explained that even though the student was a newcomer to Canada, he had been schooled in English in his home country, where the works of William Shakespeare featured quite prominently in the English literature curriculum.

The vignette in Table 6.4 illustrates how teacher expectations can be instrumental in the outcomes of the schooling experiences of their nondominant group students.

Diversity Centres

Diversity centres are spaces that focus predominantly on promoting diversity in the classroom. Creating centres, or areas of interest, are important strategies for managing classrooms, especially in contexts of diversity. The very essence of centres as commonly used by teachers rests on the idea that students are different. Recall Gardner's theory of multiple intelligences (see Chapter 1); students learn in a variety of ways and exhibit their intelligence in different ways. Centres therefore, provide students with opportunities for differential learning experiences that are based on their interests. Also, creating centres in the classroom is an excellent way to organize the physical environment of the room. Centres are individualized areas that teachers set up throughout the classroom to motivate and facilitate student learning in specific areas. Centres of interest can also serve as rest or relaxation areas. For example, a student who is having a bad day can, with the teacher's permission, relax, read, or generally sit quietly in solitude without being disruptive or bothered by anyone else. When teachers create culturally relevant centres of interest, they are in effect, empowering students from diverse backgrounds to use their skills and strengths in ways that can motivate them to learn.

Chapter 4 discussed the concept of negotiable and non-negotiable knowledge. Teachers can use the dimensions of non-negotiable knowledge as a building block for establishing centres of interest. For instance, teachers can create ICT centres (see Chapter 4) or centres for science, literacy, and mathematics. Similarly, centres can be established for geography or world issues, which should be devoted exclusively to fostering global awareness among students. Teachers can also create centres that support knowledge about indigenous people. Also, a rest or relaxation area would be where students could take a voluntary time out, particularly if it is deserved. Another empowering but often ignored strategy is the creation of prayer centres within the classrooms. While this potentially controversial (and requires permission from either the school administration or board), it is however important in contexts of student diversity because it provides a space where students of various religions can actually sit quietly and pray.

COMBATING PREJUDICE AND DISCRIMINATION

One of the most important responsibilities Canadian teachers have is fostering *prejudice reduction* in their classrooms, schools, and society. In schools, there is compelling evidence that prejudice is prevalent among school-aged children. For example in British Columbia, one survey of student opinion regarding racism found that minority students still experience racism in Canadian schools (Moodley, 1999). Some of the participating students spoke of "routine racist slurs in school corridor, classrooms and on the sports ground". The students also spoke of "Graffiti in gyms, on playground walls and toilet doors [that] sometimes include swastikas" (p. 145). Ryan (2003) in his study (see Chapter 5), confirms this pattern of racism. Unfortunately, the latter study also confirms that schools see these incidents of racism and prejudice as personality clashes, and therefore, do not give them the attention they deserve.

It is important for teachers to understand that prejudice reduction is not an activity that can be performed once and for all. It should be integrated across the curriculum in all subject areas, and teachers must constantly be on the lookout for real-time opportunities to teach it. One of the most important values for reducing prejudice in the classroom is respect. First, students must be taught how to respect one another: to accept one another along with the differences that exist among members of the classroom community, and implicitly everyone in wider society. This means that teachers must infuse their instruction with strategies that demonstrate mutual interpersonal and intercultural respect. Teachers must always show intolerance for derogatory language, put-downs, name-calling, harassment, and all such language that can become conflict triggers or result in the disempowerment of any students. Teachers must deal with this decisively and immediately, and show students that is it not permissible in their classrooms. Of course, this would all have to be done under the mandate of the school, with which teachers should be very familiar.

Banks (1999) provides several guidelines for reducing prejudice among students. First, he argues that teachers should include positive and realistic images of ethnic and racial groups in teaching materials in a consistent, natural, and integrated manner. Second, teachers should help children to differentiate the faces of members of different racial and ethnic groups. According to Banks, the best way to do this is to infuse curriculum materials with the different faces of members of different groups in society. Third, Banks argues that it is important to use resources such as films, videos, children's books, recordings, photographs, and other kinds of vicarious experiences to expose children to members of different racial and ethnic groups. Fourth, teachers should provide positive verbal and non-verbal reinforcement for the colour brown, which is generally portrayed in unflattering ways in Western societies. Five, children from different racial and ethnic groups should be involved in cooperative learning activities. Finally, students should be taught the consequences of prejudice in authentic ways.

Teaching about the unfortunate consequences of prejudice is best done in a vicarious way (Banks, 1999). One well known (albeit controversial) example of this kind of strategy is Jane Elliott's *Blue Eyes/Brown Eyes* approach to teaching about prejudice and discrimination. Elliott first used this approach in 1968 to teach her third and fourth grade students in Iowa about racism and racial inequality during the peak of the civil rights movement in the United States. In brief, this approach is based on categorizing two groups of students into hypothetically representative groups of blue- and brown-eyed people. During the first run, blue-eyed people are defined as smarter, quicker, and more likely to succeed, while brown-eyed people are defined as inferior to blue-eyed people. When she first tried this approach, Elliott gave blue-eyed group members extra privileges compared to their brown-eyed peers. To her amazement the blue-eyed group began to perform better than the brown-eyed students, even those who had done quite well in the past. A few days later, she reversed the roles and told her students that she had been wrong and that the brown-eyed students were the superior group, while members of the blue-eyed group were inferior. The situation quickly reversed itself and the brown-eyed students became much more alert than the blue-eyed students. Two important lessons emerge from Elliott's experiment. First, perceptions of discrimination and prejudice can affect people negatively. Second, prejudice and stereotyping are learned attitudes, and they can be unlearned. But more importantly, and more significant to this work, Jane Elliott has adapted her approach to the Canadian context.

In the Canadian edition, titled *Indecently Exposed* (2005), Elliott addresses Canada's unfair and unjust treatment of its First Nations peoples. Although it took some doing, the exercise helped some participants to re-evaluate and re-examine their attitudes and behaviours, and more generally, their beliefs about Canada's First Nations peoples and minorities groups. Even though this exercise was done with a group of volunteers that were fully aware of the controlled conditions of the exercise, they were nonetheless, quite overwhelmed in terms of the emotions and feelings the exercise generated. Ultimately, Jane Elliott's blue eyes/brown eyes exercise is a teachable moment at its most poignant. However, it should be emphasized that because of the potential for unfavourable reaction to this exercise by students and their parents, it is critical for teachers to first obtain the necessary permission from parents and school administration.

At a more advanced level, teachers can problematize the issue of bias and discrimination in society by asking students to read some carefully selected texts that enable them to vicariously experience prejudice. These books should include stereotypes of certain members of Canadian society. They could also be books that reflect omission — what the texts do not say about some groups of people — or that demean people on the basis of race or ethnicity. They could also be books that reflect uneven distribution of power in society such as the power imbalance between men and women in society. The goal of this kind of exercise is to give students the opportunity to deconstruct the texts (using the template in Chapter 5) and identify what makes them problematic. One extremely useful but often ignored prejudice reduction strategy is *teachable moments*.

TEACHABLE MOMENTS

One way of combating prejudice at the micro-level of the school and classroom is through teachable moments. Teachable moments are incidents that occur in classrooms that although negative in nature can be used as opportunities to teach appropriate behaviour in the area of diversity.

Vignette #1

A student of East Indian origin was chatting with a White student in a grade 5 classroom at a Catholic school. As the discussion progressed the students began to talk about their various homes, cultural practices, parents, siblings, favourite foods, etc. Their teacher, Mr. Clark, could not help overhearing the conversation. Even though the students were supposed to be engaged in a group task, he always enjoyed this type of interchange among students because it helps to build a classroom community. But, just as he was about to interrupt the conversation, the White student asked a question that stopped him in his tracks: "Why do Indians always wrap their heads in towels?" He was referring to turbans, an important symbol for many religious groups in Asia. From the silence that suddenly descended in the class, it was clear that the other students heard the question and were waiting for the response. Seeing that the East Indian student was somewhat flustered by the question, Mr. Clark redirected their attention back to the task at hand, and then moved on to examine the work of another group of students. He vaguely remembered that this East Indian student had previously complained to him that he was being teased about how his people dressed.

Commentary

This vignette is a classic case of cultural misunderstanding that deals with religion. It also pertains to ignorance. Clearly, regardless of what the White student may have had in mind, in this particular case the question appears to be the result of curiosity rather than prejudice. Prejudice would have been a compelling reason for the teacher to address, instead of avoid, the issue. Still, Mr. Clark should have seized the opportunity to explain the reason why people of various cultures and religions wear turbans. Unfortunately as a result of his avoidance, the White student and his peers may continue to hold whatever misconceptions they have about turbans, which may in turn lead to conflicts outside the purview of the teacher. Beyond providing an immediate response to the question, Mr. Clark could also have extended this teachable moment to various subject areas. For instance, the issue could have become the theme of a project on religious symbols and what they represent to people in different parts of the world. It would also be a good topic for a research project on the various religions that exist in Canada, besides Catholicism.

What else should Mr. Clark have done? He should also have used the opportunity to teach about the importance of respecting other peoples' religion, as well as the fact that every religion in Canada — Christianity, Catholicism, Judaism, Hinduism, Islam — has its representative symbols. His failure to tackle the issue head-on exemplifies how schools tacitly perpetuate prejudice and discrimination in society.

Vignette #2

Mrs. Cook is an active participant in her children's education. She always volunteered in her children's school despite her busy schedule as a mother who works both in and outside of the home. Her husband had recently changed jobs necessitating a move to a new city. Moving from a relatively homogenous small town to a city with a population of about 300 000 had been overwhelming at first. She had however, overcome her initial shock, with one exception: the diversity of the student body in her children's new school. Her daughter Susie's class was particularly diverse with children from a wide range of socio-demographic backgrounds. Notably, many children seemed to come from economically depressed homes. Susie had in fact confided that there were some who did not bring lunches to school so other students had to share. Since hearing this bit of news, Mrs. Cook had made it her duty to pack more lunch than Susie really needed. On this particular day, she was in the classroom as a volunteer during a science lesson on the advantages and challenges of computers. An interesting discussion was going on, and several students shared their views on the topic. One student opined that using computers can be more fun for some than others. Another student commented that his mother hated computers and always asked for his help. In response Susie volunteered the following: "My dad says that the Asian people in his office are very good with computers and the White people don't seem to know how to turn them on." The silence that followed was palpable, as Mrs. Cook and Mrs. Samuel, the teacher, stared at each other aghast. After what seemed like an eternity, Mrs. Samuel continued the discussion without any reference to what had just transpired.

Commentary

This was of course a missed opportunity. To begin with, Mrs. Samuel should have used Susie's comment as a foundation for a discussion on avoiding stereotyping people. It was also an unplanned opportunity to teach about multiple intelligences and the diversity of human strengths and skills. She could have pointed out that while people have different skills and capabilities, everybody is capable of learning how to use computers and technology. She could also have emphasized that Mr. Cook's office was only one context, and that it is not appropriate to generalize or make sweeping claims about a group of people, even if such views are positive.

Vignette #3

It was the middle of December. Mrs. Bandi's grade 6 class was busy preparing for the annual Christmas assembly. Most of the students in the school looked forward to this day all year and Mrs. Bandi's class was no exception. This year, grade 6 had spent a lot of time practising a musical routine they planned to unveil to the entire school during the assembly. Everyone was involved in one way or another except Jeremy. Sitting in a corner of the classroom, he was completely detached and oblivious to the excitement. When one of his fellow students asked him why he was not participating in the activities, Jeremy replied that his family did not celebrate Christmas to which another screamed, "Then you and your family will rot in hell!" Mrs. Bandi and everyone else in the class heard the comment. She was of course aware of the situation with Jeremy. Horrified, she started to speak but thought the better of it.

Commentary

Variations of this vignette are used to teach about religious diversity and tolerance in Canada, and it is a powerful hypothetical example. What a missed opportunity! This teachable moment could have been used to teach several values, including respect for others' beliefs and choices, self-restraint, and the relevant aspects of Canada's *Charter Rights and Freedoms* with (which every teacher should be conversant). For example, the provisions of Sections 2 and 15 of the *Charter*, which deal with fundamental freedoms and equality rights respectively, implicitly provide the right for students who do not wish to participate in religious activities to be excused. Similarly, the education statutes of many provinces also reaffirm such rights. Furthermore, religion in publicly funded schools has become an integral part of the debate about diversity (see Chapter 3). That is why many schools, based on community pressures, are trying to accommodate diversity, either by making Christian celebrations more secular or by providing secluded spaces for prayers during the school day. In this particular case, Mrs. Bandi could have avoided Jeremy's exclusion by designing a creative role that would have enabled him to participate in the activities in ways that did not infringe on his religious beliefs.

Vignette #4

Mrs. Ada liked giving her students group activities and tasks, and for the most part her students appeared to enjoy working together. Besides working collaboratively on an assignment, it gave everyone an opportunity to interact and talk with their peers. However, despite the popularity of group learning in the class, one student, Pascal, always appeared withdrawn and unhappy during group tasks. Usually, he simply observed the others at work, to the annoyance of his peers. Mrs. Ada had a conference with him but to no avail. She had eventually dismissed Pascal's unhappiness in group activities as a temporary problem that would eventually go away. Unfortunately, it was already the middle of the year and Pascal was as withdrawn as when the school year began. Things came to a head when a group of students refused to work with him on an in-class science project. Mrs. Ada simply moved Pascal to another group. This became a pattern whenever the class was assigned collaborative work.

Commentary

The problem in this vignette is somewhat different from the issues in the preceding vignettes. The problem is what Pascal failed to do, rather than what he did, making this a case of self-imposed exclusion. Notwithstanding that, Mrs. Ada should have worked harder to determine what the problems were. For instance, if she had conferred with Pascal's parents, she would have understood that in Pascal's culture, children value individual work more than collective work. She subsequently could have found a different way to engage Pascal, rather than always assigning him to groups. She also could have found creative ways of helping him ease into working collaboratively with his peers. One of the cooperating learning strategies TAI (above) could have been a potential solution the problem. Perhaps even more importantly, she should have used the opportunity to teach students about tolerance and acceptance.

Vignette #5

The scene is a grade 1 classroom. The students had just come in from recess and were still chatting while preparing to settle down. Amanda was happily describing, to anyone who would listen, her birthday party over the past weekend. As she talked, she passed around pictures from the party. When one of the two Black students stretched out her hand to take the pictures, Amanda stared at her hands and withheld the pictures, stating that her mother had told her that anyone looking at the pictures must have clean hands. Not understanding that Amanda was referring to her brown skin, the Black student innocently responded "But my hands are clean." Amanda, still staring at the girl's hands, simply replied "Oh, okay". Coincidentally, the teacher had watched this scene unfold, but chose to ignore it for fear that the children were too young to tackle such issues.

Commentary

Admittedly, this is one of those difficult moments that teachers dread, but in diverse contexts they must deal with them, because the case deals with skin colour and implicitly, race.

Very often, teachers have difficulty discussing issues surrounding race, particularly at the lower grades. Nieto (2004: 45) underscores this tendency towards institutionally sanctioned silence about difference in school: "[m]any times, unintentional discrimination is practiced by well-meaning teachers who fear that talking about race will only exacerbate the problem. As a consequence, most schools are characterized by a curious absence of talk about difference especially about race". Unfortunately, silence only aggravates the problem. Thus, rather than ignoring the incident, the teacher should have taken advantage of the moment to explain to her young impressionable students why people have different skin colours. It was therefore an opportunity to engage in a discussion about diversity among people (i.e., people have different skin colour just as they differ in height, size, hair colour, etc.). But most importantly, it was an opportunity for the teacher to explain that brown or dark skin should not be equated with "uncleanliness". Another important question that the vignette highlights is "When should teachers discuss such issues with students?" There is no consensus as to when to begin, but most scholars and practitioners agree that deciding when can be challenging. This is because students at the primary level do not yet have the intellectual capacity to process the complexities inherent in diversity issues, especially when it relates to race. That being said, teachers who teach young children must engage this issue as well as teach for diversity. However, such discussions must be couched in age-appropriate language.

Vignette #6

The scene is a grade 11 history class. A discussion began on the impact of Canadian government treaties with First Nations peoples on their social positioning within Canadian polity. Under the full view of the teacher, the discussion soon turned into a heated debate between three White students and the two First Nations students in the class, and both groups had dominated the discussion up to that point. This turned into an outright argument when one of the White students expressed his lack of respect for Aboriginal Canadians (using stereotypical racist language that trivialized their historical and present struggles for empowerment and self-determination). Visibly hurt and upset, the First Nations students, and a majority of their peers, challenged the insensitive comments of the White student. What followed was a shouting match that degenerated into racial slurs and insults. Concerned about everyone's safety, the teacher attempted to diffuse the situation with threats of detention, but without much success. He subsequently ordered all involved to the principal's office and continued with the lesson. At the principal's office, the First Nations' students defended their reaction and indicted the teacher for his failure to challenge and "set the White students straight".

Commentary

This is another example of an opportunity lost. To begin with, the teacher could have chastised the White students for making outright racist comments in class. One wonders about the kind of classroom culture that enabled the students to express their disrespect for First Nations peoples so blatantly. The teacher could also have used the students' comments to ease into a brief discussion of positive race relations and respect and tolerance, as well as the dangers of stereotyping people. This could have been followed with a brief lesson in history, reminding everyone of the contribution of Canada's First Nations peoples to the development of the nation.

While the teacher attempted to intervene, he failed to do so in a timely manner, and was silent on the root cause of the conflict. The teacher had an excellent (albeit unplanned) opportunity to turn an unfortunate incident into a valuable teaching tool, and so an insightful learning experience for all the class, but he did not take advantage of it. It was also a chance to model dialogical communication, in which students are reminded of the value of critical and sensitive use of language at all times, but especially in pluralistic contexts.

MODELLING BEHAVIOUR

An essential part of prejudice reduction is modelling. Just as children learn by observing the behaviour of their parents so too do students learn from their teachers' behaviours and attitudes. In fact, research has demonstrated that students learn and behave better when teachers model the kind of behaviour they expect from their students. For example, when teachers model self-respect, equity, fairness, democracy, collaboration, students are likely to embrace these values, which in turn lead to mutual respect and acceptance among students. Conversely, teachers who are prone to making derogatory remarks about some groups in society are modelling behaviour that sustains prejudice, stereotyping, and discrimination. Modelling behaviour not only involves overt actions, it also includes non-verbal behaviours, which contain cryptic, unintended messages that students notice all the same. For instance, teachers may tacitly model prejudice by condoning sexist, homophobic, or racist comments in their classrooms.

TEACHING SOCIAL JUSTICE

One of the most important things teachers can do to reduce prejudice is to teach students about social justice as early as possible. Even in the primary grades, it is quite possible to teach students about social justice, equity, and fairness in ways that introduce them to salient social issues. This also begins to prepare them for citizenship, activism, or for future advocacy for justice in Canadian society. Educators can achieve these goals by highlighting related principles whenever there's opportunity to do so — more than half the time during the course of a school day. For instance, language arts lessons, group reading sessions (i.e., the choice of books and stories), social studies, and even the sciences lend themselves quite well to teaching social justice. Similarly, lessons on the environment present unique opportunities for teaching environmental literacy and the injustices associated with environmental exploitation, particularly when it affects poor and less powerful people in society. Peterson (1994) describes one of the various strategies he uses to teach social justice in his elementary classroom:

> The underlying theme in my classroom is that the quest for social justice is a never-ending struggle. . . . I weave the various disciplines around the theme. When I read poetry and literature to the children, I often use books that raise issues about social justice and, when possible, in which the protagonists are young people working for social justice. In math, we look at everything from the distribution of wealth in the world, to the percentage of women in different occupations. The class songs and posters of the week also emphasize social struggles from around the world. . . . In addition to studying movements for social justice of the past, students discuss current problems and possible solutions (p. 37).

The overarching aims of teaching social justice are to make the classroom a community of learners, and to make it a community where students are taught progressive social values that are cognizant of Canada's diverse heritage. In other words, students are taught how respect, to appreciate people, and to value diversity in self and others (summarizing Sheets (2005), see Table 6.5). After all, schools are exceptional locales for providing students with opportunities to examine their responsibilities to one another in ways that enable them to live in a cohesive society. By learning the principles of social justice, students will come to understand the injustices inherent in hierarchical social arrangements, in which a certain few people are at the top, while many others are at the bottom.

Social justice must not be relegated to a once-in-a-while ritual that teachers feel compelled to address. It should be infused throughout their daily instructional routines. Most importantly, teachers should attempt to get some type of feedback, and so engage students in discussion. The more advanced the grade level, the easier it is for teachers to engage students in issues related to social justice. For instance, it is easier for teachers to engage in dialogue with high-school students on strategies for redressing injustices perpetuated

TABLE 6.5	Respecting and Valuing Diversity in Self and Others

- Develop lessons and use instructional resources to help students realize that even when members of a group (including groups in which they have membership), appear to be the same, there are distinct differences between the individuals of any group. At any given age, girls and boys are not at the same level of intellectual, social, and sexual maturity. People with ability differences enjoy diverse leisure activities.
- Structure activities that encourage dualistic thinkers to practise complex, higher-level thinking, and to consider multiple solutions and perspectives. Teach students how to analyze, evaluate, compare, contrast, and justify ideas on diversity issues. Ask students to use supporting data to explain and defend their points of views.
- Discuss differences and similarities in students' home traditions, routines, and rituals. Describe how birthday and religious celebrations, food, music, entertainment, sports, and art preferences, and relationships with relatives and significant others differ. Examine how the ways people express joy, sorrow, and loss vary and how they are influenced by cultural practices.
- Provide multiple opportunities for students to group heterogeneously in organized classroom activities. Encourage peer relationships that differ by gender, popularity, religious orientation, ability, ethnicity, and economic status in order to provide the broadest cross-section of social encounters.
- Involve children in age-appropriate decision making about classroom activities and rules, so they can see themselves and their actions as critical components of their school life.
- Reinforce the concept that differences contribute to the richness of the classroom community. Discuss how differing opinions help us think about the same idea in new ways. Show how creative problem solving gives us more options from which to choose. Demonstrate how the ways different students find to present knowledge of the same assignment give us more perspectives to examine.
- Watch for stereotypical images in classroom lessons, resources, and decorations. Acquire the skills needed to create, evaluate, and adapt curricular content and instruction in ways that accommodate and benefit culturally diverse students.
- Adapt community resources such as local tourism posters and postcards, cultural products, and public library materials so that students make connections from school to home to community.

Source: Adapted from Sheets, Rose Hernandez. (2005). *Diversity Pedagogy: Examining the Role of Culture in the Teaching-Learning Process*, pp. 46–47. Published by Allyn & Bacon, Boston, MA, Copyright © 2005 by Pearson Education. Adapted by permission of the publisher.

against segments of Canadian society (on the basis of race, social class, gender, sexual orientation, religion, etc.), because they have the intellectual capacity and experience to engage the topic. Finally since, as argued throughout this work, schools are implicated in systemic oppression and social injustice, it is logical that schools should take the lead in making Canada a discrimination- and prejudice-free society.

Summary

Despite increasing diversity in Canadian schools, many teachers continue to organize their routines and manage their classrooms in conventional ways that ignore the reality of contemporary classrooms. Guided by the overarching question "How can teachers engage all learners in diverse contexts?", the chapter focused on providing practical instructional and classroom strategies to enrich the schooling experiences of all students, especially those that have been marginalized. The major position of the chapter is that to make a difference in the lives of their students, teachers must create alternative visions of their classrooms. These visions must go beyond the traditional views that are incongruent with recent demographic trends in Canadian society. Moreover, in creating a community of learners, teachers must draw on the diverse experiences and perspectives of students to critically engage them in the teaching and learning process.

Although only conceptually discrete, the first part of the chapter examined empowering pedagogical strategies from a sequential perspective: the pre-instructional, the instructional, and the post-instructional stages. Each stage highlights corresponding teacher activities that can enhance schooling experiences for all students. The second part of the chapter explored effective assessment and classroom management strategies in contexts of student diversity, the main thrust being that disciplinary and assessment strategies must be developed in ways that are fair and socially just. Since prejudice reduction is a critical aspect of teaching for empowerment in multicultural and multilingual contexts, strategies for reducing prejudice, as well as for teaching social justice to students at any level, were also discussed. To emphasize the argument in the chapter, hypothetical vignettes that simulate potential conflict situations in diverse contexts were also discussed. Collectively, these teachable moments, or unplanned opportunities, that present themselves in class should be seen by teachers as valuable tools for exploring diversity-related issues in heterogeneous classrooms.

Key terms

Assessment	Differentiated instruction	Instructional activities
Post-instructional analysis	Pre-instructional activities	Prejudice reduction
		Teachable moments

Questions to Guide Reflective Practice

1. Critics of standardized tests argue that they are biased against certain groups of students. What are your views of the current wave of high-stakes testing that is sweeping across Canada?

2. Do you share the view that if not dealt with effectively, cultural differences can be conflict triggers in the classroom?

3. Other than the ideas that are advanced in the chapter, suggest ways of making Canadian classrooms more welcoming for students from diverse backgrounds.

4. To what extent should schools be involved in teaching students about tolerance in Canadian society?

Case Study Analysis: Chapter Opening Vignette

1. Assume that you are the principal of Cascadia Secondary School. How would you address this potentially explosive situation?

2. To what extent should the school administration be held accountable for the problems facing the new students?

3. To what extent should the teachers be held accountable for the problem?

4. To what extent do you think that the refugee students' exclusion is self-imposed?

5. Besides the obvious problem of intercultural misunderstanding, what other issues are involved in this vignette? Justify your answer.

6. Discuss this vignette with a group of your peers. Is there consensus in your opinions of the issues addressed in the vignette?

7. Identify the role that both groups of parents can play in resolving the problem.

Test Your Knowledge

1. If you have never taken one, arrange to take an IQ test. How well did you perform? Do you think the test is culturally biased?

2. Does your province require students to take any form of standardized test? At what grade levels are these tests administered? What are students' success rates in the tests?

3. If you are not one yourself, interview several teachers or prospective teachers you know. What are their perceptions of standardized tests and your province's student assessment policies?

4. Do school boards in your province have a formal policy of teaching students prejudice reduction?

5. Using the discussion in this chapter as a foundation, develop a plan for making diverse classrooms into communities of learners.

6. There are other cooperative learning strategies besides those discussed in this chapter. Research and identify at least three other approaches. Can these be used in diverse contexts?

For Further Reading

Anyon, J. (2005). *Radical possibilities: Public Policy, Urban Education and a New Social Movement*. New York: Routeledge.

Gillburn, D. (2004). Ability, Selection, and Institutional Racism in Schools. In M. Olssen (Ed.), *Culture and Learning: Access and Opportunity in the Classroom* (pp. 279–298). Charlotte: Information Age Publishing Inc.

Grant, C., and Sleeter, C. (2007). *Turning on Learning: Five Approaches for Multicultural Teaching Plans for Race, Class, Gender and Disability,* 4th Ed. Hoboken: John Wiley Sons.

Gronlund, N., and Cameron, I. (2004). *Assessment of Student Achievement.* Toronto: Pearson Education.

hooks, bell. (2003). *Teaching Community: Pedagogy of Hope.* New York: Routledge.

Sheets, R. (2005). *Diversity Pedagogy: Examining the Role of Culture in the Teaching-Learning Process.* Boston: Pearson Education.

Slavin, R. (1983). *Cooperative Learning.* New York: Longman.

Websites of Interest

www.canteach.ca Online Resources for Educators with a Focus on Canada

www.collectionscanada.ca/multicultural Multicultural Resources and Services (for Educators)

www. diversitylearning.ca Resources on Diversity Learning (Lesson Plans and Learning Activities)

www.metisresourcecentre.mb.ca Métis Resource Centre of Manitoba

www.bullying.org Website on Bullying

www.cyberbullying.ca Website on Cyberbullying

www.albertaassociationformulticulturaleducation.ca Alberta Association for Multicultural Education

CHAPTER 7

Policy and Training Issues

- ❏ Why Develop Just Educational Policies?
- ❏ Progressive Social and Educational Policies
- ❏ Social Policies Affecting Diversity
- ❏ Training Teachers
- ❏ Leadership Matters
- ❏ School Board Action

VIGNETTE

It was the school district's year end educators' conference and workshop — an annual forum that provides teachers and administrators an opportunity to engage in constructive interchange about important issues. The issues usually range from specific problems in individual schools to noteworthy district events and achievements during the course of the year. For the most part, both groups tend to agree on the issues, except when it is particularly contentious. This year's focus issue involves how to deal with increasing student diversity. Opinions diverged into two predominant views — those who see schools as sites for ameliorating social conditions through progressive educational policies, and those who see the role of the school as teaching standardized core knowledge. During lunch on the second day, a group of teachers and principals were discussing and sharing ideas. The conversation soon turned to the problems that some Aboriginal children, from a nearby reserve,

were experiencing in school. One principal from a school with a significant number of First Nations students expressed his dilemma: How much should teachers in his school integrate the students' culture and worldviews into the provincially mandated curriculum? No clear consensus emerged. Another principal declared that he felt compelled to encourage his teachers to adopt the board's policy of integrating student cultures "as much as possible", while a teacher argued that there were no minority students in her class, and so she did not consider it necessary to address diversity issues at all. Others urged the principal to follow the board's policies even though most acknowledged that these were quite vague. Another group felt that the principal should, following due consultation with his superintendent, initiate some contextualized solutions. The debate progressed with no resolution in sight, when it suddenly dawned on one of the teachers that the problem was the imprecise nature of the province's policies, which made it almost impossible to implement mandated guidelines in any meaningful way. Moreover, the central office would need to revise its policy in order to give teachers a clearer mandate for making their classrooms inclusive. Even more problematic, diversity policies seemed to vary significantly from one board to another: Based on discussions she has had with teachers in other districts, the problem was not just localized. She thought it was time for the provincial government to develop a comprehensive diversity policy for schools.

INTRODUCTION: POLICY MATTERS

The above vignette reflects a common theme in discussions among educators about public and educational *policy* in Canada. Quite often, policies and the various education statutes adopted by the provinces lack clarity and precision, and so, are subject to a wide range of interpretations. Few would query the assertion that ideally educators should have substantive professional autonomy as they carry out their responsibilities. Also, it is logical that as long as standard policies and guidelines to regulate education are developed, they should be precise, clear, and accessible to the target group. The previous chapter examined some specific activities and practices that educators ought to adopt to provide meaningful instructional experiences to their diverse students. This chapter focuses on policy issues as integral aspects of any broad agenda for supporting diversity in schools. It also examines the role of administrators and school boards. As argued in the preceding chapters, teachers' conception and understanding of diversity issues are critical to initiating transformative praxis in schools, but such awareness should begin during their professional training. Consequently, this chapter also explores issues surrounding preservice training.

It is important to understand the concept of policy, at least at a cursory level, but defining policy can be daunting as there are competing definitions. Sorting through the various conceptualizations, Delaney (2002) identifies core elements of a policy that are relevant to this volume, and to this chapter in particular. A policy can be viewed as a formulated act that is based on achieving a set objective which is sanctioned by an institutional body or authority. Thus, a policy that is aimed at supporting diversity in schools should be an officially initiated and institutionally sanctioned mandate. It should provide a framework by which educators can be held accountable for their actions while they promote diversity. In short, policy is a document that serves as a blueprint for practice. In particular, educational policies serve as guides for how education is organized, including what happens in the classroom. Underscoring the importance and power of educational policies, Young, Levin, and Wallin (2007) contend that

> policies shape the structure of schools, the resources that are available in schools, the curriculum, the teaching staff, and, to a considerable extent, the round of daily activities. Policies determine how much money is spent, by whom and on what, how teachers are paid, how students are evaluated, and most other aspects of schools as we know them (p. 68).

In effect, policies determine who teaches, what is taught, and where and how it is taught. In the complex policy environment that educators must navigate, clear guidelines make the adoption and implementation of policies much more feasible.

One major problem with policies is that the relationship between a policy mandate and its adoption is not linear, since formulating a policy does not guarantee its adoption — at least not in the way it was intended. For example, many teachers tend to support progressive educational policies in principle, but fail to adopt them in practice. Moreover, as the discussion in the opening vignette demonstrates, when policies are not precise they can be subject to different interpretations and thus, disparate implementations. So what influences the adoption and efficacy of a policy?

Bascia (2001) has identified several policy variables which can affect individual pedagogical practices, as well as education more generally. The first variable is change. There is a natural tendency to attempt to solve societal problems through education, even though, paradoxically, reform initiatives contribute to the politicization of pedagogy, the curriculum, and the general direction of education. Like schools, educational policies are often assumed to be neutral and objective phenomena that place a premium on the interest of every student. The reality, however, is that policies are never value free, as power politics and ideology often permeate their enactment.

A second variable that shapes policy and practice is durability — the structural features of educational systems that persist over time, despite attempts at reform. Examples of enduring educational structures include standardized curricula, a leaning toward organizing schools using the bureaucratic ideologies of business, the sorting of students by age and ability, and importantly, the dominance of Eurocentric and White male ideologies in education. A third factor that can impact on educational policy is the inherent complexity in implementation because it is difficult to mandate what really matters to people (Bascia, 2001; Fullan, 1993). Ultimately, policy making is about change, and change is an incubator for conflict and power struggle between stakeholders. In his seminal work *Change Forces*, Fullan (1993) talks about the complexity and "messiness" of the change process. Change is even messier when a proposed policy challenges the status quo, such as the dominant group's notion of what counts as valid knowledge, or what constitutes progressive educational policies.

Provincial and school board policies tend to be quite vague about diversity and education — for the most part leaving micro-level practitioners the arduous task of making sense of it all. Given the increasing diversity in Canadian classrooms, school systems desperately need explicit and inclusive guidelines to help educators provide optimum educational experiences for all students.

WHY DEVELOP JUST EDUCATIONAL POLICIES?

There are various reasons why it is imperative to develop just social and educational policies in Canada and other pluralistic Western countries: These are *ideological*, *strategic and practical*, and *fundamental rights* reasons. It is important to point out that while these concepts are discussed separately here for conceptual clarity, they are in reality interconnected.

Ideological Reasons

Although the word ideology — a deep seated belief about the way the world works — often has a negative connotation, in this context it refers to an ideal situation: Canadians developing a collective orientation that values diversity enough to create policies to support it. These policies would lay the foundation for creating a just and equitable society. Canada prides itself as being a historically tolerant society, even though early social policies were grounded in assimilationist ideologies. Currently, Canada ostensibly adheres to diversity as a social policy, but (as argued throughout this book) the voices of some groups have been silenced as a consequence of unjust social policies. Unfortunately, this is incongruent with what Canada purports to stand for, and amounts to democratic (Henry and Tator, 2006), dysconscious (King, 1991), or subliminal (Fleras and Elliott, 2003) racism. In general these kinds of discriminatory ideologies and their related practices tend to exist just beneath the surface and are dysfunctional and destructive to the life chances of some groups in society. For example, some Canadians may profess egalitarianism and a commitment to diversity, but will oppose affirmative policies to empower minorities and other oppressed groups (Fleras and Elliott, 2003). These are the same people who invoke reverse discrimination in response to government initiatives designed to support diversity, such as employment equity.

Strategic and Practical Reasons

A second reason why it is necessary to develop fair social and educational policies is to safeguard the strategic and practical interests of subordinated groups, and Canadian society in general. For example, although the Government of Canada implemented the *Employment Equity Act* in 1985 (revised in 1995) as a way of diversifying the workforce, Statistics Canada data (2002) show that there is still an under-representation of visible minorities in the labour force. Similarly, Canadian women in general, and visible minority women in particular, have not enjoyed equitable distribution of resources within Canadian society (Bannerji, 2000). Enacting socially just policies would help remedy this imbalance. One of the goals of policy makers at all levels of the system should be ensuring that students whose interests have been poorly served by the educational system will remain in school. The importance of developing just and fair educational policies cannot be emphasized enough. In a 21st Century world that emphasizes human capital as an asset, it is a great waste of human potential to continue to support the kind of education that limits life chances, and by extension, students' ability to contribute to Canadian society to their fullest potential (Radwanski, 1987).

Fundamental Rights Reasons

Enacting just social and educational policies is also a matter of fundamental human rights which, as argued in Chapter 2, are entrenched in the Canadian *Charter of Rights and Freedoms* and in international conventions to which Canada is a signatory. Moreover, several sections of the *Charter*, and in particular section 15, include special provisos that legitimize special social programs for empowering groups that historically have been marginalized in Canadian society.

PROGRESSIVE SOCIAL AND EDUCATIONAL POLICIES

One thing that both implicitly and explicitly spans the discussions in this book is the need for a socially just society empowered through educational policies and practices. Many progressive writers have argued that the starting point for change must be to enact *just educational policies* that truly reflect the Canadian mosaic. Anything else would amount to a gross miscarriage of justice for those who are negatively impacted. So, what constitutes just educational policies?

For the purposes of this book, just educational policies are mandates that enfranchise those who have been excluded from equitable access to empowering education by structural, social, and political processes that are embedded in institutionally sanctioned practices. Moreover, to be considered as just and fair, an educational policy must meet several criteria. First, the policy must aim to empower all stakeholders who traditionally have been at the fringes of power in Canadian society. Second, it must be developed and implemented in ways that will make a tangible difference in the lives of its intended beneficiaries. Although not easily perceived by most people, policies often determine people's quality of life. Take for instance the case of people who live in poverty. Social policies often create or exacerbate conditions that sustain their position of marginality. We often fail to ask ourselves a fundamental question: "Why would people live in poor neighbourhoods such as the impoverished Toronto neighbourhood that McLaren (2007) describes (see Chapter 3)?" Why would people send their children to poor schools with limited resources? The answer is very straightforward — they have no choice. Given the choice, everyone would attend the best school, live in the best neighbourhood, and have a quality of life that is second to none. The reality is that the structural forces legitimized by policies act to maintain the status quo and the social class divide. Another example is language issues in Canada, as provincial policies often address the needs of language minority students in superficial and minimally effective ways (Corson, 2001; Duffy, 2003). A just language policy would protect the linguistic interests (including the speech patterns and discourse norms) of minority students. Without such policies, existing patterns of educational inequality will be reproduced over several generations of families from nondominant groups.

Third, for a policy to be considered socially just there must be evidence that the interests of those most in need have been carefully addressed during its planning and development and that all stakeholders have been duly consulted prior to implementation. As presented in Chapter 1, the principles of social justice require that in cases where people have been traditionally marginalized, their needs must be given greater consideration. An example of this principle at work can be seen in the federal government's employment equity policy, which is designed to eliminate discriminatory employment practices, as well as increase employment opportunities for designated groups in Canadian society. Another example of how unfair social policies affect education and life chances concerns First Nations peoples. Many northern communities of Aboriginal Canadians face tremendous difficulty when recruiting and retaining teachers. Despite attractive salaries, many do not remain for extended periods due to the deplorable social conditions in these communities. First Nations children, who unfortunately can least afford it, suffer the most from high attrition rates among teachers who are recruited to teach them. Indeed, as the United Nations has argued, Canada's relationship with its First Nations peoples is a dark shadow in its history and an excellent example of why public policies should be just and inclusive.

Overall, just educational policies include a conscientizing component that serves as foundation for enabling minority groups to question ideological orthodoxies that devalue their status. Reconstituting the lived experiences and historical and social positioning of Canada's peripheral groups requires informed agency, which as Freire (1970) suggests is a socially learned phenomenon that is significantly enhanced by the knowledge acquired through education.

SOCIAL POLICIES AFFECTING DIVERSITY

From a policy perspective, responses to diversity in Canada have been evolutionary. Chapter 1 outlines typical programmatic responses to diversity in Canadian schools. This section examines the various policy frameworks that influence Canadian diversity. Canada's policy response to diversity can be classified into three ideologically grounded phases, each marking a different historical epoch that is inextricably linked to immigration and the search for a Canadian identity. These are **assimilation**, **benevolent accommodation**, and **cultural pluralism**.

Assimilation as Social Policy

Assimilation, which is a one-way process of deliberate or unconscious absorption (Fleras and Elliott, 2003), was Canada's earliest diversity policy. However, assimilation is never une affaire classé, or completely accomplished. What emerged in Canada during the early years of its evolution as a nation-state was overt Anglo-conformity, in which Eurocentric ideologies prevailed over other worldviews. During this period, diversity policies were predominantly manifest in vigorous programs to assimilate the First Nations peoples and in racist immigration policies aimed at ensuring that Canada remained exclusively White. During this period, several immigration policies and orders-in-council were passed to exclude those who were considered racially, culturally, and physically unfit to become Canadians (see Chapter 2). Consistent with the social policy, educational policies were assimilationist and aimed to create an illusive "melting pot". Eventually, assimilation as a social policy lost its lustre as a guiding principle because "the social and political climate that once dismissed group differences as a liability to overcome through assimilation has given way to positive definitions of diversity as liberating and empowering" (Fleras and Elliott, 2003: 13). Canada's assimilationist policies lasted until the end of World War II, which ushered in new diversity policies.

Benevolent Accommodation as Social Policy

Post-war policies inadvertently contributed to the growth of Canadian diversity because they were benevolently accommodating, in that they were designed to accept some of the refugees and displaced people from the war. However, despite this benevolent turn, educational policies were still ideologically designed to assimilate and inculcate the spirit of patriotism and good citizenship (Joshee, 2004; Osborne, 1999). The civil rights movement in the United States in the 1960s prompted further change in immigration policies to include erstwhile excluded groups of immigrants. But most significantly, Quebec's Quiet Revolution ultimately led to the policy that made Canada a multicultural country within a bilingual framework. This finally gave supporters of diversity as social policy during the 1970s and 1980s, the formal and legal platform from which to advocate policies that promote Canadian diversity.

Pluralism as Social Policy

The adoption of the official policy of multiculturalism ushered in Canada's de jure identity as a pluralistic nation state. As a social policy, cultural pluralism has come to define what Canada stands for. Although once dismissed as untenable and divisive, it is now considered the most viable social policy within the Canadian polity. Cultural pluralism has evolved according to national and global exigencies. Chronologically speaking, two particular variations are relevant here: social justice and, as some would argue, **social cohesion**, which is the current trend (Joshee, 2004). Both policy perspectives are briefly discussed below.

Social Justice as Social Policy

The period between the late 1970s and the1990s was marked by attempts to consolidate Canada's image as a cultural mosaic. This mosaic was to be tolerant of its diverse groups and establish the policies and structural and social frameworks to support diversity. Thus, significant attention was devoted to developing policies that promoted social justice. Educationally, these policies were manifested in programs such as heritage language instruction and multicultural and anti-racist education programs (see Chapter 2). Moreover, many provincial ministries (or departments) of education adopted curriculum documents that were inclusive and reflected the emerging consensus of Canada as a diverse and multicultural society (Wright, 2000).

Social Cohesion as Social Policy

Currently, Canada's official diversity policy remains, in principle, the expansion of immigration quotas. However, unlike the previous two decades, official support from provincial governments for diversity seems to have waned, giving way to policies that are deliberately geared towards social cohesion (Joshee, 2004). Moreover, the increasing influence of neoconservative ideologies in the social, and by default the educational, arena has undermined much of the progress that was made during preceding decades (Joshee, 2004). Like many Western nations (and the world in general), Canada is facing the dilemma of balancing unity and diversity. The problem as Banks (2006: 152) formulates it is that "unity without diversity results in hegemony and oppression; diversity without unity leads to Balkanization and the fracturing of the nation-state". Banks argues that a major challenge facing many countries is how to juxtapose inclusive public policies (that integrate the voices and experiences of diverse groups) with the goal of creating a coalescing national identity. Collaterally, this same challenge is facing educational systems in Canada.

A current trend and potential solution to this problem, at least as it relates to education, is to emphasize policies satisfactory to everyone (Wright, 2000). For example in a document prepared by the Department of Canadian Heritage, one of the contributors posited that

> an emphasis on a culture of equal rights for all Canadians could be developed as the core of a new Canadianess. A patriotism based on the *Charter of Rights* would be more appealing than anti-racism, because it emphasizes the positive contributions towards justice to be made rather than negative behaviour to be penalized or ostracised. . . . (cited in Wright, 2000: p. 87).

Also, most curricular documents now focus on providing the basics with minimal attention to diversity issues. For example, in many provinces during the 1990s, policy makers made concerted effort to address issues of equity and social justice in the school curriculum. In particular, during its NDP government in the 1990s, the Ontario Ministry of Education paid extensive attention to issues of discrimination and inequity in schools. So much so, that in 1993, it became mandatory for every school to develop and implement policies that promoted ethno-cultural diversity, anti-racism, and equity.

However, the Conservative government that came into power in 1995 de-emphasized equity and diversity issues. Currently, curriculum documents barely make reference to such issues, nor is adequate attention paid to programs that support minority students (Corson 2001; Rezai-Rashti, 2003; Dei et al., 2000; Bascia, 2001). For example, reductions in government educational spending have resulted in reduced ESL programs in schools (Bascia, 2001). This was not previously the case, when even moderately proficient students had access to special ESL programs. Bascia (2001) describes the current status of ESL programs in some Ontario jurisdictions:

> In the schools we visited, the low status of ESL programs relative to the "regular" school curriculum was obvious. Even while administrators we spoke with expressed a personal commitment to ESL programming in their schools, its subordinate position was played out and reinforced by a variety of structural and normative factors. In the elementary schools this manifested in terms of the dominance of the prescribed curriculum and a lack of attention to linguistic and cultural diversity in "regular" classrooms. . . . The space allocated to ESL programs was inadequate and of poor quality. In the secondary school, ESL classes were assigned to particularly shabby rooms and portables some distance away from the main building (p. 258).

Duffy (2003) has expressed similar concerns about the status of ESL programs and the academic support that is provided to immigrant students across Canada. Duffy's warning, the consequence of his research work, underscores the potential social cost to all Canadians of neglecting programs that provide additional educational support to new immigrants. While more encouraging than Bascia's 2001 and Duffy's 2003 findings above, the results of another Canadian study that examined ESL students' academic and social support needs from their perspectives as well as those of their teachers in a south-western Ontario high school, also suggest the need for more funding and infrastructural support for ESL programs (Kruczek, 2007).

One of the instruments through which provincial governments influence education and diversity policies is the curriculum. Unfortunately, the curriculum is often presented as standardized knowledge, or as a collection of facts, which is separate from learners and the context in which learning takes place (Kincheloe, 2005). Moreover, this "universal" knowledge is transmitted to students with only minor change from time to time to accommodate new developments in various subject areas. Yet, as many theorists have argued, the curriculum is more than a course of study. It should encompass a more embracing view of student's experiences as individuals and the ways they relate to the world around them. Just educational policies require that such perspectives undergird curriculum policies in pluralistic societies such as Canada.

TRAINING TEACHERS

Chapter 4 argues that one of the reasons educators do not easily embrace progressive educational policies is their initial professional training. One area policy initiatives need to address therefore is teacher education programs. As diversity continues to be a permanent feature of Canadian classrooms, those who teach will have to learn ways of addressing the issue, not after the fact, but even before they begin to practise their profession. This means that during their tenure as preservice students, novice teachers must learn what it entails to teach in diverse contexts.

What kind of initial training do teachers require to prepare them to teach in diverse classrooms? Teacher education programs focus on subject area specialization and general teaching methodologies, but new teachers need to learn how to identify the hidden curriculum (see Chapter 4). Beginning with an interrogation of their own programs, as Cochran-Smith (2000) argues, teacher education programs should be deconstructed and read as "text" to uncover omissions and inclusions that are informed by hegemonic assumptions about minoritized groups, as well as other diversity-related issues:

> As text, teacher education is dynamic and complex — much more than a sequence of courses, a set of fieldwork experiences, or the readings and written assignments that are required for certification or credentialing purposes . . . [It] also means examining its subtexts, hidden texts, and intertexts — reading between the lines as well as reading under, behind, through and beyond them . . . scrutinizing what is absent from the main texts and what themes are central to them . . . (p. 167).

Novice teachers who are able to critique their own programs for hidden messages that foster oppression are more likely to be aware of and sensitive to the needs of their diverse students. Such understanding would inform the choices they make in their classrooms. However, studies have shown that teacher candidates are reluctant to embrace progressive educational ideologies. Why is this case?

Barriers to Teacher Candidate Adoption of Progressive Paradigms

There are several reasons why some teacher candidates are reluctant to embrace progressive views about diversity and education. First, preservice students tend to see social difference as a problem rather than a resource. This is significant because teacher worldviews and belief systems have a significant influence on their practice and how they treat their students. This basic assumption explains why many teacher education courses begin with helping students identify their personal and educational philosophies.

Second, they tend to equate cultural or racial difference with other types of difference such as intelligences, personality types, learning differences, etc. (Levine-Rasky, 1998). One must be careful not to minimize the importance of other kinds of difference, as these are integral to a holistic conceptualization of diversity (see Chapter 1). Differences involving race and culture do, however, require a different kind of knowledge-base, which teacher education programs may fail to provide (Solomon and Allen, 2001; Gay, 2000; Nieto, 2002; Milner, 2003).

Third, teacher candidates usually do not understand the language, culture, or particular circumstances of their diverse students, nor do they understand how some school-based problems and inequalities are historically, socially, and politically constructed. Prospective teachers need to be made aware that educators often become entangled (sometimes inadvertently) in political struggles that emanate from wider society, as various stakeholders compete for control of education and public knowledge. The everyday choices that teachers make are sometimes based on ideological tendencies towards hegemony in content, pedagogy, and student participation.

Fourth, like some practising teachers, many teacher candidates make the erroneous assumption that not all students can learn, and so attribute student underachievement exclusively to personal and family variables. Additionally, they tend to subscribe to ideologies that are difficult to change. As Levine-Rasky (1998) argues

> It is prevalent among prospective teachers to persist in interpreting social difference and inequality through the lens of meritocracy in which success is directly related to individual achievement and talent irrespective of environmental or broader social factors such as racial discrimination, poverty, unequal treatment in public institutions, language barriers and other patterns of oppression (pp. 90, 91).

Other research corroborate Levine-Rasky's assertion. For example, a study by Solomon et al. (2005) investigated teacher candidate perceptions and understanding of "Whiteness" and *White privilege* in Canadian society through a discourse analysis of student responses to Peggy McIntosh's (1990) article *White Privilege* (see Chapter 1). The study found that candidates from different racial and cultural backgrounds have different perceptions of oppression and White privilege. The researchers also found a tendency towards the denial of such privileges using various strategies: ideological incongruence, liberalist notions of individualism and meritocracy, and the negation of White capital.

Briefly, ideological incongruence is a discrepancy between beliefs and the actual reality of practicalizing those beliefs. Thus, while some teachers may believe in critical pedagogy, they have difficulty adopting and implementing its principles in practice.

The second strategy, liberalist notions of individualism and meritocracy, suggests that White teacher candidates tend to subscribe to the ideology that sees a linear correlation between hard work and educational success, to the neglect of other variables. Finally, the third strategy, the negation of White capital, indicates that teacher candidates tend to deny the "existence of white privilege and its attendant capital and material benefits" (Solomon et al., 2005, p. 157). Other scholars have drawn similar conclusions (e.g., Delpit, 2006; James, 2003; Dei et al., 2000). Based on an introspective analysis of his experiences as a White educator in the United States, Howard (2006) has this to say about White privilege:

> Reflecting back on [my] experience, I realize that members of the dominant group in any society do not necessarily have to know anything about these people who are not like them. For our survival and the carrying on of the day-to-day activities of our lives most Whites . . . do not have to engage in any meaningful connection with people who are different. This privileged isolation is not a luxury available to people who live outside of dominance and must, for their survival, understand the essential social nuances of those in power" (pp. 14–15).

To a certain extent, the denial of the possession of privilege and power helps members of the majority group to normalize dominance. According to social dominance theory, individuals normalize dominance through the social positionality syndrome to immunize themselves against collective guilt. Also, people see and interpret social phenomena through different lenses according to their social positioning. As proponents of social dominance theory state, how individuals view themselves, construct reality, and make meaning of their lives is usually connected to their position within the hierarchies of dominance and subordination. For example, many non-Aboriginal Canadians often absolve themselves of guilt that results from the unjust treatment of First Nations peoples by placing the blame on their ancestors — even though the same injustices persist. Most First Nations peoples would of course see things differently from their vantage point as the oppressed.

While the general literature on teacher education is replete with discussions of the lack of preparation of White teacher candidates for teaching in pluralistic contexts, as Nieto (2002) points out, teacher education programs must focus on preparing *all* students. While the experiences of visible minority teachers may help them to understand the concept of marginality, they do not automatically imbue in them the expertise to teach diverse students without the requisite training. Citing her own teaching experiences from elementary through university classrooms, Nieto (2002) relates that it is not unusual to see minority teachers treat students from their own communities in the same manner of which they are so critical when the perpetrator is from the dominant group. This is not to understate the importance of diversifying the teaching profession as discussed below. Rather, the point is that all teacher candidates (regardless of their background, gender, etc.), need intensive authentic cross-cultural and diversity training to prepare them to teach for diversity in Canadian classrooms.

Another important point is that a course on diversity is often conflict laden, as sensitive issues are deconstructed and reconstructed in an attempt to unmask social oppression and change the status quo. Nieto's (2002) description of a graduate course on multicultural education she taught provides a compelling example of what can happen in these courses:

> [A]lmost from the beginning there was conflict in the class room. The conflict was due not just to the resistance and anger of several white students but also to the feeling on the part of some students from culturally subordinated backgrounds that their particular difference should have precedence in our considerations of diversity. . . . After what for some had been years of trying to hide and downplay their diversity here is a place where differences were accepted and affirmed. . . . The class was permeated by rage and this rage sometimes translated into clamours for dominance. Many of the white students squirmed uneasily in their seats or exploded with exasperation whenever the topics of racism and institutional oppression came up (p. 237).

In the Canadian context, Solomon et al., (2005) have also described a similar experience in their work with teacher candidates who often exhibit discomfort when class discussions revolve around issues of oppression, domination, racism, marginalization, and colonialism.

Another factor that can make a difference to teacher candidates' understanding is field experience — factor, a significant part of their training. It is essential that teacher candidates, regardless of their future teaching plans, acquire some practical experience of teaching across race, gender, ethnicity, linguistic differences, etc. While all discussion of equity must begin at the theoretical level in teacher education, we must always remember that theory informs practice and vice versa. In the words of Entwistle (1996: 27), "The continuous process of interrogating our practice with theory and refining our theory in the crucible of practice, is the condition of our growth as both theorists and practitioners".

What should teacher candidates know to be able to teach a diverse student population? The simple answer is, of course, everything that is discussed in this volume. However, for the purposes of this chapter, scholars have identified several broad competency areas on which teacher education programs should focus (Bennett, 2007; Gay, 2000; hooks, 2003; Ladson-Billings, 1994; Levine-Rasky, 1998; Milner, 2003; Villegas and Lucas, 2002, etc.). These issues include interrogating forms of institutional racism and discrimination, teacher candidate expectations about student achievement, developing critical affirming and inclusive perspectives on the curriculum, and critical pedagogical strategies (see Chapter 4). Also, teacher candidates require in-depth knowledge of student assessment in diverse contexts, as well as student- and parent-teacher collaboration. In sum, teacher education programs should be reconceptualized to provide novice teachers with opportunity for substantive engagement with social justice issues and diversity-oriented pedagogy. Described variously as diversity pedagogy (Sheets, 2005), culturally responsive teaching (Gay, 2000; Villegas and Lucas, 2002), and culturally relevant pedagogy (Ladson-Billings, 1994), diversity-oriented pedagogy involves all the practices teachers adopt to enable diverse students to become academically and socially successful. Gay (2000: 44) summarizes the constituents of diversity-oriented pedagogy (or culturally responsive teaching): "culturally responsive pedagogy validates, facilitates, liberates, and empowers ethnically diverse students by simultaneously cultivating their cultural integrity, individual abilities, and academic success. It is anchored on four foundational pillars of practice". These pillars of practice are teacher attitudes and expectations, effective cross-cultural communication, the infusion of diverse cultural content into the curriculum, and critical pedagogy.

Teachers who embrace diversity-oriented pedagogy are agents of change, and thus able to make a profound difference in the lives of their students. As Villegas and Lucas (2002) assert, teachers who are agents of change believe that their role transcends technical expertise

TABLE 7.1	A Critically Reflective Chart about Race for Preservice Teachers	
	Critical Question	**Reflective Purposes and Significance**
1	How will my race influence my work as a teacher with students of colour?	This question challenges preservice teachers to reflect on the privileges and/or the lack thereof that have enabled their work and/or hindered it based solely on race. In this way, teachers come to understand past experiences and

TABLE 7.1	*(Continued)*

		instances that they are able to directly link to race in pursuit of consciousness and competence.
2	How will my students of colour's race influence my role and work as the teacher?	This question requires preservice teachers to reflect on the way students might perceive them as the teacher whose race may or may not be different to theirs. Teachers may start to become more sensitive to the issues that students have (not guessing or speculating per se) but becoming cognizant of the fact that they may need to be sensitive to differences that are consequences of race.
3	What is the impact of race on my beliefs? (Teacher educators should explore more specific questions relative to this central question.)	This question requires preservice teachers to reflect about the issues that may have been hidden previously. Consequently, these issues may become more overt through their deliberation, and teachers may be brought to realities that allow them to either deal with them by changing themselves or not (decision making).
4	How do I, as a teacher, situate myself in the education of others, and how do I negotiate the power structure in my class to allow students to feel a sense of worth?	With these questions come awareness that guides the manner in which preservice teachers think about planning lessons and enacting them for students. Pre-service teachers may decide that, considering their personal race and that of their students, a different approach is best suited. In addition, these questions challenge preservice teachers to negotiate the power structure in the learning environment.
5	What may be the issues most important to my students and me? What may be the nature of race on these issues?	This question challenges preservice teachers to think about becoming (re)searchers in their environment with race as a focus.
6	To what degree is my role as teacher and my experiences superior to the experiences and expertise of students, and is there knowledge to be learned from my constituents?	This question requires preservice teachers to reflect on coming to terms with intellectual negotiations that should exist in the classroom considering race.
7	How do I situate and negotiate the students' knowledge, experiences, expertise, and race with my own?	This question challenges preservice teachers to begin deciding if they are willing to negotiate expertise with their students. In addition, it allows teachers to pursue comfortable balances in the learning environments with race as a focus.
8	Am I willing to speak about race on behalf of those who might not be present in the conversation BOTH inside and outside of school, and am I willing to express the injustices of race in conservative spaces?	This question challenges preservice teachers to not separate their personal and professional philosophies. If they believe that oppression is wrong and display this belief at school, then they are challenged to think about how they would portray this with their discourse and actions outside of school resulting in a form of social justice.

Source: Milner, H. Richard (2003). Reflection, Racial Competence and Critical Pedagogy: How Do We Prepare Preservice Teachers to Pose Tough Questions? *Race, Ethnicity and Education.* 6 (2), 193–208. Reprinted by permission of the publisher (Taylor & Francis Ltd.; http://www.informaworld.com).

and encompasses the struggle to promote equity in society. As agents of change, teachers (including those in training) must model the principles of social justice in their class-rooms. As Ayers (1998) eloquently puts it

> Teaching for social justice is teaching that arouses students, engages them in a quest to iden-tify obstacles to their full humanity, to their freedom, and then to drive, to move against those obstacles. And so the fundamental message of the teacher for social justice is: you can change the world (p. xvii).

Successful teaching in pluralistic societies also requires that teachers understand the salient issues concerning race and identity, since these often present particular challenges to teachers who find themselves teaching students that are different from themselves. Milner (2003) suggests that a critical aspect of learning to teach in multicultural settings is for preservice teachers to learn ways of asking themselves critical questions about race and identity (see Table 7.1) and to assess how the answers might impact on their practices.

Teaching Style

There is one more issue requiring attention which must be addressed during teacher apprenticeship — teaching style. Preservice teachers have to learn the importance of cul-tural congruence in teaching students from nondominant backgrounds, as learning styles vary both at the individual and group level (see Chapter 1). The teaching styles of many Canadian teachers are based on middle-class conservative norms that emphasize competi-tion, linear thinking, task orientation, and focus on parts rather than on the whole. This contrasts sharply with the learning styles of students from minority cultures, girls, and working-class children, which tend to emphasize personal interaction and attention to the whole. Where teaching styles differ markedly from learning styles, students do not do as well as when there is a correspondence between their modes of learning and how they are taught. Erickson (2001) suggests educators pay attention to this part of the invisible cul-ture, as it is often problematic in contexts of diversity.

LEADERSHIP MATTERS

The role of administrators receives less attention than it should in discourses on teaching for diversity in Canadian schools. Although leadership practices significantly shape school culture and member beliefs about their responsibilities, the skill sets that adminis-trators need to lead in diverse educational environments are often neglected. Studies con-firm the importance of school leaders in implementing and sustaining inclusive socially just policies, but leaders cannot successfully accomplish these objectives using orthodox models of leadership. What kind of leadership is required in diverse educational contexts? While there several potential models, I propose *diversity-oriented leadership*.

Diversity-Oriented Leadership

Diversity-oriented (educational) leadership (DOL) requires training that embraces change in theory and in practice. Overall, it is transformative and eclectic (Egbo, 2005), inclusive (Ryan, 2006), emancipatory and liberatory (Corson, 2000) and social justice oriented (Shields, 2004; Brown, 2004). Despite differences among these models, they all advocate leadership for social justice and diversity, and adhere to the idea of transformative change, which is cognizant of the power differentials among groups in society. They also ask uncomfortable questions of taken-for-granted assumptions about educational policies, administrative practices, and power and knowledge, with the ultimate goal of increasing the life chances of those they serve. Such leaders adopt educational policies and practices premised on the idea of building a just society. They also see redemptive possibilities in social structures: They believe that while structures can be oppressive, they also hold the potential for change. Diversity-oriented leaders often reject the notion of students as at-risk, disadvantaged, and culturally different. Rather, they embrace more positive metaphors that see minority students who, like other students, have needs that schools have the moral and ethical responsibility to determine, understand, and address (Reyes and Wagstaff, 2005). Studies have found that leaders who embrace diversity and successfully educate students from nondominant backgrounds tend to embrace collaborative governance, humanistic leadership philosophies, community empowerment, and critical theory and promote dialogue (Ryan, 2006; Reyes and Wagstaff, 2005; Brown, 2004; May, 1994). There are several dimensions to diversity-oriented leadership: the inclusive, eclectic, transformative, and emancipatory dimensions as discussed below, and as shown in Table 7.2.

Inclusive Dimension

DOL is inclusive in that it values the voices of all stakeholders in the educational enterprise. In particular, it aims to include the voices of students from marginalized communities, as well as that of their families. It also embraces inclusive leadership, which Ryan (2006) describes as

> a collective process in which everyone is included or fairly represented . . . [it is] an array of practices, procedures, understandings, and values that persist over time . . . inclusive leadership relies on many different individuals who contribute in their own often humble ways . . . to make things happen (pp. 16, 17).

This means that whenever critical decisions are made, principals ought to seek the opinions of all voices of the diverse communities within which their schools are located. For instance, school leaders in urban settings must understand that while they can make decisions arbitrarily, the best results can only be achieved through collaboration with parents and community members. Ryan (2001) describes how the principals of two schools he studied foster inclusion through community outreach that involves understanding and respecting the cultural nuances of the immigrant and First Nations communities they serve:

> She learned over time, and after some errors, that there were certain protocols that helped her communicate with the Somali community in her school area. She discovered that it helped if she learned who the "men in charge were" or which people were willing to be spokespeople. She found out that communications were facilitated if she connected with these people or with others who had been in the country for longer periods of time. Edward, on the other hand, discovered that developing a good relationship with the nearby Native community required that he connect not only with the parents of students, but also with the elders. He came to recognize the importance of elders in Native culture, and as a result, found ways to convey this respect in his overtures to the community (p. 9).

As the two principals above demonstrate, inclusive leaders are constantly seeking ways of communicating with and empowering students and diverse families as members of the learning community.

Eclectic Dimension

DOL is eclectic in that it explores various models of democratic and humanistic leadership, to develop an individualized, contextualized, and contingent leadership model that is cognizant of the specific needs of the learning community. By critically examining different models of leadership, diversity-oriented leaders can embrace the idea of a hybridized leadership model that promotes the interest of their students, while enabling them to determine which paradigms are most likely to promote diversity. However, an eclectic method should not be construed as subscribing to a relativistic approach in which anything goes. On the contrary, it simply means that critically inclined administrators veer away from narrow conceptions of leadership, and focus on the bigger picture — to improve the life chances of all their students, especially those from nondominant groups.

Transformative Dimension

In this analysis, the word transformative is utilized for a profound change in consciousness, in the sense used by Freire (1970) and Mezirow (1990). Such a change involves critical reflection, and probing questioning resulting in a shifting of perspectives, which in turn acts as a force for social praxis (see Chapter 4). Leadership involves the exercise of influence, where typically, one individual is able to shape the decision-making processes that affect organizational goals. This situation confers significant power, which can be put to positive use or can lead to injustice. Diversity-oriented leaders employ power to positive use by ensuring that everyone in the school community has a voice in the decision-making process. To make a difference in the lives of students from marginalized communities, educational decision makers must move beyond orthodox ideologies that sustain existing power structures and exclude the powerless (especially those from cultures that are not valued in mainstream society). However, before transformation can occur, leaders must first critique both existing and unorthodox practices. As Furman and Shields (2005) argue, injustices have to be identified before praxis can occur. Furthermore leaders must begin by interrogating their taken-for-granted assumptions about schooling and society, and re-align their perspectives, after which they should initiate critical praxis (see Chapter 5). Brown (2004) asserts

> If . . . educational leaders have engaged in self-directed learning, critical reflection, and rational discourse concerning their underlying assumptions about practice, the next logical step is to integrate these assumptions into an informed theory of practice (i.e., social action) (p. 97).

Educators in culturally and linguistically diverse settings have to deal with issues that create ethical dilemmas for them, since solutions to some problems may require paradigm shifts. For example, how far should educators go, or indeed how much can they allow, in the name of cultural accommodation? How can they resolve the distinction between what is and what ought to be?

TABLE 7.2	Matrix of Diversity-Oriented (Educational) Leadership (DOL)			
DIMENSION	Inclusive	Eclectic	Transformative	Emancipatory
Inclusive	Involves all stakeholders in decision making	Draws on various leadership theories	Ultimate goal is to impact positively on students life chances	Encourages dialogue between all members of the school
	Embraces Distributive Leadership Promotes Community Participation	Solicits ideas from various sources	Embraces critical pedagogical strategies	Promotes "critical consciousness" in teachers and students
Eclectic	Teachers/students voices matter	Context specific Makes connections between theory and Practice	Diversifies the teaching and support staff Open to divergent views	Embraces all students' culture Leads the change process
	Encourages student leadership		Sees the big picture	
Transformative	Promotes Teacher leadership	Understands change theories	Conducts regular diversity audits	Embraces leadership pratices for change
	Fosters a community of learners	Uses understanding of change processes to initiate change	Engages in critical self–reflection	Promotes social justice
			Develops Progressive Policies	Is the lead critical pedagogist
Emancipatory	Challenges traditional practices	Understands power dynamics in society Take risks	Encourages empowering practice among teachers	Understands uneven power relations in society
	Acts as an advocate for students	Changes undesirable educational practices	Institutionalizes change	interrogates unjust educational policies and practices

Emancipatory Dimension

Differing from the other dimensions of DOL, the emancipatory dimension concerns the task of raising critical awareness and consciousness among those who have been marginalized. This is along the lines of Freire's (1970) idea of conscientization, and it also involves agency, or advocacy, for change. When people become emancipated, they begin to ask critical questions about their lives, their positions in society, the social spaces they occupy, and how structural forces empower and disempower. This enables students and teachers, under the guidance of the principal, to see structures and issues in a different light than they would ordinarily. These new understandings facilitate their ability to change oppressive social structures, such as those that are embedded in the educational system. Leaders must encourage critical activities, critical teaching, and extracurricular activities that enable students to not only experience but to engage learning. As Reyes and Wagstaff (2005) point out, leadership is a most powerful intervening variable, and it can be the determining factor for whether schools are successful with their students, especially those from diverse backgrounds. Emancipatory practices enable school leaders to transcend their mundane and technical responsibilities to embrace diverse voices.

SCHOOL BOARD ACTION

All levels of government within Canada share a responsibility for developing equitable social and educational policies. We often think of policies as operational guidelines that come from the very top of government bureaucracy. In reality, policies are enacted at various levels of school systems — the provincial (ministry) level, the board level, and at the micro-level of the school — although the second and third levels are guided by provincial policies. Since the adoption of the policy of multiculturalism, and as a consequence of community pressure, many Canadian school boards have variously instituted diversity policies aimed at abating prejudice and promoting tolerance. However, much still needs to be done since policies are now shifting to align with neoconservative beliefs.

Progressive discourse on changing schools for diversity tends to centre on provincial policies and school practices to the neglect of school boards. As the branch of education that is closest to schools and communities, school boards have a significant role to play in the empowerment of minority students. Although recent educational reform in Canada has significantly reduced the power of boards of education, they remain powerful instruments for educating and enacting policies that influence the way schools are managed and organized, including setting policies that are based on core beliefs. A board's core beliefs are important because they lead to commitment, which in turn is a building block for action (McAdam, 2006).

Orientation towards Diversity

Very often, the educational system itself (at the government and board levels) puts up barriers that prevent teachers from embracing alternative ways of teaching. For instance, at the macro-level, curricular documents are developed in ways that exclude the voices of certain segments of society and in ways that frustrate anti-oppressive paradigms. Teachers are unable to cross this barrier and make the necessary changes because the curriculum does not allow them. Consequently, when school boards and districts do not embrace cultural diversity as policy, it affects the extent to which teachers are able to embrace culturally relevant practices. While provinces legislate and enact core policies, school boards cause these policies to be implemented by their actions through their own collateral and context-specific policies. A board that is committed to promoting a paradigm within its own sphere of influence, develops policies and structures that lead to the realization of the board's commitment.

Hiring Policies

As discussed earlier, most Canadian teachers are White, monolingual educators from middle class backgrounds who are teaching a student population that is increasingly diverse in race, language, culture, ethnicity, ability, and social class. According to the Canadian Teachers Federation (2002), while many Canadian urban areas serve students from diverse ethno-cultural backgrounds, only a small fraction of minorities are represented in the teaching and administrative force or on school boards. Thus, diversifying the teaching force is essential to any program that aims to promote diversity in Canadian classrooms.

What are the specific advantages of diversifying the teaching staff? First, students from diverse backgrounds need to see themselves reflected in the school of which they are an integral part. The psychological impact of minority students seeing only White teachers in their school is significant. Second, minority teachers are in a position to provide diverse students the support that they may not receive from White teachers (due to cultural discontinuity). Third, minority students are more likely to ask for help from teaching staff who are like them (and whom they believe understand their historical, cultural, and individual experiences), thus reducing some of the disconnect they feel in a predominantly White institution. Fourth, and most important, diversifying the staff enriches the educational experiences of all students as it provides teachers who teach from different perspectives, i.e., beyond the monofocal lenses through which teachers of European backgrounds often teach. Fifth, by diversifying their staff, school systems would be implementing what they often endorse in principle. More often than not, talk about diversifying the school staff focuses on mainstream teachers who teach diverse students. Just as it is important to diversify the teaching staff, it is necessary to ensure the diversity of the support and non-teaching staff because they too interact with students on a regular basis.

Capacity Building

Capability building is targeted investment in material, intellectual, and human resources (Delaney, 2002). Within education, the purpose of building capacity is to improve practice for the benefit of those who are being served by the system. One way this can be done is through supporting professional development. Fortunately, many school boards now provide this kind of support, especially for newly recruited teachers. More often than not however, these workshops do not address the issues of teaching in contexts of diversity. School boards play a significant role through the policies they adopt and the nature of the support they provide to teachers. Professional training is required for teachers to become cognizant of and to adopt progressive educational practices in their classrooms.

Beside the provision of professional learning support, building capacity has direct bearing on teacher leadership. It is impossible for teachers to meet the needs of their diverse students without expanding the general conceptualization of teaching beyond its usual connotation as a technical activity that only involves classroom instruction. This expanded vision enables teachers to assume leadership roles during their interactions with students and their families and empowers them to renegotiate their power relations with principals and other educational stakeholders. In this way, they can provide extended support to students, particularly those from nondominant groups (Bascia, 1994; Ryan, 2006; McAdam, 2006).

Teachers who provide substantive support for their minoritized students are those who feel uncomfortable with the status quo. They are critical teachers who, as Kincheloe (2005) explains,

> see a socially constructed world and ask what forces construct the consciousness and the ways of seeing of the actors who live in it. Why are some constructions of educational reality embraced and officially legitimized by the dominant culture while others are repressed? (p. 12)

Preventing Unfair De Facto Policies

De facto policies are unwritten and unofficial policies that become part of the culture of a school or any organization. In schools, these policies tend to impact negatively on students whose families do not have the social capital and advocacy skills to intervene. For example, Chapter 1 discusses how Black students are now considered athletically superior to their White counterparts. This has had unintended consequences for Black students in pluralistic Western societies, including Canada. It is now an unstated policy to socialize Black students out of the classroom and into the gym by encouraging them to spend inordinate amounts of time on sports. This inadvertently reinforces the students' belief in an unrealistic future in professional sports. This vision of a potentially huge pay off, which in all probability will not happen, leads them to completely immerse themselves in sports and results in academic disengagement. Solomon (1994) summarizes the dysfunctional consequences of Black students becoming immersed in sports subculture in school:

> First, it interferes with their academic progress; students miss classes, shortcut homework, and do poorly on exams. Second, black students who are preoccupied with sports become marginal in other areas of school life especially those that are academically oriented, such as speech, drama, or student government (p. 192).

This is of course, not a stated policy, but exists nonetheless in our schools, especially those with a significant population of minority students. Many boards of education have attempted to change this subculture by requiring a mandatory level of academic success to permit participation in sports. However, this is often a minimal level of achievement that most students can easily manage to achieve. Unfortunately, mediocre academic performance is not enough to reverse the likelihood that these students will eventually occupy marginal positions within the labour force. This is congruent with the argument put forward by Bowles and Gintis (1976) in which they advance the view that educational systems are organized along hierarchies that are reflective of people's expected future role within the labour force (see Chapter 1).

Thus, while de facto policies may be informal, they are quite pervasive in Canadian schools, and can potentially have catastrophic consequences. Finally, de facto policies are usually very subtractive in the sense that their effects are usually negative and felt most by marginalized students.

A related issue is enacting policies that have not been carefully studied for potential consequences. As Apple (2006) argues, policies often have significant unperceived consequences, because even educational reforms implemented with good intentions have unforeseen effects that can be quite problematic. An example of how policies can go awry is the high-stakes school testing that has been instituted in many jurisdictions across Canada and the United States. Research shows these testing policies have had unintended consequences that reinforce inequity and exclusion. Another example of how policies can become dysfunctional in practice is zero tolerance disciplinary policies. These were adopted in the wake of increasing school violence and are now proven to be discriminatory because they disproportionately affect minority students (Henry and Tator, 2006).

Summary

The goal of promoting diversity in Canadian schools cannot be achieved without practical and structural changes being made to social and educational policies at all levels of the government and the relevant sectors of society. This chapter presents arguments that policy and training matters are critical components of educational responses to diversity in Canadian schools. The chapter also argues that improving the life chances of diverse students is also a matter of national interest, given emerging patterns of global cooperation and competition. Although not a panacea for the problems that face minoritized groups in Canadian schools, just educational policies are catalysts for praxis-oriented transformation since they legitimize educators striving to adopt progressive educational practices. In addition, training prospective teachers and administrators in ways that enable them to embrace transformative perspectives is an essential part of any intervention agenda. The chapter also argues that even the preservice teacher practicum must be designed to contribute to candidates' critical awareness of power issues in society. It should show how these issues intersect with teaching and learning so that they can become change agents for promoting equity, fairness, and empowerment in their classrooms. The overall thrust of the chapter is that empowering minority groups depends on linkage between critical theory and practice via policies that advance understanding of the relationship between education and the empowerment of marginalized groups. Policy development should promote a mélange of praxis-oriented policies that serve the best interests of all students, including marginalized groups who have so far been excluded. However, in formulating new policies, policy makers and other stakeholders must avoid making simplistic generalizations about Canada's minoritized groups, since they do not constitute a monolithic body. Progressive educational policies within the Canadian context should reflect a more equitable distribution of power in society.

Key Terms

Assimilation	Benevolent accommodation	Capacity building
Cultural pluralism	Diversity-oriented leadership	Fundamental rights policy
Just educational policies	Social cohesion	White privilege

Questions to Guide Reflective Practice

1. What role should provincial governments play in fostering inclusive educational environments?

2. Should the roles of teachers and administrators be guided by provincial mandates, or should educators exercise their professional autonomy in developing guidelines for dealing with diversity in schools?

4. To what extent do "implementation issues" facilitate and/or limit the creation of inclusive educational environments?

5. To what extent should teacher pedagogical practices regarding diversity be driven by policy?

6. Develop a hypothetical policy for dealing with diversity issues in Canadian schools.

7. One of the subtexts of this chapter is that policies are essential to conducting the business of education. From your own perspective, why is it beneficial for teachers and principals to understand the concept of policy, as well as its impact on their day-to-day activities?

Case Study Analysis: Chapter Opening Vignette

1. What are the key policy and diversity issues raised in this vignette?

2. How should teachers and administrators approach diversity issues in schools?

3. How can school boards benefit from the conversation between teachers and administrators?

4. What advice would you offer the principal who is at a crossroads about how much she should advocate the integration of First Nations culture into the curriculum?

5. In your opinion, which provisions and tools should provinces provide to assist school boards in addressing the issues raised in the vignette?

6. How can provinces better account for the variability among school districts when developing educational policies?

7. Along with some of your peers, replicate the debate in this vignette. Divide yourselves into two camps. One group should support inclusive educational policies while the other opposes them. At the end of the debate, determine whether there is common ground.

8. What is the implicit issue in this vignette?

9. How can you relate critical pedagogy as discussed in Chapter 4 to the central issue in this vignette?

Test Your Knowledge

1. Does your local school board have a diversity policy? What is the nature of the policy? Do you believe that the policy will achieve its intended results?

2. The legislated policies governing education can be found in provincial education Acts, Statutes, or Regulations. Conduct an analysis of your province's *Education Act.* Is there legislation that specifically addresses the following dimensions of diversity: religion, cultural difference, disability, language diversity, sexual orientation, racial difference, and gender?

3. How are educational policies enacted in your province?

4. React to the statement "Policies are blueprints for action."

5. From your reading of the chapter, identify and discuss several indicators of just educational policies.

6. Based on the discussion in the chapter, how would you describe diversity-oriented leadership?

For Further Reading

Anyon, J. (2005). *Radical Possibilities: Public Policy, Urban Education and a New Social Movement.* New York: Routledge.

Apple, M. (2000). Racing Toward Educational Reform. In R. Mahalingam and C. McCarthy (Eds.). *Multicultural Curriculum* (pp. 84–107). New York: Routledge.

Apple, M., and Buras, K. (Eds.) (2006). *The Subaltern Speak: Curriculum, Power, and Educational Struggles.* New York: Routledge.

Banks, J., and Banks, C. M. (Eds.). (2004). Handbook of Research on Multicultural Education, 2nd Edition. San Francisco: Jossey-Bass.

Corson, D. (2000). Emancipatory Leadership. *International Journal for Leadership in Education,* 3 (2): 93–120.

Entwistle, H. (2001) The Relationship between Educational Theory and Practice: A New Look. In W. Hare and J. Portelli (Eds.). *Philosophy of Education: Introductory Readings,* 3rd Edition. Calgary: Detselig Enterprises.

Gay, G. (2000). *Culturally Responsive Teaching: Theory, Research, Practice.* New York: Teachers College Press.

hooks, bell. (2003). *Teaching Community: A Pedagogy of Hope.* New York: Routledge.

Johnston, I., and Carson, T. (2000). The Difficulty with Difference in Teacher Education: Toward a Pedagogy of Compassion. *Alberta Journal of Educational Research,* 46(1): 75, 1–9.

Kincheloe, J. (Ed.) (2005). *Classroom Teaching: An Introduction.* New York: Peter Lang Publishing.

Ladson-Billings, G., and Tate, W. (Eds.). (2006) *Education Research in the Public Interest: Social Justice, Action, and Policy* (pp.173–198). New York: Teachers College Press.

Milner, H. (2003). Reflection, Racial Competence and Critical Pedagogy: How Do We Prepare Preservice Teachers to Pose Tough Questions? *Race, Ethnicity and Education,* 6(2): 193–208.

Shields, C. (2004). Dialogic Leadership for Social Justice: Overcoming Pathologies of Silence. *Educational Administration Quarterly,* 40(1): 111–134.

Stone, D. (1997). *Policy Paradox: The Art of Political Decision Making.* New York: W. W. Norton Company.

Taylor, J. (1995). Non-Native Teachers Teaching in Native Communities. In Marie Battiste and Jean Barman (Eds.), *First Nations Education in Canada: The Circle Unfolds* (pp. 224–244). Vancouver: UBC Press.

Villegas, A. M., and Lucas, T. (2002). *Educating Culturally Responsive Teachers: A Coherent Approach.* Albany: State University of New York Press.

Websites of Interest

www.cepan.ca The Canadian Education and Policy Administration Network

www.cea-ace.ca/res.cfm Canadian Education Association — Research and Policy

www.canadianeducationalpolicystudies.ca Canadian Educational Policy Studies — Contains Education Policy Documents

www.educationpolicy.org Education Policy Institute

www.lab.brown.edu/tdl/tl-strategies/crt-research.shtml Focus on Teaching Diverse Learners Culturally Responsive Teaching

Moving Forward

VIGNETTE

John Zeak had been teaching at Mountain Elementary School for only a few months. Like all new teachers, he had faced several challenges. While he enjoyed working with his grade 7 students, he had found it somewhat challenging to deal with Josh Simms, a likable student whose tendency to harass others was a source of concern. Josh seemed particularly intent on offending everyone whom he believed was different from him. This included the girls and several minority students in the class. He had the knack of finding something disparaging to say about those he harassed. He was also constantly disrespectful of the teacher. At first John Zeak had ignored what he assumed was attention-seeking behaviour that would play itself out as the school year progressed. After all, was he not constantly reminding his students that such behaviour was not acceptable in his class? Josh would eventually "get it" he rationalized. Things did not work out that way and Josh's harassment of some of his peers continued to escalate. Zeak found that he was constantly trying to resolve conflicts that Josh had initiated. As Josh's bullying became increasingly disruptive and

intolerable, he invited Josh's parents to a face-to-face meeting to discuss the problem. He had hoped that they could collaboratively devise a course of action to teach Josh tolerance and respect for others. To his amazement, Josh's parents seemed unconcerned and dismissive of the problem. In fact, Mr. Simms informed John Zeak in no uncertain terms that he was not to be bothered in future about issues that "do not matter". Meanwhile, there was no change in Josh's behaviour. One particular incident eventually forced the issue. During a group activity, Josh had continuously pestered Celeste, one of the few First Nations students in the class. After several unsuccessful interventions, John Zeak threatened him with suspension at the end of the day if he did stop the harassment. Josh reacted negatively, yelling out, "Quit bugging me! I am exercising my free speech! My parents told me that under the *Charter of Rights and Freedoms*, I can say whatever I like." Zeak was shocked at Josh's misinterpretation of the *Charter*: sure, he had a right to free speech, but not by trampling on the rights of others. Exasperated by Josh's outburst and rudeness before the entire class, John Zeak decided to follow through with his threat of suspension, which he had a legal right to do under the province's education statute. He was not about to allow prejudice to thrive in his class. The next morning, John Zeak was summoned to the principal's office and was surprised to find Josh and his parents in conference with Mr. Thompson, the principal. Mr. Thompson explained that Mr. and Mrs. Simms were about to initiate legal action against him, the principal, and the school board for the violation of their son's fundamental rights to self-expression. As far as they were concerned, Josh's behaviour had not warranted suspension. John Zeak was speechless. He now understood how and from where Josh had learned his prejudice. No, he thought, Mr. Simms is wrong and these issues matter. He wondered how many other students in his class shared Josh's feelings. If he had failed to reach Josh, his strategies for teaching about diversity, mutual respect, and tolerance were clearly not working. What was he doing wrong? He had to find more proactive and results-oriented strategies. Regardless of the outcome of this particular incident, he had to move forward; he would not be discouraged because too much was at stake.

INTRODUCTION: RETHINKING THE WAY "WE DO SCHOOLS"

There is debate in prevailing scholarship over what constitutes social justice, the sources of injustices in school and society, and the educators' role in changing the status quo in Canada and the Western world. Certain groups of students continue to experience negative and unfair treatment that relegates them to the unenviable position of the "other". With this in mind, critical areas should be addressed in order to help diverse learners? These critical areas can be summarized as philosophical orientation, curriculum content, the process of teaching, and the context of teaching. A central theme in this chapter is that it is the way these broad areas are *qualitatively* addressed by teachers which will make a difference moving forward. John Zeak in the vignette above makes a profound statement: He is right, there is too much at stake for all educators not to rethink their approaches to teaching and learning in contemporary Canadian schools. This final chapter of the book, therefore, examines these broad areas individually, from the perspective of directions for future action.

PHILOSOPHICAL ORIENTATIONS: CONFRONTING ORTHODOXY

Chapter 5 argues that teachers and administrators must regularly conduct critical self-analysis, which should culminate in perspective realignment. However, change in perspectives also requires that educators and administrators examine and change their philosophical orientations to teaching, as required. This change may well induce a paradigm shift away from traditional and conservative views of schooling and society. Teachers have to re-evaluate their basic beliefs and assumptions about students, and education. In effect teachers who wish to make a difference have two options: continue to reinforce *orthodox* thinking or embrace transformation-oriented thinking. This book's underlying premise is that educational systems cannot continue to organize themselves in orthodox ways that reinforce exclusionary practices, i.e., in ways that silence those whose cultural capital is considered less valuable than the middle-class values disseminated in schools. Thus, educators must problematize educational knowledge by asking such questions as "Whose interests do schools represent? Whose "ways of knowing" are privileged and whose are devalued? To what extent do Canadian educational policies and practices promote equity and fairness?" and "How can the status quo be challenged?" Visionary educators must have a thorough grounding in what constitutes fairness and social justice, which means meeting people's needs as required, rather than giving everybody an equal share of social resources. But it is not enough to understand these principles, teachers must also implement them in authentic ways as they strive to meet the individual needs of their diverse students. Rejecting orthodox practice also means that educators must eschew the usual practice of labelling students as "at risk", "difficult to educate", etc. Besides the obvious psychological implications of such dichotomization, labelling impacts on teachers' communication and interaction patterns with such students, and on how the curriculum is delivered to the various groups of students within the same classroom. Therefore, traditional methods of teaching (those based solely on the notion of immutable universals) are no longer justifiable given the fluid nature of the world (including student diversity and educational policies). While some teachers are cognizant of this and endeavour to integrate diverse perspectives into the content they teach, they generally use an add-on approach that differs only minimally from traditional approaches to teaching and learning. Reconstituting the way things are done in school should therefore involve a fundamental shift in thinking. That is from orthodox thinking to a transformation-oriented conceptualization of issues, which should manifest in the infusion of diversity issues across the curriculum in constructive and dynamic ways. The basic differences between orthodox and transformation-oriented thinking are outlined in Table 8.1. Also, the following example further illustrates the differences. One of your students who constantly shows concern for the poor and downtrodden comes to school with a newspaper clipping about the appalling condition of some First Nations communities in the Northwest Territories. A teacher who thinks in traditional ways will only acknowledge the student's interest in the story as commendable and then move on to other things whereas a teacher who is truly interested in changing the status quo would not only encourage the student to

TABLE 8.1	Elements of Orthodox Compared with Transformation-Oriented Thinking
Orthodox (Traditional) Thinking	**Transformation-Oriented Thinking**
• Believes in the banking perspective of teaching, in which students are treated as depositories of information	• Questions and engages the curriculum and encourages students to do the same. Sees a link between peoples' experiences and how knowledge is constructed
• Adopts traditional pedagogies and reinforces the status quo	• Embraces and adopts progressive pedagogies such as critical and diversity pedagogy, and diversity-oriented teacher research.
• Believes in teacher-centred approaches	• Believes that knowledge is co-created and makes the classroom a community of learners
• Ignores the intersection of privilege and social positioning in academic achievement	• Understands that privilege contributes to educational success
• Sees education as a meritocracy and views educational successes solely as a function of individual hard work	• Understands that a myriad of interacting variables, including unfair policies and practices, contribute to academic success
• Believes in the value-free notion of education and teaching	• Understands that teaching is a politically charged activity
• Subscribes to the illusion of colour blindness	• Recognizes individual differences, but rejects deterministic views of who can succeed in school
• Sees student diversity as a problem to be "managed" or overcome	• Sees student diversity as a resource that can enrich the quality of teaching and learning for all
• Sees the curriculum as a neutral and universal document	• Sees the curriculum as a cultural artifact that represents the worldviews of the dominant group

develop strategies for improving the situation, he or she would make the story the nexus of a major class project.

EMPOWERMENT THROUGH THE CONTENTS OF THE CURRICULUM

Various chapters throughout this book have touched on the issue of the curriculum. This chapter explores how teachers can infuse *diversity issues across the curriculum (DIAC)* through the contents they teach as a natural extension of their quest to make learning a worthwhile experience for all students.

Diversity Issues across the Curriculum (DIAC)

DIAC involves a purposeful attempt to integrate diverse perspectives into what is formally taught in school. It is a pedagogical strategy for pervasive curriculum intervention that is intended to provide students with the appropriate knowledge, skills, attitudes, and moral orientation required to live in a pluralistic nation and a globalized world. This means that every subject is to be taught in racially, culturally, linguistically, and gender inclusive ways that challenge orthodox knowledge and position alternative discourse as valued knowledge that all children should have access to. While some topics lend themselves more to integration into the curriculum than others, virtually all subject areas can be adapted to meet student learning needs. Chapter 4 discusses the concepts of negotiable and non-negotiable knowledge as models of what schools should teach in a pluralistic society, and an increasingly globalized world. Teachers can use this framework as a starting point for integrating diversity issues across the curriculum. Even when they must adhere to standardized curricula, teachers can still integrate DIAC as they teach the various subject areas. In that instance, the goal is not to change the curriculum, but rather to expand it based on the contextual needs of the students. Ideally, in order to successfully implement DIAC teachers must first **deconstruct** the curriculum (that is, critically examine and engage the contents [Ladson-Billings, 2006]) and then *reconstruct* it to identify the missing information. Filling in the gaps may require inserting the voices of those who have been left out of the curriculum.

How does DIAC work in practice? Recall the case of the student who came to school with the newspaper clipping discussed above. This is a good example of how teachers can integrate DIAC as part of their instructional activities. The newspaper story can be inserted into virtually every lesson and unit that will be taught. For example, students could be asked in social studies or language arts to use the issue as the basis of a journal writing activity that deals with ways of improving the lives of First Nations peoples, and perhaps ways of improving the lives of the downtrodden in other parts of the world. Similarly, the same story can be integrated into a lesson in health education by exploring the health and psychological implications of poor social conditions in Canada's Aboriginal communities. It can become part of a math unit if students are asked to research statistical information about Canada's Aboriginal peoples. The story can also be used to teach a lesson in history and geography (depending on the grade level). Similarly, a teacher whose particular interest is in integrating diversity issues from a global perspective could discuss the lives of those who are living under similar conditions in other parts of the world, and then have the students propose ways of changing the situation. By adopting this approach to DIAC, the teacher is using a newspaper clipping to teach students global awareness, critical thinking skills, cross-cultural awareness and sensitivity, **empathy**, poverty, social justice, research, and advocacy skills. The teacher is also providing the students with the opportunity to critique undesirable social conditions, thus enabling them to discuss and develop ideas for creating a just Canadian society.

While some teachers may feel that the above approach is overtly political and therefore should not be a constituent part of classroom activities or practices, it is worth emphasizing that teaching is a political activity for all the reasons already outlined in Chapter 5. Moreover, the role of an educational system cannot be separated from its historical context, nor can it be viewed apart from the larger political and economic structures of which it is an integral part. The above is only an example of how DIAC can be integrated into lessons, other instances will abound.

Ideally, for DIAC to be effective, it should be addressed at all levels of the educational system. First, at the policy making or ministry level curriculum developers must not only address diversity issues in determining what students should be taught (see Chapter 4), they should also address how these issues will be integrated in actual instruction. As Dei et al. (2000) argue

> In creating a multi-voiced counter narrative, a new curriculum of learning must be redesigned to reflect alternate realities and worldviews. Schooling must be reoriented to reflect the contributions of non-European cultures to scientific academic work. . . . The partial readings of human development, which have denied the accomplishments and achievements of these groups, must be addressed (p. 183).

It is during curriculum development that the Dei et al. charge should first be addressed. Second, DIAC should also be addressed at the board level. School boards must ensure that teachers are provided the necessary resources to enable them to implement DIAC. Third and most important, teachers should integrate DIAC as discussed above, at the micro-level.

EMPOWERMENT THROUGH THE PROCESS OF TEACHING

In empowering diverse learners, whether we speak in terms of racial or language minorities, immigrant or refugee students, etc., praxis-oriented initiatives must give students a voice, foster their intellectual growth, affirm student identities, and focus on the needs of the individual.

Giving Students a Voice

Reforms that intend to create an inclusive learning environment for diverse students can be implemented by giving them a voice as important members of the learning community. As Freire (1970) argues, a pedagogy that purports to be truly liberating and empowering cannot be successful without the participation of those who are to be empowered. Enabling everyone one to speak is a starting point for changing undesirable educational practices (Ryan, 2006). It is ironic that in Canada, which considers itself a pluralistic democracy (Myer, 2006), some groups still do not have the voice that the constitution explicitly guarantees. The prevailing culture in Canadian schools represents the privileged collective voice of the dominant group. This is the voice that educators must interrogate in order to empower diverse learners (see Chapter 1). To counteract social reproduction in Canadian schools, teachers must diverge from the persistent pattern of silencing the voices of students from disadvantaged communities. McLaren (2007) underscores the importance of voice in empowering groups that are at the periphery of the school system:

> I would argue along with Henry Giroux that a critical and affirming pedagogy has to be constructed around the stories that people tell, the ways in which students and teachers author meaning, and the possibilities that underlie the experiences that shape their voices. It is around the concept of *voice* that a theory of both teaching and learning can take place, one that points to new forms of social relations and to new and challenging ways of confronting everyday life (p. 244) [emphasis in original].

The concept of voice as used here refers to collective agency and power that facilitates student ability to engage the system in profound and meaningful ways. But, empowering diverse learners does not solely depend on making students part of the dialogue for change. Teachers should also be given a voice that they can leverage to initiate praxis. As micro-level practitioners, it is through the mediation of teachers' voices that undesirable school and classroom practices can be challenged and altered. Also, by using their voices in positive ways, teachers can contribute significantly to restructuring colonizing societal processes that operate both inside and outside the school.

Affirming Students' Identity

A critical element in empowering diverse learners is affirming their identity. Our identity is an integral part of who we are, and in all practical applications, contributes to how we construct knowledge (see Chapter 1). It is important to remember that some of the academic challenges that minoritized students face are directly linked to the negation of their identity. The bulk of this book is devoted to exploring the ways that educators can affirm the identities of diverse students to increase their academic success and ultimately their life chances. This is also a central argument in the works of writers who advocate progressive educational paradigms such as multicultural education, anti-racist education, critical pedagogy, diversity pedagogy, and culturally relevant teaching (e.g., Banks, 2001; Bennett, 2007; McLaren, 2007; Dei, 1996; Villegas and Lucas, 2002; Gay, 2000; Ladson- Billings, 1994; Delpit, 2006; Fleras and Elliott, 2003; Henry and Tator, 2006). Affirming identities should therefore be a moral agenda that guides the actions of educators in contexts of student diversity.

Fostering Intellectual Growth

One important strategy that teachers can use to empower diverse learners is to foster their intellectual growth. Quite often teachers subscribe to the deficit model of achievement, seeing students from certain racial and ethno-cultural groups as incapable or limited in their abilities (Gillborn, 2004). Consequently there is reduced expectation, which in turn prevents them from supporting the intellectual growth of these students. As we have already seen in the boxed vignette in Chapter 6, expectations are indeed powerful determinants of teacher judgment of a student's abilities. The vignette also suggests that student ability, often assumed to be innate in many Western societies (see Chapter 1) may be significantly influenced by experience and the kinds of knowledge to which students are exposed. The teachers who assumed that an excellent critique of Shakespeare was not written by the Black immigrant student (whom they judged as least likely to have studied Shakespearian literature) made a common error. Such ill-considered beliefs lead only to the further disadvantaging of students from nondominant backgrounds.

Ladson-Billings (2006) argues that in order for teachers to move their students from a level of mediocrity to one of possibilities, teachers must see future leaders, neurosurgeons, Nobel Laureates, and social justice advocates among their students. To achieve this, they must move from a state of sympathy to a state of empathy. Such a mental state requires teachers to "feel with the students rather than feeling for them. Feeling with the students builds a sense of solidarity between the teacher and students but does not excuse students from working hard in pursuit of excellence". Excellence and critical pedagogical practices are not mutually exclusive — for instance, by adopting culturally relevant pedagogies, teachers explore all possible avenues to ensure that their students perform to the best of their abilities. Moreover, as Kalantzis and Cope (1999) argue, students need a rigorous curriculum if they are to gain any kind of meaningful access to social rewards. Whereas most critical educators argue for making the curriculum relevant to the experience of students, Kalantzis and Cope caution that

> diversifying curriculum in the interest of 'relevance' is to create a new streaming in a pseudo-democratic garb. Students who would have failed in a comprehensive, traditional curriculum now pass in what everyone . . . know[s] to be 'Mickey-mouse' courses. . . . All too easily, and in the name of cultural self-esteem, this can end in a celebratory multiculturalism of spaghetti and polka; a multiculturalism that trivializes culture and is more concerned with the affirmation of difference than with what students need in linguistic-cognitive terms if they are to gain some degree of broader social access (pp. 260–261).

Based on the understanding that people learn best when their learning is linked to their experiences, critical teaching practices are ultimately about fostering intellectual growth and academic excellence in all learners. When teachers decide that students are incapable of performing certain tasks or are operating below a predetermined level of intellectual ability, their desire to help the students grow intellectually is considerably reduced. This is most unfortunate because our contemporary information-based society demands that teachers deliver intellectually challenging curricula. Indeed, as schools must now prepare students for technology and jobs that may not yet exist, promoting intellectual growth among all students should be the sine qua non for all educators.

Individualized Attention

While this book deals extensively with issues from a group standpoint, it should also be obvious that the individual is as important as the group. It is at the individual level that teachers are able to indeed reach students. Teachers must treat each student as an individual human being requiring special attention whenever necessary, as it is in fact good teaching to pay attention to individual differences. While this book devotes considerable space to teaching students culturally relevant knowledge and pedagogy, it is important to point out that educating students in a multicultural society does not mean typecasting them into preconceived notions of how they are supposed to act. According to Delpit (2006)

> The question is not necessarily how to create the perfect "culturally matched" learning situation for each ethnic group, but rather how to recognize when there is a problem for a particular child

and how to seek its cause in the most broadly conceived fashion. Knowledge about culture is but one tool that educators may make use of when devising solutions for a school's difficulty in educating diverse children (p. 167).

On a similar tack, traditional assumptions about learning that contribute to "teaching less instead of teaching more" (Delpit, 2006) must be replaced with more progressive beliefs about the potential of every child to learn.

THE CONTEXT OF TEACHING

In contextualizing teaching and the way forward, this work adopts a perspective that sees the context of teaching and learning extending beyond the classroom to include the communities from which schools draw their students. This conception of the context includes strategies that teachers can adopt to provide a safe, warm, and caring learning environment for all learners, in addition to those that schools can use to reach out to their communities. It includes the strategies for classroom management discussed in Chapter 6, as well as those for disciplining students.

The Importance of Empathy

All propositions in this book are aimed at empowering diverse learners and all students in pluralistic societies. It is, however, difficult to achieve these goals if students are not taught how to empathize with their peers. Although not explicitly stated, the theme of empathy runs through this book. Whether we talk of teaching global awareness, critical thinking skills, or prejudice reduction and respect for others, empathy is an important precursor to developing these themes. For example, Chapter 5 briefly broaches this subject when discussing the issue of global awareness. It bears emphasizing that it is difficult to teach tolerance, anti-racism, multiculturalism, and all the other empowering frameworks discussed in this book if students fail to embrace the value of empathy. Empathy is our ability to understand and be compassionate about other people's experiences. As Howard (2006) describes it

> Empathy means "to feel with". [It] requires the suspension of assumptions, the letting go of ego, and the release of the privilege of non-engagement. . . .[It] is the antithesis of dominance. It requires all of our senses and focuses our attention on the perspective and worldview of another person (p. 77).

The issue of empathy is particularly relevant in discourses on diversity. It is through empathy that students from dominant society can understand the experiences of their peers from Canada's diverse communities. But it is not only students who need to develop an ethic of empathy. For example, it is difficult for Whites to comprehend what people of other races have experienced, but empathy can enable them to relate enough to understand. Speaking from the perspective of a White educator in the United States, Howard (2006) contends that while it is difficult for teachers to fully experience the realities of the everyday life of minoritized groups, they can however "on occasion share a part of the journey together, occupy the same craft for a time and learn to see the view through each others' eyes." This in essence is what Canadian educators must do in order to teach for diversity. In fact, Villegas and Lucas (2002) suggest that the development of empathy should begin in teacher education programs, by using the experiences of prospective teachers who have encountered various forms of oppression as a teaching tool. In order to nurture empathy in their students, teachers themselves must learn to respond to students in an empathetic way. For example, many students in urban schools have had traumatic experiences before coming to Canada: war, refugee status, severe poverty. All these students come to school with various types of challenges that may impact on how they respond to teachers, their peers, and the education system in general. Responding empathetically to these students will contribute significantly to improving their school experiences.

Teaching the Ethic of Care

Related to empathy is the idea of profound caring, which beyond the state of simply understanding, propels teachers to act as advocates of their students. This refers to the ethic of care that teachers at all levels are morally bound to extend to their students and to model. As Noddings (2005: 18) argues, "teachers not only have to create caring relations in which they are the carers . . . they also have a responsibility to help their students develop the capacity to care". In her book *In a Different Voice: Psychological Theory and Women's Development,* Gilligan (1982) argues that while women generally ascribe to an "ethic of care" men tend to subscribe to an "ethic of justice". Although Gilligan distinguishes between these two types of ethics, from a pedagogical perspective all teachers — men and women alike — are expected to demonstrate an ethic of care towards their students. Like Gilligan, Noddings (2005) in her pioneering work on the linkages between interpersonal relationships and positive educational outcomes puts caring at the centre of any meaningful educational change in the contemporary context of student heterogeneity. Manning (1999) provides a précis of the implications of an ethic of caring for teachers:

> There is a special kind of relationship awareness that characterizes an ethic of care . . . So I see my student as a fellow human and a fellow learner. I recognize that he is in need of my help and that I am able to give it. I recognize my role as a teacher and the special obligation this implies. Next, I see him as a member of the classroom community. . . . Finally, I acknowledge the web of personal relationships that can either support or undermine his academic success . . . [A]n ethic of care requires a response on my part. It is not enough to stare at my student and imagine him in a sympathetic way . . . I must make my caring concrete in the actions that I take to respond to his need (p. 119).

Thus, seeing their students as co-sharers of a given space will increase interpersonal bonds between teachers and their students. These transcend not only static sympathy, but make teachers more committed to working towards change in the lives of students, both in and outside the school. The ethic of care enables teachers to act and become advocates for their students. It raises their expectations for their students, and encourages them to become involved in their communities and create vital networks of teacher-parent-community relationships. The ethic of care helps teachers to model appropriate behaviour, nurture healthy, cross-cultural relationships, and above all, work towards increasing the life chances of all students, and in particular those that have been traditionally marginalized.

Community Outreach

Diverse learners come from communities that can be empowered only to the extent that schools encourage collaboration. It is extremely difficult to reach students without collaborating with their families. An earlier chapter explicates the importance of school-family collaboration if school systems hope to meet the needs of students from diverse backgrounds. Community outreach is an important strategy for developing these partnerships. Teachers send home newsletters on a regular basis, but as result of language barriers, the target parents may not be able to read them. This is a common problem in immigrant communities. However, what many schools in Canada do, resources permitting, is send home various translations of the newsletters. Teachers can also take advantage of their students as potential translators. For example, during teacher-parent interviews, students can act as translators (depending of course on the issue to be discussed). It is also important for teachers and principals to attend community functions, and generally make their presence felt within the community.

Community outreach includes inviting parents and community members to come into the classroom to participate in any way that they can. Parents can either help or observe their children at work. Even those who lack language skills should be encouraged to support their children by their very presence in class. Encouraging community members to come into the classroom sends an important signal: Schools are open to power sharing and are willing to work collaboratively with them.

The key to school-community collaboration is building a rapport based on trust. To build community relationships, educators should go out and get to know their school communities and visit First Nations Friendship centres, Greek Association centres, Somalian Community centres, etc. One effective strategy for fostering community outreach is the use of community counsellors. Dei et al. (2000: 212) report that the school board they examined in the Greater Toronto Area employed community liaison counsellors to

- provide support for non-English speaking parents and students
- assist in academic placement based on first language screening
- address concerns about race, culture, and religion in schools' policy and practice
- help parents understand and adapt to the Canadian educational system
- provide pertinent information to teachers, administrators, and school counsellors on the specific needs of their particular communities
- mediate conflicts and concerns among families, schools, and communities.

The dual role of community liaison counsellors as both community advocates and board employees, however, can be challenging. According to Dei et al. "[a]dvocacy for students being their primary concern, often puts counsellors at odds with either parents or the Board. Balancing student, parent and community needs with Board requirements makes their role politically challenging and often contentious".

Professional Development and Life-Long Learning

This book discusses extensively the role of teachers in empowering diverse learners. It also argues that Canadian diversity is not a choice — it is a reality with which school systems and all educators must deal. The degree of success that teachers experience in teaching diverse learners depends on the knowledge they have about teaching such students. It is therefore essential that teachers develop their own theories, perspectives, paradigms, and strategies for dealing with diversity. Doing this requires that they become lifelong learners, as well as regular participants in professional development programs. As Howard (2006) contends, educators, especially White teachers, in multicultural, multiracial, and multilingual settings cannot teach what they do not know.

DIVERSE COMMUNITIES AS AGENTS OF CHANGE

Chapter 5 argues that schools and teachers cannot initiate change without co-opting the participation of the White dominant group. Just as it argues that members of the dominant group must become allies of school systems in order to change the status quo, it is critical that members of minoritized communities themselves become agents of change. The strategies proposed in this book can only be partially successful unless disadvantaged groups develop agency in the sense advocated by progressive educators. Indeed, throughout history transformative change never occurred without advocacy and agency on the part of those who are most affected by oppressive social structures, including the educational institutions that reinforce inequality. Unfortunately, many members of the affected communities are often reluctant or unable to act. Through hegemony, some members of disadvantaged communities internalize societal perceptions of their status, leading to a resigned acceptance and normalization of their status.

Nevertheless, it must be emphasized that becoming advocates for change and social justice does not preclude changing patterns of unproductive behaviour. For instance, the practice of Black students discouraging one another from succeeding in school because they are "acting White" is counterproductive, even though such behaviour may be a response to oppressive schooling (Ogbu, 1987). Research has clearly established that many minority families value education very highly and want their children to acquire higher education. School systems must provide members of Canada's marginalized communities with opportunities to participate in their children's education in more meaningful ways. This is essential because they cannot change the system if they do not understand what goes on within it. Based on his research work among a group of White and visible minority students in British Columbia, Orlowski (2001) argues that racism and discrimination remains problematic in Canada and urges everyone (especially educators) to work towards changing the status-quo. He also argues that

> the most effective way to lessen white hegemonic power includes a collective effort on the part of all the minorities. If they hope to be successful in creating a more liberatory Canadian society, these groups will simply have to forget about the ancient social hierarchies that they have experienced (p. 264).

Members of Canadian society who have a subordinate status, and have experienced marginality relative to the two European charter groups, cannot leave the issue of change to chance, nor make it the sole responsibility of "advocates" for equity and social justice. Canada's diverse communities, both at the individual and group levels, must also become agents of change as we move forward.

DIVERSITY AND STUDENTS WITH DISABILITIES

The bulk of this book is devoted to issues of cultural, racial, and linguistic diversity, as well as to socio-economic and gender-based differences among students (see Chapter 1). However there is one dimension of diversity — students with special needs — that has so far not been explored and which deserves attention (although it cannot be examined fully in this text). Few works put students with special needs and diversity together, although they are interconnected in very important ways. First, both are concerned with issues such as access to fair and equitable education, equitable representation in the curriculum, language discrimination, and fair measures of performance (Sleeter and Puente, 2001). In effect, both are concerned with promoting equity and social justice in schools and society. Second, some writers argue that the overrepresentation of students from minoritized backgrounds in special education classes is a reflection of wider societal beliefs about the nature of intelligence, what schools should teach, and how students and parents should relate to schools (Sleeter and Puente, 2001; Harry and Klingner, 2006). Third, special education programs by their very nature are exclusionary, and consequently contribute to reproducing inequalities in society. Fourth, another problem that faces special education programs and situates them firmly in the realm of equity is that schools are often poorly equipped to teach students with special needs. Fifth is the controversial practice of organizing special programs for students who are considered exceptionally gifted. This practice remains a source of equity-related debate — the central argument being that labelling some students as gifted or talented implicitly means that other are less well intellectually endowed. Sixth, as argued in the preceding chapters, minority students are disproportionately represented in special programs. Very often, students that have minor behavioural problems are classified as special needs, simply as a function of their racial or cultural background. Sleeter and Puente (2001) argue compellingly that the main point of convergence in discourses on diversity and special education is the overwhelming representation of minority students in special education classes. A report from the Civil Rights Project at Howard University (cited in Bennett, 2007) which has some relevance to the Canadian context, identified variables that contribute to the over-representation of racial minorities in special education programs. These include an over-identification of minority students as needing special education, the mainstreaming of minority, rather than White, students into special education classes, the quality of evaluation, support, and services that result in erroneous placement, and flawed individualized education programs.

Throughout the history of Canadian schooling, dealing with students with special needs has always presented its own set of challenges. Historically for reasons related to easy access, Canadian students with special needs were segregated into their own classrooms, which made it easier to provide them with the specialized attention they needed. However, during the last several decades there has been an ideological shift in thinking about how students with special needs should be treated or grouped for instruction. This trend towards "mainstreaming" or "inclusion" means that for the most part, students with special needs are integrated into regular classrooms. Osborne (1999) and Winzer (2005) advance several reasons why Canadian students with special needs are now being mainstreamed:

1. The segregation of these students leads to stereotyping. Rather than being seen as those who face challenges in learning, they are classified as people who cannot learn at all.

2. Segregation cuts the students off from society, and thus does not prepare them adequately for life outside of their classrooms.

3. Grouping these students into their own special classrooms tends to lower teachers' expectations of them because they are seen as people who can perform only the most basic academic tasks.

4. Segregating them into their own special classrooms tended to facilitate their being labelled as needing special help, even though their problems may not be directly related to academic ability. For example, as Osborne argues, students who are deaf or blind and segregated are considered learning disabled, yet their problem is simply related to visual or auditory impairment. Similarly, students who exhibit some behavioural problems may be considered mentally challenged, but their problem is not really one of ability, but rather a question of attitude.

5. Segregating students makes it easier to avoid looking for different ways of assisting them because they are considered as limited in ability.

6. The principles of educational equity demand that all students should have equal opportunity to learn with their peers.

Segregation of students amounts to an infringement of their human rights because (no matter their level of ability) students with special needs are human beings and citizens and are therefore entitled to the rights and privileges thereof. Moreover, the rights of students with special needs are protected under the *Charter of Rights and Freedoms*. Winzer (2005) summarizes the link between the philosophy of inclusion or mainstreaming to civil rights especially with regards to the United States:

> Special education is intimately connected to common views of social justice. The provision of less restrictive, more natural integrated environments for students with disabilities is an out growth of a social philosophy about individual civil rights that is so critical in the United States. Proponents argue that special classes are discriminatory and unequal and in violation of the democratic ethos that allows equal access to education for all students. That is, removal from the mainstream of education is inherently restrictive and limiting, and the right to be educated with one's peers is a civil right (p. 44).

While there is significant support for integrating students with special needs into regular classrooms, there is also some resistance to the idea. For example, teachers who do not have training in special education often argue that they do not have the expertise to accept such students in their class (Ryan, 2006). Opponents also see integration as additional work for teachers.

However, despite the trend to integrate special needs students into "regular" classrooms, there are nonetheless special education classes, which are designed to accommodate students who have been identified as having some learning disabilities. The number of students who are identified as having learning disabilities such as autism, dyslexia, attention deficit disorder (ADD), and attention deficit hyperactivity disorder (ADHD) has increased dramatically. These last two categories tend to be behaviour related, and typically have an over-representation of minority students, especially boys (Harry and Klingner, 2006).

Another group that usually predominates in special education classes is students that have some form of language-related difficulties, even though for the most part, these language problems are generally about difficulties in enunciating mainstream language (Egbo, 2001). Some writers note how challenging it is to determine the extent to which limited language proficiency is the result of difficulty in learning a second language versus learning disabilities. Therefore, the process of evaluation is problematically imprecise as one bilingual assessor interviewed by Harry and Klingner, (2006) acknowledges

My role as a bilingual assessor is to determine if the child's difficulties are due to [learning a second language] or due to other factors. Sometimes it might be something I don't know. Sometimes I don't have all of the facts in front of me. Sometimes the discrepancy is so thin. Maybe if they give him more time, he'll make it. Maybe we will give him 2 years and with more time we'll see a change. Maybe sometimes we know that 2 years will not help. Sometimes it is just kind of [a] struggle to see (p. 117).

What is disconcerting about comments such as the above is that the consequence of imprecise identification is erroneous categorization of students as special needs learners. Similarly, students from low socio-economic backgrounds tend to be over-represented in special education classes (Harry and Klinger, 2006). The intention is not to underrate the importance of diagnosing special needs students. Rather, the point is that when identifying students with what Bennett (2007) refers to as the "soft" cases of exceptionalities, i.e., those with behaviour-related diagnoses such as ADD and ADHD, it is prudent to proceed with caution. Delpit (2006) provides an example of why caution is essential. The case involves one of her former students who, in the first grade, was identified as requiring special needs placement. Delpit acknowledges that the student did experience considerable academic difficulty (particularly in mathematics). When she got to know him better, she found that even at the age of seven he had some adult responsibilities at home. For instance, he was solely responsible for taking care of a sister who was suffering from cerebral palsy, a drug incapacitated mother, and the household chores. He was also responsible for doing the family shopping and had become quite adept at handling money. Still, he could not perform some basic mathematical tasks in school. The discrepancy between this student's demonstrated ability at home and his limited academic achievement highlights the problems of what the curriculum sometimes presents and of how schools determine ability and skills. It also illustrates the problem of treating most students using a one-size-fits-all approach. Students differ considerably, and teachers have to find ways of reaching each one of them as a unique individual.

Returning to the issue of labelling, Bennett (2007) argues that

Successful teachers in inclusive classrooms . . . [discard] the ethnocentric view that low-income and ethnic-minority students are "culturally disadvantaged" and "at risk". They reject the idea that anyone who has not had the "normal" advantages of a middle-income home life is culturally deprived. They realize that a "deficit" view is harmful because it focuses on where our students *aren't* and blinds us to where they *are* (pp. 258–259). [emphasis in original]

In effect, labelling puts blinders on teachers and prevents them from exploring the vast region of possibilities that is their students. Consider the following vignette: The family of sixth grader Chelina had immigrated to Canada from Latin American a few years earlier and settled in Quebec. Chelina was experiencing considerable difficulty learning French, so much so that there was consensus among the experts who evaluated her that she might have some form of learning disorder. In addition to her difficulties with the language, she seemed to be obsessed with various objects in the class. Her dismayed teacher could not understand why Chelina was always tinkering with, or closely examining, the objects that captured her interest. On a number of occasions, she had tried to redirect Chelina's attention back to the task at hand by taking away such objects. She had discussed the issue with some of her colleagues, all of whom were of the opinion that Chelina's obsession was probably indicative of some form of psychological trauma that might be linked to her home life. Little was known about her family life except that her father worked in one of the local factories. This was an unfortunate omission because had the teacher probed a little further, she would have discovered that Chelina's father had been an engineer in their native country before immigrating to Canada as a political refugee. She would also have learned that stringent recertification requirements and his limited proficiency in French had so far prevented him from practising his profession in Canada. Furthermore, she would have understood that Chelina's obsession with objects was the result of her fervent desire to follow in her father's footsteps, i.e., to become an engineer. This case is a good example of why educators must not rush to label students.

CONCLUSION

This volume attempts to build a theory of practice that educators can adopt to initiate social change. The intent is to propose a progressive paradigm of dealing with diversity in Canadian schools. In so doing, several frameworks and models of teaching in contexts of student diversity have been explored. The rationale for exploring various frameworks is based on the recognition that teaching for diversity in authentic and life-changing ways depends on the adoption of an eclectic framework that integrates elements of various models across the curriculum. The work argues that educators must learn to ask uncomfortable questions about taken-for-granted assumptions about educational policies, the nature of learning, and what constitutes valid knowledge, with the ultimate goal of increasing the life chances of those they serve. At the same time, teachers and other educators must also address the issues of fairness, legitimacy, impartiality, and mutual advantage with respect to educational policy and practice. Ultimately, a body of knowledge that has been developed from the perspective of the dominant group can favour only dominant group students. Acknowledged or not, there are procedural rules for how we educate children and the existence of these rules is not in itself problematic. What many argue is unacceptable, is that these rules often reflect only the monolithic views of the dominant groups in Canadian society. This book also argues that schools must reconceptualize the way they are organized and implement mechanisms for sharing power among all stakeholders, especially students from nondominant group backgrounds and their families. The continued exclusion of their voices is blatantly contrary to Canada's chosen identity as a cultural mosaic. Furthermore, in the words of Howard (2006: 143) who writes within the context of the United States, the transformative agenda for all educators involves "dismantling the dominance paradigm and . . . envisioning, creating and modelling a better future, a new social paradigm that honors diversity and ensures greater equity for all . . . people".

While acknowledging that individuals do have a role to play in engendering their own academic and future success, teachers must recognize how a legacy of privilege contributes to the school success of students from the dominant group. Conversely, it must be clearly understood that a history of marginality underlies the negative schooling experiences of students from nondominant communities. The assumption that a predetermined biological or cultural propensity towards failure is the root cause of academic underachievement among some groups of students is no longer a tenable position. It is useful at this stage to highlight some of the issues raised in the book:

- Given that diversity is a stable Canadian reality, examining the relationships between race, culture, gender, and socio-economic status must be a critical starting point for initiating policies and programs that are geared towards *teaching for diversity in Canadian schools*. It is a widely accepted premise that social positioning, privilege, and the knowledge that is reproduced in schools (at least in Western and pluralistic societies such as Canada) intersect in complex ways that affect school success.

- There is compelling evidence to show that minority students have a tenuous relationship with schools as a function of systemic racism, exclusionary educational practices, and Eurocentric ideologies that not only negate their identities but also devalue their cultural capital.

- A myriad of variables account for differential school achievement between various groups of students, and between boys and girls. While cognizant that there is as much intra-group diversity as there are inter-group differences, taking people's backgrounds, learning styles, and worldviews into consideration must be part of critical teaching practices.

- While the explicit goal of schools is to socialize and educate the next generation, and the content required is generally stipulated in the formal curriculum, a substantive amount of what students learn is not openly stated — even though this implicitly conveyed knowledge, or the hidden curriculum, underpins student and teacher behaviour in Canadian schools.

- Historically, Canada has always been a culturally and linguistically diverse society. However, responses to diversity by successive Canadian governments, social institutions, and the public at large are typically influenced by prevailing social ideologies. More importantly, the contemporary demographic profile of Canadian society has always been inextricably linked to immigration policy.

- Canadian schools mirror the diversity in wider society, especially in large urban centres. Consequently, and also as a result of constitutional provisions in the *Charter of Rights and Freedoms*, social and educational policies have been developed to address Canadian diversity and to ostensibly equalize educational and social opportunities for all.

- Progressive educators, and this book, argue that while significant progress has been made towards empowering students from diverse backgrounds, more still needs to be done at all levels of the educational system, especially at the micro-level of the classroom. Furthermore, educational policies and practices must be grounded in the principles of fundamental human rights and social justice, — which reject monocultural and assimilationist educational ideologies in pluralistic societies such as Canada.

- The goal of promoting diversity in Canadian schools cannot be achieved without practical and structural changes to social and educational policies at all levels of the government, and relevant sectors of society. To this extent, policy matters.

Finally, this work argues that authentic change can occur only when teachers and other educators embrace inclusive and anti-bias paradigms and demonstrate an unwavering commitment to social justice. With this in mind, I urge all educators to let transformative praxis begin.

Key Terms

Deconstruction   Diversity issues across the   Empathy
                          curriculum (DIAC)

Questions to Guide Reflective Practice

1. With regard to teaching for diversity, what in your opinion should be the future direction for teachers? Develop a comprehensive future-oriented strategy to guide your own practice.

2. Based on your reading of this chapter and the book, how can long-term strategies for empowering diverse learners be developed?

3. This chapter argues that the issue of students with special needs intersects with other diversity issues. To what extent do you agree with this assertion? Justify your answer.

4. How can schools maintain a critical balance between preserving group interests and the interests of the individual?

5. How would you characterize the over-representation of minority students in special education programs? Do you believe that it is the result of systemic racism or a true reflection of the situation? How can schools change this trend?

Case Study Analysis: Chapter Opening Vignette

1. Assess John Zeak's handling of the case. Did he do everything he could have done to avoid the escalation of the situation?

2. If you were John Zeak what, if anything, would you have done differently?

3. What is the major error that John Zeak made in this situation that all teachers, especially those that are new to the profession, should avoid?

4. If you were the principal how would you resolve this conflict?

5. Briefly outline an action plan for dealing with students who are prejudiced like Josh.

6. Explain your understanding of John Zeak's comment "there was too much at stake".

Test Your Knowledge

1. Research and identify the policies that guide special education programs in your province. To what extent are special needs students "mainstreamed" in your local schools?

2. Discuss the advantages and disadvantages of integrating students with special needs into "regular" classrooms with a group of your peers. What is the opinion of the majority?

3. Research what extent placement patterns of students with special needs in your province reflect the view that minoritized students are over-represented in special education programs.

4. Interview some special education specialists. What are their views on the practice of "mainstreaming"?

5. Find out what schools in your community are doing to make schools spaces that foster equity, student empowerment, and collaboration among all relevant stakeholders.

6. The chapter argues that one way of empowering diverse students and their communities is through community outreach. What is your local school board's policy for facilitating the participation of members of the diverse communities in the schools within its jurisdiction?

For Further Reading

Bennett C. I. (2007). *Comprehensive Multicultural Education: Theory Practice*, 6th Edition. Boston: Pearson Education.

Delpit, L. (2006). *Other People's Children: Cultural Conflict in the Classroom*. New York: The New Press.

Gay, G. (2000). *Culturally Responsive Teaching: Theory, Research Practice*. New York: Teachers College Press.

Gillborn, D. (2004). Ability, Selection, and Institutional Racism in Schools. In M. Olssen (Ed.), *Culture and Learning: Access and Opportunity in the Classroom* (pp. 279–298). Charlotte: Information Age Publishing Inc.

Grossman, H. (1995). *Teaching in a Diverse Society*. Needham Heights: Allyn Bacon.

Harry, B., and Klingner, J. (2006). *Why Are so Many Minority Students in Special Education?* New York: Teachers College Press.

Howard, G. R. (2006). *We Can't Teach What We Don't Know: White Teachers, Multiracial Schools*, 2nd Edition. New York: Teachers College Press.

McLaren, P. (2007). *Life in Schools: an Introduction to Critical Pedagogy in the Foundations of Education*, 5th Edition. Boston: Pearson Education.

Osborne, K. (1999). *Education: A Guide to the Canadian School Debate–Or Who Wants What and Why?* Toronto: Penguin Canada.

Websites of Interest

www.edu.gov.on.ca/eng/general/elemsec/speced/speced.html Ontario Ministry of Education Website

www.ibwebs.com/canadian.htm Canadian Special Education Website

www.specialeducation.ab.ca/ Alberta Teachers' Association — Special Education Council

www.neads.ca National Educational Association of Disabled Students (NEADS)

www.ethnocultural.ca Canadian Ethnocultural Council

www.cmef.ca Canadian Multicultural Education Foundation

APPENDIX

Canadian Charter of Rights and Freedoms

Whereas Canada is founded upon principles that recognize the supremacy of God and the rule of law:

GUARANTEE OF RIGHTS AND FREEDOMS

1. The *Canadian Charter of Rights and Freedoms* guarantees the rights and freedoms set out in it subject only to such reasonable limits prescribed by law as can be demonstrably justified in a free and democratic society.

FUNDAMENTAL FREEDOM

2. Everyone has the following fundamental freedoms:
    (a) freedom of conscience and religion;
    (b) freedom of thought, belief, opinion and expression, including freedom of the press and other media of communication;
    (c) freedom of peaceful assembly; and
    (d) freedom of association.

DEMOCRATIC RIGHTS

3. Every citizen of Canada has the right to vote in an election of members of the House of Commons or of a legislative assembly and to be qualified for membership therein.
4. (1) No House of Commons and no legislative assembly shall continue for longer than five years from the date fixed for the return of the writs of a general election of its members.
    (2) In time of real or apprehended war, invasion or insurrection, a House of Commons may be continued by Parliament and a legislative assembly may be continued by the legislature beyond five years if such continuation is not opposed by the votes of more than one-third of the members of the House of Commons or the legislative assembly, as the case may be.
5. There shall be a sitting of Parliament and of each legislature at least once every twelve months.

MOBILITY RIGHTS

6. (1) Every citizen of Canada has the right to enter, remain in and leave Canada.

   (2) Every citizen of Canada and every person who has the status of a permanent resident of Canada has the right

   (a) to move to and take up residence in any province; and

   (b) to pursue the gaining of a livelihood in any province.

   (3) The rights specified in subsection (2) are subject to

   (a) any laws or practices of general application in force in a province other than those that discriminate among persons primarily on the basis of province of present or previous residence; and

   (b) any laws providing for reasonable residency requirements as a qualification for the receipt of publicly provided social services.

   (4) Subsections (2) and (3) do not preclude any law, program or activity that has as its object the amelioration in a province of conditions of individuals in that province who are socially or economically disadvantaged if the rate of employment in that province is below the rate of employment in Canada.

LEGAL RIGHTS

7. Everyone has the right to life, liberty and security of the person and the right not to be deprived thereof except in accordance with the principles of fundamental justice.

8. Everyone has the right to be secure against unreasonable search or seizure.

9. Everyone has the right not to be arbitrarily detained or imprisoned.

10. Everyone has the right on arrest or detention

    (a) to be informed promptly of the reasons therefor;

    (b) to retain and instruct counsel without delay and to be informed of that right; and

    (c) to have the validity of the detention determined by way of *habeas corpus* and to be released if the detention is not lawful.

11. Any person charged with an offence has the right

    (a) to be informed without unreasonable delay of the specific offence;

    (b) to be tried within a reasonable time;

    (c) not to be compelled to be a witness in proceedings against that person in respect of the offence;

    (d) to be presumed innocent until proven guilty according to law in a fair and public hearing by an independent and impartial tribunal;

    (e) not to be denied reasonable bail without just cause;

    (f) except in the case of an offence under military law tried before a military tribunal, to the benefit of trial by jury where the maximum punishment for the offence is imprisonment for five years or a more severe punishment;

    (g) not to be found guilty on account of any act or omission unless, at the time of the act or omission, it constituted an offence under Canadian or international law or was criminal according to the general principles of law recognized by the community of nations;

(h) if finally acquitted of the offence, not to be tried for it again and, if finally found guilty and punished for the offence, not to be tried or punished for it again; and

(i) if found guilty of the offence and if the punishment for the offence has been varied between the time of commission and the time of sentencing, to the benefit of the lesser punishment.

12. Everyone has the right not to be subjected to any cruel and unusual treatment or punishment.

13. A witness who testifies in any proceedings has the right not to have any incriminating evidence so given used to incriminate that witness in any other proceedings, except in a prosecution for perjury or for the giving of contradictory evidence.

14. A party or witness in any proceedings who does not understand or speak the language in which the proceedings are conducted or who is deaf has the right to the assistance of an interpreter.

EQUALITY RIGHTS

15. (1) Every individual is equal before and under the law and has the right to the equal protection and equal benefit of the law without discrimination and, in particular, without discrimination based on race, national or ethnic origin, colour, religion, sex, age or mental or physical disability.

(2) Subsection (1) does not preclude any law, program or activity that has as its object the amelioration of conditions of disadvantaged individuals or groups including those that are disadvantaged because of race, national or ethnic origin, colour, religion, sex, age or mental or physical disability.

OFFICIAL LANGUAGES OF CANADA

16. (1) English and French are the official languages of Canada and have equality of status and equal rights and privileges as to their use in all institutions of the Parliament and government of Canada.

(2) English and French are the official languages of New Brunswick and have equality of status and equal rights and privileges as to their use in all institutions of the legislature and government of New Brunswick.

(3) Nothing in this Charter limits the authority of Parliament or a legislature to advance the equality of status or use of English and French.

16.1. (1) The English linguistic community and the French linguistic community in New Brunswick have equality of status and equal rights and privileges, including the right to distinct educational institutions and such distinct cultural institutions as are necessary for the preservation and promotion of those communities.

(2) The role of the legislature and government of New Brunswick to preserve and promote the status, rights and privileges referred to in subsection (1) is affirmed.

17. (1) Everyone has the right to use English or French in any debates and other proceedings of Parliament.

(2) Everyone has the right to use English or French in any debates and other proceedings of the legislature of New Brunswick.

18. (1) The statutes, records and journals of Parliament shall be printed and published in English and French and both language versions are equally authoritative.

(2) The statutes, records and journals of the legislature of New Brunswick shall be printed and published in English and French and both language versions are equally authoritative.

19. (1) Either English or French may be used by any person in, or in any pleading in or process issuing from, any court established by Parliament.

(2) Either English or French may be used by any person in, or in any pleading in or process issuing from, any court of New Brunswick.

20. (1) Any member of the public in Canada has the right to communicate with, and to receive available services from, any head or central office of an institution of the Parliament or government of Canada in English or French, and has the same right with respect to any other office of any such institution where

(a) there is a significant demand for communications with and services from that office in such language; or

(b) due to the nature of the office, it is reasonable that communications with and services from that office be available in both English and French.

(2) Any member of the public in New Brunswick has the right to communicate with, and to receive available services from, any office of an institution of the legislature or government of New Brunswick in English or French.

21. Nothing in sections 16 to 20 abrogates or derogates from any right, privilege or obligation with respect to the English and French languages, or either of them, that exists or is continued by virtue of any other provision of the Constitution of Canada.

22. Nothing in sections 16 to 20 abrogates or derogates from any legal or customary right or privilege acquired or enjoyed either before or after the coming into force of this Charter with respect to any language that is not English or French.

MINORITY LANGUAGE EDUCATIONAL RIGHTS

23. (1) Citizens of Canada

(a) whose first language learned and still understood is that of the English or French linguistic minority population of the province in which they reside, or

(b) who have received their primary school instruction in Canada in English or French and reside in a province where the language in which they received that instruction is the language of the English or French linguistic minority population of the province,

have the right to have their children receive primary and secondary school instruction in that language in that province.

(2) Citizens of Canada of whom any child has received or is receiving primary or secondary school instruction in English or French in Canada, have the right to have all their children receive primary and secondary school instruction in the same language.

(3) The right of citizens of Canada under subsections (1) and (2) to have their children receive primary and secondary school instruction in the language of the English or French linguistic minority population of a province

    (a) applies wherever in the province the number of children of citizens who have such a right is sufficient to warrant the provision to them out of public funds of minority language instruction; and

    (b) includes, where the number of those children so warrants, the right to have them receive that instruction in minority language educational facilities provided out of public funds.

ENFORCEMENT

24. (1) Anyone whose rights or freedoms, as guaranteed by this Charter, have been infringed or denied may apply to a court of competent jurisdiction to obtain such remedy as the court considers appropriate and just in the circumstances.

    (2) Where, in proceedings under subsection (1), a court concludes that evidence was obtained in a manner that infringed or denied any rights or freedoms guaranteed by this Charter, the evidence shall be excluded if it is established that, having regard to all the circumstances, the admission of it in the proceedings would bring the administration of justice into disrepute.

GENERAL

25. The guarantee in this Charter of certain rights and freedoms shall not be construed so as to abrogate or derogate from any aboriginal, treaty or other rights or freedoms that pertain to the aboriginal peoples of Canada including

    (a) any rights or freedoms that have been recognized by the Royal Proclamation of October 7, 1763; and

    (b) any rights or freedoms that now exist by way of land claims agreements or may be so acquired.

26. The guarantee in this Charter of certain rights and freedoms shall not be construed as denying the existence of any other rights or freedoms that exist in Canada.

27. This Charter shall be interpreted in a manner consistent with the preservation and enhancement of the multicultural heritage of Canadians.

28. Notwithstanding anything in this Charter, the rights and freedoms referred to in it are guaranteed equally to male and female persons.

29. Nothing in this Charter abrogates or derogates from any rights or privileges guaranteed by or under the Constitution of Canada in respect of denominational, separate or dissentient schools.

30. A reference in this Charter to a Province or to the legislative assembly or legislature of a province shall be deemed to include a reference to the Yukon Territory and the Northwest Territories, or to the appropriate legislative authority thereof, as the case may be.

31. Nothing in this Charter extends the legislative powers of any body or authority.

APPLICATION OF CHARTER

32. (1) This Charter applies

    (a) to the Parliament and government of Canada in respect of all matters within the authority of Parliament including all matters relating to the Yukon Territory and Northwest Territories; and

    (b) to the legislature and government of each province in respect of all matters within the authority of the legislature of each province.

  (2) Notwithstanding subsection (1), section 15 shall not have effect until three years after this section comes into force.

33. (1) Parliament or the legislature of a province may expressly declare in an Act of Parliament or of the legislature, as the case may be, that the Act or a provision thereof shall operate notwithstanding a provision included in section 2 or sections 7 to 15 of this Charter.

  (2) An Act or a provision of an Act in respect of which a declaration made under this section is in effect shall have such operation as it would have but for the provision of this Charter referred to in the declaration.

  (3) A declaration made under subsection (1) shall cease to have effect five years after it comes into force or on such earlier date as may be specified in the declaration.

  (4) Parliament or the legislature of a province may re-enact a declaration made under subsection (1).

  (5) Subsection (3) applies in respect of a re-enactment made under subsection (4).

CITATION

34. This Part may be cited as the *Canadian Charter of Rights and Freedoms*.

Glossary

Aboriginal peoples   Descendants of the original inhabitants of North America. There are three distinct groups of Aboriginal peoples: the Métis, First Nations peoples and the Inuit.

Action research   Systematic investigation conducted by teachers and other educators who gather information about their own teaching for the purposes of improving practice. Teacher Diversity Research is a variant of action research (see below).

Administrator Diversity Awareness Compass (ADAC)   An analytical and diagnostic tool that enables school leaders to conduct diversity-related self and institutional analysis. This tool may facilitate school administrators' ability to create inclusive learning environments for all students.

Afrocentric schools   Schools in Canada and the United States that rely on a curriculum that is based on the heritage, history, culture and epistemology of people of African descent. Pedagogically, Afrocentric schools embrace a holistic view of education that encourages students to be subjects in their learning experience rather than objects. The ultimate goal is to better meet the needs of Black students.

Anti-racism   A term that is used to describe a process of change that advocates the elimination of individual, institutional, and systemic racism unequal power relations in pluralistic societies like Canada and the United States.

Anti-racist education   Advocates the elimination of discriminatory educational practices through changes in schools' curricula, policies and practices. Anti-racism theorists and educators believe that racism is at the root of some of the problems minority students experience in school.

Assessment   Diagnostic, formative or summative appraisals used to make educational decisions about students' performance. i.e. weaknesses, strengths, progress. Assessments are also used to evaluate curriculum effectiveness and accuracy. Assessment features prominently in diversity and education discourse, and significantly impacts the educational attainment of students.

Assimilation   The complete adoption of the values and cultures of a group by an individual or group from a different culture. It usually results in attitudinal and behavioral changes and a rejection of the values, attitudes and beliefs of one's original cultural group. Assimilation may be voluntary, forced or can occur indirectly through programs and initiatives that encourage minority group members to adopt dominant group culture. In Canada, (cultural) assimilation implies either Anglo or Franco conformity.

Benevolent accommodation   A description of policies and strategies that are aimed at assisting refugees and other newcomers in which the relationship between the giver and the receiver is one of "benefactor" and "dependant" respectively.

Bilingual education   A term used to describe an educational approach that involves the use of two languages of instruction to teach a student — the student's primary language and a second language. There are various models of bilingual education.

Bilingualism   A term that is generally used to denote fluency in two languages. In Canada, bilingualism refers to the legal and constitutionally established status of English and French as the official and equal languages of the country.

Bio-diversity   The variability of all things on earth and the ecology for which they are composed. Bio-diversity includes all terrestrial and aquatic organisms.

Canadian Charter of Rights and Freedoms
Adopted in 1982 as part of the Constitution, the Charter guarantees Canadians various fundamental rights and freedoms, including freedom of conscience and religion, freedom of expression, of beliefs, of democratic rights, of liberty and security and a plethora of legal rights. The Charter also outlaws discrimination based on categories such as race, national or ethnic origin, colour, religion, sex, age, or mental or physical disability. It also reaffirms Canada's official bilingualism and multiculturalism.

Capacity building   Actions taken towards improving practice for the benefit of those who are directly affected by such practices. In education, capacity building may also be achieved through professional development.

Conscientization   A term popularized by critical educator Paulo Freire, it refers the process of learning that facilitates individuals' abilities to recognize and understand the social, political and economic contradictions present in society at a deep, rather than a superficial, level. Ideally, conscientization leads to action–becoming critical of one's social environment and actively participating in eradicating unjust practices and policies.

Criterion-referenced assessment   An assessment strategy in which students' performance is measured against set criteria rather than against the performance of their peers.

Critical language awareness   An approach that helps students identify and understand the ways language, power, and ideology are interconnected. Teachers can model critical language awareness by paying attention to their own language practices in and out of school.

Critical multicultural education   A variant of multicultural education that advocates radical structural and institutional changes in society through education. Its main focus is on radical transformation of societal structures that exclude some segments of society.

Critical pedagogy   A school of thought that advocates the examination of the ways power mediates academic success and how challenge and interrogation can interrupt the control dominant society has over educational knowledge. The ultimate goal of critical pedagogy is to eliminate oppression as well as to create a fair and just society through meaningful changes in educational practices.

Critical theory   A school of thought that critiques what it views to be historically based patterns of oppression and domination in society. At the same time, it proposes an alternative view of society that offers possibilities for changing social structures and institutions such as schools.

Critical thinking   The deliberate process of reasoning that enables people to move from a restricted to a more abstract level of thinking. Critical thinking involves critical reflection, probing, questioning, and the reconfiguration of information in ways that appeal to people's experiences and meaning systems.

Cross-cultural communication   The exchange of information between a sender and receiver who are of different cultural backgrounds. Cross-cultural communication can be verbal or non-verbal. When a culture-related disconnect occurs between people of different cultures cross-cultural *mis*communication occurs.

Cross-cultural sensitivity audits   A process for examining educators' sensitivity to culture-related needs of their students as well as to what extent these needs have been met in their teaching and school practices.

Culture   Ideas, beliefs, values and behavioural patterns, knowledge-base and traditions of a group of people who share a common ancestry—history, geography, language, racial religious variables etc. These, in turn, are transmitted from one generation to another.

Cultural deprivation theory   A theory that stipulates that factors originating from students' home environment or cultural backgrounds such as value systems and lack of motivation on the part of the students constrain their ability to achieve success in school.

Cultural diversity Different or variable ways of knowing, perceiving and interpreting reality or making sense of the world by a group of people based on their culture or heritage (see also definition of culture above).

Cultural capital The knowledge-base, habits, patterns of language use, skills and attitudes that people learn as a result of being part of a social class. According to one of its major proponents, Pierre Bourdieu, some forms of cultural capital are more valued than others. Moreover, schools reinforce the cultural capital of the dominant group.

Cultural habitus Refers to social class-based dispositions that a person possesses, which inform his or her behaviour.

Cultural pluralism Cultural pluralism refers to the process whereby two or more cultural and ethnic groups co-exist through compromise and mutual respect for one another. The term is often used interchangeably with multiculturalism. Canada's policy of multiculturalism, the various provincial human rights codes and *The Canadian Charter of Rights and Freedoms* (see Appendix) all promote cultural pluralism.

Culturally relevant pedagogy Popularized by Gloria Ladson-Billings, this is an approach to teaching academic knowledge that builds on what students already know based on their culture, thus making them active participants in the learning process in authentic ways.

Deconstruction Literally means to "take apart". It refers to the act of critically examining a taken-for-granted concept or idea for the purposes of exposing its contradictions and inconsistencies.

Dialogical classroom communication A pattern of communication in which both the teacher and his or her students are able to freely express themselves in a "community of learners".

Diaspora A term used to refer to the dispersion of ethnic peoples, languages and cultures once concentrated in a specific location.

Differentiated instruction Targeted instructional strategies that enable teachers to meet the individual needs of students. Teachers may assess needs based on students' interests, strengths, skills and readiness. Success in using differentiated instruction depends on teachers providing students with multiple options to appropriate tasks.

Discrimination Differential and treatment and denial of rights and liberties on the basis of race, gender, nationality, sexual orientation, religion, and disability. Discrimination by individuals or institutions lead to unequal access to health care, education, employment, etc.

Diversity A term used to describe the various forms of differences among people, such as race, gender, ability, religion, socioeconomic status, and sexual orientation. The term is also used to describe differences in the environment.

Diversity audits Self-initiated assessment conducted by school administrators that test the extent to which a school supports and promotes diversity. These audits attempt to foster a theory of inclusion built on the linkages between institutional structures, leadership practices and student empowerment.

Diversity issues across the curriculum (DIAC) The practice of integrating diversity issues consistently into all subject areas in schools.

Diversity-oriented leadership A model of leadership that is inclusive, eclectic, transformative, emancipatory and social justice-oriented. Diversity-oriented leadership encourages diversity while challenging taken-for-granted assumptions about leadership practices.

Diversity pedagogy Refers to a philosophical perspective that views the relationship between culture and cognition as central to understating the relationship between the teaching and learning process. Its main focus is on the ways teachers' and students' behaviour influence how knowledge is co-created (Sheets, 2005).

Dominant group A term used to describe the groups that possess the most privilege and controls the social, political, and economic power within a given society. Within the Canadian context, the dominant group is considered to be White, male, Christian and English-speaking citizens.

Dominant narratives An institutionally sanctioned way of thinking, talking, and viewing the world (often that of the privileged or dominant group), which become accepted as the norm.

Eclectic leadership A critical model of leadership that draws on several progressive approaches to empower members of a learning community, especially those from disadvantaged backgrounds.

Emancipatory possibilities Describes an educational intervention framework that has the potential to liberate and empower the oppressed.

Empathy Ability to understand and be compassionate about other people's experiences.

English as a Second Language (ESL) Language acquisition program that is specifically designed to teach students for whom English is not a native language. Depending on the context, there are several models of ESL programs.

Environmental scan In this context, the term refers to the process of appraising the makeup of the student body in a school in order to know who they are. The overarching goal of environmental scanning is to help educators make informed decisions about appropriate pedagogical strategies, materials, language support, community partnerships, etc. that are necessary for positive learning outcomes for all students.

Ethnic group A group of people, who through shared history and cultural traits such as language, artifacts, values, etc., have a shared identity. An essential characteristic of an ethnic group is a sense of peoplehood (Banks and Banks, 2001).

Ethnicity The common beliefs, behaviour and traditions of a group of people sharing a common ancestry, historical experiences and heritage including linguistic, religious and racial identities.

Ethnographic study A study that attempts to examine people's behaviour in relation to those around them in specific cultural sites. In the context of this book, a classroom is assumed to be a "cultural site" in which the teacher and his or her students interact with one another as cultural beings.

Eurocentric ideologies Principles that suggest the superiority of Europe and European worldviews. These principles are usually transmitted in social institutions like schools. In Canada, Eurocentric beliefs and ideologies are the standard by which other cultures are judged.

Explicit curriculum The knowledge, behaviours and attitudes (usually articulated in curriculum documents) that the school intentionally teaches students.

First Nations peoples One of the three distinct groups of Aboriginal Peoples. There are 633 First Nation Bands representing 52 nations or cultural groups and over 50 languages.

Focused observation A process in Teacher Diversity Research that identifies a specific problem or issue and concentrates on observing or studying the phenomenon.

French immersion A bilingual education program in which a significant portion of curriculum instruction is in French.

Fundamental rights Rationale for fair and just social policies based on the tenets and characteristics of fundamental human rights as enacted by the United Nations as well as through national human rights codes.

Global awareness The acquisition of knowledge and understanding of societies and environments beyond one's local community and country. Global awareness is grounded in the need to understand the ways in which people and societies are interconnected.

Haptics A form of non-verbal communication that involves touch.

Hegemony   A form of social control that is not based on force. It relies on false consensus that reinforces the power of the dominant group without making the process of control obvious.

Heritage languages   A term used to describe non-English, Non-French and non-Aboriginal languages spoken by other Canadians. As part of the multiculturalism policy, the federal government provides some resource support for heritage language instruction.

Hidden curriculum   What the school unintentionally teaches students through the contents of the curriculum, routines and expected behavioural norms.

Inclusive language   The use of language that avoids the deliberate or intentional exclusion of particular groups in society.

Indigenous knowledge   The worldviews, ways of knowing and cumulative knowledge of a particular group usually acquired through cultural transmission. Indigenous knowledge is comprised of various areas, including ecological, humanistic and spiritual knowledge.

Intercultural education   Education that fosters cross-cultural understanding. Its purpose is generally to foster peace and mutual understanding.

Interdisciplinary knowledge   Knowledge that results from, and can be applied to, two or more disciplines.

International covenants   International agreements that guide the ways in which certain issues are handled worldwide. Many covenants such as the Universal Declaration of Human Rights and the International Convention Against All Forms of Racial Discrimination seek to safeguard the rights and freedoms of citizens of the world, especially those that have been traditionally marginalized. These include women First Nations peoples and minorities.

Just educational policies   Fair and inclusive educational policies that are geared towards empowering those who have been marginalized and oppressed by the educational system.

Kinesics   A type of nonverbal communication pattern that deals with the study of body language.

Liberal-democratic ideology   A political school of thought that emphasizes equality, individualism and meritocracy. As a consequence, adherents tend to oppose special treatment for even groups that have been traditionally marginalized in society.

Life chances   The options and opportunities that society and social institutions such as schools offer to individuals under the right conditions. Life chances has two main elements—ligatures, which are bonds that people develop through immersion in the same social contexts, and options, which are opportunities that are provided by social institutions such as schools.

Linguistic pluralism   The paradigm that depicts nonofficial languages as useful tools for instruction, which can be used in conjunction with official languages in schools. Linguistic pluralism encourages the idea that nonofficial languages have a place in educational instruction that goes beyond their usual categorization as "resources".

Meritocracy   An ideological view of society (and social institutions) as a level playing field in which everyone has an equal chance to succeed regardless of their background, social advantage or disadvantage. Under this arrangement, school failure is attributed solely to individual ability and effort to the exclusion of other variables such as history of domination and inequitable access to social rewards.

Minority group   A group of people who make up a small proportion of the total population and are physically, socially or culturally different from the majority group. These differences sometimes serve as grounds for discrimination, exclusion, and subjugation.

Monocultural education   Education that is based on a singular worldview, e.g. Eurocentric ideology.

Mosaic   A metaphor used to describe the social arrangement in Canada in which various racial and ethnic groups subscribe to a Canadian identity while maintaining their cultural identities. It is based on an "image of a patterned entity comprising disparate and distinct elements arranged into a cohesive whole" (Fleras and Elliott, 2003). The concept is often considered the reverse of the "melting pot" ideology, in which various cultures meld together to create a seemingly cohesive national culture and identity.

Multiculturalism   A political doctrine with corresponding principles in which diversity is acknowledged as a desirable social arrangement. Canada's inter-group relations are founded on this doctrine as manifested in the official identity of Canada as a "Multicultural society within a Bilingual framework" (Pierre Trudeau, 1971).

Multicultural education   A term used to describe a wide range of educational reforms that aim to restructure the curriculum in order to foster respect for cultural diversity and difference among students as well as provide equal educational opportunities for all students. There are various models of multicultural education ranging from what is generally considered as superficial to critical (radical) multicultural education.

Multilingualism   Proficiency in more than two languages.

Mutual resistance   A behaviour that occurs when a teacher and his or her student are no longer able to tolerate each other's perceived biases and uncooperative attitudes and therefore take an oppositional stand. It often leads to culture-related conflicts between teachers and students in diverse contexts.

Negotiable knowledge   Context specific knowledge that is geared towards promoting local values and epistemologies. Dimensions of negotiable knowledge include community-centered values, local ecosystem, language, cultural heritage, and community awareness.

Non-negotiable knowledge   Essential knowledge that all students must acquire in a diverse society. Non-negotiable knowledge has several dimensions which include, although are not limited to, culturally relevant academic knowledge, critical multicultural/intercultural education, global awareness, and critical language awareness, indigenous knowledge, critical thinking, and basic academic knowledge.

Norm-referenced assessment   An assessment technique that measures students' achievement against those of their peers.

Official language minorities   The official *Languages Act of Canada* (1969/1988) gives French-speaking Canadians who live outside Quebec and English-speaking Canadians who live in Quebec the right to education and access to services in French and English respectively.

Oppositional subcultures   Counter cultures and attitudes that people develop in response to perceived oppression by the dominant culture.

Paralinguistic   A form of communication which involves vocal effects that affect speech production.

Peace education   Education that is philosophically and pedagogically geared towards promoting values that encourage and foster peaceful co-existence among all individuals nationally and internationally. The main objectives of peace education are to reduce prejudice while promoting human rights, tolerance, diversity and identity validation.

Perspectives re-alignment   Positive change in thinking that occurs as a result of individuals engaging in critical self-analysis. Educators who wish to contribute to meaningful change to empower culturally, linguistically, economically and socially disadvantaged students should ideally undergo perspective realignment through a process that involves critical self-reflection.

Policy   Courses of action designed by institutional bodies or authorities for the purposes of meeting specified objectives. In many instances, policy also serves as guiding principles towards the attainment of a specific goal.

Post-instructional analysis   The reflection that takes place after instruction. Specifically, it is the stage at which teachers decide what teaching strategies to reinforce, refine, modify or eliminate. It is also used to determine the degree of instructional success.

Praxis   A process that involves linking reflection with action for the purposes of initiating social change.

Pre-instructional activities   Refers to the preparatory activities that precede instruction. For the purposes of this book, this stage involves content planning and comprehensive content analysis for biases in language and resources.

Prejudice   A preformed, usually unfavourable opinion about someone or a group that is made without consideration of the facts. Prejudice is often a precursor for discrimination.

Prejudice reduction   Strategies and activities that encourage the elimination of prejudice. It should be integrated across curriculums and in all subject areas.

Privilege   The taken-for-granted experiences of opportunity, rights, freedoms, benefits and advantages enjoyed by members of the dominant group in a given society, and often denied to nondominant, minority or disadvantaged groups.

Proxemics   The study of non-verbal communication that deals with personal distance.

Race   A term used to describe a group of people of common ancestry with physical characteristics that are distinguishable from that of individuals of other lineages. These physical characteristics include skin colour, hair texture and facial features, shape of eyes, etc. Race is used as a basis for designating social categories into which people are grouped. Also, it is sometimes used as the basis for discrimination and exclusion.

Racism   Prejudicial attitudes and action towards a person or group from another race. A characteristic tenet of racism is the idea that one group is superior while the other is inferior. Racism can be individual, institutional or systemic (see also systemic discrimination).

Social cohesion   Grounded in the idea of a common good for all, social cohesion is, in theory, the process of maintaining social order through mutual understanding, respect, equal opportunities, and fair access to social resources in a given society. In practice, this is not often the case.

Social justice   A concept founded on the idea that all people and groups within a society are to be afforded equal access to freedoms, liberties, opportunities and participation within their societies.

Social reproduction   The condition through which the values, traditions and ideologies of the dominant or majority group becomes institutionalized and as a result, creates economic, political and social inequalities in societies. As institutions of socializations, schools contribute to social reproduction. At the same time, they hold the greatest potential for effecting positive social change.

Stereotyping   A process of generalization that ascribes the same characteristics to a group of people without consideration for individual differences. Stereotypes can be misleading because they are normally based on misconceptions about race, culture, gender, sexual orientation, religion, language, ability, physical appearance and other human attributes.

Structural audits   The process through which educators assess the extent to which the needs of all students (and their families) are being met by schools' diversity-oriented practices such as hiring policies, school programs and curriculum, instructional resources and disciplinary policies.

Structural functionalism   A sociological paradigm that states that the primary function of the various aspects (parts) of society is to maintain equilibrium. Structural functionalism sees the various institutions in society as interrelated in so far as they all play an important role in overall maintenance and stability.

Systemic discrimination   Institutionalized discrimination through practices and policies that overtly appear neutral but are intentionally or unintentionally exclusionary and biased towards members of minority groups. Systemic discriminatory practices and policies ultimately act as barriers to the social and educational advancement of disadvantaged groups.

Teachable moments   Unplanned incidents which occur in classrooms (mostly during instruction) that provide teachers instant opportunities to teach desirable behaviours and attitudes such as respect, tolerance and empathy.

Teacher diversity research   A multi-step variant of action research that seeks to initiate change through teachers' study of their diversity related teaching practices. It encourages teachers to better understand the ways in which their action and teaching practices empower or disempower their diverse students.

Teacher Diversity Awareness Compass (TDAC) A multi-dimensional framework designed to facilitate the process of self-analysis and awareness of diversity issues in teachers. TDAC has several dimensions: critical self-analysis, role reversal or role playing the "other", attitude and values appraisal, perspectives review and re-alignment and self-directed transformative action.

Transcultural education   The educational paradigm that encourages individuals to acknowledge the world outside of their own as well as to address the challenges inherent in a globalized world.

Transformative action   Actions directed at improving the life chances of students from marginalized communities.

Transformative learning   The type of learning that results in profound changes in the learner's perspectives/consciousness. Transformative learning encourages learners to adopt a more critical view of the world.

Transformative practice   Teaching practices that are aimed towards effecting educational and social change.

Transformative praxis   A change-oriented social or pedagogical action (see also praxis).

Triggers   Used in this context to describe activities that enable teachers and administrators to initiate self-analysis, particularly in contexts of student diversity.

Unilingualism   The use of, or reliance on one language for the purposes of instruction.

Visible minorities   The official term used to describe non-White, non-Aboriginal and non-Caucasian racial minorities in Canada. Specifically, the Employment Equity Act defines visible minorities as "persons, other than Aboriginal peoples, who are non-Caucasian in race or non-white in colour". These include Chinese, South Asian, Black, Filipino, Latin American, Southeast Asian, Arab, West Asian, Korean, Japanese, Visible minority, and Multiple visible minority.

White privilege   The concept that White people have opportunities and advantages that are often taken for granted based on the colour of their skin. These same opportunities and advantages are not given to non-White members of society.

Xenophobia   An irrational fear of foreigners or strangers, their cultures and customs. It is often the basis of intergroup distrust and conflicts.

References

Ableser, J. (2007). Life Beyond Multiple Choice Tests: Alternative and Authentic Assessment. In K. Smith (Ed.), *Teaching, Learning, Assessing: A Guide for Effective Teaching at College and University* (pp. 143–161). Oakville: Mosaic Press.

Aboud, F. (1992). Children and Prejudice: Conceptual Issues. In K. Moodley (Ed.), *Beyond Multicultural Education: International Perspectives*. Calgary: Detselig Enterprises Ltd.

Allahar, A. (1998). Race and Racism: Strategies of Resistance. In V. Satzewich (Ed.), *Racism and Social Inequality in Canada: Concepts, Controversies and Strategies of Resistance* (pp. 335–353). Toronto: Thompson Educational Publishing.

Allgood, I. (2001). The Role of the School in Deterring Prejudice. In C. Diaz (Ed.), *Multicultural Education in the 21st Century* (pp. 184–207). New York: Addison Wesley Longman.

Allingham, N. (1993). Anti-Racist Secondary School English Curriculum. In *Anti-Racist Education: Selected Readings and Resources*. The Ontario Educational Communications Authority.

Althusser, L. (1971). *Ideology and Ideological State Apparatus*. London: New Left Books.

American Association of University Woman (AAUW). (1998). *Gender Gaps: Where schools still fail our children*. Washington, D.C.

Anyon, J. (1980). Social Class and the Hidden Curriculum of Work. *Journal of Education*, 162(1): 67–92.

Anyon, J. (1981). Social Class and School Knowledge. *Curriculum Inquiry*, 11(1): 3–42.

Anyon, J. (1997). *Ghetto Schooling: A Political Economy of Urban Educational Reform*. New York: Teachers College Press.

Anyon, J. (2005). *Radical Possibilities: Public Policy, Urban Education and a New Social Movement*. New York: Routledge.

Aoki, T., Werner, W., Dahlie, J., and Connors, B. (1984). Whose Culture? Whose Heritage? Ethnicity Within Canadian Social Studies Curricula. In J. Mallea and J. Young (Eds.), *Cultural Diversity and Canadian Education: Issues and Innovations*. Ottawa: Carleton University Press.

Apple, A. (2004). Race and the Politics of Educational Reform. In M. Olssen (Ed.), *Culture and Learning: Access and Opportunity in the Classroom* (pp. 299–314). Charlotte: Information Age Publishing Inc.

Apple, M. (1982) *Education and Power*. Boston: Routledge and Kegan, Paul.

Apple, M., Kenway, J., and Singh, M. (2005). *Globalizing Education: Policies, Pedagogies, and Politics*. New York: Peter Lang.

Apple, M., and Buras, K. L. (Eds.). (2006). *The Subaltern Speak: Curriculum, Power, and Educational Struggles*. New York: Routledge.

Arhar, J. M., Holly, M. L., and Kasten, W. C. (2001). *Action Research for Teachers: Traveling the Yellow Brick School*. New Jersey: Prentice Hall.

Ariza, E. N. W. (2006). *Not for ESOL Teachers: What Every Classroom Teacher Needs to Know about the Linguistically, Culturally, and Ethnically Diverse Student*. Boston: Pearson Education.

Au, K., and Mason, J. (1981). Social Organizational Factors in Learning to Read: The Balance of Rights Hypothesis. *Reading Research Quarterly*, 17: 334–354.

Ayers, W. (1998). Forward. Popular Education: Teaching for Social Justice In W. Ayers, J. A. Hunt, and T. Quinn (Eds.),

Teaching for Social Justice, pp. xvii–xxv. New York: Teachers College Press.

Ball, S., and Vincent, C. (2001). New Class Relations in Education: The Strategies of the 'Fearful' Middle Classes. In J. Demaine (Ed.), *Sociology of Education Today*, (pp. 180–195). New York: Palgrave Macmillan.

Banks, C. A. M. (2001). Becoming a Cross-Cultural Teacher. In C. F. Diaz (Ed.), *Multicultural Education in the 21st Century* (pp. 171–183). New York: Addison-Wesley Educational Publishers.

Banks, J. A. (1988). Approaches to Multicultural Curriculum Reform. *Multicultural Leader*, 1(2): 1–3.

Banks, J. A. (1991). Teaching Multicultural Literacy to Teachers. *Teaching Education*, 4(1): 135–144.

Banks, J. A. (1999). *An Introduction to Multicultural Education*. Boston: Allyn & Bacon.

Banks, J. A. (2004). *Diversity and Citizenship Education: Global Perspective*. San Francisco: John Wiley & Sons.

Banks, J. A. (2006). Democracy, Diversity, and Social Justice: Educating Citizens for the Public Interest in a Global Age. In G. Ladson-Billings and W. F. Tate (Eds.), *Education Research in the Public Interest: Social Justice, Action, and Policy* (pp.141–157). New York: Teachers College Press.

Bannerji, H. (2000). *The Dark Side of the Nation: Essays on Multiculturalism, Nationalism and Gender*. Toronto: Canadian Scholars' Press Inc.

Barakett, J., and Cleghorn, A. (2000). *Sociology of Education: An Introductory View from Canada*. Scarborough: Prentice Hall.

Baron, D. (1997). Hooked on Ebonics. Available online: www.english.uiuc.edu/baron/essays/ebonics.htm

Bar-Tal, D. (2002). The Elusive Nature of Peace Education. In G. Salomon and B. Nevo (Eds.), *Peace Education: The Concept, Principles and Practices around the World* (pp. 27–36). Mahwah: Lawrence Erlbaum Associates.

Bascia, N. (1994). Teacher Leadership under Difficult Conditions: Personal and Professional Costs and Benefits. *Orbit*, 25(4): 16–17.

Bascia, N. (2001). Pendulum Swings and Archaeological Layers: Educational Policy and the Case of ESL. In J. P. Portelli and R. P. Solomon (Eds.), *The Erosion of Democracy in Education: Critique to Possibilities* (pp. 269–296). Calgary: Detselig Enterprises.

Battiste, M. (2000). Maintaining Aboriginal Identity, Language, and Culture in Modern Society. In M. Battiste (Ed.), *Reclaiming Indigenous Voice and Vision* (pp. 192–208). Vancouver: UBC Press.

Battiste, M. (October 31 2002). *Indigenous Knowledge and Pedagogy in First Nations Education: A Literature Review with Recommendations*. Paper prepared for the National Working Group on Education and the Minister of Indian and Northern Affairs Canada (INAC). Ottawa: Indian and Northern Affairs Canada.

Battiste, M., and Henderson, J. Y. (2000). *Protecting Indigenous Knowledge and Heritage: A Global Challenge*. Saskatoon: Purich.

Beckles, H. (1997). *General History of the Caribbean Volume III*. In F. Knight (Ed.), Paris: UNESCO Publishing.

Begley, P. (1999). Guiding Values for Future School Leaders. *Orbit*, 30(10): 19–23.

Bellamy, L. A., and Guppy, N. (1991). Opportunities and Obstacles for Women in Canadian Higher Education. In J. Gaskell and A. McLaren, *Women and Education*. Calgary: Detselig.

Bennett, C. I. (1992). Strengthening Multicultural and Global Perspectives in Curriculum. In K. Moodley (Ed.), *Beyond Multicultural Education: International Perspectives* (pp. 171–199). Calgary: Detselig Enterprises.

Bennett, C. I. (2007). *Comprehensive Multicultural Education: Theory and Practice*, 6th Edition, Boston: Allyn and Bacon.

Bennett, K., and LeCompte, M. (1995). *The Way Schools Work: A Sociological Analysis of Education*. New York: Longman Inc.

Bernal, M. (1987). *Black Athena: Afrosiastic Roots of Classical Civilization,* Volume 1. New Brunswick: Rutgers University Press.

Bernhard, J., and Freire, M. (1999). What Is My Child Learning at Elementary School? Culturally Contested Issues between Teachers and Latin American Families. *Canadian Ethnic Studies*, 31(3): 72–94.

Bernstein, B. (1977). *Class, Codes and Control, Volume 3. Towards a Theory of Educational Transmission,* 2nd Edition. London: Routledge and Kegan Paul.

Bissoondath, N. (2002). *Selling Illusions: The Cult of Multiculturalism in Canada.* Toronto: Penguin.

Bjerrum-Nielsen, H., and Davies, B. (1997). The Construction of Gendered Identity through Classroom Talk. In Davies, B., and Corson, D. (Eds.), *Encyclopedia of Language and Education,* Volume 3. *Oral Discourse and Education* (pp. 125–135). Dordrecht: Kluwer Academic Publishers.

Blades, D., Johnston I., and Simmt, E. (2001). Ethnocultural Diversity and Secondary School Curriculum. *Directions: Research Reviews from the Canadian Race Relation Foundation.* 1: 30–41.

Bodkin, B. (2004). Responding to the Complexity of Boys' Learning: Promising Practices from School Districts. *Orbit*, 34(1): 30–32.

Bombardieri, M. (January 17, 2005). Summer's Remarks on Women Draw Fire. *The Boston Globe*, retrieved April 5, 2007. Available online: www.boston.com/news/local/articles/ 2005/01/17/summers_remarks_on_women _draw_fire.html

Bouchard, P., Boily, I., and Proulx, M. C. (2003). *School Success by Gender: A Catalyst for the Masculinist Discourse.* Ottawa: Status of Women Canada. Available online:www.swc-cfc.gc.ca/ pubs/pubspr/0662882857/ 200303_0662882857_e.pdf

Bourdieu, P. (1977). Cultural Reproduction and Social Reproduction. In J. Karabel and A. Halsey (Eds.), *Power and Ideology in Education*. New York: Oxford University Press.

Bourdieu, P. (1991). *Language and Symbolic Power*. Cambridge: Polity Press.

Bourdieu, P., and Passeron, J. (1977). *Reproduction in Education, Society and Culture*. London: Sage Publications.

Bowles, S., and Gintis, H. (1976). *Schooling in Capitalist America*. New York: Basic Books.

Brant, C. (1990). Native Ethics and Rules of Behaviour. *Canadian Journal of Psychiatry*, 35(6): 534–539.

Brascoupé, S., and Mann, H. (June, 2001). *A Community Guide to Protecting Indigenous Knowledge* (R2-160/2001E). Ottawa: Minister of Indian Affairs and Northern Development.

Brown, K. (2004). Leadership for Social Justice and Equity: Weaving a Transformative Framework and Pedagogy. *Educational Administration Quarterly*, 40(1): 77–108.

Bullivant, B. (1989). The Pluralist Dilemma Revisited. In G. Verma (Ed.), *Education For All: A Landmark in Pluralism*. London: Falmer Press.

Burbules, N., and Bruce, B. (2000). Theory and Research in Teaching as Dialogue. In V. Richardson (Ed.), *Handbook of Research on Teaching,* 4th Edition. Washington, D. C. American Educational Research Association.

Burnet, J. (1984). Myths and Multiculturalism. In R. J. Samuda, J. W. Berry, and M. Laferriere (Eds.), *Multiculturalism in Canada: Social and Educational Perspectives*. Toronto: Allyn and Bacon Inc.

Canadian Heritage (2003). Aboriginal Languages Initiative (ALI) Evaluation, Final Report. Avalable online: www.pch.gc.ca/progs/em-cr/eval/ 2003/2003-pdf/ALI_03_eval_e.pdf

Canadian Race Relations Foundations (2005) Glossary of Terms. Available online: www.crr.ca/divers-files/ englossary-feb2005.pdf

Carlsson-Paige, N. & Lantieri, L. (2005). A Changing vision of education. In N. Noddings (Ed.). *Educating Citizens for Global Awareness*. New York: Teachers College Press.

Carr, P., and Klassen, T. (1997). Different Perceptions of Race in Education: Racial Minority and White Teachers. *Canadian Journal of Education,* 22: 67–81.

Carrington, B., and Bonnett, A. (1997). The Other Canadian 'Mosaic'—'Race' Equity Education in Ontario and British Columbia. *Comparative Education*, 33(3): 411–431.

Carringon, B., Bonnet, A., Nayak, A., Short, G., Skelton, C., Smith, F., Tomlim, R., and Demaine, J. (2001). Teachers and the Question of Ethnicity. In J. Demaine (Ed.), *Sociology of Education Today* (pp. 100–118). New York: Palgrave Macmillan.

Casella, R. (2005). What is Zero Tolerance? In W. Hare and J. P. Portelli (Eds.), *Key Questions for Educators* (pp. 128–130). Halifax: Edphil Books.

Chancer, L. S., and Watkins, B. X. (2006). *Gender, Race, and Class: An Overview.* Malden: Blackwell Publishing Ltd.

Chrétien, Jean. (June 2000). Statement of Prime Minister of Canada on Canadian Diversity. Available online : www.pch.gc.ca/progs/multi/respect_e.cfm

Citizenship and Immigration Canada. (2001). *Strategic Policy, Planning and Research. Facts and Figures 2000: Immigration Overview*. Ottawa: Public Works and Government Services Canada.

Citizenship and Immigration Canada. (2004). *Annual Report to Parliament on Immigration 2003*. Retrieved July 4, 2006, from www.cic.gc.ca/english/pub/ immigration2003.html

Citizenship and Immigration Canada. (n.d.). *Facts and Figures 2003: Immigration Overview Permanent and Temporary Residents*. Retrieved July 4, 2006, from www.cic.gc.ca/english/pub/facts2003/ overview/index.html

Citizenship and Immigration Canada. (August 2006). *OP5: Overseas Selection and Processing of Convention Refugees Abroad Class and Members of the Humanitarian-protected Persons Abroad Classes*. Retrieved April 5, 2007, from www.cic.gc.ca/manuals-guides/ english/op/op05e.pdf

Citizenship and Immigration Canada (CIC), 2007 Annual Report to Parliament on Immigration. Available online www.cic.gc.ca/english/resources/ publications/annual-report2007/ introduction.asp

Clarke, P. (2005). Religion, Public Education and the Charter: Where Do We Go Now? *McGill Journal of Education,* 40(3): 351–381.

Coates, J. (2004). *Women, Men, and Language: A Sociolinguistic Account of Gender Differences in Language*. London: Longman.

Cochran-Smith, M. (2000). Blind Vision: Unlearning Racism in Teacher Education. *Harvard Educational Review,* 70: 157–190.

Cohen, E., Brody, C., and Sapon-Shevin, M. (Eds.). (2004). *Teaching Cooperative Learning: The Challenge for Teacher Education*. Albany: State University of New York Press.

Cole, E. (1998). Immigrant and Refugee Children: Challenges and Opportunities for Education and Mental Health Services. *Canadian Journal of School Psychology,* 14(1): 36.

Cook, V. (Ed.). (2003). *The Effects of the Second Language on the First*. Clevedon: Multilingual Matters.

Corson, D. (1993). *Language, Minority Education and Gender: Linking Social Justice and Power.* Clevedon: Multilingual Matters/Toronto: OISE Press.

Corson, D. (1995). *Discourse and Power in Educational Organizations.* Toronto: OISE Press.

Corson, D. (1998). *Changing Education for Diversity.* Buckingham: Open University Press.

Corson, D. (2001). *Language Diversity and Education.* Mahwah: Lawrence Erlbaum Associates.

Coulson, A. (2002). Delivering Education. In E. P. Lazear (Ed.), *Education in the Twenty-First Century* (pp. 105–146). Stanford: Hoover Institution Press.

Council of Ministers of Education, Canada. (2002). *SAIP School Achievement Indications Program: Writing III.*

Available online: www.cmec.ca/publications/index.en.stm

Cranton, P. (1994). *Understanding and Promoting Transformative Learning: A Guide to Educators of Adults.* San Francisco: Jossey Bass.

Cummins, J. (1986). Empowering Minority Students: A Framework for Intervention. *Harvard Educational Review,* 56(1): 18–36.

Cummins, J. (1996). *Negotiating Identities.* Los Angeles: California Association for Bilingual Education.

Cummins, J. (2000). *Language, Power and Pedagogy: Bilingual Children in the Crossfire.* Clevedon: Multilingual Matters.

Cummins, J. (2001). *Negotiating Identities: Education for Empowerment in a Diverse Society,* 2nd Edition. Los Angeles: California Association for Bilingual Education.

Cummins, J., Bismilaa, V., Chow, P., Cohen, S., Giampapa, F., and Leoni, L. (2005). Affirming Identity in Multilingual Classrooms. *Educational Leadership,* 63(1): 38–43.

Cummins, J., and Danesi, M. (1990). *Heritage Languages: The Development and Denial of Canada's Linguistic Resources.* Toronto: Our Schools Our Selves Education Foundation.

Curtis, B., Livingstone, D., and Smaller, H. (1992). *Stacking the Deck and the Streaming of Working-Class Kids in Ontario Schools.* Toronto: Our Schools, Our Selves: 124–136.

Dahrendorf, R. (1979). *Life Chances.* Chicago: University of Chicago Press.

Daniel, P. (2001). Towards an Intercultural Curriculum: An Example from the Atlantic Coast of Nicaragua. *Journal of Teaching and Learning,* 1(1): 1–16.

Dei, G. J. S. (1996). *Anti-Racism Education: Theory and Practice.* Halifax: Fernwood Publishing.

Dei, G. J. S., James, I. M., Karumanchery, L. L., James-Wilson, S., Zine, J. (2000). *Removing the Margins: The Challenges and Possibilities of Inclusive Schooling.* Toronto: Canadian Scholars' Press.

Dei, G. J. S., Mazzuca, J., McIsaac, E., and Zine, J. (1997). *Reconstructing Dropout: A Critical Ethnography of the Dynamics of Black Students' Disengagement from School.* Toronto: University of Toronto Press.

Delaney, J. G. (2002). *Educational Policy Studies: A Practical Approach.* Calgary: Detselig Enterprises.

Delpit, L. (2006). *Other People's Children: Cultural Conflict in the Classroom.* New York: The New Press.

De Mejia, A. M. (2002). *Power, Prestige and Bilingualism: International Perspectives on Elite Bilingual Education.* Clevedon: Multilingual Matters.

Diaz, C. F. (2001). The Third Millennium: A Multicultural Imperative for Education. In C.F. Diaz (Ed.), *Multicultural Education in the 21st Century* (pp. 1–10). New York: Addison-Wesley Educational Publishers.

Dickinson, G. M., and Dolmage, W. R. (1996). Education, Religion and Courts in Ontario. *Canadian Journal of Education/ Revie canadiennne de l'education,* 21(4): 363–383.

Dirks, G. E. (1984). A Policy within a Policy: The Identification and Admission of Refugees to Canada. *Canadian Journal of Political Science,* 17(2): 279–307.

Driedger, L. (2003). *Race and Ethnicity: Finding Identities and Equalities,* 2nd Edition. Don Mills, Ontario: Oxford University Press.

Duffy, A. (2003). *Class Struggles: Public Education and the New Canadian.* The Atkinson Charitable Foundation. Retrieved June 22, 2006, from http:atkinsonfoundation.ca/files/duffyrev.pdf

Durkheim, E. (1956). *Education and Sociology.* New York: The Free Press.

Dworkin, R. (1978). *Taking Rights Seriously.* London: Duckworth.

Edwards, V. (1997). Teacher-Pupil Talk in Multi-Ethnic Classrooms. *Encyclopedia of Language and Education, Vol. 3, Oral Discourse and Education:* 95–103.

Egbo, B. (2001). Differential Enunciation, Mainstream Language and the Education of Immigrant Minority Students: Implications for Policy and Practice. *Journal of Teaching and Learning*, 1(2): 47–61.

Egbo, B. (2005). Emergent Paradigm: Critical Realism and Transformative Research in Educational Administration. *McGill Journal of Education*. 40(2): 267–284.

Egbo, B. (2006). *Research on, and Strategies for Leadership in Contexts of Student Diversity: A "Compass" for Action*. Paper presented at the American Educational Research Association (AERA), Annual Meeting. San Francisco: April 7–11.

Egbo, B. (2007) Teaching for Inclusion in University Classrooms. In K. Smith (Ed.), *Teaching, Learning, Assessing: A Guide for Effective Teaching at College and University* (pp. 29–38). Oakville: Mosaic Press.

Entwistle, H. (1996). The Relationship between Educational Theory and Practice: A New Look. In W. Hare and J. P. Portelli (Eds.), *Philosophy of Education: Introductory Readings*. Calgary: Detselig Enterprises.

Epstein, J. (2001). *School, Family, and Community Partnerships: Preparing Educators and Improving Schools*. Boulder: Westview Press.

Erickson, F. (2001). Culture in Society and in Educational Practices. In J. Banks and C. McGee Banks (Eds.) *Multicultural Education: Issues and Perspectives*, 4th Edition. New York: John Wiley and Sons.

Fairclough, N. (1992). *Critical Language Awareness*. London: Longman.

Fleras, A., and Elliott, J. (1992). *Multiculturalism in Canada: The Challenge of Diversity*. Scarborough: Nelson Canada.

Fleras, A., and Elliot, J. (2003). *Unequal Relations: An Introduction to Race and Ethnic Dynamics in Canada,* 4th Edition. Toronto: Prentice-Hall.

Furman, G. C., and Shields, C. M. (2005). How Can Educational Leaders Promote and Support Social Justice and Democratic Community in Schools? In W. Firestone and C. Riehl (Eds.), *A New Agenda for Research in Educational Leadership* (pp. 119–137). New York: Teachers College Press.

Freeman, R. D. (1996). Dual Language Planning at Oyster Bilingual School: "It's Much More than Language". *TESOL Quarterly*, 30: 557–582.

Freeman, R. D. (1998). *Bilingual Education and Social Change*. Clevedon: Multilingual Matters.

Freeman, C. E. (2004). *Trends in Educational Equity of Girls and Women: 2004 (NCES 2005–016)*. U. S. Department of Education, National Center for Education Statistics. Washington, D. C. U. S. Government Printing Office.

Freire, P. (1970). *Pedagogy of the Oppressed*. New York: Herder and Herder.

Freire, P. (1998). *Pedagogy of Freedom: Ethics, Democracy, and Civic Courage*. Lanham: Rowan & Littlefield.

Freire, P. (2002). *A Pedagogy of Hope: Reliving Pedagogy of the Oppressed*. New York: Continuum.

Friesen, J. (1992). Multiculturalism in Canada: Hope or Hoax? *Multicultural Education Journal*. 10(1): 1–48.

Froese-Germain, B. (1999). *Standardized Testing: Undermining Equity in Education*. Ottawa: Canadian Teachers' Federation.

Froese-Germain, B. (2004). Are Schools Really Shortchanging Boys? Reality Check on the Gender Gap. *Orbit*, 34(1): 3–5.

Fullan, M. (1993). *Change Forces: Probing the Depths of Educational Reform*. London: Falmer.

Gallas, K. (1998). *Sometimes I Can Be Anything: Power, Gender and Identity in a Primary Classroom*. New York: Teachers College Press.

Gamarnikow, E., and Green, A. (2003). School Diversification Policy Under New Labour. In C. Vincent (Ed.), *Social Justice, Education and Identity* (pp. 209–223). London: RoutledgeFalmer.

Gardner, Howard. (1999). *Intelligence Reframed: Multiple Intelligences for the 21st Century*. New York: Basic Books.

Gaskell, J., and Eyre, L. (2004). Gender Equity and Education Policy in Canada, 1970-2000. *Orbit,* 34(1): 6–8.

Gay, G. (2000). *Culturally Responsive Teaching: Theory, Research & Practice.* New York: Teachers College Press.

Gewirtz, S. (2001). Rethinking Social Justice: A Conceptual Analysis. In J. Demaine (Ed.), *Sociology of Education Today,* (pp. 180–195). Houndsmill: Palgrave Publishers.

Ghosh, R. (2002). *Redefining Multicultural Education,* 2nd Edition. Scarborough: Thomson Learning.

Ghosh, R., and Abdi, A. (2004). *Education and the Politics of Difference: Canadian Perspective.* Toronto: Canadian Scholars' Press.

Ghuman, P. (1980). Punjabi Parents and English Education. *Education Research,* 22(1): 121–130.

Ghuman, P., and Wong, R. (1989). Chinese Parents and English Education. *Education Research,* 31(2): 134–141.

Gibson, L. (1998). Teaching as an Encounter with Self: Unraveling the Mix of Personal Beliefs, Education Ideologies and Pedagogical Practices. *Anthropology and Education Quarterly,* 29(3): 360–371.

Gibson, M. (1976). Approaches to Multicultural Education in the U.S.: Some Concepts and Assumptions. *Anthropology and Education Quarterly,* 7(4): 7–18.

Gibson, M. (1987). The School Performance of Immigrant Minorities: A Comparative View. *Anthropology and Education Quarterly,* 18: 262–267.

Gillborn, D. (2004). Ability, Selection, and Institutional Racism in Schools. In M. Olssen (Ed.), *Culture and Learning: Access and Opportunity in the Classroom* (pp. 279–298). Greenwich: Information Age Publishing.

Gilligan, C. (1982). *In a Different Voice: Psychological Theory and Women's Development.* Cambridge: Harvard University Press.

Giroux, H. (1983). *Theory and Resistance in Education: A Pedagogy For the Opposition.* South Hadley: Bergin and Garvey Publishers, Inc.

Giroux, H. (1992). *Border Crossings: Cultural Worker and the Politics of Education.* New York: Routledge.

Giroux, H. (2002). Democracy, Freedom, and Justice after September 11th: Rethinking the Role of Educators and the Politics of Schooling. *Teachers College Record,* 104(6): 1138–1162.

Goddard, T. (1997): Monocultural Teachers and Ethnoculturally Diverse Students. *Journal of Education Administration and Foundations,* 12(1): 30–45.

Goldstein, T., and Selby, D. (Eds.). (2000). *Weaving Connections: Education for Peace, Social and Environmental Justice.* Toronto: Sumach Press.

Government of Canada (2001). About what??

Government of Ontario (2000) Safe Schools Act. Available online: www.ontla.on.ca/bills/bills-files/ 37_Parliament/Session1/b081ra.pdf

Grant, C. A., and Sleeter, C. E. (2007). *Turning on Learning: Five Approaches for Multicultural Teaching Plans for Race, Class, Gender and Disability,* 4th Edition. Danvers: John Wiley & Sons.

Grenier, L. (1998). *Working with Indigenous Knowledge: A Guide for Researchers.* Ottawa: International Development Research Centre. Retrieved January 26, 2007, from www.idrc.ca/openebooks/ 847–3/

Gronlund, N., and Cameron, I. (2004). *Assessment of Student Achievement.* Toronto: Pearson Education.

Grossman, H. (1995). *Teaching in a Diverse Society.* Needham Heights: Allyn & Bacon.

Hall, S. (1993). Cultural Identity and Diaspora. In W. Patrick, and L. Chrisman (Eds.), *Colonial Discourses and Postcolonial Theory: A Reader* (pp. 392–403). New York: Columbia University Press.

Hampton, M., and Roy, J. (1998). Strategies for Facilitating Success of First Nations Students. *Canadian Society for the Study of Higher Education,* 32(3): 1–28.

Handler, R. (1988). *Nationalism and the Politics of Culture in Quebec.* Madison: University of Wisconsin Press.

Hannah, J. (1999). Refugee Students at College and University: Improving Access and Support. *International Review of Education,* 45(2): 153–166.

Harper, H. (1997). Difference and Diversity in Ontario Schooling. *Canadian Journal of Education/Revue canadienne de l'éducation*, 22(2): 192–206.

Harris, I. M. (1996). Peace Education in an Urban School District in the United States. *Peabody Journal of Education*, 71(3): 63–83.

Harry, B., & Klingner, J. (2006). *Why Are So Many Black Students in Special Education? Understanding Race and Disability in Schools.* New York: Teachers College Press.

Hayes, K. (1992). Attitudes Towards Education: Voluntary and Involuntary Immigrants From the Same Families. *Anthropology and Education Quarterly*, 23(3): 250–267.

Heath, S. B. (1983). *Way with Words: Language, Life and Work in Communities.* Cambridge: Cambridge University Press.

Heit, M., and Blair, H. (1993). Language Needs and Characteristics of Saskatchewan Indian and Métis Students: Implications for Education. In S. Morris, K. McLeod, and M. Danesi (Eds.), *Aboriginal Languages and Education: The Canadian Experience* (pp. 103–128). Oakville: Mosaic Press.

Henderson, J. Y. (2000). Postcolonial Ghost Dancing: Diagnosing European Colonialism. In M. Battiste (Ed.), *Reclaiming Indigenous Voice and Vision* (pp. 57–75). Vancouver: UBC Press.

Henry, F., and Tator, C. (2006). *The Color of Democracy: Racism in Canadian Society.* Toronto: Nelson Thomson.

Henze, R., Katz, A., Norte, E., Sather, S. E., and Walker, E. (2002). *Leading for Diversity: How School Leaders Promote Positive Interethnic Relations.* Thousand Oaks: Corwin Press.

Herrnstein, K. J., and Murray, C. (1994). *The Bell Curve: the Reshaping of American Life by Differences of Intelligence.* New York: Free Press.

Hirsch, E. D. (1987). *Cultural Literacy: What Every American Needs to Know.* Boston: Houghton-Mifflin.

hooks, bell. (1994). *Teaching to Transgress.* New York: Routledge.

hooks, bell. (2003). *Teaching Community: A Pedagogy of Hope.* New York: Routledge.

Howard, G. R. (2006). *We Can't Teach What We Don't Know: White Teachers, Multiracial Schools,* 2nd Edition. New York: Teachers College Press.

Howard, R. (1980). Contemporary Canadian Refugee Policy: A Critical Assessment. *Canadian Public Policy*, 6(2): 361–373.

Howe, E. R. (2003). Curriculum, Teaching and Learning Within the Context of Comparative, International and Developmental Education. *Canadian and International Education*, 30(1): 1–14.

Hurtado, S., Milem, J., Clayton-Pedersen, A., and Allen, W. (1999), Enacting Diverse Learning Environments: Improving the Climate for Racial/Ethnic Diversity in Higher Education. *ASHE-ERIC Higher Education Reports*, 26(8): 1–116.

Igoa, C. (1995). *The Inner World of the Immigrant Child.* New York: St. Martin's Press.

Iram, Y. (Ed.). (2006). *Educating Toward a Culture of Peace.* Charlotte: Information Age Publishing.

Irvine, J. J. (1990). Black Students and School Failure: Policies, Practices, and Prescriptions. New York: Greenwood Press.

Irving, M. (2006) Practicing What We Teach: Experiences with Reflective Practice and Critical Engagement. In J. Landsman and W. L. Chance (Eds.), *White Teachers/Diverse Classrooms: A Guide to Building Inclusive Schools, Promoting High Expectations, and Eliminating Racism* (pp. 221–233). Sterling: Stylus Publishing.

Isajiw, W. (1999). *Understanding Diversity: Ethnicity and Race in the Canadian Context.* Toronto: Thompson Educational Publishing.

Isoki, S. (2001). Present Company Excluded, of Course . . . Revisited. In C. James and A. Shadd (Eds.), *Talking about Identity: Encounters in Race, Ethnicity, and Language* (pp. 60–71). Toronto: Between the Lines.

James, C. E. (2003). *Seeing Ourselves: Exploring Race, Ethnicity and Culture.*

Toronto: Thompson Educational Publishing, Inc.

James, C. E. (2004). Assimilation to Accommodation: Immigrants and the Changing Patterns of Schooling. *Education Canada*, 44(4): 43–45.

Jensen, A. R. (1969). How Much Can We Boost IQ and Scholastic Achievement? *Harvard Educational Review*, 39: 1–23.

Johnston, I., and Carson, T. (2000). The Difficulty with Difference in Teacher Education: Toward a Pedagogy of Compassion. *Alberta Journal of Educational Research*, 46(1): 75, 1–9.

Jones, V., and Jones, L. (2004). *Comprehensive Classroom Management: Creating Communities of Support and Solving Problems,* 7th Edition. Boston: Pearson Education.

Jordan, C., and Rodriguez, V. (2004). Family and Community Connections with Schools . . . Why Bother. *Orbit,* 34(3): 3–6.

Joshee, R. (2004). Citizenship and Multicultural Education in Canada: From Assimilation to Social Cohesion. In J. A. Banks (Ed.), *Diversity and Citizenship Education* (pp. 127–155). San Francisco: John Wiley & Sons.

Jossey-Bass. (2002). *The Jossey-Bass Reader on Gender in Education*. San Francisco: Jossey-Bass Publishing.

Kalantzis, M. and Cope, B. (1999). Multicultural Education: Transforming the Mainstream. In S. May (Ed.), *Critical Multiculturalism: Rethinking Multicultural & Anti Racist Education* (pp. 245–276). London: Falmer Press.

Kaprielian-Churchill, I. (1996). Refugees and Education in Canadian Schools. *International Review of Education*, 42(4): 349–365.

Katz, H., and McCluskey, K. (2003). Seeking Strength-based Approaches in Aboriginal Education: The "Three Stars and a Wish" Project. *McGill Journal of Education*, 38(1): 116.

Kauffman, J. M., Mostert, M. P., Trent, S. C., & Hallahan, D. P. (2002). *Managing Classroom Behavior: A Reflective Case-Based Approach,* 3rd Edition. Boston: Allyn & Bacon.

Khayatt, D. (2000). Talking Equity: Taking up Differences in the Classroom. In C. James (Ed.), *Experiencing Difference* (pp. 258–270). Halifax: Fernwood Publishing.

Kincheloe, J. L. (2005a). *Critical Pedagogy: Primer*. New York, NY: Peter Lang Publishing.

Kincheloe, J. L. (2005b). Issues of Power, Questions of Purpose. In J. L. Kincheloe (Ed.), *Classroom Teaching: An Introduction* (pp. 25–52). New York: Peter Lang Publishing.

King, J. E. (1991). Dysconscious Racism: Ideology, Identity, and the Miseducation of Teachers. *The Journal of Negro Education*, 60(2): 133–146.

Knoblauch, C., and Brannon, L. (1993). *Critical Teaching and the Idea of Literacy*. Portsmouth: Boynton/Cook Publishers.

Kohl, H. (1994). *"I Won't Learn From You" and Other Thoughts on Creative Maladjustment*. New York: The New Press.

Kohli, W. (2005). What is Social Justice Education? In W. Hare and J. P. Portelli (Eds.), *Key Questions for Educators* (pp. 98–100). Halifax: Edphil Books.

Kronowitz, E. L. (2008). *The Teacher's Guide to Success: Teaching Effectively in Today's Classrooms*. Boston: Pearson Education.

Kruczek, J. (2007). *A Case Study of ESL High School Students' Perceptions of Their Experiences: Identifying Language Minority Students' Support Needs in A Diverse Classroom*. University of Windsor: Unpublished Masters Thesis.

Ladson-Billings, G. (1994). The Dreamkeepers: Successful Teachers of African American Children. San Francisco: Jossey-Bass.

Ladson-Billings, G. (2006). Introduction. In G. Ladson-Billings & W. F. Tate (Eds.), *Education Research in the Public Interest: Social Justice, Action, and Policy* (pp. 1–13). New York: Teachers College Press.

Lambert, W. (1975) Culture and Language as Factors in Learning and Education. In A. Wolfgang (Ed.), *Education & Immigrant Students: Issues and Answers*. Toronto: Ontario Institute for Studies in Education.

Landsman, J. (2006). When Truth and Joy are at Stake: Challenging the Status Quo in the High School English Class. In J. Landsman and Chance W. L. (Eds.), *White Teachers/Diverse Classrooms: A Guide to Building Inclusive Schools, Promoting High Expectations, and Eliminating Racism* (pp. 221–233). Sterling: Stylus Publishing.

Landsman, J., and Lewis, C. W. (Eds.). (2006). *White Teachers/Diverse Classrooms: A Guide to Building Inclusive Schools, Promoting High Expectations, and Eliminating Racism*. Sterling: Stylus Publishing.

Larkin, J. (1994). *Sexual Harassment: High School Girls Speak Out*. Toronto: Second Story Press.

Leavitt, R. M. (1993). Language and Cultural Content in Native Education. In S. Morris, K. McLeod and M. Danesi (Eds.), *Aboriginal Languages and Education: The Canadian Experience* (pp. 1–15). Oakville: Mosaic Press.

Lee, K. (2000). *Urban Poverty in Canada: A Statistical Profile*. Ottawa: Canadian Council on Social Development.

Levin, B. (1995). Educational Responses to Poverty. *Canadian Journal of Education*, 20: 211–224.

Levin, B. (2004). A Recommitment to Equity in Education. *Education Canada,* 44(2): 16.

Levin, M. A. (1994). New Wine in Old Bottles: The Limits of School Reformation. *Orbit*, 25(4): 45–48.

Levine-Rasky, C. (1998). Pre-service Teacher Education and the Negotiation of Social Difference. *British Journal of Sociology of Education*, 9(1): 89–112.

Lippi-Green, R. (1997). *English with an Accent: Language, Ideology and Discrimination in the United States*. London: Routledge.

Litner, B., Rossiter, A., and Taylor, M. (1992). The Equitable Inclusion of Women in Higher Education: Some Consequences for Teaching. *Canadian Journal of Education,* 17(3): 286–302.

Loppie, C. (2007). Learning from the Grandmothers: Incorporating Indigenous Principles into Qualitative Research. *Qualitative Health Research*, 17(2): 276–284.

Lupul, M. (1987). The Contributions of Language Policies and Programs to Multicultural Education. In McLeod, K. (Ed.), *Multicultural Education: A Partnership*. Toronto: CCMIE/OISE Press.

Magsino, R. (1985). The Right to Multicultural Education: A Descriptive and Normative Analysis. *Multiculturalism*, 9(1): 4–9.

Magsino, R. (1989). Multiculturalism in Schools: Is Multicultural Education Possible and Justifiable? In S. Morris (Ed.), *Multicultural and Intercultural Education: Building Canada*. Calgary: Detselig Enterprises.

Malik, K. (1996). *The Meaning of Race: Race, History, and Culture in Western Society*. New York: New York University Press.

Manitoba Education and Training. (1993). *Policy for Heritage Language Instruction*. Manitoba: Manitoba Education and Training.

Marshall, C., and Oliva, M. (2006). Building the Capacities of Social Justice Leaders. In C. Marshall, and M. Oliva (Eds.), *Leadership for Social Justice: Making Revolutions in Education* (pp. 1–15). Boston: Pearson Education.

Martin, Y. M. (1996). Religion in Schools: Legally Speaking. *Education Canada*, 36(4): 42. Retrieved October 3, 2006, from CBCA Education Database.

May, S. (1994). *Making Multicultural Education Work*. Clevedon: Multilingual Matters.

May, S. (1999). Critical Multiculturalism and Cultural Difference: Avoiding Essentialism. In S. May (Ed.), *Critical Multiculturalism: Rethinking Multicultural & Anti Racist Education* (pp. 11–41). London: Falmer Press.

Maynes, B. (2001). Educational Programming for Children Living in Poverty: Possibilities and Challenges. In J. P. Portelli and R.P. Solomon (Eds.), *The Erosion of Democracy in Education: Critique to Possibilities* (pp. 269–296). Calgary: Detselig Enterprises.

McAdams, D. (2006). *What School Boards Can Do: Reform Governance for Urban Schools*. NewYork: Teachers College.

McIntosh, P. (1990). White Privilege: Unpacking the Invisible Knapsack. *Independent School*, Winter: 31–36.

McKenzie, K. B., and Scheurich, J. (2004). Equity Traps: A Useful Construct for Preparing Principals to Lead Schools that are Successful with Racially Diverse Students. *Educational Administration Quarterly*, 40(5): 601–632.

McLaren, P. (1980). *Cries from the Corridor: The New Suburban Ghettos*. Toronto: Metheun.

McLaren, P. (2007). *Life in Schools. An Introduction to Critical Pedagogy in the Foundations of Education*. Boston: Pearson Education.

Merton, R. K. (1957). *Social Theory and Social Structure*. New York: Free Press.

Mezirow J., and Associates (1990). *Fostering Critical Reflection in Adulthood: A Guide to Transformative and Emancipatory Learning*. San Francisco: Jossey-Bass Publishers.

Mezirow J., and Associates (2000). *Learning as Transformation: Critical Perspectives on a Theory in Progress*. San Francisco: Jossey-Bass Publishers.

Mills, G. E. (2003). *Action Research: A Guide for the Teacher Researcher,* 3rd Edition. Upper Saddle River: Pearson Education.

Milner, H. (2003). Reflection, Racial Competence and Critical Pedagogy: How Do We Prepare Pre-service Teachers to Pose Tough Questions? *Race, Ethnicity and Education*. 6(2): 193–208.

Moodley, K. (1999). Antiracist Education through Political Literacy: the Case of Canada. In S. May (Ed.), *Critical Multiculturalism: Rethinking Multicultural & Anti Racist Education* (pp. 138–152). London: Falmer Press.

Morgan, E. (2001). Religious Equality Comes to Ontario Education. *Orbit*, 32(2).

Morse, H. (2000). It Takes a Whole Village to Raise a Child: Poverty & Partnerships. *CAPHERD*, 66(1), 15–17.

Morris, S., McLeod, K., and Danesi, M. (1993). *Aboriginal Languages and Education: The Canadian Experience*. Oakville: Mosaic Press.

Morrison, D., Luther, M., and McCullough, J. (1991). Language Programming with Dialect Students. *Orbit,* 22: 8–9.

Murphy, P., and Ivinson, G. (2004). Gender Difference in Educational Achievement: A Socio-cultural Analysis. In M. Olssen (Ed.), *Culture & Learning: Access & Opportunity in the Curriculum* (pp. 365–386). Greenwich: Information Age Publishing.

National Coalition of Advocates for Students. (1994). *Delivering on the Promise: Positive Practices for Immigrant Students*. Boston: National Coalition of Advocates for Students.

Ng, R. (1995). Teaching against the Grain: Contradictions and Possibilities. In R. Ng, P. Staton, and J. Scane, (Eds.), *Anti-racism, Feminism, and Critical Approaches to Education* (pp. 124–168). Toronto: OISE Press.

Nickels, B., and Piquemal, N. (2005). Cultural Congruence in the Education of and Research with Young Aboriginal Students: Ethical Implications for Classrooms Researchers. *Alberta Journal of Educational Research*, 51(2): 118–134.

Nieto, S. (2001). We Speak in Many Tongues: Language Diversity and Multicultural Education. In Carlos Diaz (Ed.), *Multicultural Education in the 21*st *Century* (pp. 152–170). New York: Addison Wesley Longman.

Nieto, S. (2002). *Language, Culture and Teaching: Critical Perspectives for a New Century*. Mahwah: Lawrence Erlbaum Associates Publishers.

Nieto, S. (2004). *Affirming diversity: The sociopolitical context of multicultural education*. (4th Ed.). Boston: Pearson Education.

Nieto, S., and Bode, P. (2008). Affirming Diversity: The Sociopolitical Context of Multicultural Education, 5th Edition. Boston: Pearson Education.

Noddings, N. (2005a). Global Citizenship: Promises and Problems. In N. Noddings, *Educating Citizens for Global Awareness* (pp. 1–21). New York: Teachers College Press.

Noddings, N. (2005b). *The Challenge to Care in Schools: An Alternative Approach to Education*. New York: Teachers College Press.

O'Connor, C., and Deluca Fernandez, S. (2006). Race, Class, and Disproportionality: Reevaluating the Relationship between Poverty and Special Education Placement. *Educational Researcher*, 35(6): 6–11.

Ogbu, J. (1987). Variability in Minority School Performance: A Problem in Search of an Explanation. *Anthropology and Education Quarterly*, 18: 312–334.

Ogbu, J. (1992). Understanding Cultural Diversity and Learning. *Educational Researcher*, 21(8): 5–14.

Omi, M., and Winant, H. (1993). On the Theoretical Concept of Race. In C. McCarthy and W. Crichlow (Eds.), *Race Identity and Representation in Education* (pp. 3–10). New York: Routledge.

Orfield, G., Frankenberg, E.D., and Lee, C. (2003). The Resurgence of School Segregation. *Educational Leadership*, 60(4): 16–20.

Orlowski, P. (2001). Ties That Bind and Ties That Blind: Race and Class Intersections in the Classroom. In C. James and A. Shadd (Eds.) *Talking about Identity: Encounters in Race, Ethnicity and Language* (pp. 250–266). Toronto, ON: Transcontinental Printing.

Osborne, K. (1999). *Education: A Guide to the Canadian School Debate–Or Who Wants What and Why?* Toronto: Penguin/McGill Institute.

Ouellet, F. (1992). Education in a Pluralistic Society: Proposal for an Enrichment of Teacher Education. In K. Moodley (Ed.), *Beyond Multicultural Education: International Perspectives* (pp. 281–302). Calgary: Detselig Enterprises.

Ovando, C. J. (2001). Language, Diversity and Education. In J. A. Banks and C. A. McGhee Banks (Eds.), *Multicultural Education: Issues and Perspectives,* 4th Edition. (pp. 268–291). New York: John Wiley & Sons, Inc.

Paley, V. G. (2000). *White Teacher*. Cambridge: Harvard University Press.

Palmer, P. J. (1998). *The Courage to Teach: Exploring the Inner Landscape of a Teacher's Life*. San Francisco: Jossey-Bass Publishers.

Parkay, F. W., Stanford, B. H, Vaillancourt, J. P., and Stephens, H. C. (2005). *Becoming a Teacher*. Toronto: Pearson.

Parsons, T. (1951). *The Social System*. New York: Free Press.

Parsons, T. (1959). The School Class as a Social System: Some of its Functions in American Society, *Harvard Educational Review*, 29: 297–315.

Paul, R. (1995). *Critical Thinking: How to Prepare Students for a Rapidly Changing World*. Santa Rosa: Foundation for Critical Thinking.

Paul, R., and Elder L. (2004). *The Miniature Guide to Critical Thinking: Concepts and Tools*. Dillon Beach: The Foundation for Critical Thinking.

Paul, R., and Elder L. (2006). How to Improve Student Learning: 30 Practical Ideas (Based on Critical Thinking Concepts & Principles). Dillon Beach: The Foundation for Critical Thinking.

Peters, M., Lankshear, C., and Olssen, M. (Eds.). (2003). *Critical Theory and the Human Condition*. New York: Peter Lang.

Peterson, B. (1994). Teaching for Social Justice: One Teacher's Journey. In B. Bigelow, L. Christensen, S. Karp, B. Miner, and B. Peterson (Eds.), *Rethinking Our Classrooms: Teaching for Equity and Justice,* Volume 1, pp. 30–38, Milwaukee: Rethinking Schools.

Picot, G., and Hou, F. (2003). *The Rise in Low Income Rates among Immigrants in Canada*. Statistics Canada, Analytical Studies Branch Research Paper Series, 11F0019MIE2003198: Ottawa: Statistics Canada.

Pike, G. (2000). A Tapestry in the Making: The Strands of Global Education. In T. Goldstein and D. Selby (Eds.), *Weaving Connections: Educating for Peace, Social and Environmental Justice* (pp. 218–241). Toronto: Sumach Press.

Ponting, J. R. (1998). Racism and Stereotyping of First Nations. In V. Satzewich (Ed.), *Racism and Social*

Inequality in Canada: Concepts, Controversies & Strategies of Resistance (pp. 269–299). Toronto: Thompson Educational Publishing.

Pope, G. A., Wentzel, C., Braden, B., and Anderson, J. (2006). Relationships between Gender and Alberta Achievement Test Scores during a Four-Year Period. *Alberta Journal of Educational Research*, 52(1): 4–15.

Porter, J. (1965). *The Vertical Mosaic: An Analysis of Social Class and Power in Canada*. Toronto: University of Toronto Press.

Power, C. N. (2000). Global Trends in Education. *International Education Journal*, 1(3): 152–163.

Price, V. (2006). I Don't Understand Why My African American Students Are Not Achieving. In J. Landsman and Chance W. L. (Eds.), *White Teachers/Diverse Classrooms: A Guide to Building Inclusive Schools, Promoting High Expectations, and Eliminating Racism* (pp. 122–136). Sterling: Stylus Publishing.

Prouty, D., Trites Botkin, N. (1995). *For Angela*. (Video) National Film Board of Canada.

Radwanski, G. (1987). *The Ontario Study of the Relevance of Education and the Issue of Dropouts*. Ontario: Ministry of Education.

Rawls, J. (1972). *A Theory of Justice*. Cambridge, MA: Harward University Press.

Reagan, T. (2005). *Non-Western Educational Traditions: Indigenous Approaches to Educational Thought and Practice,* 3rd Edition. Mahwah: Lawrence Erlbaum Associates.

Reyes, P., and Wagstaff, L. (2005). How Does Leadership Promote Successful Teaching and Learning for Diverse Students? In W. A. Firestone and C. Riehl (Eds.), *A New Agenda for Research in Educational Leadership* (pp. 81–100). New York: Teachers College Press.

Rezai-Rashti, G. (1995). Multicultural Education, Anti-racist Education, and Critical Pedagogy: Reflection on Everyday Practice. In R. Ng, P. Staton, and J. Scane,

(Eds.), *Anti-racism, Feminism, and Critical Approaches to Education* (pp. 3–19). Toronto: OISE Press.

Rezai-Rashti, G. (December 29, 2003). Educational Policy Reform and its Impact on Equity Work in Ontario: Global Challenges and Local Possibilities, *Education Policy Analysis Archives*, 11(51). Retrieved March 20, 2007, from http://epaa.asu.edu/epaa/v11n51/.

Riffel, J., and Levin, B. (1994). Dealing with Diversity: Some Propositions from Canadian Education. *Education Policy Analysis*, 2(2): 14.

Royal Commission on Aboriginal Peoples, (1996). *Report of the Royal Commission of Aboriginal Peoples*, Volume 2 and 3. Ottawa: Canada Communication Group.

Royal Commission on Bilingualism and Biculturalism. (1970). *Report of the Royal Commission on Bilingualism and Biculturalism, Book IV: The Cultural Contribution of Other Ethnic Groups*. Ottawa: Queen's Printer.

Ruck, M., and Wortley, S. (2002). Racial and Ethnic Minority High School Students' Perception of School Disciplinary Practices: A Look at Some Canadian Findings. *Journal of Youth and Adolescence,* 31(3): 185–195.

Ruiz, R. (1984). Orientations in Language Planning. *Journal of the National Association for Bilingual Education*, 8: 15–34.

Rushton, J. P. (1997). *Race, Evolution, and Behaviour: A Life History Perspective*. New Brunswick, NJ: Transaction Publishers.

Russell, C. L., Bell, A., and Fawcett, L. (2000). Navigating the Waters of Canadian Environmental Education. In T. Goldstein and D. Selby (Eds.), *Weaving Connections: Educating for Peace, Social and Environmental Justice* (pp. 196–217). Toronto: Sumach Press.

Ryan, J. (2001). Promoting Inclusive School-Community Relationships: Administrator Strategies for Empowering and Enabling Parents in Diverse Contexts. *Journal of Teaching and Learning,* 2 (1): 1–20.

Ryan, J. (2003). Educational Administrators' Perceptions of Racism in Diverse School Contexts. *Race, Ethnicity and Education,* 6(2): 145–164.

Ryan, J. (2006). *Inclusive Leadership*. San Francisco: Jossey-Bass.

Sadker, M., and Sadker, D. (1986). Sexism in the Classroom: From Grade School to Graduate School. *Phi Delta Kappan,* 67: 512–515.

Sadker, M., and Sadker, D. (2002). The Miseducation of Boys. In S. Bailey (Ed.), *The Jossey-Bass Reader on Gender in Education* (pp. 182–203). San Francisco: John Wiley & Sons.

Sadker, D., and Sadker, M. (2004). *Teachers, Schools, and Society,* 7th Edition. McGraw-Hill.

Salomon, G. (2002). The Nature of Peace Education: Not All Programs are Created Equal. In G. Salomon and B. Nevo (Eds.) *Peace Education: The Concept, Principles and Practices around the World* (pp. 3–14). Mahwah: Lawrence Erlbaum Associates.

Samuel, E., and Burney, S. (2003). Racism, eh? Interactions of South Asian Students with Mainstream Faculty in a Predominately White Canadian University. *Canadian Journal of Higher Education,* 33: 81–114.

Sapon-Shevin, M. (2004). Introduction. In E. G. Cohen, C. M. Brody, and M. Sapon-Shevin *Teaching Cooperative Learning: The Challenge for Teacher Education* (pp. 1–10). Albany: State University of New York Press.

Scott, F. B. (2001). *Teaching in a Multicultural Setting: A Canadian Perspective*. Toronto: Prentice Hall.

Sears, C. (1998). *Second Language Students in Mainstream Classrooms: A Handbook for Teachers in International Schools*. Clevedon: Multilingual Matters.

Semali, L. M., and Kincheloe, J. L. (1999). What is Indigenous Knowledge and Why Should We Study It? In L. M. Semali and J. L. Kincheloe (Eds.), *What is Indigenous Knowledge? Voices from the Academy* (pp. 3–58). New York: Falmer Press.

Shakeshaft, C. (1986). A Gender at Risk. *Phi Delta Kappan,* 67: 499–503.

Sheets, R. H. (2005). *Diversity Pedagogy: Examining the Role of Culture in the Teaching-Learning Process*. Boston: Pearson Education.

Shields, C. (2003). *Good Intentions Are not Enough: Transformative Leadership for Communities of Difference*. Lanham: Scarecrow.

Shields, C. (2004). Dialogic Leadership for Social Justice: Overcoming Pathologies of Silence. *Educational Administration Quarterly*, 40(1): 111–134.

Shor, I. 1992. *Empowering Education: Critical Teaching for Social Change*. Chicago: University of Chicago Press.

Skrla, L., Scheurich, J., Garcia, J., and Nolly, G. (2004). Equity Audits: A Practical Leadership Tool for Developing Equitable and Excellent Schools. *Educational Administration Quarterly*, 40(1): 113–161.

Skutnabb-Kangas, T. (2000). *Linguistic Genocide in Education – or Worldwide Diversity and Human Rights?* Mahwah: Lawrence Erlbaum Associates.

Slavin, R. E. (1983). *Cooperative Learning*. New York: Longman Inc.

Sleeter, C. E., and Puente, R. (2001). Connecting Multicultural and Special Education. In C.F. Diaz (Ed.), *Multicultural Education in the 21st Century* (pp. 109–119). New York: Addison-Wesley Educational Publishers.

Solomon, R. P. (1994) Academic Disengagement: Black Youth and the Sports Subculture from a Cross-National Perspective. In L. Erwin & MacLennan (Eds.). *Sociology of Education in Canada: Critical Perspectives on Theory, Research and Practice*. pp. 188–199. Toronto: Copp Clark Longman Ltd.

Solomon, R. P., and Allen, A. M. (2001). The Struggle for Equity, Diversity, and Social Justice in Teacher Education. In J. P. Portelli and R. P. Solomon (Eds.), *The Erosion of Democracy in Education: Critique to Possibilities* (pp. 269–296). Calgary: Detselig Enterprises.

Solomon, R. P., Portelli, J. P., Daniel, B. J. and Campbell, A. (2005). The Discourse of

Denial: How White Teacher Candidates Construct Race, Racism, and "White Privilege". *Race, Ethnicity and Education*, 8(2): 147–169.

Solomon, R. P., and Levine-Rasky, C. (1996). When Principle Meets Practice: Teachers' Contradictory Responses to Anti-racist Education. *Alberta Journal of Educational Research*, 42(1): 19–33.

Sowell, T. (2002). *The Education of Minority Children.* In E. P. Lazear (Ed.), *Education in the Twenty-First Century* (pp. 79–92). Stanford: Hoover Institution Press.

Spender, D. (1982). *Invisible Women: the Schooling Scandal.* London: Writers and Readers Publishing Cooperative Society.

Starratt, R. J. (2003). *Centering Educational Administration: Cultivating Meaning, Community, Responsibility.* Mahwah: Lawrence Erlbaum Associates.

Statistics Canada. (2002). Profile of Languages in Canada: English, French and Many Others. Ottawa: Statistics Canada. Available online: www.statcan.ca/bsolc/english/bsolc?catno = 96F0030X2001005

Statistics Canada. (2003). *Canada's Ethnocultural Portrait: The Changing Mosaic, 2001 Census* (96F0030XIE2001008). Ottawa. Retrieved April, 7, 2006, from www12.statcan.ca/english/census01/products/analytic/companion/etoimm/canada.cfm

Statistics Canada. (2004). Youth in Transition Survey. Available online: www.statscan.ca

Statistics Canada. (2005). Population projections of visible minority groups, Canada, provinces and regions 2001–2017, Catalogue 91-541-XIE, Ottawa: Statistics Canada. Available online: www.statcan.ca/english/freepub/91-541-XIE/91-541-XIE2005001.pdf

Statistics Canada. (2006). Report of the Pan-Canadian Education Indicators Program 2005. Catalogue no. 81-582-XPE. Ottawa: Statistics Canada.

Statistics Canada. (January 2003). *2001 Census: Analysis Series Aboriginal Peoples of Canada: A Demographic Profile* (96F0030XIE2001007). Ottawa: Minister of Industry.

Statistics Canada. (2007). Portrait of the Canadian Population in 2006, 2006 Census. Ottawa: Statistics Canada, Catalogue no. 97–550-XIE. Available online: www12.statcan.ca/english/census06/analysis/popdwell/pdf/97–550-XIE2006001.pdf

Stone, D. (1997). *Policy Paradox: The Art of Political Decision Making.* New York: W.W. Norton & Company.

Suarez-Orozco, M. (1991). Immigrant Adaptation to Schooling. In M. Gibson and J. Ogbu (Eds). *Minority Status and Schooling: A Comparative Study of Immigrants and Involuntary Minorities.* NewYork: Garland Publishing, Inc.

Sunderland, J. (2000). New Understandings of Gender and Language Classroom Research: Texts, Teacher Talk and Student Talk. *Language Teaching Research,* 4: 149–173.

Sweet, L. (2005) Accommodating Religious Difference: The Canadian Experience. In C. James (Ed.) *Possibilities & Limitations: Multicultural Policies and Programs in Canada.* Halifax: Fernwood Publishing.

Tator, C., and Henry, F. (1991). *Multicultural Education: Translating Policy into Practice.* Ottawa: Department of Multiculturalism and Citizenship.

Taylor, A., and Krahn, H. (2005). Aiming High: Educational Aspirations of Visible Minority Immigrant Youth. Canadian Social Trends (Winter). Ottawa: Statistics Canada. Available online: www.statcan.ca/english/freepub/11-008-XIE/2005003/articles/8966.pdf

Taylor, C. (1992). The Politics of Recognition. In C. Taylor and A. Guttman (Eds.), *Multiculturalism and 'The Politics of Recognition': An Essay.* Princeton: Princeton University Press.

Taylor, J. (1995). Non-Native Teachers Teaching in Native Communities. In M. Battiste and J. Barman (Eds.), *First Nations Education in Canada: The Circle Unfolds* (pp. 224–244). Vancouver: UBC Press.

Thompson, J. (1991). Introduction. In J. Thompson (Ed.), *Language and Symbolic Power*. Cambridge: Polity Press.

Toronto District School Board. (2006). *School Matters: A Parent's Guide to the TDSB*. Available online: www.tdsb.on.ca/communications/publications/school_matters/school_matters.html

Troyna, B. (1987). Beyond Multiculturalism: Towards the Enactment of Anti-Racist Education in Policy, Provision and Pedagogy. *Oxford Review of Education,* 13: 307–320.

Troyna, B. (1993). *Racism and Education: Research Perspectives*. Toronto: OISE Press.

Tye, K. (2003). Global Education as a Worldwide Movement. *Phi Delta Kappan*, 85(2): 165–169.

United Nations (1951) *Refugee Convention*, Article 1(A)(2): United Nations. The Geneva Convention.

Van Manen, M. (2003). On the Epistemology of Reflective Practice. *Teachers and Teaching: Theory and Practice*, 1(1): 33–50.

Vibert, A. B., Portelli, J. P., Shields, C., and Larocque, L. (2002). Critical Practice in Elementary Schools: Voice, Community, and a Curriculum of Life. *Journal of Educational Change*, 3: 93–116.

Villegas, A. M., and Lucas, T. (2002). *Educating Culturally Responsive Teachers: a Coherent Approach*. Albany: State University of New York Press.

Vincent, C. (Ed.). (2003). *Social Justice, Education and Identity*. New York: Routledge/Falmer Press.

Vygotsky, L. (1962). *Thought and Language*. Cambridge: MIT Press.

Watt-Cloutier, S. (May 24, 2006). Don't Abandon the Arctic to Climate Change. *The Globe and Mail*. Retrieved from March 10 2007, from www.globeandmail.com

Wilkinson, L., and Hebert, Y. (2003). The Values Debate, Citizenship Policy and Education in Canada: What World do we Want? In W. Kymlicka (Ed.), *Citizenship, Values, and Responsibilities*. Special Issue of Canadian Diversity/Diversite Canadienne, 2(1): 39–41.

Williams, D. (1990). Is the Post-secondary Classroom a Chilly One for Women? A Review of the Literature. *Canadian Journal of Higher Education* 20(3): 30–42.

Willinsky, J. (2004). Keep the Whole World at Your Fingertips: Education, Globalization, and the Nation. *Education Canada*, 45(1): 24–26.

Winzer, M. (2005). *Children with Exceptionalities in Canadian Classrooms*. Toronto: Prentice Hall.

Winzer, M., & Grigg, N. (1992). Classroom management. *In Educational Psychology in the Canadian Classroom* (pp. 574–621). Scarborough, ON: Prentice-Hall.

Woolfolk A. (1995). Educational Psychology. (6th Edition). Boston: Allyn and Bacon.

Wotherspoon, T. (1998). *The Sociology of Education in Canada: Critical Perspectives*. Toronto: Oxford University Press.

Wright, O. M. (2000). Multicultural and Anti-Racist Education: The Issue of Equity. In T. Goldstein and D. Selby (Eds.), *Weaving Connections: Educating for Peace, Social and Environmental Justice* (pp. 57–98). Toronto: Sumach Press.

Young, I. M. (1990). Justice and the Politics of Difference. Princeton, NJ: Princeton University Press.

Young, J. C. (1984). Education in Multicultural Society: What Sort of Education? What Sort of Society? In J. R. Mallea and J. C. Young, *Cultural Diversity and Canadian Education: Issues and Innovations* (pp. 412–430). Ottawa: Carleton University Press.

Young, J., Levin, B., and Wallin, W. (2007). *Understanding Canadian Schools: An Introduction to Educational Administration*, 4th Edition. Toronto: Thomson Publishing.

Zhang, C., Ollila, L., and Harvey, B. (1998). Chinese Parents' Perceptions of Their Children's Literacy and Schooling in Canada. *Canadian Journal of Education*, 23(2): 182–190.

Zine, J. (2002). Inclusive Schooling in a Plural Society: Removing the Margins. *Education Canada*, 42(3): 36–39.

Index